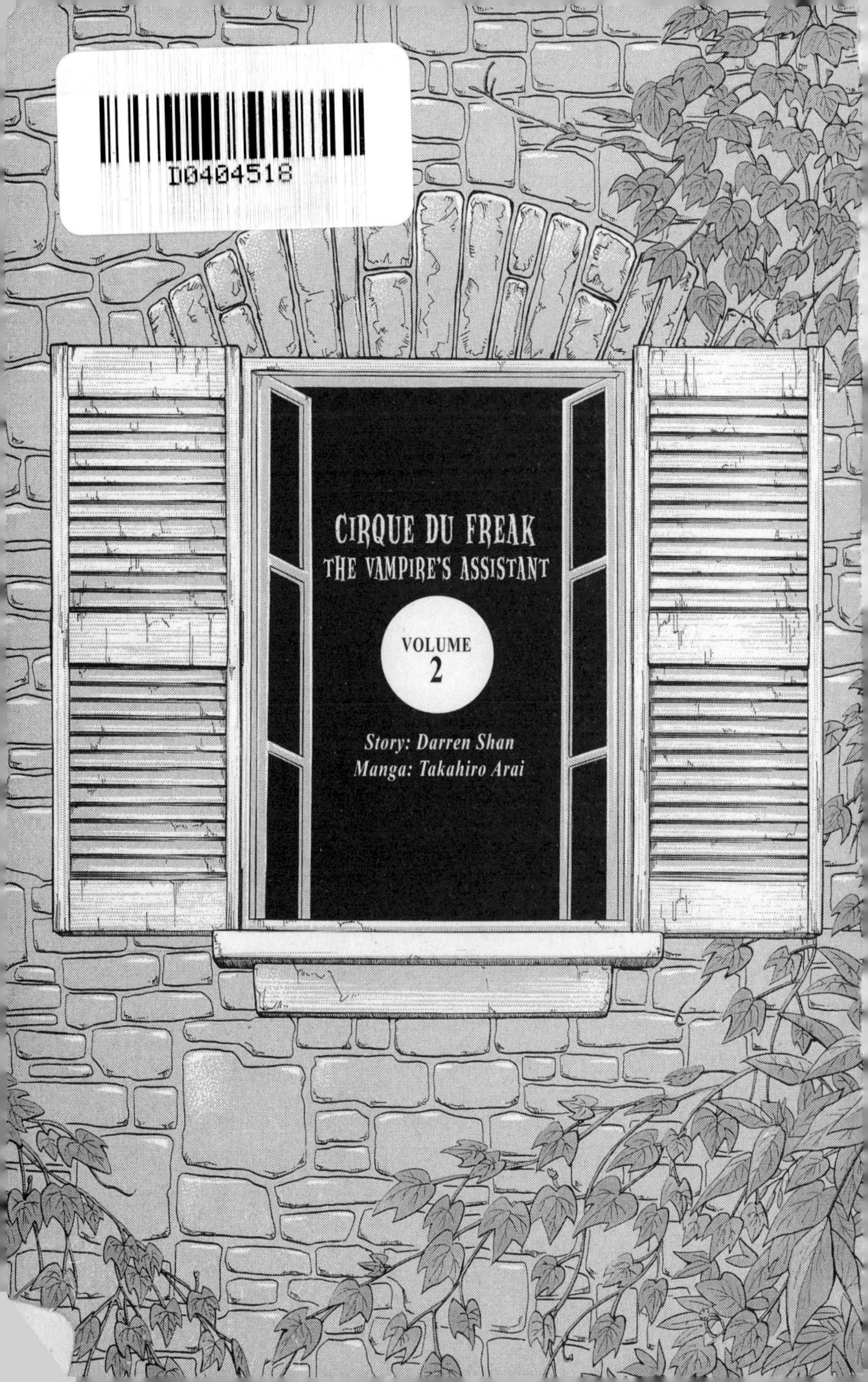
CIRQUE DU FREAK
THE VAMPIRE'S ASSISTANT
VOLUME 2
Story: Darren Shan
Manga: Takahiro Arai

A SUMMARY OF CIRQUE DU FREAK:

DARREN SHAN LEADS THE LIFE OF A HEALTHY, HAPPY YOUNG BOY...BUT HIS FATE TAKES A TURN FOR THE WORSE ON THE NIGHT HE GOES TO SEE THE CIRQUE DU FREAK WITH HIS BEST FRIEND, STEVE. WHEN THE CIRQUE'S POISONOUS SPIDER BITES STEVE ON THE NECK, DARREN MUST ASK THE SPIDER'S OWNER, THE VAMPIRE LARTEN CREPSLEY, FOR HELP. MR. CREPSLEY IS ABLE TO FULFILL DARREN'S REQUEST, BUT THERE IS A FEE TO BE PAID—DARREN MUST BECOME A VAMPIRE! HIS PEACEFUL LIFE GONE, DARREN MUST NOW VENTURE INTO THE NIGHT ON A JOURNEY WITH HIS NEW VAMPIRE MASTER...

CIRQUE DU FREAK 2
CONTENTS

CHAPTER 5: THE LIFE OF A VAMPIRE.................3

CHAPTER 6: TO CIRQUE DU FREAK..................21

CHAPTER 7: FRIEND NUMBER TWO 41

CHAPTER 8: MR. TINY....................................59

CHAPTER 9: A TINY URGE TO KILL..................77

CHAPTER 10: A CONDITION FOR SAM.............95

CHAPTER 11: A FALSE CONFESSION.................113

CHAPTER 12: THE LAST NIGHT 131

CHAPTER 13: BLOOD AND SPIRIT..................153

CHAPTER 14: TOGETHER WITH SAM................171

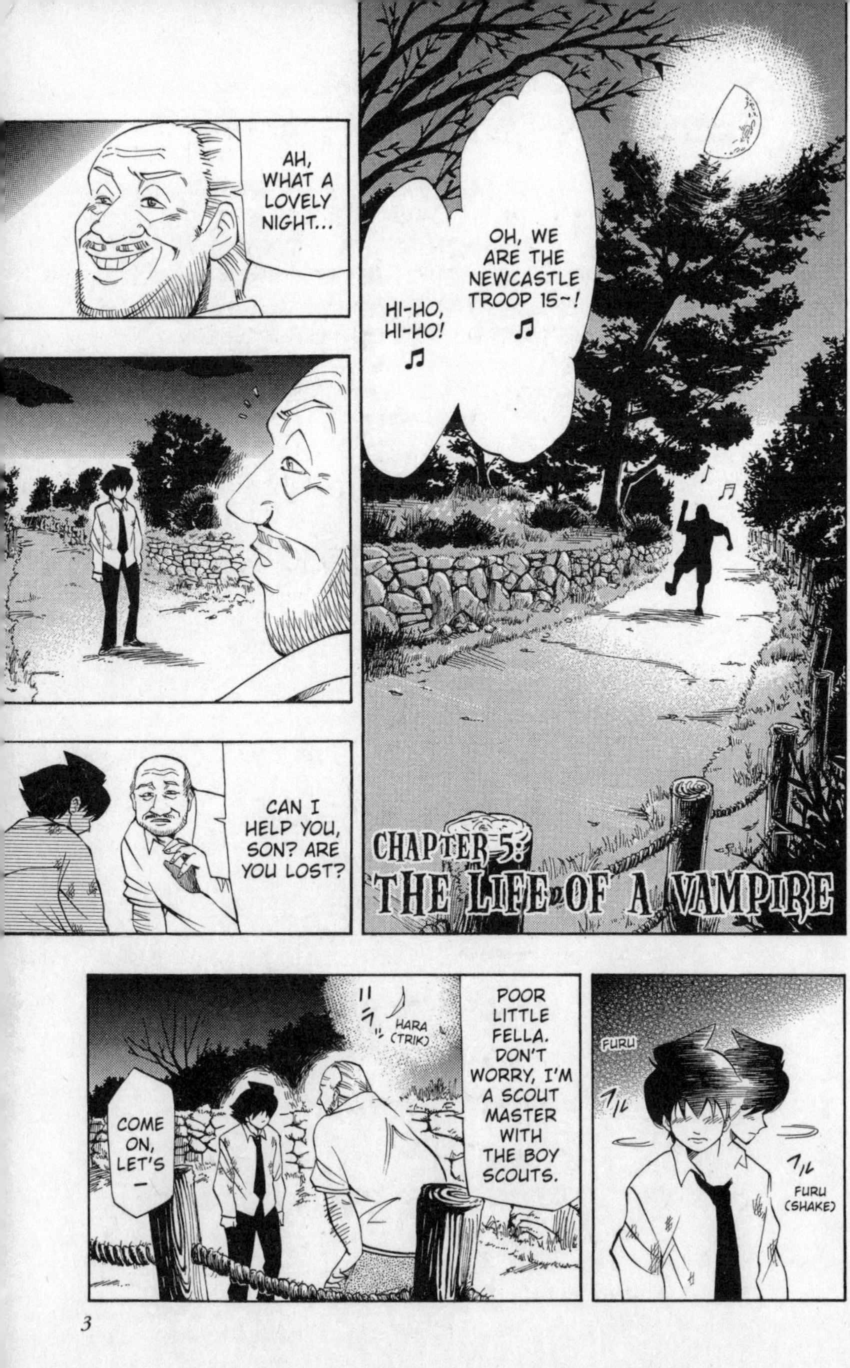
OH, WE ARE THE NEWCASTLE TROOP 15~! ♫
HI-HO, HI-HO! ♫
CHAPTER 5:
THE LIFE OF A VAMPIRE
AH, WHAT A LOVELY NIGHT...
CAN I HELP YOU, SON? ARE YOU LOST?
FURU
FURU (SHAKE)
HARA (TRIK)
POOR LITTLE FELLA. DON'T WORRY, I'M A SCOUT MASTER WITH THE BOY SCOUTS.
COME ON, LET'S —

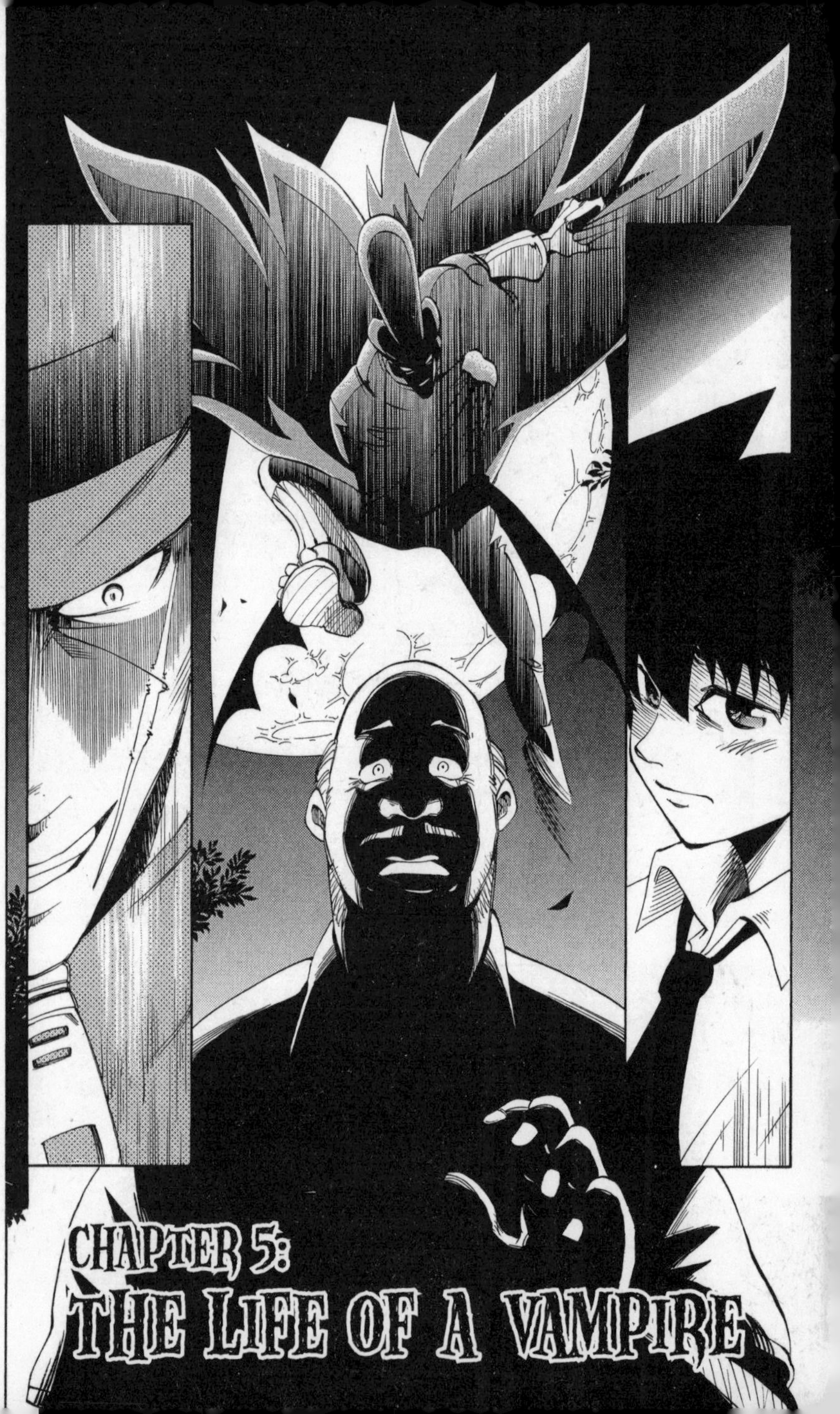
CHAPTER 5:
THE LIFE OF A VAMPIRE

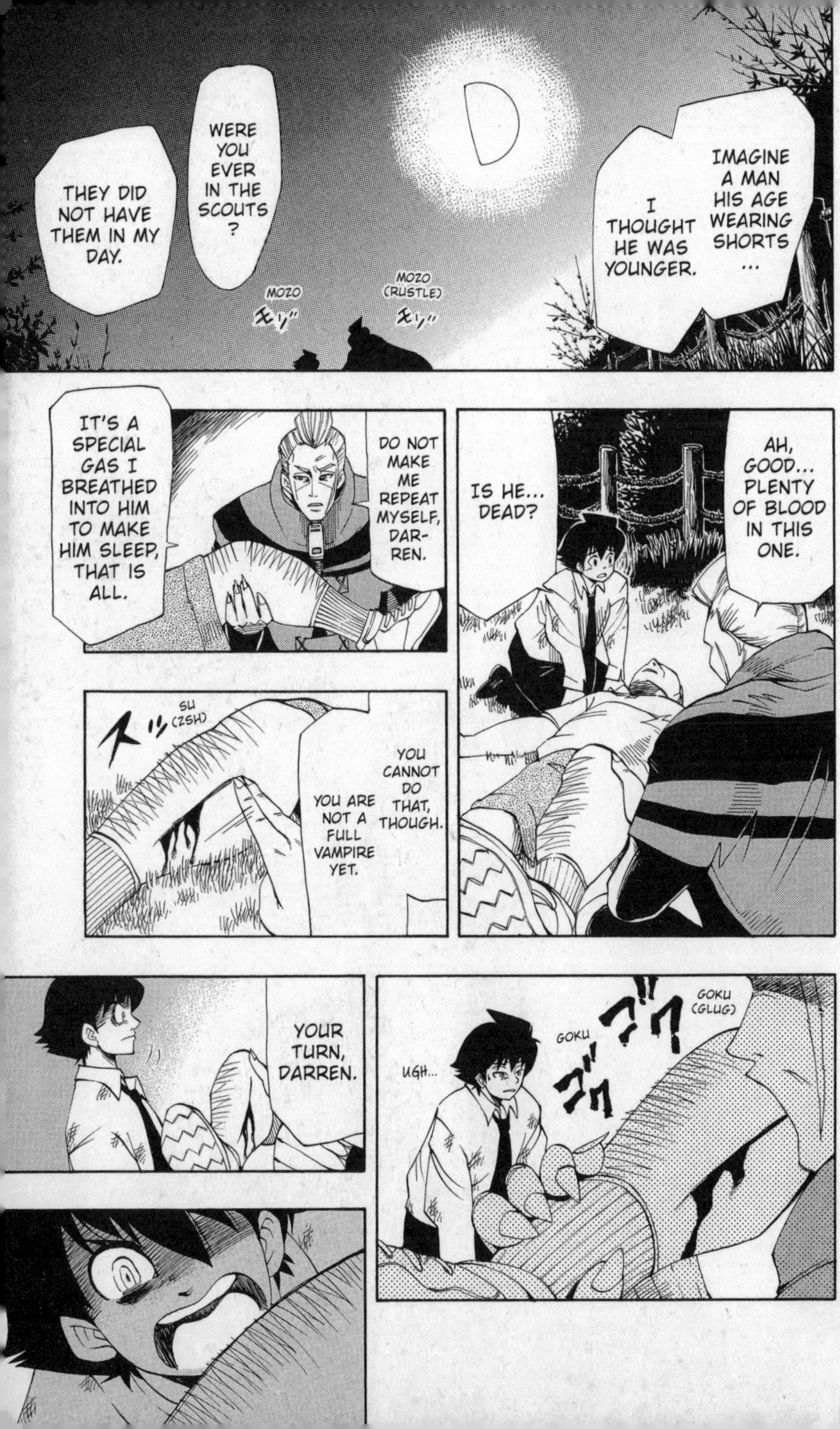
IMAGINE A MAN HIS AGE WEARING SHORTS...
I THOUGHT HE WAS YOUNGER.
MOZO (RUSTLE)
MOZO
WERE YOU EVER IN THE SCOUTS?
THEY DID NOT HAVE THEM IN MY DAY.
AH, GOOD... PLENTY OF BLOOD IN THIS ONE.
IS HE... DEAD?
DO NOT MAKE ME REPEAT MYSELF, DAR-REN.
IT'S A SPECIAL GAS I BREATHED INTO HIM TO MAKE HIM SLEEP, THAT IS ALL.
YOU CANNOT DO THAT, THOUGH.
YOU ARE NOT A FULL VAMPIRE YET.
SU (ZSH)
GOKU (GLUG)
GOKU
UGH...
YOUR TURN, DARREN.

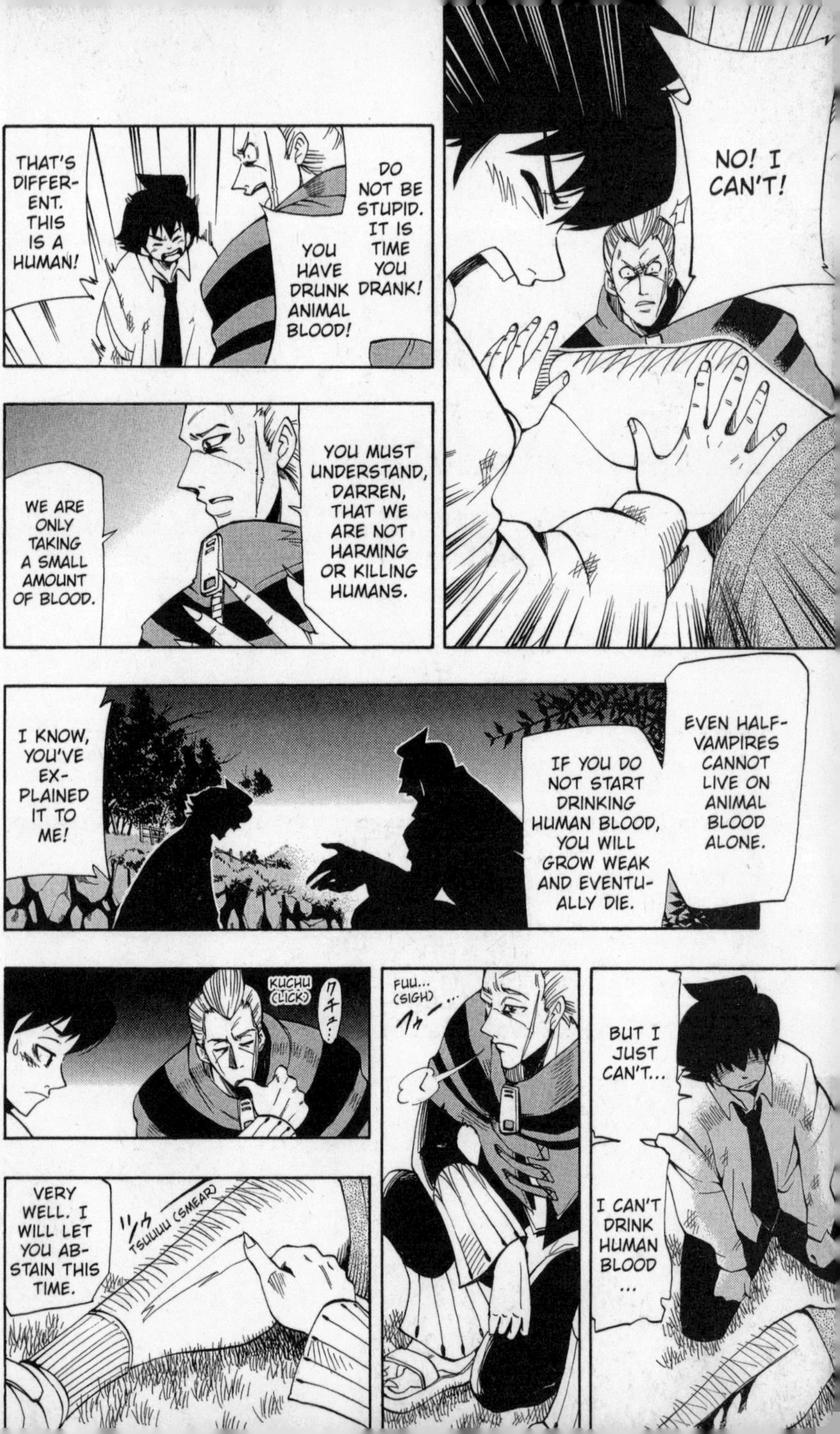
NO! I CAN'T!
DO NOT BE STUPID. IT IS TIME YOU DRANK!
YOU HAVE DRUNK ANIMAL BLOOD!
THAT'S DIFFER-ENT. THIS IS A HUMAN!
YOU MUST UNDERSTAND, DARREN, THAT WE ARE NOT HARMING OR KILLING HUMANS.
WE ARE ONLY TAKING A SMALL AMOUNT OF BLOOD.
EVEN HALF-VAMPIRES CANNOT LIVE ON ANIMAL BLOOD ALONE.
IF YOU DO NOT START DRINKING HUMAN BLOOD, YOU WILL GROW WEAK AND EVENTU-ALLY DIE.
I KNOW, YOU'VE EX-PLAINED IT TO ME!
BUT I JUST CAN'T...
I CAN'T DRINK HUMAN BLOOD ...
FUU... (SIGH)
KUCHU (LICK)
VERY WELL. I WILL LET YOU AB-STAIN THIS TIME.
TSUUUU (SMEAR)

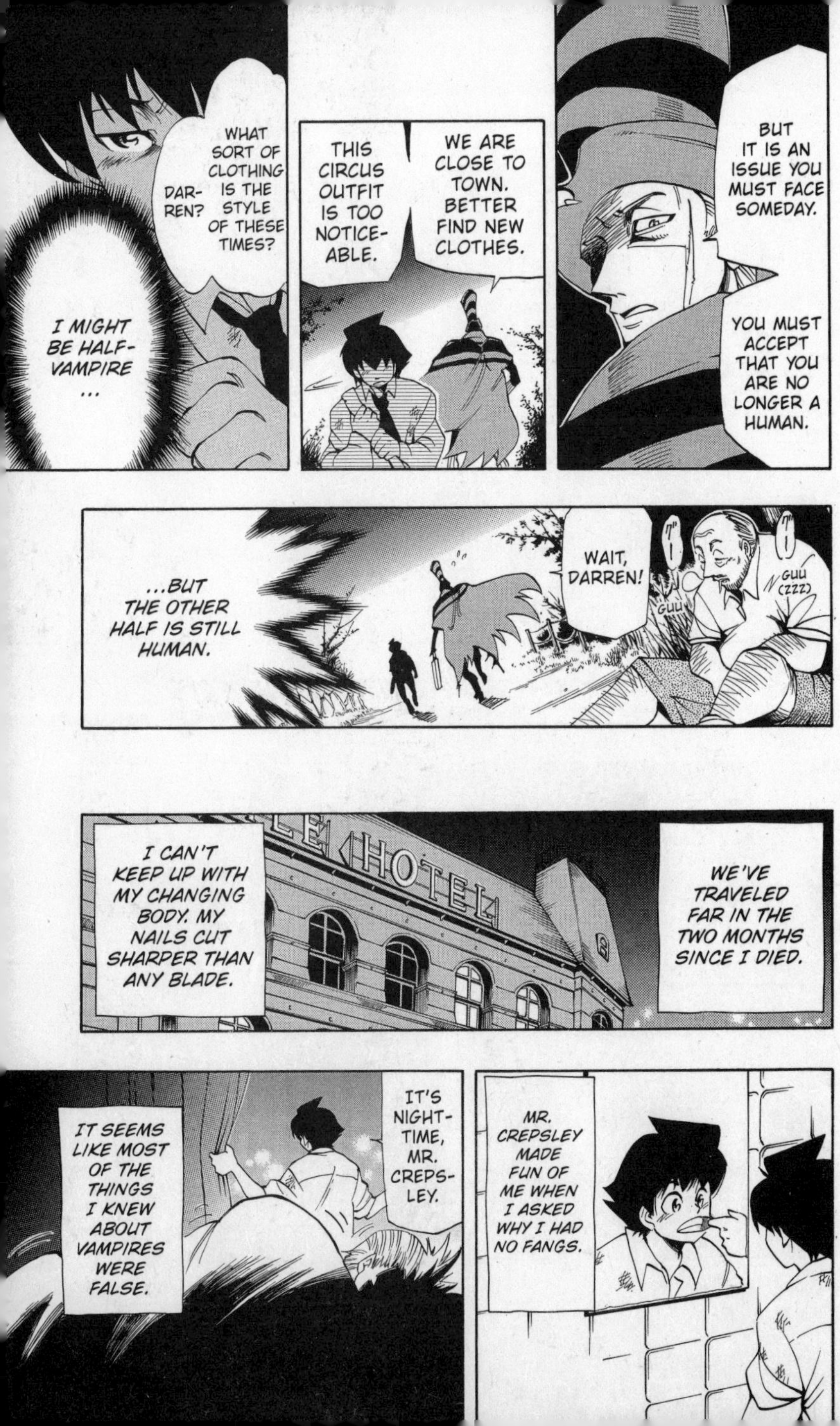
BUT IT IS AN ISSUE YOU MUST FACE SOMEDAY.
YOU MUST ACCEPT THAT YOU ARE NO LONGER A HUMAN.
WE ARE CLOSE TO TOWN. BETTER FIND NEW CLOTHES.
THIS CIRCUS OUTFIT IS TOO NOTICE-ABLE.
WHAT SORT OF CLOTHING IS THE STYLE OF THESE TIMES?
DAR-REN?
I MIGHT BE HALF-VAMPIRE ...
WAIT, DARREN!
GUU (ZZZ)
GUU
...BUT THE OTHER HALF IS STILL HUMAN.
WE'VE TRAVELED FAR IN THE TWO MONTHS SINCE I DIED.
LE HOTEL
I CAN'T KEEP UP WITH MY CHANGING BODY. MY NAILS CUT SHARPER THAN ANY BLADE.
MR. CREPSLEY MADE FUN OF ME WHEN I ASKED WHY I HAD NO FANGS.
IT'S NIGHT-TIME, MR. CREPS-LEY.
IT SEEMS LIKE MOST OF THE THINGS I KNEW ABOUT VAMPIRES WERE FALSE.

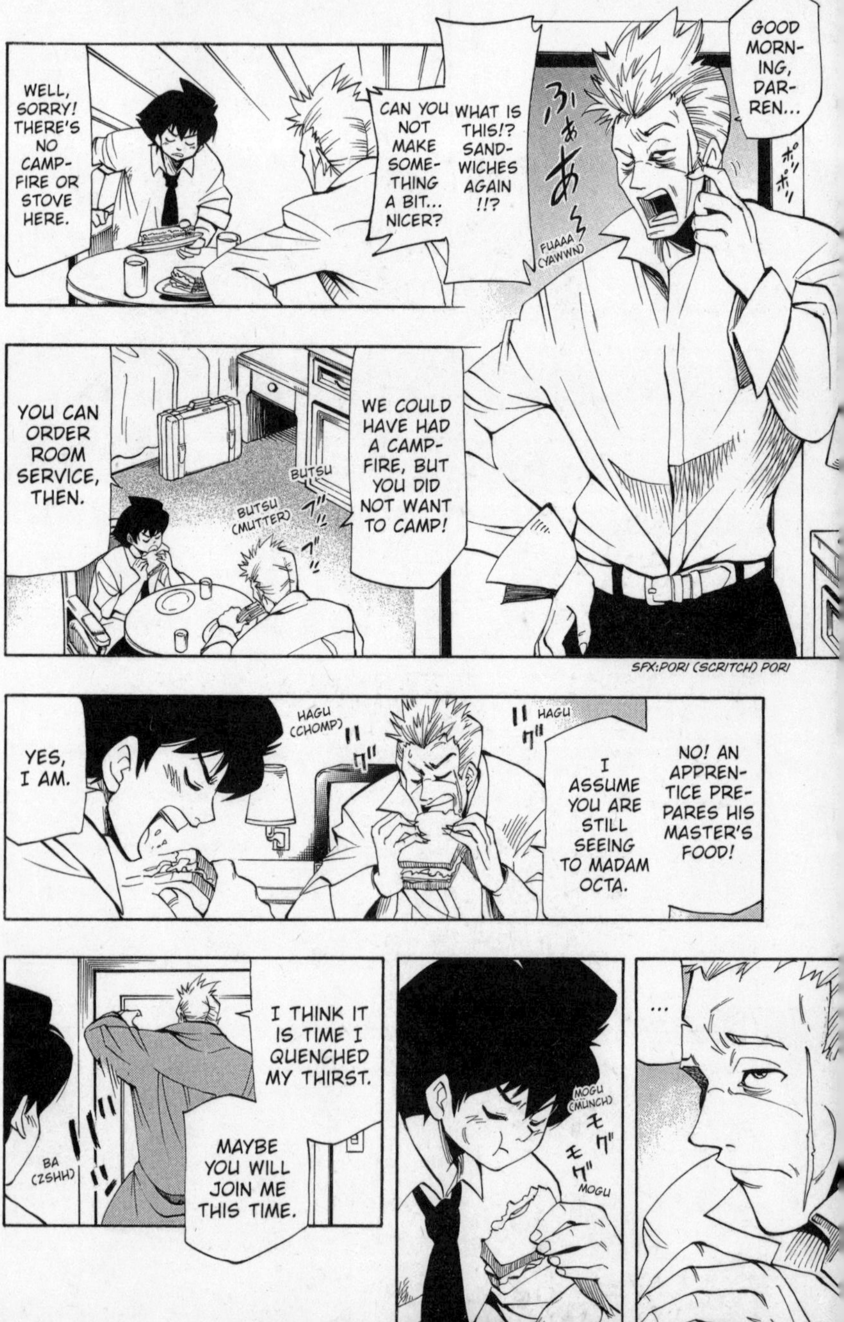
GOOD MORN-ING, DAR-REN...
FUAAA (YAWWN)
SFX:PORI (SCRITCH) PORI
WHAT IS THIS!? SAND-WICHES AGAIN !!?
CAN YOU NOT MAKE SOME-THING A BIT... NICER?
WELL, SORRY! THERE'S NO CAMP-FIRE OR STOVE HERE.
WE COULD HAVE HAD A CAMP-FIRE, BUT YOU DID NOT WANT TO CAMP!
BUTSU
BUTSU (MUTTER)
YOU CAN ORDER ROOM SERVICE, THEN.
NO! AN APPREN-TICE PRE-PARES HIS MASTER'S FOOD!
I ASSUME YOU ARE STILL SEEING TO MADAM OCTA.
HAGU
HAGU (CHOMP)
YES, I AM.
...
MOGU (MUNCH)
MOGU
I THINK IT IS TIME I QUENCHED MY THIRST.
MAYBE YOU WILL JOIN ME THIS TIME.
BA (ZSHH)

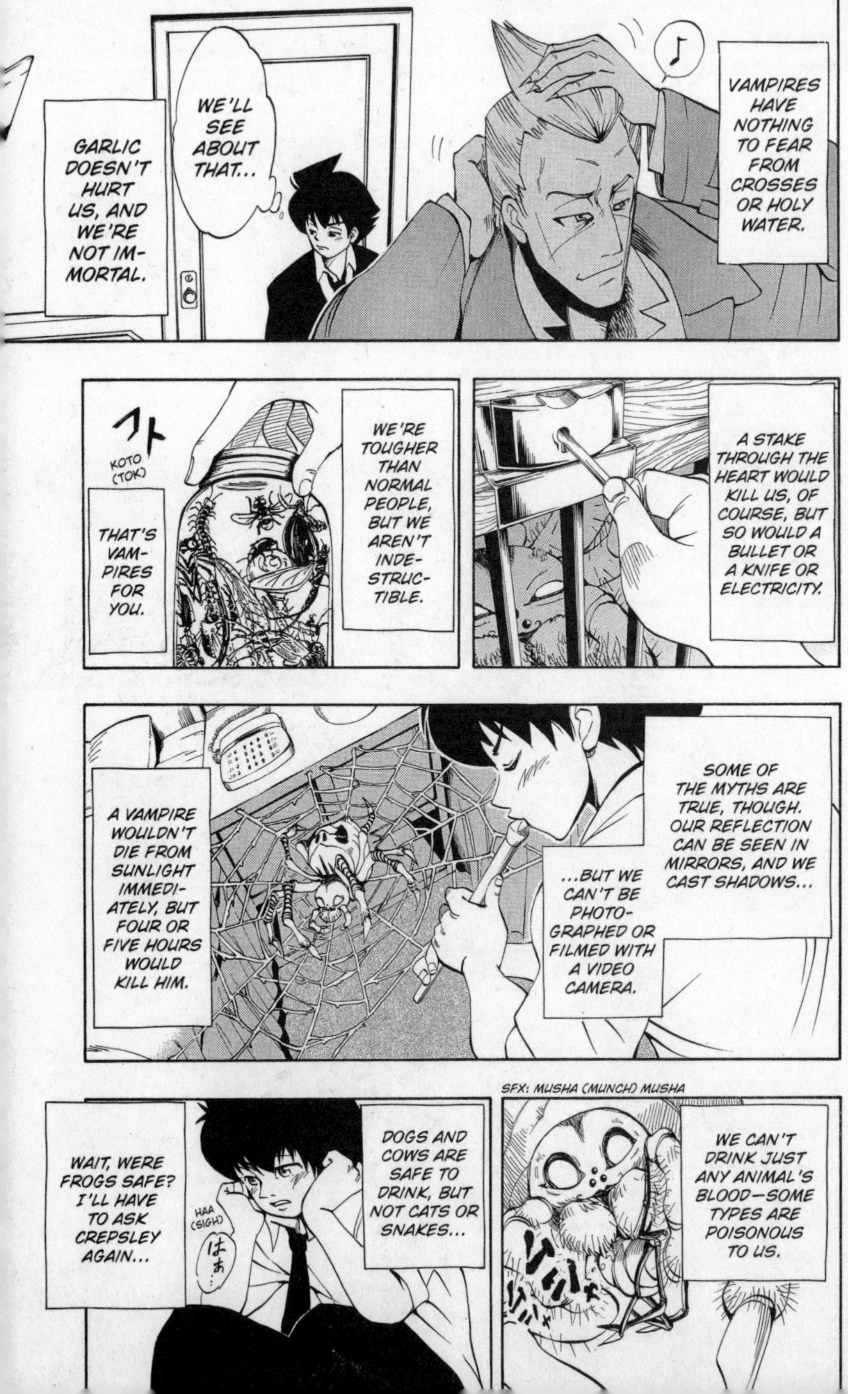

VAMPIRES HAVE NOTHING TO FEAR FROM CROSSES OR HOLY WATER.
WE'LL SEE ABOUT THAT...
GARLIC DOESN'T HURT US, AND WE'RE NOT IM-MORTAL.
A STAKE THROUGH THE HEART WOULD KILL US, OF COURSE, BUT SO WOULD A BULLET OR A KNIFE OR ELECTRICITY.
WE'RE TOUGHER THAN NORMAL PEOPLE, BUT WE AREN'T INDE-STRUC-TIBLE.
コト
KOTO (TOK)
THAT'S VAM-PIRES FOR YOU.
SOME OF THE MYTHS ARE TRUE, THOUGH. OUR REFLECTION CAN BE SEEN IN MIRRORS, AND WE CAST SHADOWS...
...BUT WE CAN'T BE PHOTO-GRAPHED OR FILMED WITH A VIDEO CAMERA.
A VAMPIRE WOULDN'T DIE FROM SUNLIGHT IMMEDI-ATELY, BUT FOUR OR FIVE HOURS WOULD KILL HIM.
SFX: MUSHA (MUNCH) MUSHA
WE CAN'T DRINK JUST ANY ANIMAL'S BLOOD—SOME TYPES ARE POISONOUS TO US.
DOGS AND COWS ARE SAFE TO DRINK, BUT NOT CATS OR SNAKES...
HAA (SIGH)
はぁ...
WAIT, WERE FROGS SAFE? I'LL HAVE TO ASK CREPSLEY AGAIN...

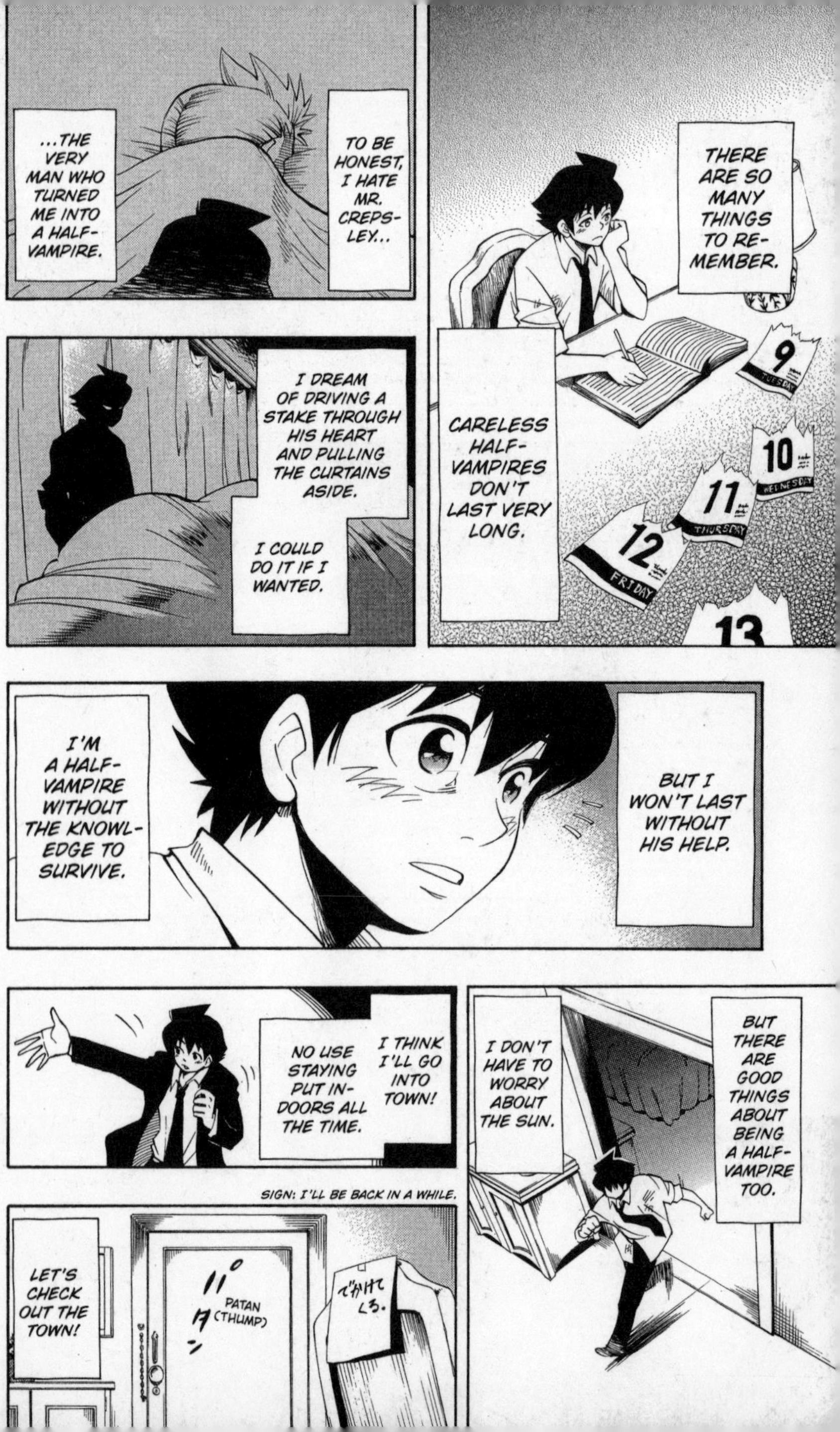
THERE ARE SO MANY THINGS TO REMEMBER.
CARELESS HALF-VAMPIRES DON'T LAST VERY LONG.
9 TUESDAY
10 WEDNESDAY
11 THURSDAY
12 FRIDAY
13
TO BE HONEST, I HATE MR. CREPSLEY...
...THE VERY MAN WHO TURNED ME INTO A HALF-VAMPIRE.
I DREAM OF DRIVING A STAKE THROUGH HIS HEART AND PULLING THE CURTAINS ASIDE.
I COULD DO IT IF I WANTED.
BUT I WON'T LAST WITHOUT HIS HELP.
I'M A HALF-VAMPIRE WITHOUT THE KNOWLEDGE TO SURVIVE.
BUT THERE ARE GOOD THINGS ABOUT BEING A HALF-VAMPIRE TOO.
I DON'T HAVE TO WORRY ABOUT THE SUN.
I THINK I'LL GO INTO TOWN!
NO USE STAYING PUT INDOORS ALL THE TIME.
SIGN: I'LL BE BACK IN A WHILE.
でかけてくる。
パタン
PATAN (THUMP)
LET'S CHECK OUT THE TOWN!

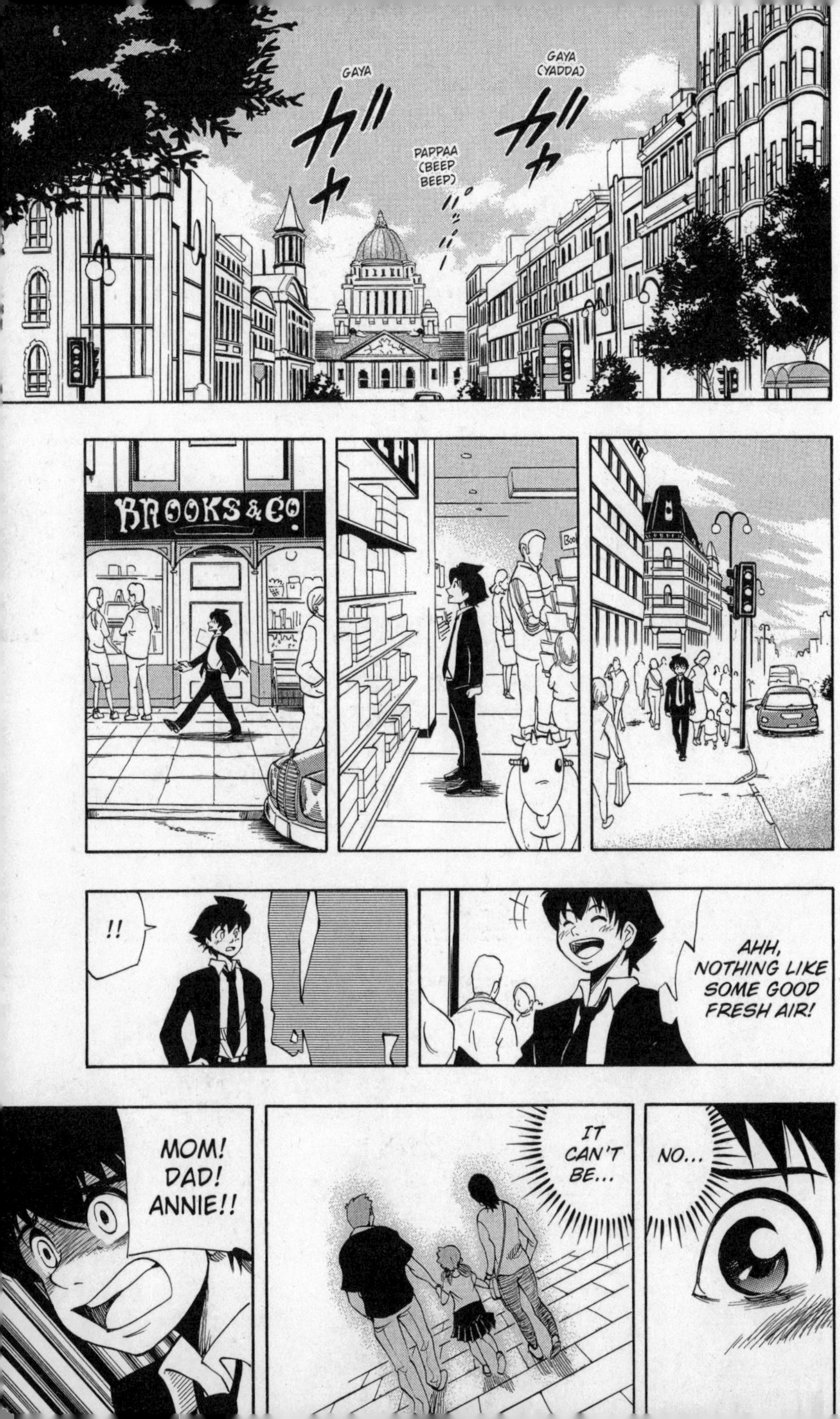
GAYA (YADDA)
PAPPAA (BEEP BEEP)
GAYA
BROOKS&CO
AHH, NOTHING LIKE SOME GOOD FRESH AIR!
!!
NO...
IT CAN'T BE...
MOM! DAD! ANNIE!!

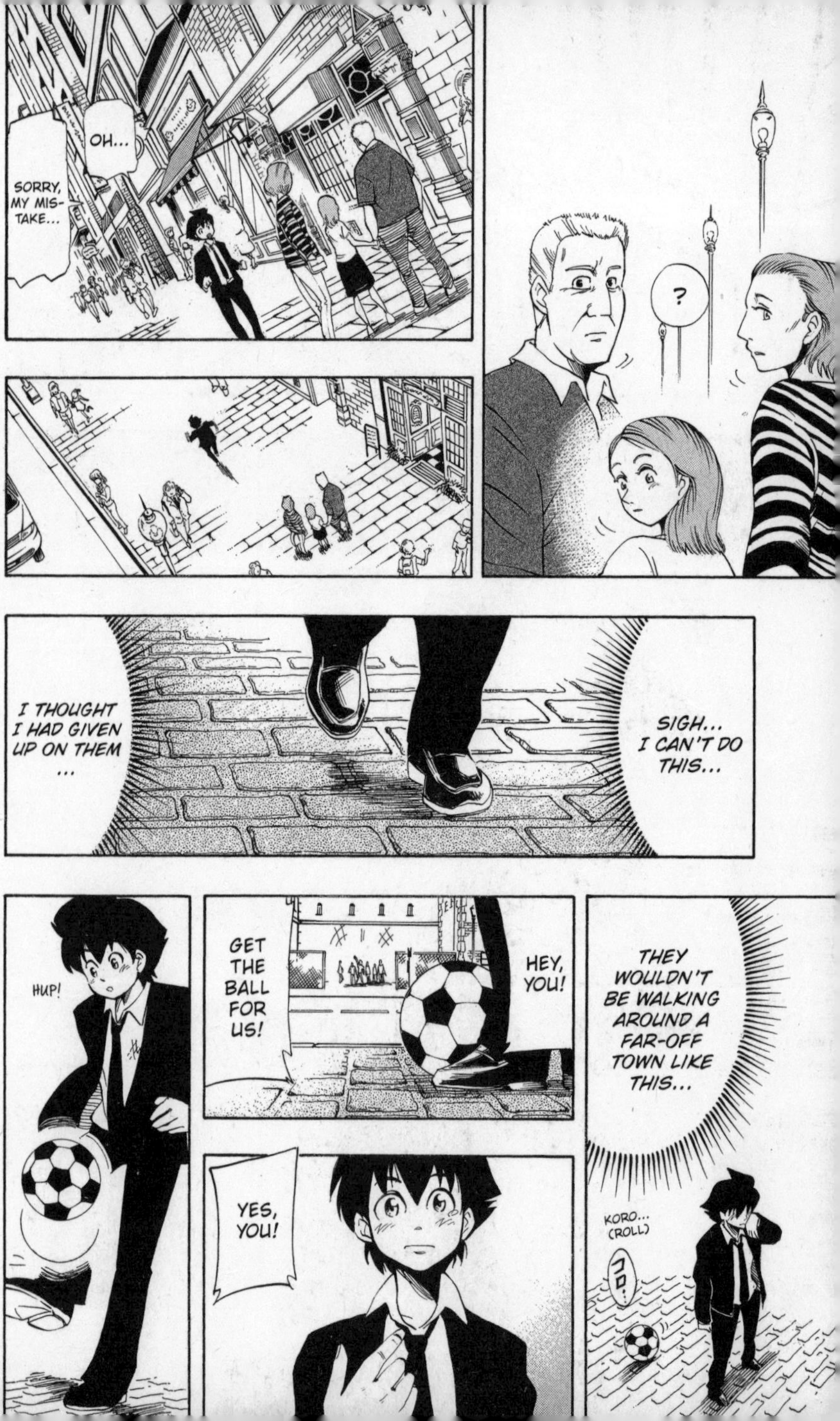
?
OH...
SORRY, MY MIS-TAKE...
SIGH... I CAN'T DO THIS...
I THOUGHT I HAD GIVEN UP ON THEM ...
THEY WOULDN'T BE WALKING AROUND A FAR-OFF TOWN LIKE THIS...
KORO... (ROLL)
コロ…
HEY, YOU!
GET THE BALL FOR US!
YES, YOU!
HUP!

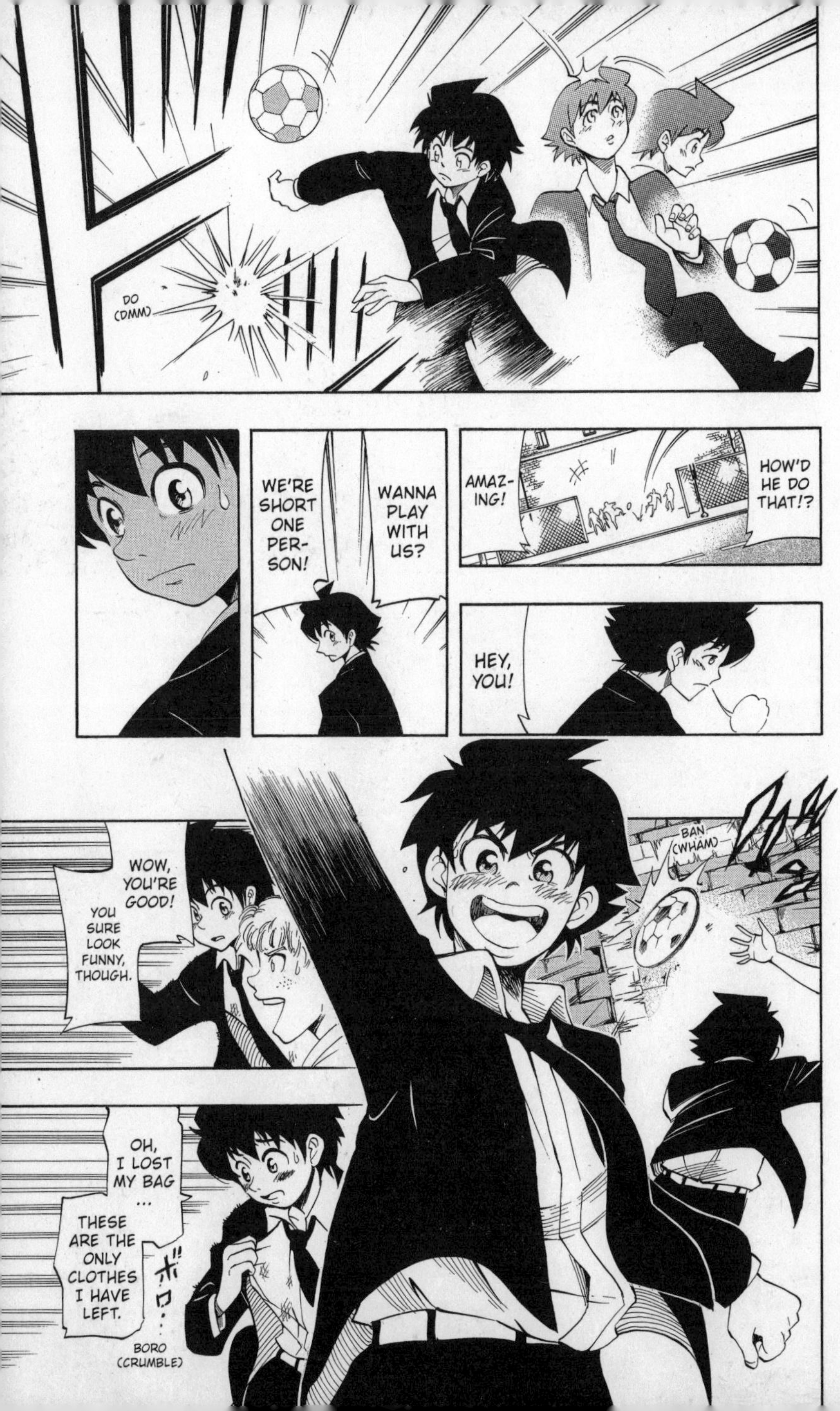

DO (DMM)
HOW'D HE DO THAT!?
AMAZ-ING!
HEY, YOU!
WANNA PLAY WITH US?
WE'RE SHORT ONE PER-SON!
BAN (WHAM)
WOW, YOU'RE GOOD!
YOU SURE LOOK FUNNY, THOUGH.
OH, I LOST MY BAG ...
THESE ARE THE ONLY CLOTHES I HAVE LEFT.
ボロ・・・
BORO (CRUMBLE)

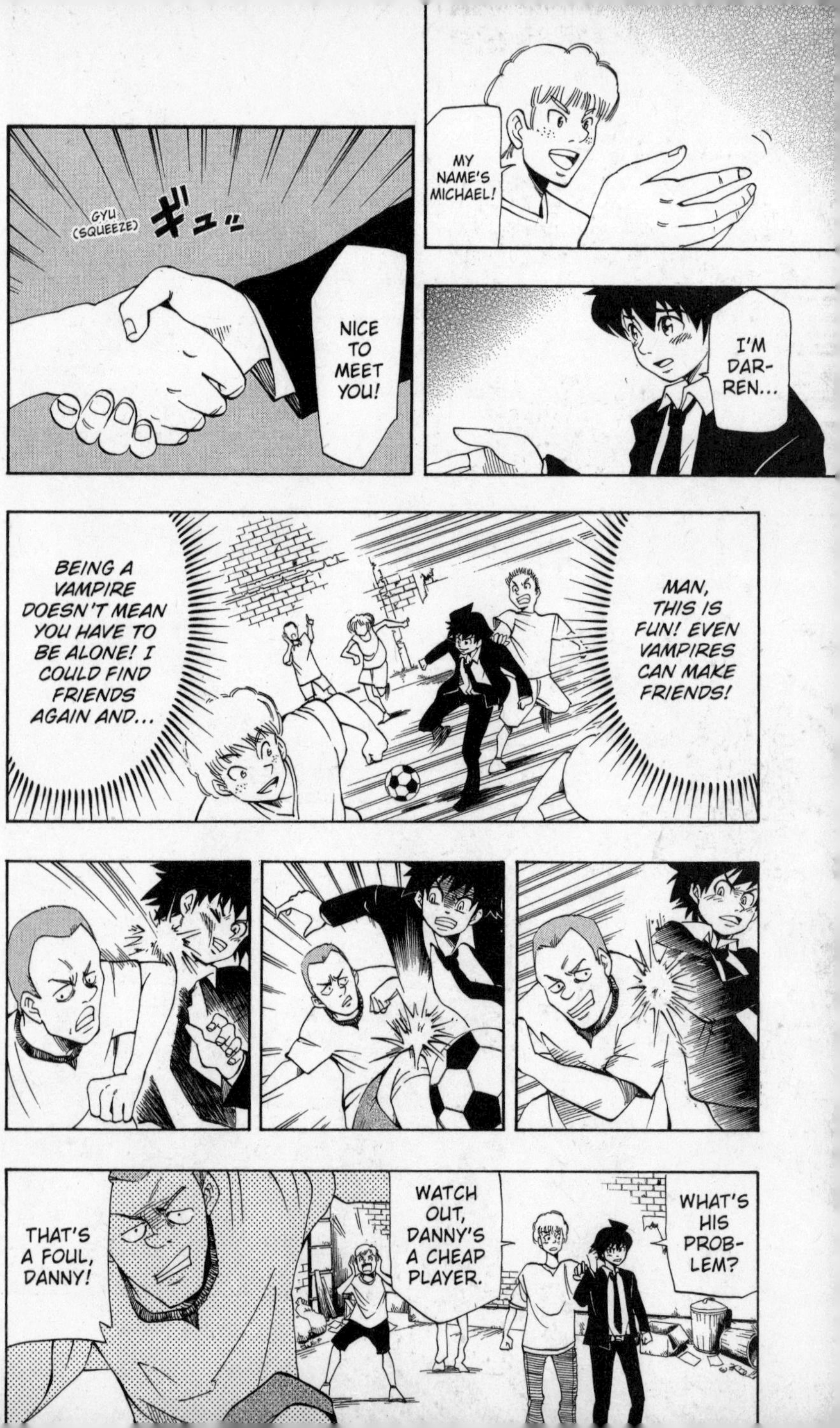

MY NAME'S MICHAEL!
I'M DAR-REN...
GYU (SQUEEZE)
ギュッ
NICE TO MEET YOU!
MAN, THIS IS FUN! EVEN VAMPIRES CAN MAKE FRIENDS!
BEING A VAMPIRE DOESN'T MEAN YOU HAVE TO BE ALONE! I COULD FIND FRIENDS AGAIN AND...
WHAT'S HIS PROB-LEM?
WATCH OUT, DANNY'S A CHEAP PLAYER.
THAT'S A FOUL, DANNY!

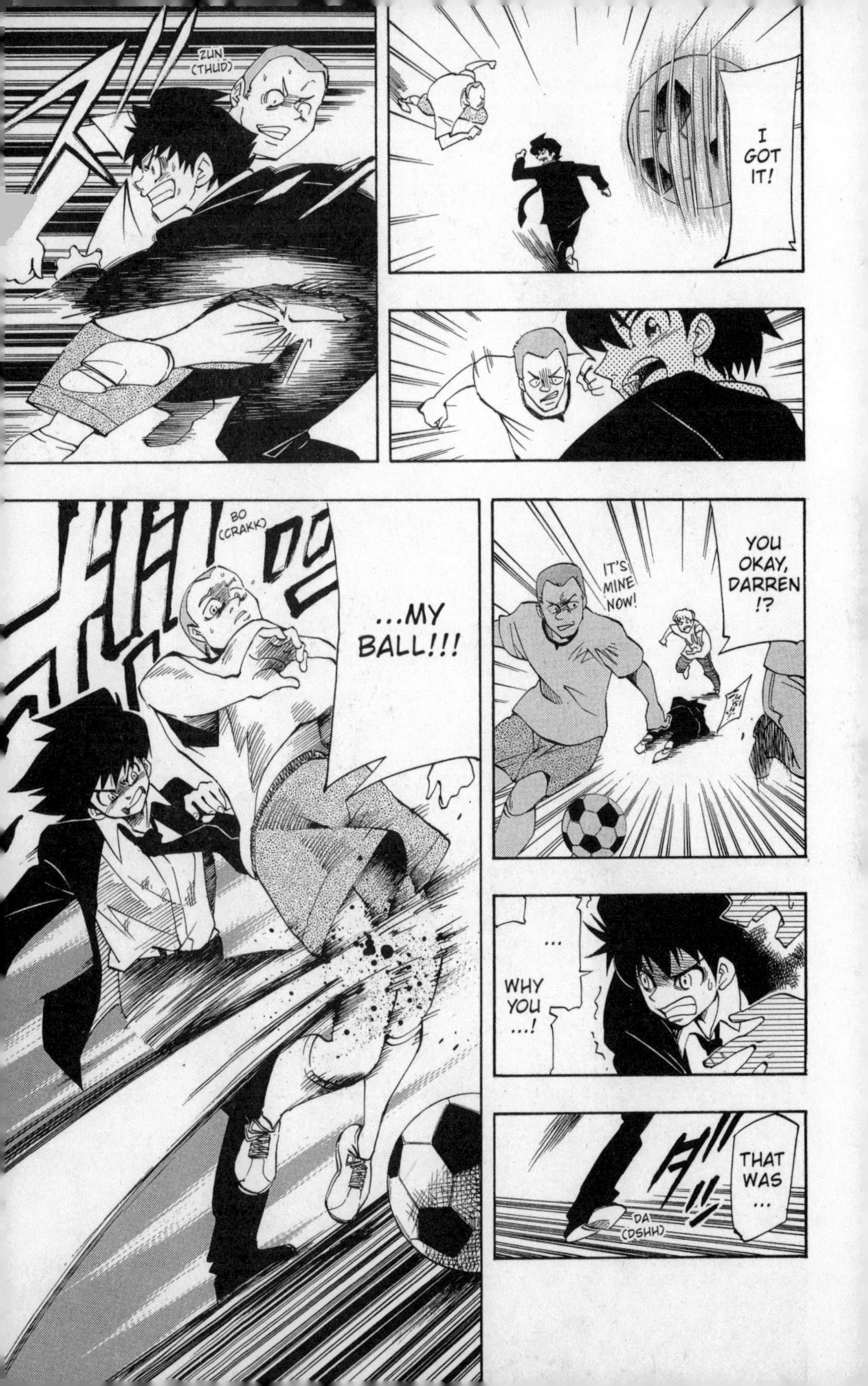

I GOT IT!
ZUN (THUD)
YOU OKAY, DARREN!?
IT'S MINE NOW!
... WHY YOU ...!
THAT WAS ...
DA (DSHH)
BO (CRAKK)
...MY BALL!!!

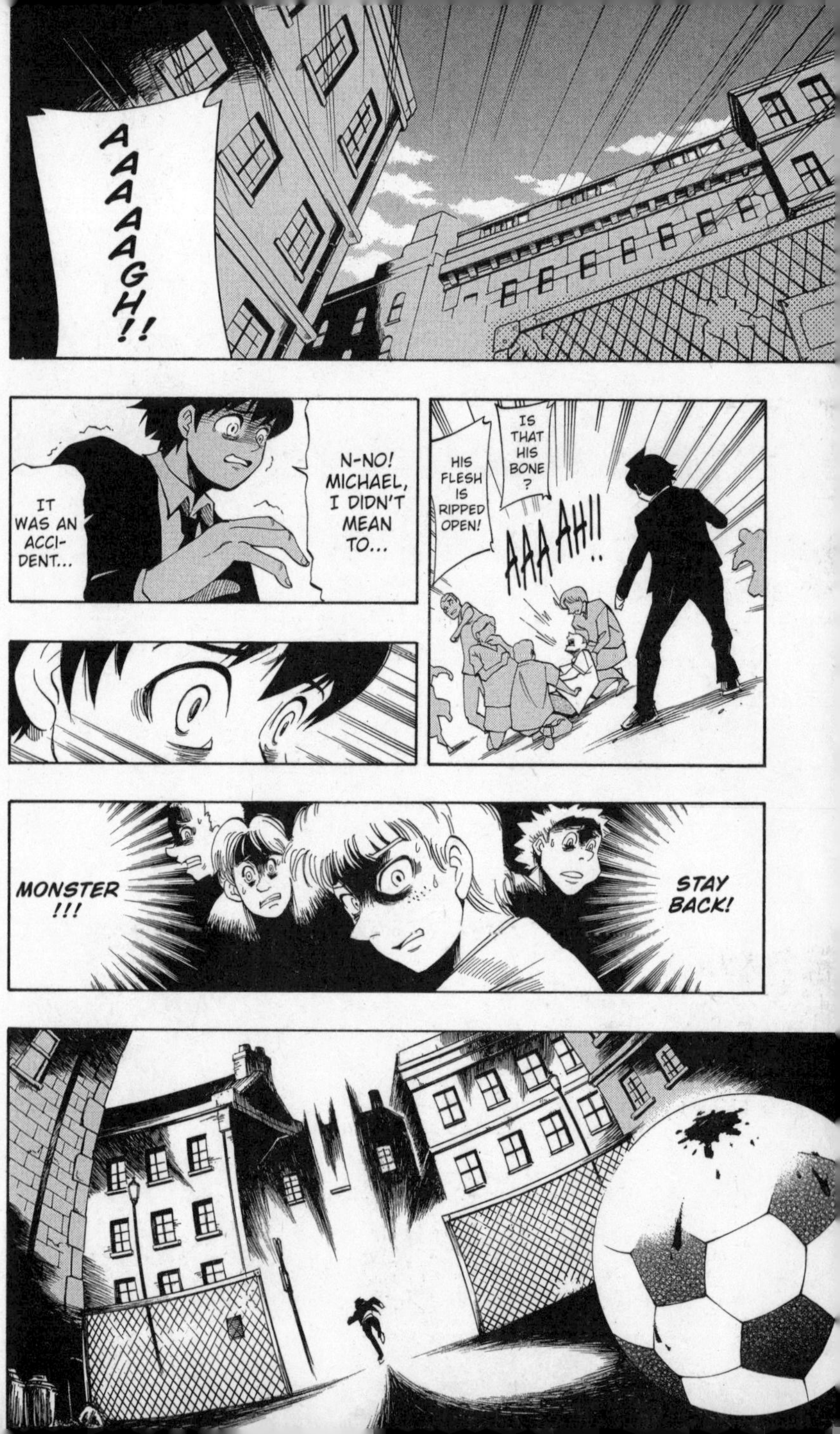
AAAAAGH!!
IS THAT HIS BONE?
HIS FLESH IS RIPPED OPEN!
AAAAH!!
N-NO! MICHAEL, I DIDN'T MEAN TO...
IT WAS AN ACCI-DENT...
STAY BACK!
MONSTER!!!

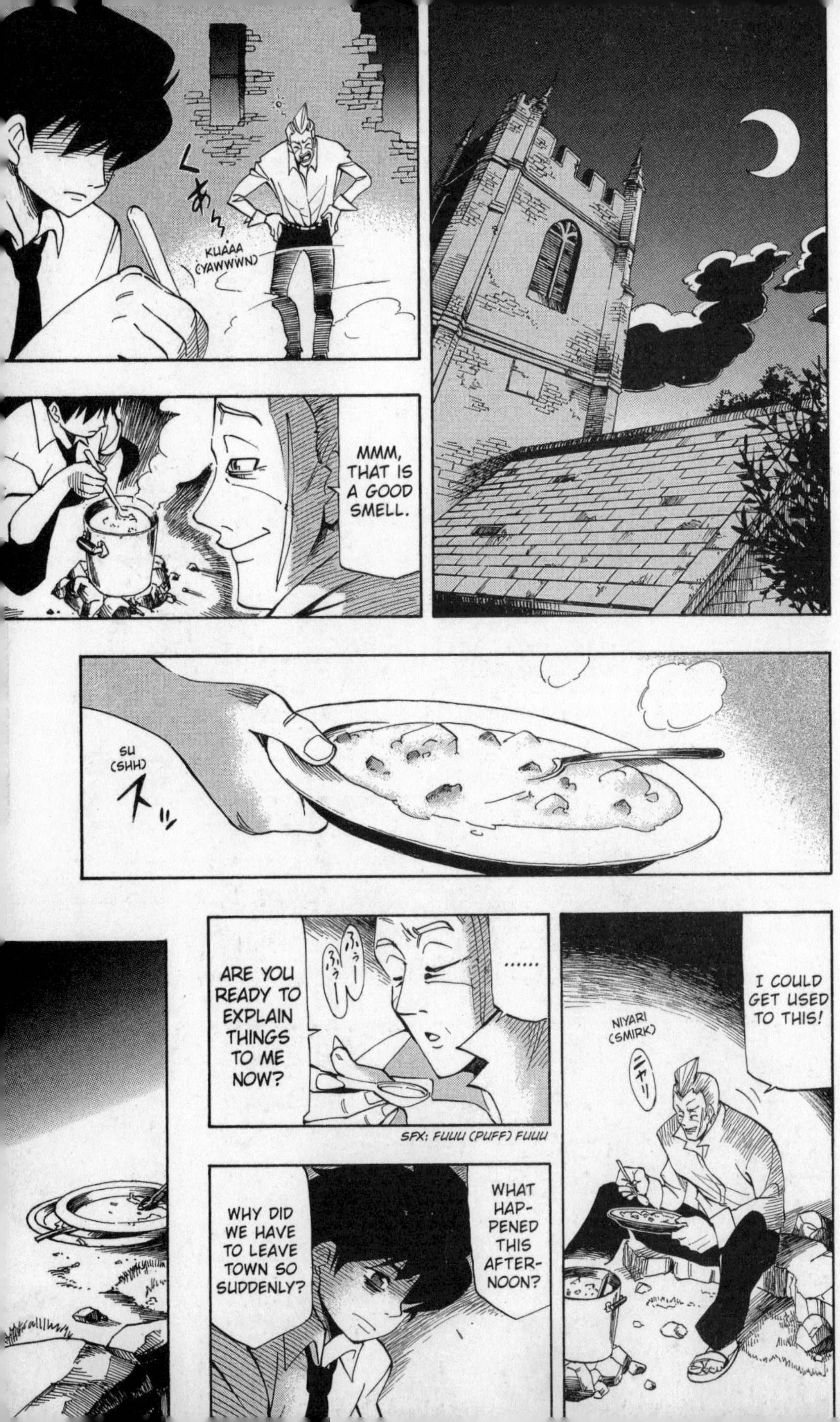
KUAAA (YAWWWN)
MMM, THAT IS A GOOD SMELL.
SU (SHH)
ス
I COULD GET USED TO THIS!
NIYARI (SMIRK)
ニヤリ
......
ARE YOU READY TO EXPLAIN THINGS TO ME NOW?
SFX: FUUU (PUFF) FUUU
WHAT HAPPENED THIS AFTERNOON?
WHY DID WE HAVE TO LEAVE TOWN SO SUDDENLY?

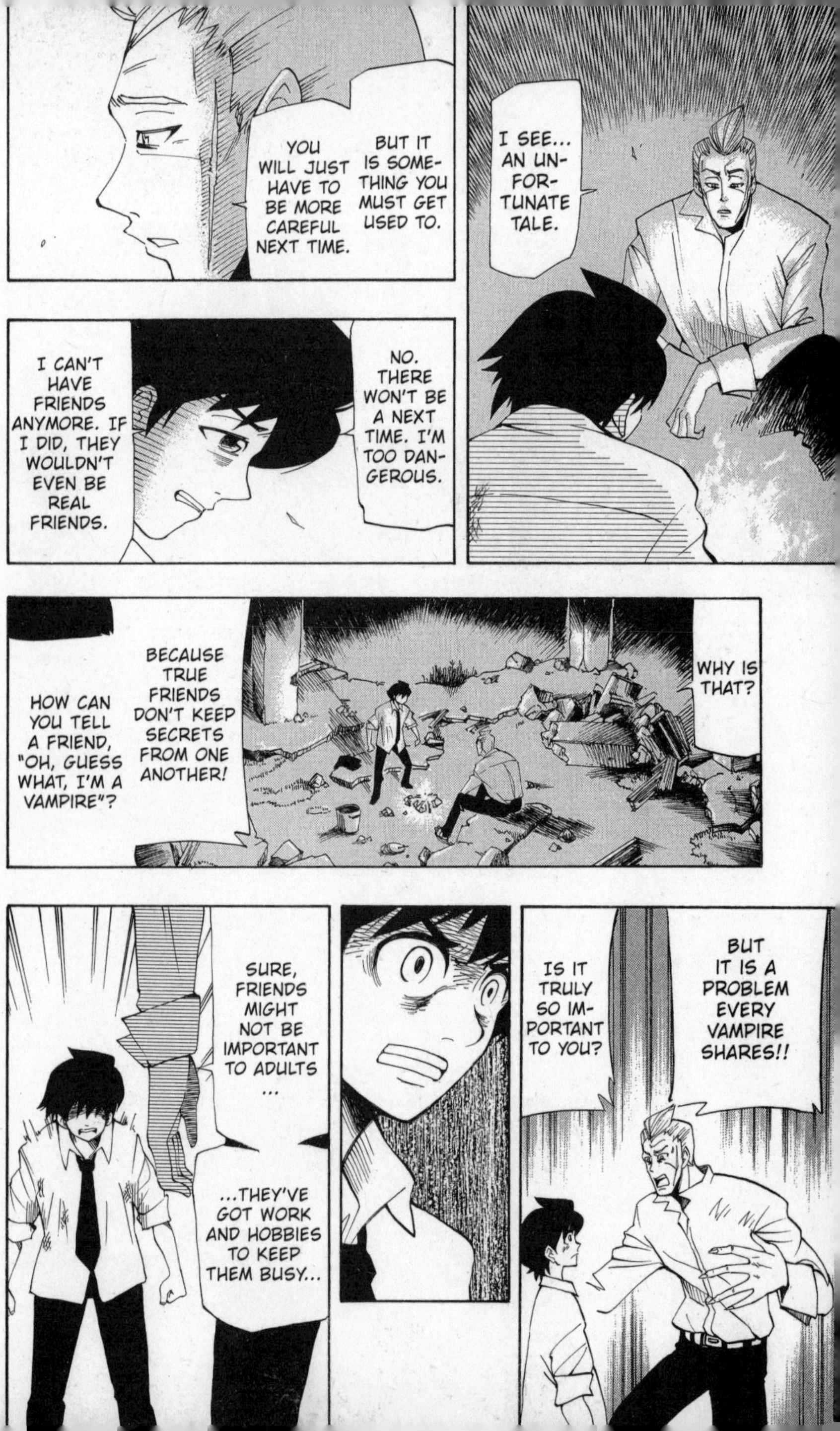
I SEE... AN UN-FORTUNATE TALE.
BUT IT IS SOME-THING YOU MUST GET USED TO.
YOU WILL JUST HAVE TO BE MORE CAREFUL NEXT TIME.
NO. THERE WON'T BE A NEXT TIME. I'M TOO DAN-GEROUS.
I CAN'T HAVE FRIENDS ANYMORE. IF I DID, THEY WOULDN'T EVEN BE REAL FRIENDS.
WHY IS THAT?
BECAUSE TRUE FRIENDS DON'T KEEP SECRETS FROM ONE ANOTHER!
HOW CAN YOU TELL A FRIEND, "OH, GUESS WHAT, I'M A VAMPIRE"?
BUT IT IS A PROBLEM EVERY VAMPIRE SHARES!!
IS IT TRULY SO IM-PORTANT TO YOU?
SURE, FRIENDS MIGHT NOT BE IMPORTANT TO ADULTS ...
...THEY'VE GOT WORK AND HOBBIES TO KEEP THEM BUSY...

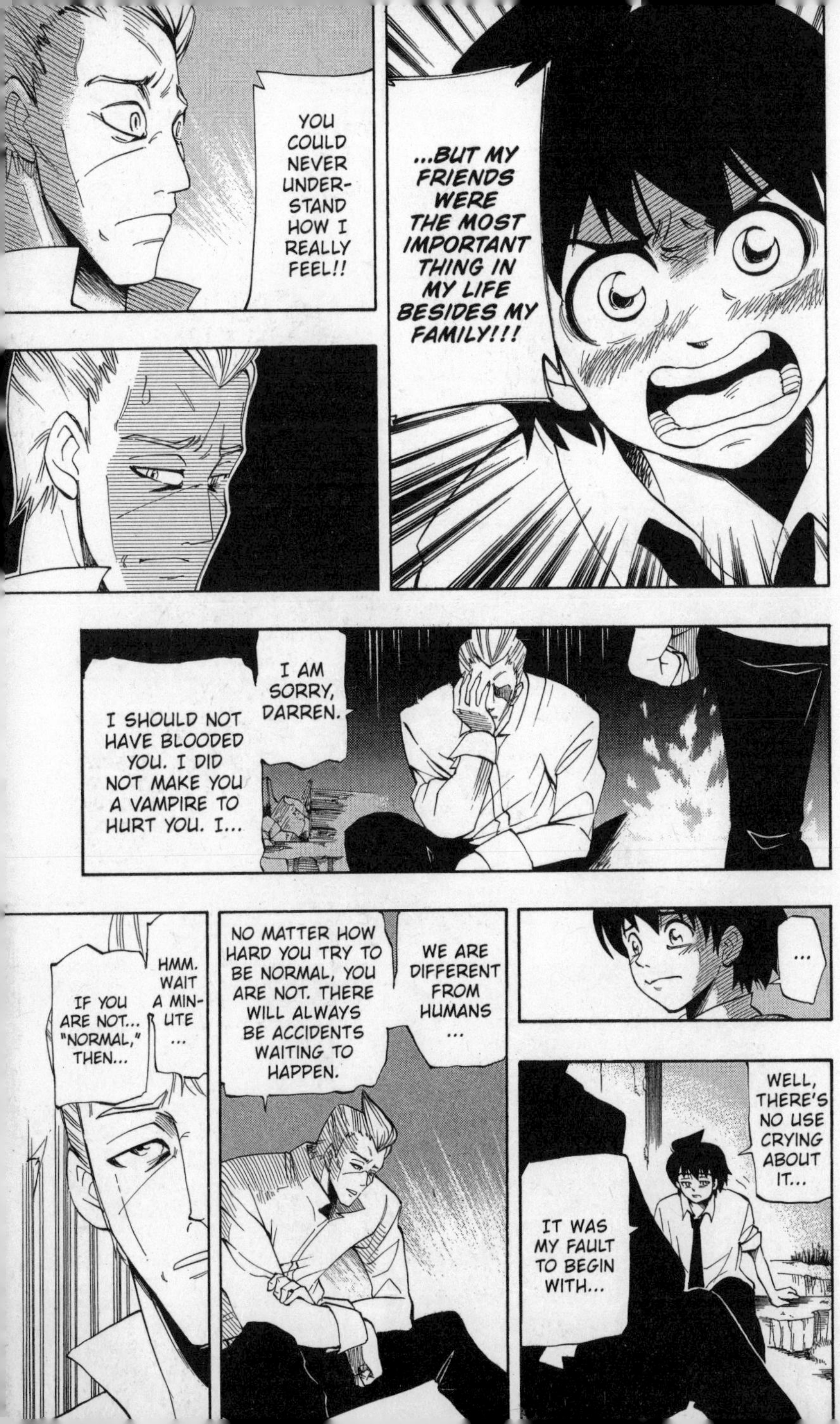
...BUT MY FRIENDS WERE THE MOST IMPORTANT THING IN MY LIFE BESIDES MY FAMILY!!!
YOU COULD NEVER UNDER-STAND HOW I REALLY FEEL!!
I AM SORRY, DARREN.
I SHOULD NOT HAVE BLOODED YOU. I DID NOT MAKE YOU A VAMPIRE TO HURT YOU. I...
...
WELL, THERE'S NO USE CRYING ABOUT IT...
IT WAS MY FAULT TO BEGIN WITH...
WE ARE DIFFERENT FROM HUMANS ...
NO MATTER HOW HARD YOU TRY TO BE NORMAL, YOU ARE NOT. THERE WILL ALWAYS BE ACCIDENTS WAITING TO HAPPEN.
HMM. WAIT A MIN-UTE ...
IF YOU ARE NOT... "NORMAL," THEN...

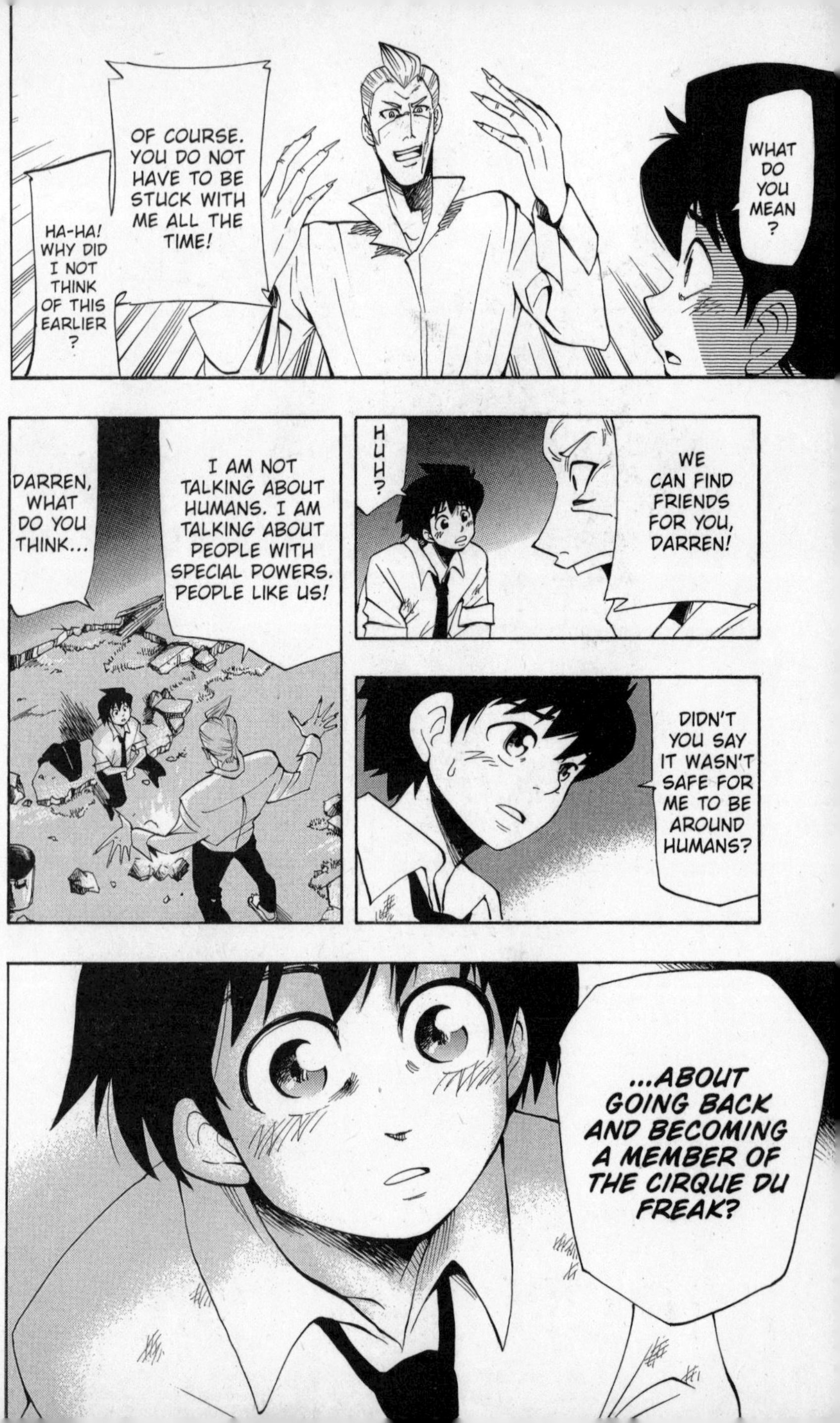
WHAT DO YOU MEAN?
OF COURSE. YOU DO NOT HAVE TO BE STUCK WITH ME ALL THE TIME!
HA-HA! WHY DID I NOT THINK OF THIS EARLIER?
WE CAN FIND FRIENDS FOR YOU, DARREN!
HUH?
DIDN'T YOU SAY IT WASN'T SAFE FOR ME TO BE AROUND HUMANS?
I AM NOT TALKING ABOUT HUMANS. I AM TALKING ABOUT PEOPLE WITH SPECIAL POWERS. PEOPLE LIKE US!
DARREN, WHAT DO YOU THINK...
...ABOUT GOING BACK AND BECOMING A MEMBER OF THE CIRQUE DU FREAK?

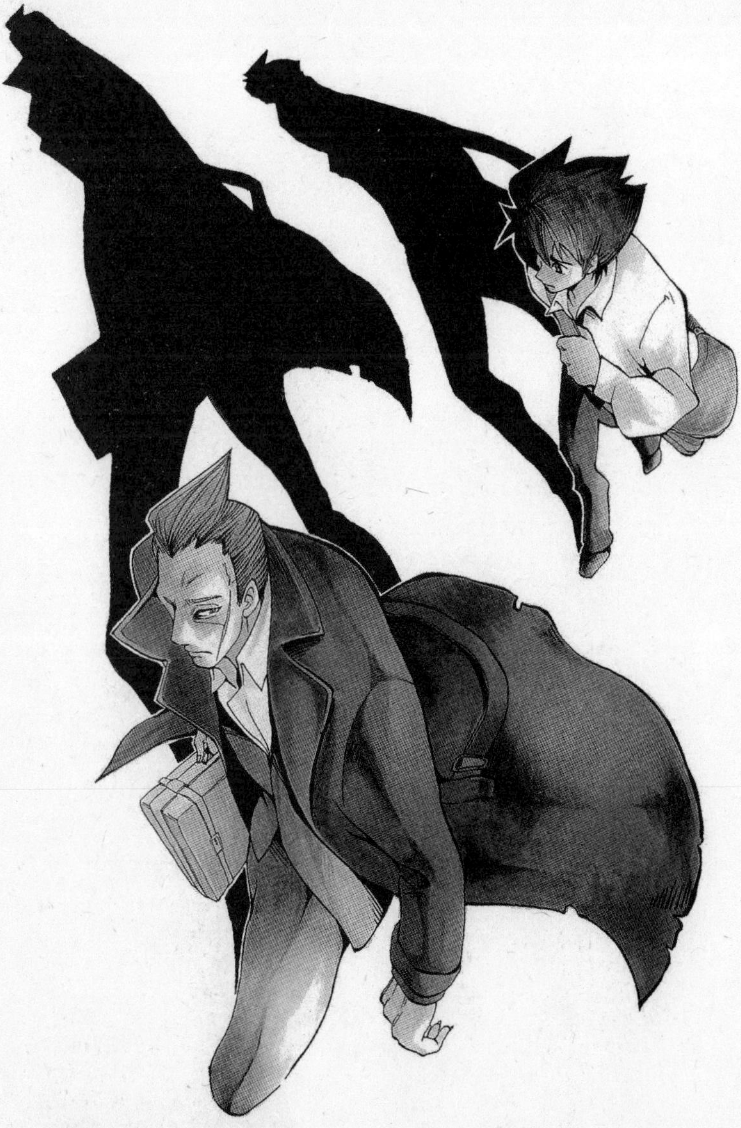

CHAPTER 6:
TO CIRQUE DU FREAK

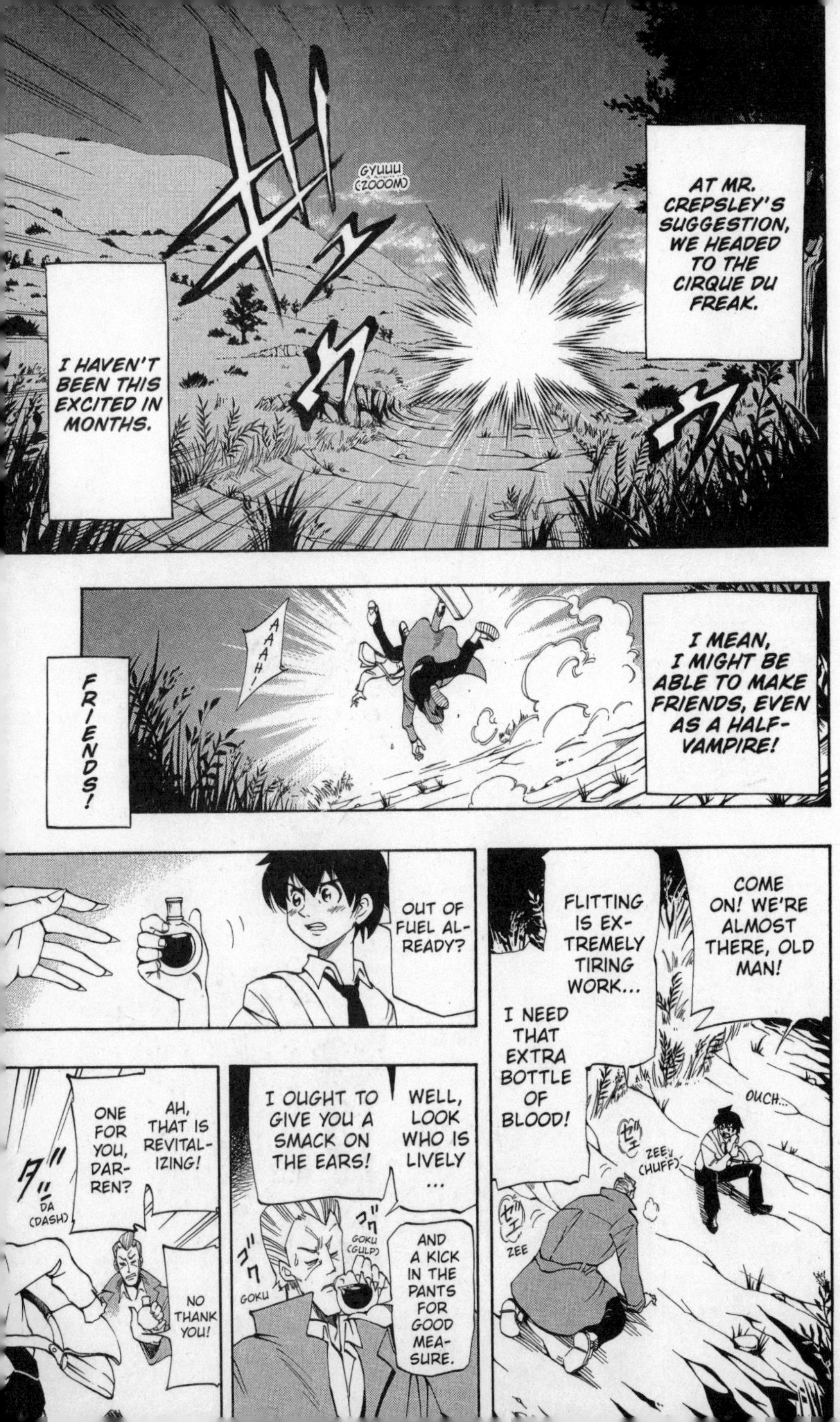
AT MR. CREPSLEY'S SUGGESTION, WE HEADED TO THE CIRQUE DU FREAK.
GYUUU (ZOOOM)
I HAVEN'T BEEN THIS EXCITED IN MONTHS.
I MEAN, I MIGHT BE ABLE TO MAKE FRIENDS, EVEN AS A HALF-VAMPIRE!
AAAH!
FRIENDS!
COME ON! WE'RE ALMOST THERE, OLD MAN!
FLITTING IS EXTREMELY TIRING WORK...
I NEED THAT EXTRA BOTTLE OF BLOOD!
OUCH...
ZEE (CHUFF)
ZEE
OUT OF FUEL ALREADY?
WELL, LOOK WHO IS LIVELY ...
I OUGHT TO GIVE YOU A SMACK ON THE EARS!
GOKU (GULP)
GOKU
AND A KICK IN THE PANTS FOR GOOD MEASURE.
AH, THAT IS REVITALIZING!
ONE FOR YOU, DARREN?
DA (DASH)
NO THANK YOU!

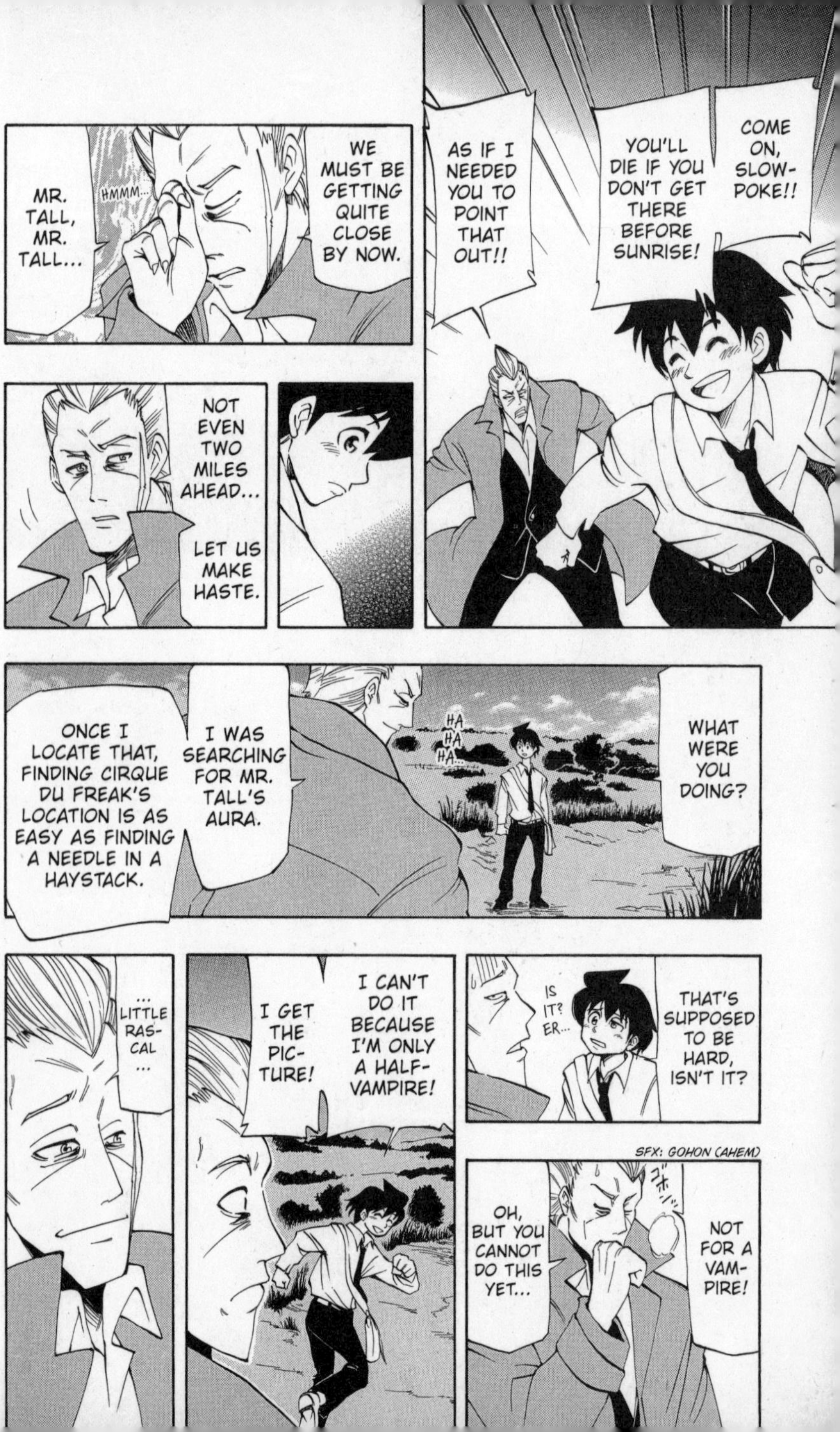
COME ON, SLOW-POKE!!
YOU'LL DIE IF YOU DON'T GET THERE BEFORE SUNRISE!
AS IF I NEEDED YOU TO POINT THAT OUT!!
WE MUST BE GETTING QUITE CLOSE BY NOW.
HMMM...
MR. TALL, MR. TALL...
NOT EVEN TWO MILES AHEAD...
LET US MAKE HASTE.
WHAT WERE YOU DOING?
HA HA HA...
I WAS SEARCHING FOR MR. TALL'S AURA.
ONCE I LOCATE THAT, FINDING CIRQUE DU FREAK'S LOCATION IS AS EASY AS FINDING A NEEDLE IN A HAYSTACK.
THAT'S SUPPOSED TO BE HARD, ISN'T IT?
IS IT? ER...
SFX: GOHON (AHEM)
NOT FOR A VAMPIRE!
OH, BUT YOU CANNOT DO THIS YET...
I CAN'T DO IT BECAUSE I'M ONLY A HALF-VAMPIRE!
I GET THE PICTURE!
...LITTLE RASCAL...

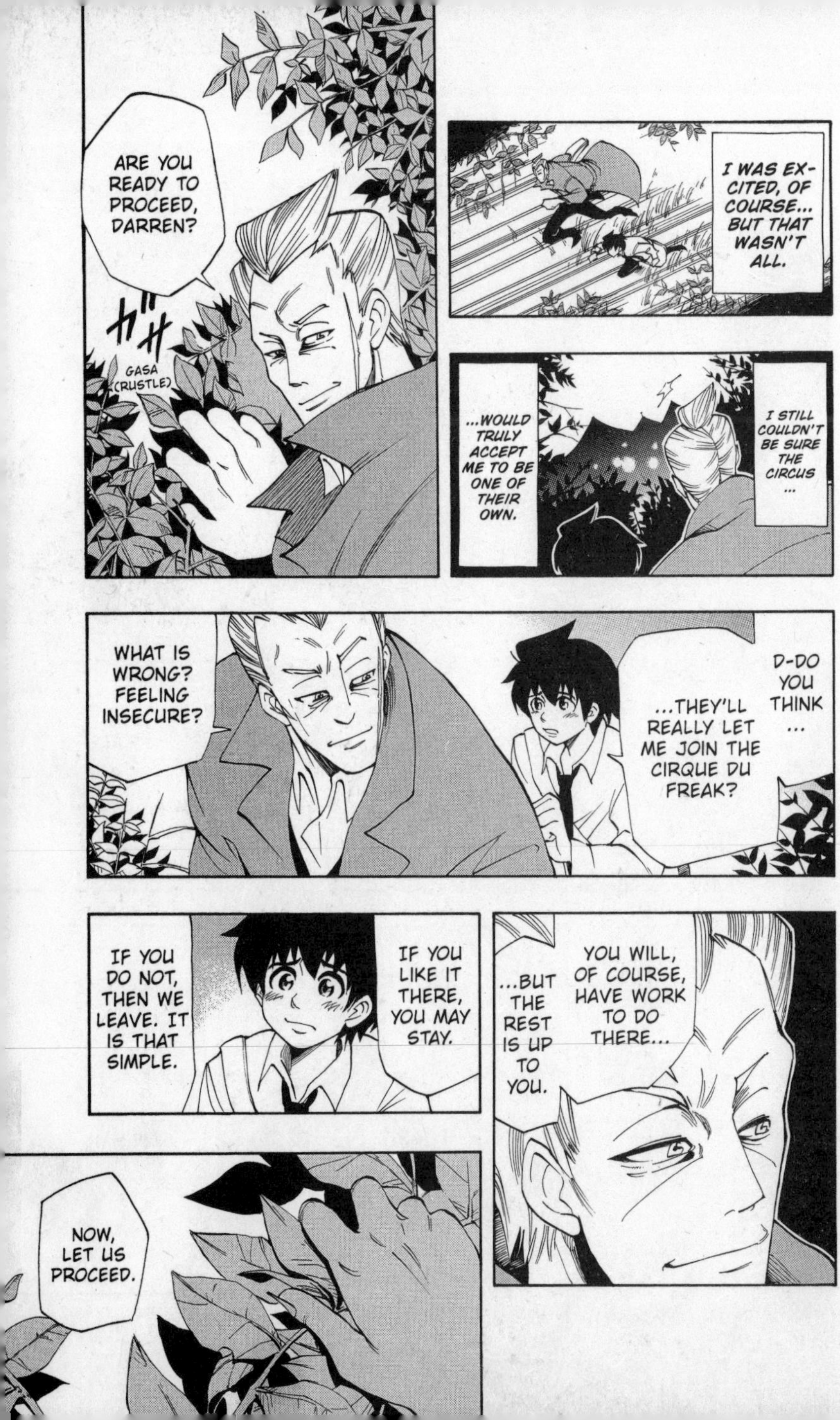
I WAS EXCITED, OF COURSE... BUT THAT WASN'T ALL.
I STILL COULDN'T BE SURE THE CIRCUS ...
...WOULD TRULY ACCEPT ME TO BE ONE OF THEIR OWN.
ARE YOU READY TO PROCEED, DARREN?
GASA (RUSTLE)
D-DO YOU THINK ...
...THEY'LL REALLY LET ME JOIN THE CIRQUE DU FREAK?
WHAT IS WRONG? FEELING INSECURE?
YOU WILL, OF COURSE, HAVE WORK TO DO THERE...
...BUT THE REST IS UP TO YOU.
IF YOU LIKE IT THERE, YOU MAY STAY.
IF YOU DO NOT, THEN WE LEAVE. IT IS THAT SIMPLE.
NOW, LET US PROCEED.

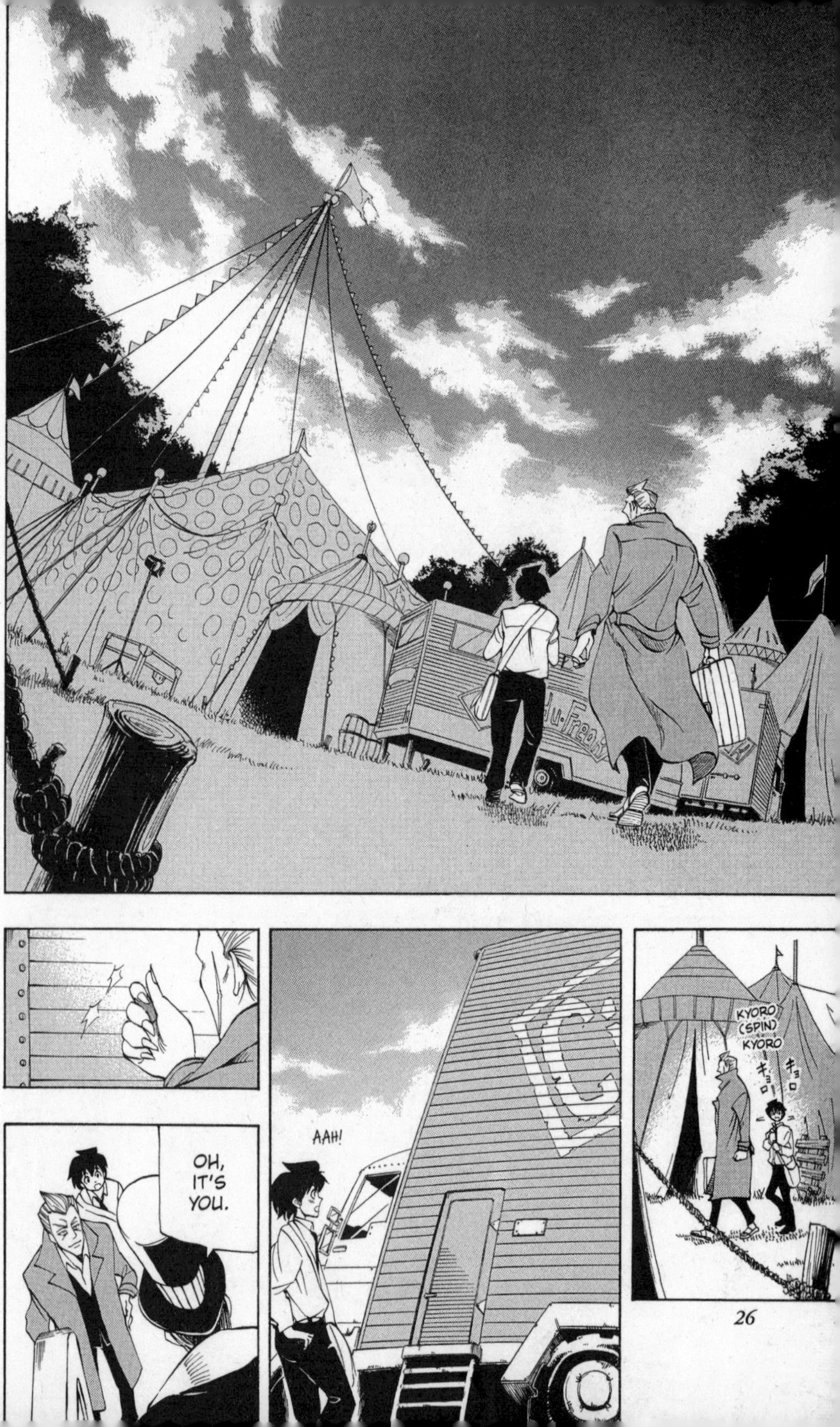
KYORO (SPIN) KYORO
キョロ キョロ
AAH!
OH, IT'S YOU.

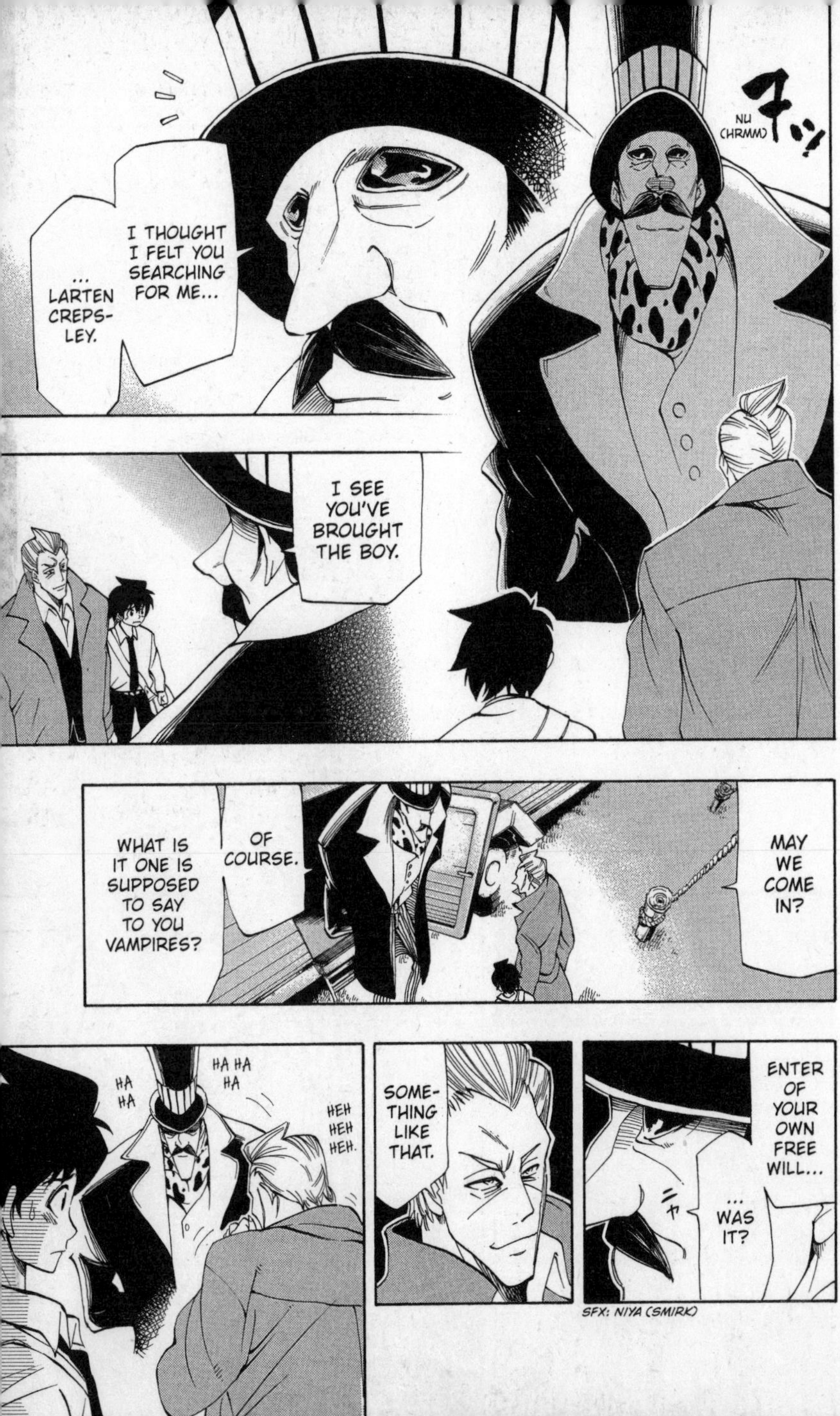
ヌッ
NU (HRMM)
I THOUGHT I FELT YOU SEARCHING FOR ME...
... LARTEN CREPS-LEY.
I SEE YOU'VE BROUGHT THE BOY.
MAY WE COME IN?
OF COURSE.
WHAT IS IT ONE IS SUPPOSED TO SAY TO YOU VAMPIRES?
ENTER OF YOUR OWN FREE WILL...
ニャ
... WAS IT?
SOME-THING LIKE THAT.
HEH HEH HEH.
HA HA HA
HA HA
SFX: NIYA (SMIRK)

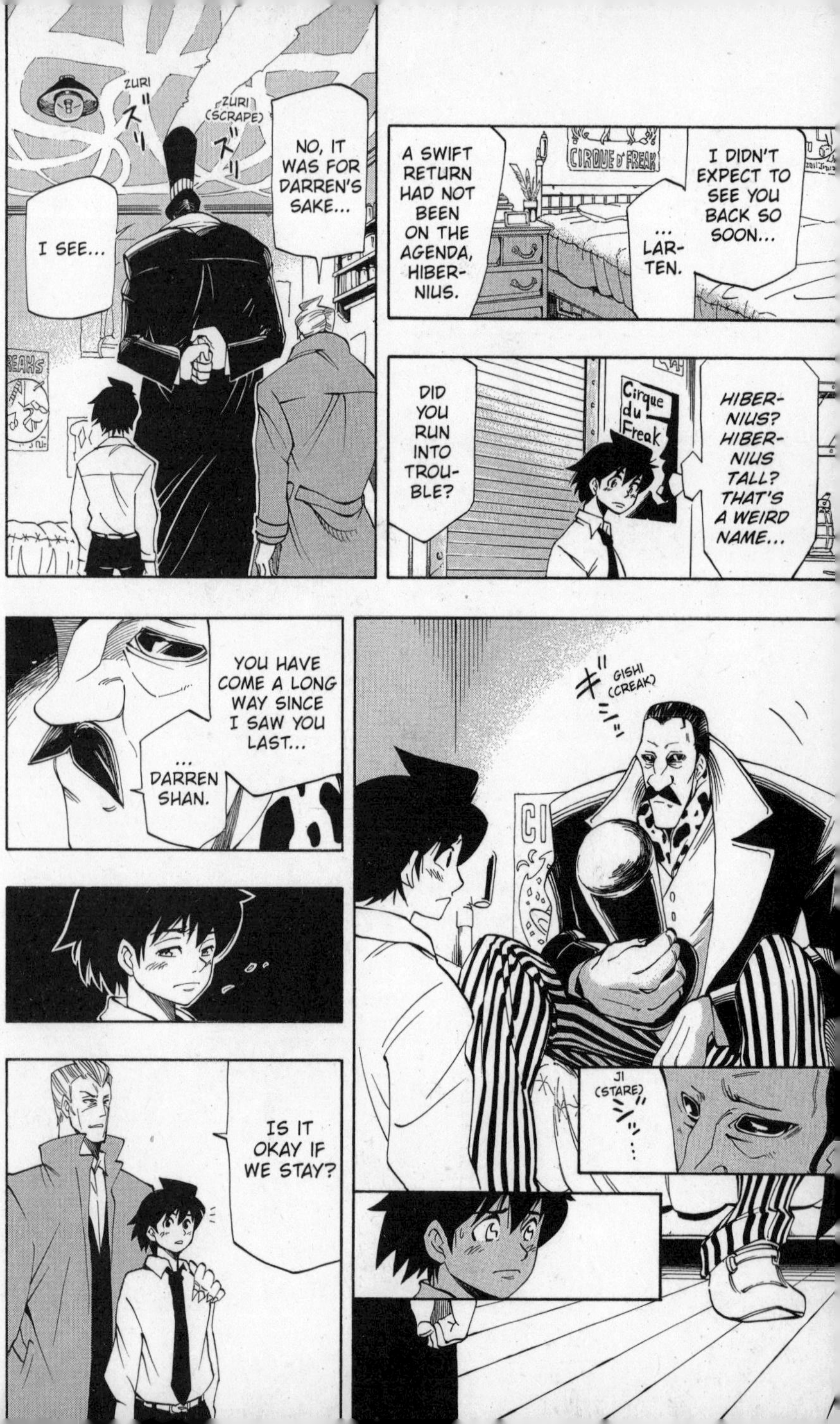

I DIDN'T EXPECT TO SEE YOU BACK SO SOON...
... LARTEN.
A SWIFT RETURN HAD NOT BEEN ON THE AGENDA, HIBERNIUS.
CIRQUE D'FREAK
HIBERNIUS? HIBERNIUS TALL? THAT'S A WEIRD NAME...
Cirque du Freak
DID YOU RUN INTO TROUBLE?
ZURI
ZURI (SCRAPE)
NO, IT WAS FOR DARREN'S SAKE...
I SEE...
GISHI (CREAK)
JI (STARE)
YOU HAVE COME A LONG WAY SINCE I SAW YOU LAST...
... DARREN SHAN.
IS IT OKAY IF WE STAY?

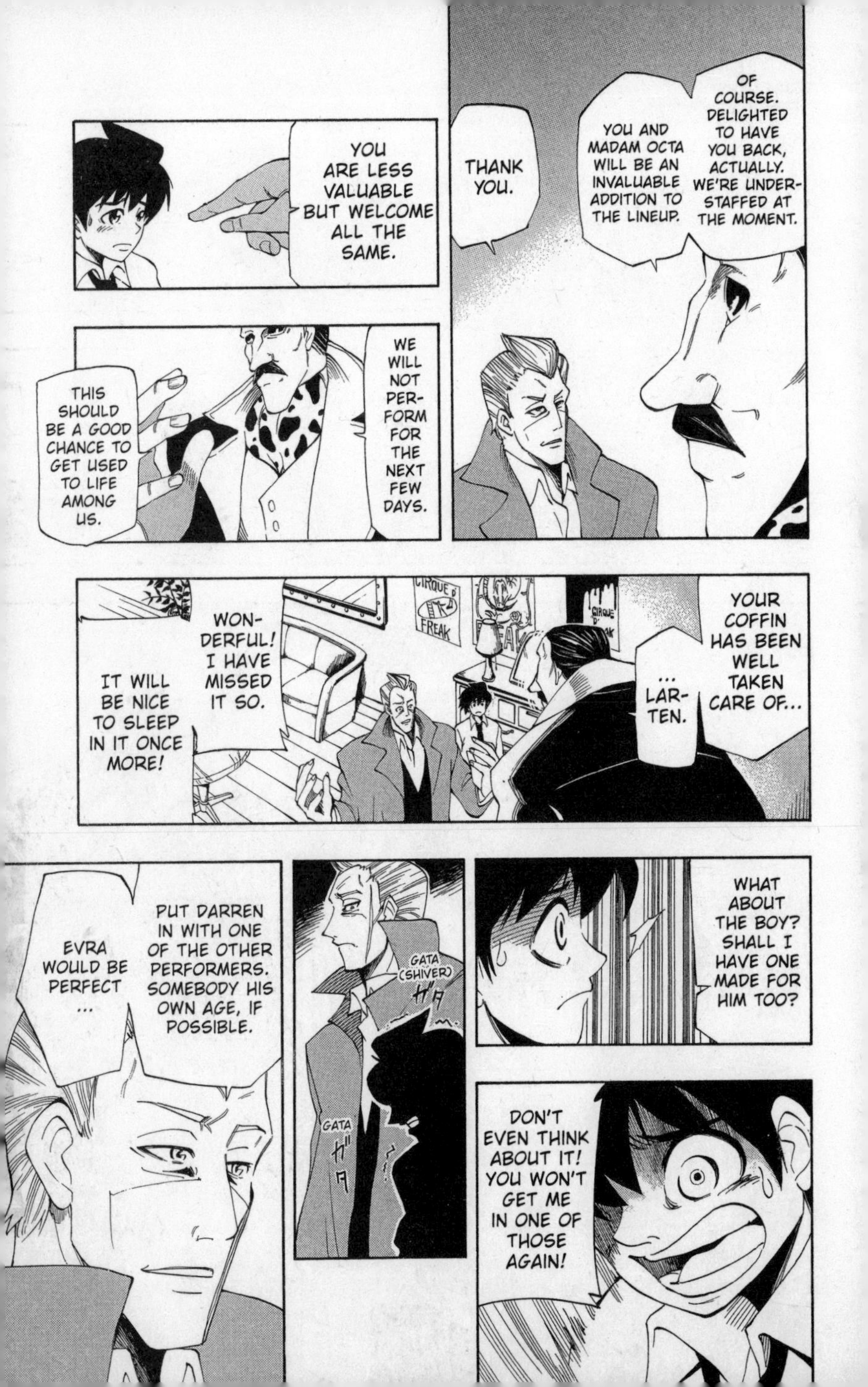
OF COURSE. DELIGHTED TO HAVE YOU BACK, ACTUALLY. WE'RE UNDER-STAFFED AT THE MOMENT.
YOU AND MADAM OCTA WILL BE AN INVALUABLE ADDITION TO THE LINEUP.
THANK YOU.
YOU ARE LESS VALUABLE BUT WELCOME ALL THE SAME.
WE WILL NOT PERFORM FOR THE NEXT FEW DAYS.
THIS SHOULD BE A GOOD CHANCE TO GET USED TO LIFE AMONG US.
YOUR COFFIN HAS BEEN WELL TAKEN CARE OF...
... LAR-TEN.
CIRQUE D' FREAK
WON-DERFUL! I HAVE MISSED IT SO.
IT WILL BE NICE TO SLEEP IN IT ONCE MORE!
WHAT ABOUT THE BOY? SHALL I HAVE ONE MADE FOR HIM TOO?
DON'T EVEN THINK ABOUT IT! YOU WON'T GET ME IN ONE OF THOSE AGAIN!
GATA (SHIVER)
GATA
PUT DARREN IN WITH ONE OF THE OTHER PERFORMERS. SOMEBODY HIS OWN AGE, IF POSSIBLE.
EVRA WOULD BE PERFECT ...

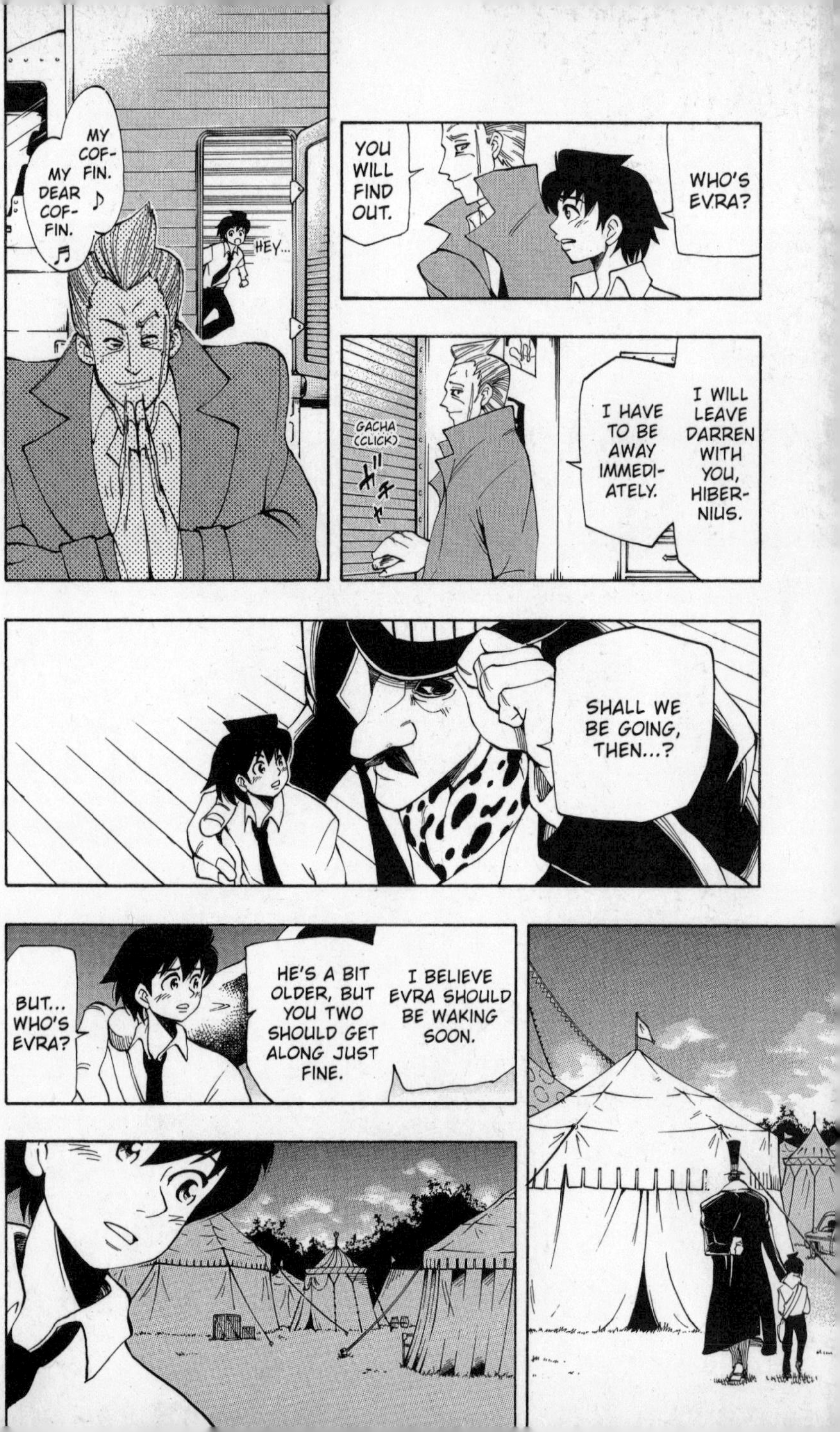
WHO'S EVRA?
YOU WILL FIND OUT.
I WILL LEAVE DARREN WITH YOU, HIBERNIUS.
I HAVE TO BE AWAY IMMEDIATELY.
GACHA (CLICK)
MY COF-FIN. ♪ MY DEAR COF-FIN. ♬
HEY...
SHALL WE BE GOING, THEN...?
I BELIEVE EVRA SHOULD BE WAKING SOON.
HE'S A BIT OLDER, BUT YOU TWO SHOULD GET ALONG JUST FINE.
BUT... WHO'S EVRA?

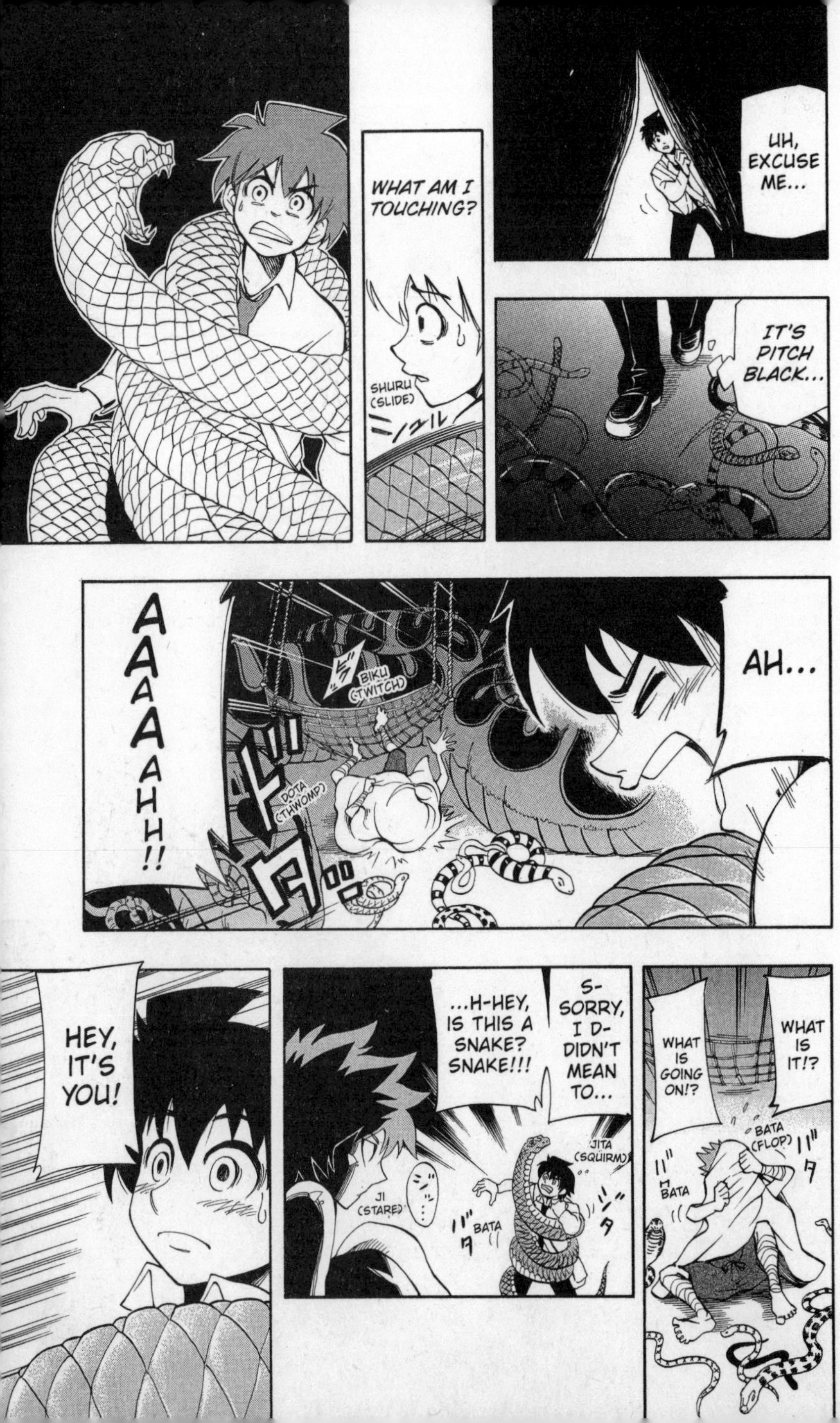
UH, EXCUSE ME...
IT'S PITCH BLACK...
WHAT AM I TOUCHING?
SHURU (SLIDE)
AH...
BIKU (TWITCH)
AAAAAAHH!!
DOTA (THWOMP)
WHAT IS IT!?
WHAT IS GOING ON!?
BATA (FLOP)
BATA
S-SORRY, I D-DIDN'T MEAN TO...
...H-HEY, IS THIS A SNAKE? SNAKE!!!
JITA (SQUIRM)
JI (STARE)
BATA
HEY, IT'S YOU!

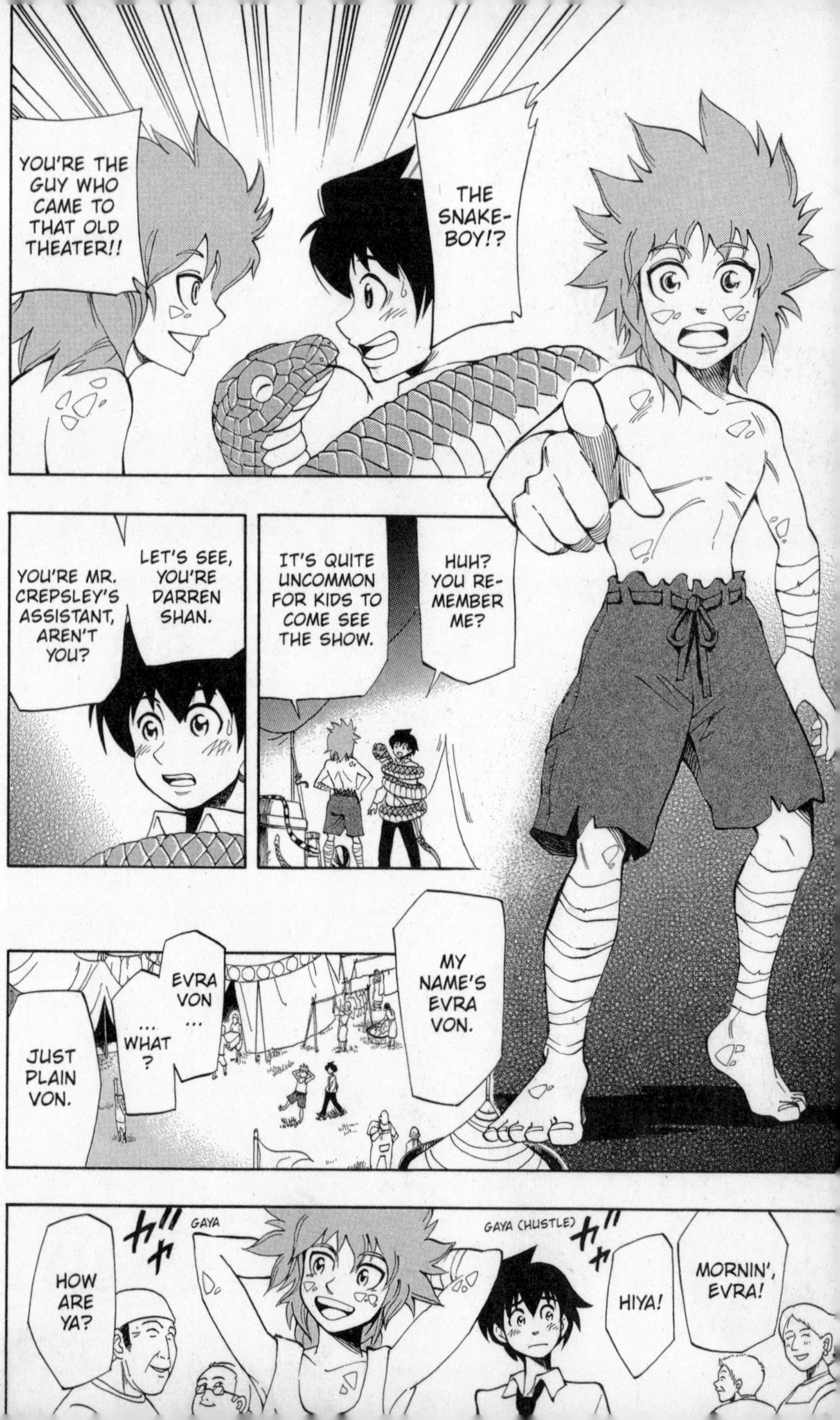
THE SNAKE-BOY!?
YOU'RE THE GUY WHO CAME TO THAT OLD THEATER!!
HUH? YOU RE-MEMBER ME?
IT'S QUITE UNCOMMON FOR KIDS TO COME SEE THE SHOW.
LET'S SEE, YOU'RE DARREN SHAN.
YOU'RE MR. CREPSLEY'S ASSISTANT, AREN'T YOU?
MY NAME'S EVRA VON.
EVRA VON ...
... WHAT ?
JUST PLAIN VON.
MORNIN', EVRA!
HIYA!
GAYA (HUSTLE)
GAYA
HOW ARE YA?

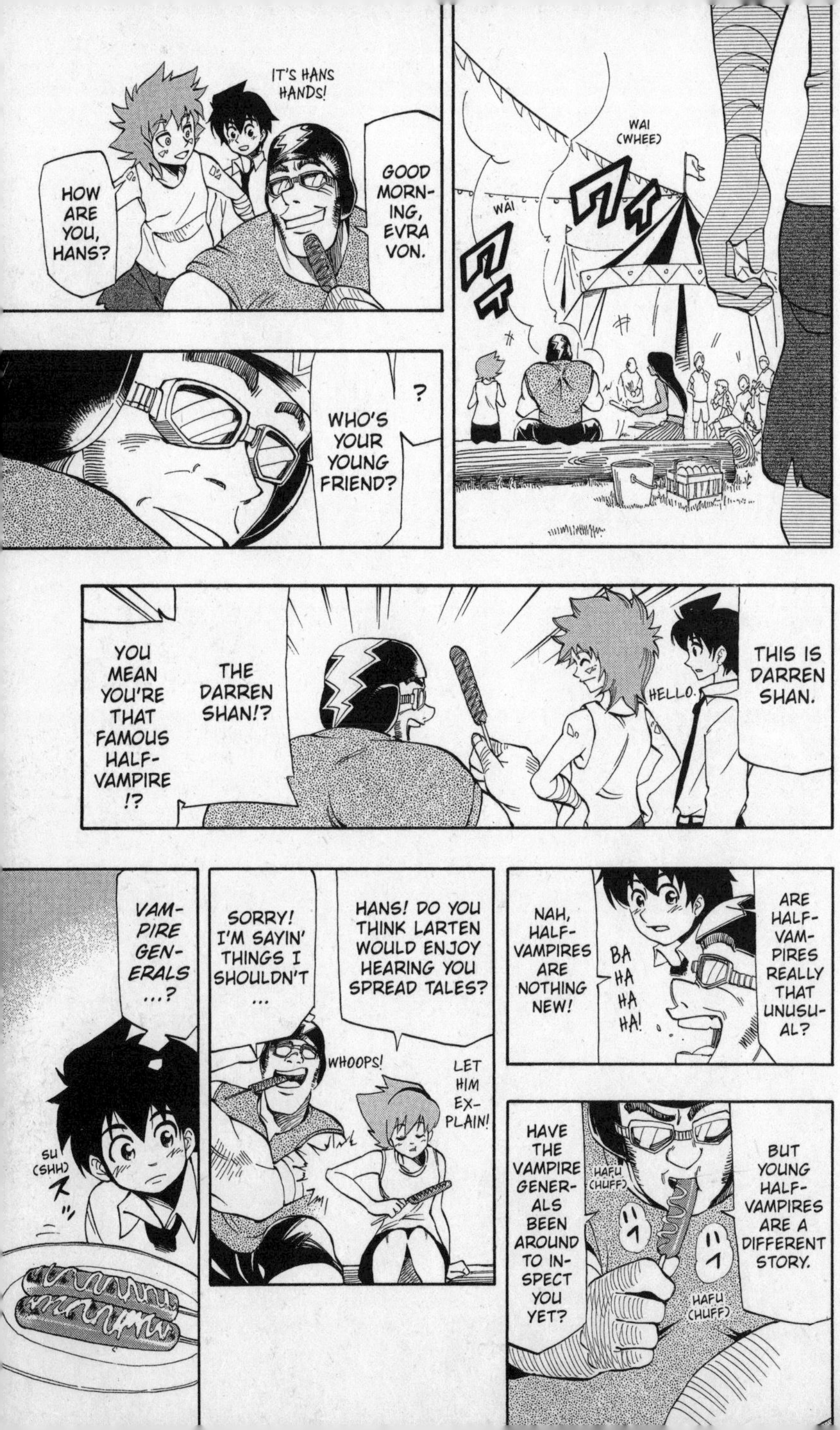
GOOD MORNING, EVRA VON.
IT'S HANS HANDS!
HOW ARE YOU, HANS?
WAI (WHEE)
WAI
?
WHO'S YOUR YOUNG FRIEND?
THIS IS DARREN SHAN.
HELLO.
THE DARREN SHAN!?
YOU MEAN YOU'RE THAT FAMOUS HALF-VAMPIRE!?
ARE HALF-VAMPIRES REALLY THAT UNUSUAL?
BA HA HA HA!
NAH, HALF-VAMPIRES ARE NOTHING NEW!
BUT YOUNG HALF-VAMPIRES ARE A DIFFERENT STORY.
HAFU (CHUFF)
HAFU (CHUFF)
HAVE THE VAMPIRE GENERALS BEEN AROUND TO INSPECT YOU YET?
HANS! DO YOU THINK LARTEN WOULD ENJOY HEARING YOU SPREAD TALES?
LET HIM EXPLAIN!
WHOOPS!
SORRY! I'M SAYIN' THINGS I SHOULDN'T ...
VAMPIRE GENERALS ...?
SU (SHH)

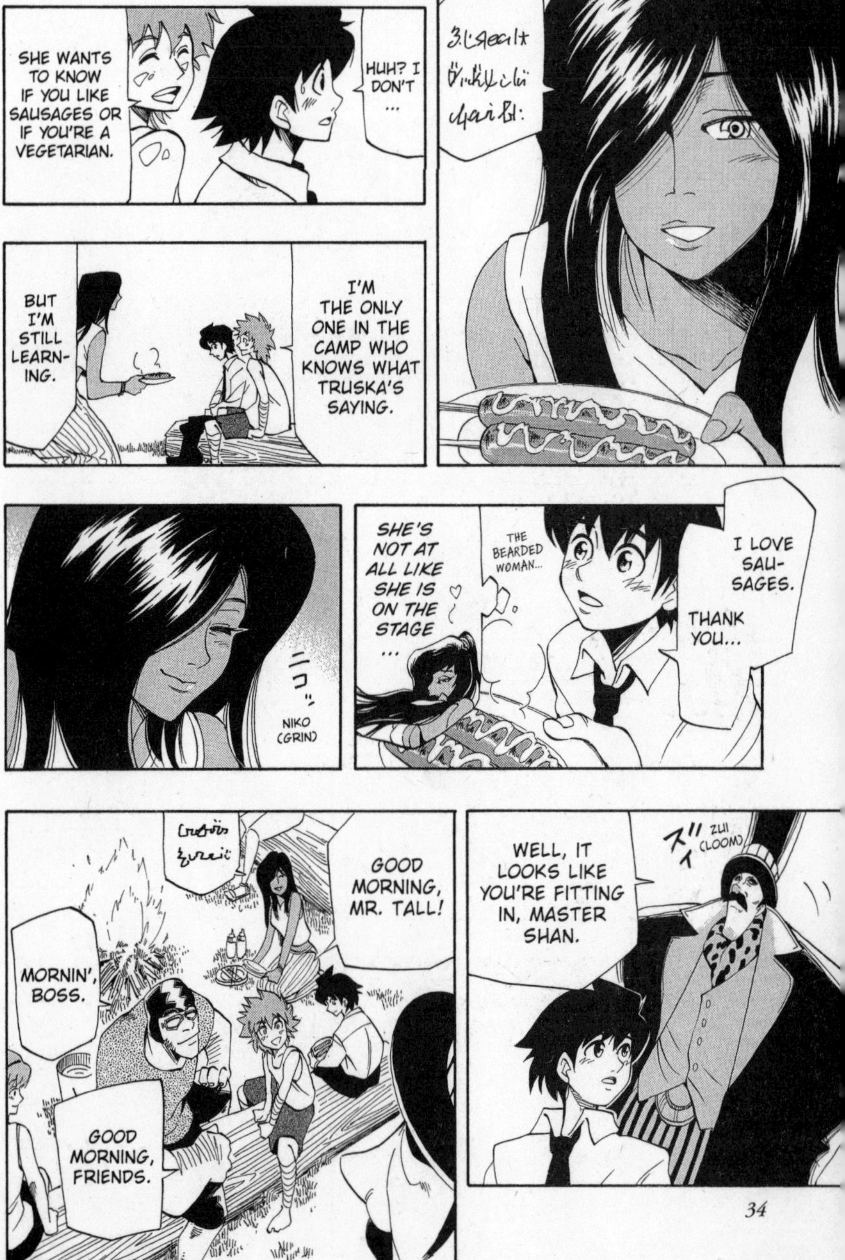
HUH? I DON'T ...
SHE WANTS TO KNOW IF YOU LIKE SAUSAGES OR IF YOU'RE A VEGETARIAN.
I'M THE ONLY ONE IN THE CAMP WHO KNOWS WHAT TRUSKA'S SAYING.
BUT I'M STILL LEARNING.
I LOVE SAUSAGES.
THANK YOU...
THE BEARDED WOMAN...
SHE'S NOT AT ALL LIKE SHE IS ON THE STAGE ...
ニコッ
NIKO (GRIN)
ズイ
ZUI (LOOM)
WELL, IT LOOKS LIKE YOU'RE FITTING IN, MASTER SHAN.
GOOD MORNING, MR. TALL!
MORNIN', BOSS.
GOOD MORNING, FRIENDS.

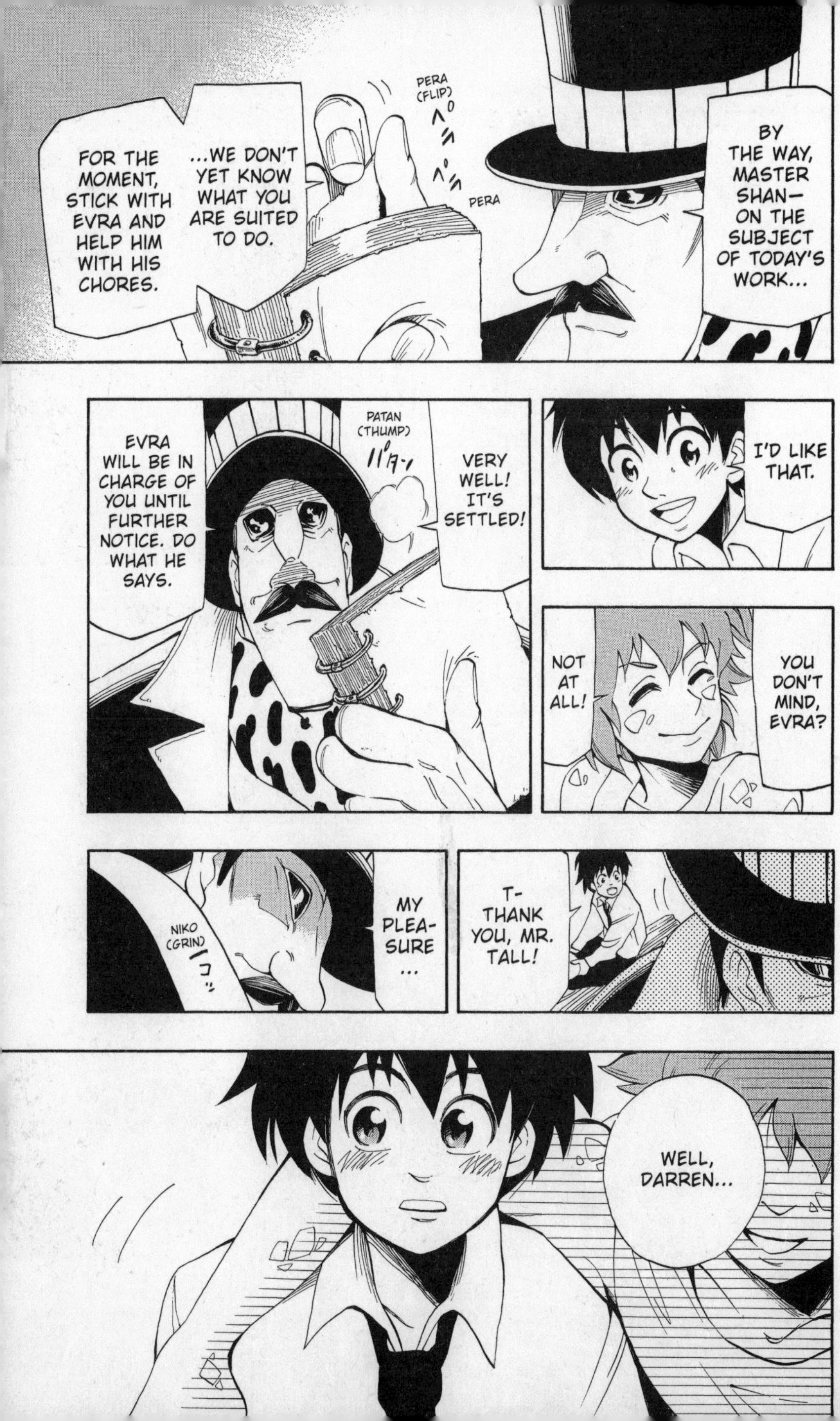

BY THE WAY, MASTER SHAN— ON THE SUBJECT OF TODAY'S WORK...
PERA (FLIP)
PERA
...WE DON'T YET KNOW WHAT YOU ARE SUITED TO DO.
FOR THE MOMENT, STICK WITH EVRA AND HELP HIM WITH HIS CHORES.
I'D LIKE THAT.
YOU DON'T MIND, EVRA?
NOT AT ALL!
VERY WELL! IT'S SETTLED!
PATAN (THUMP)
EVRA WILL BE IN CHARGE OF YOU UNTIL FURTHER NOTICE. DO WHAT HE SAYS.
T-THANK YOU, MR. TALL!
MY PLEASURE...
NIKO (GRIN)
WELL, DARREN...

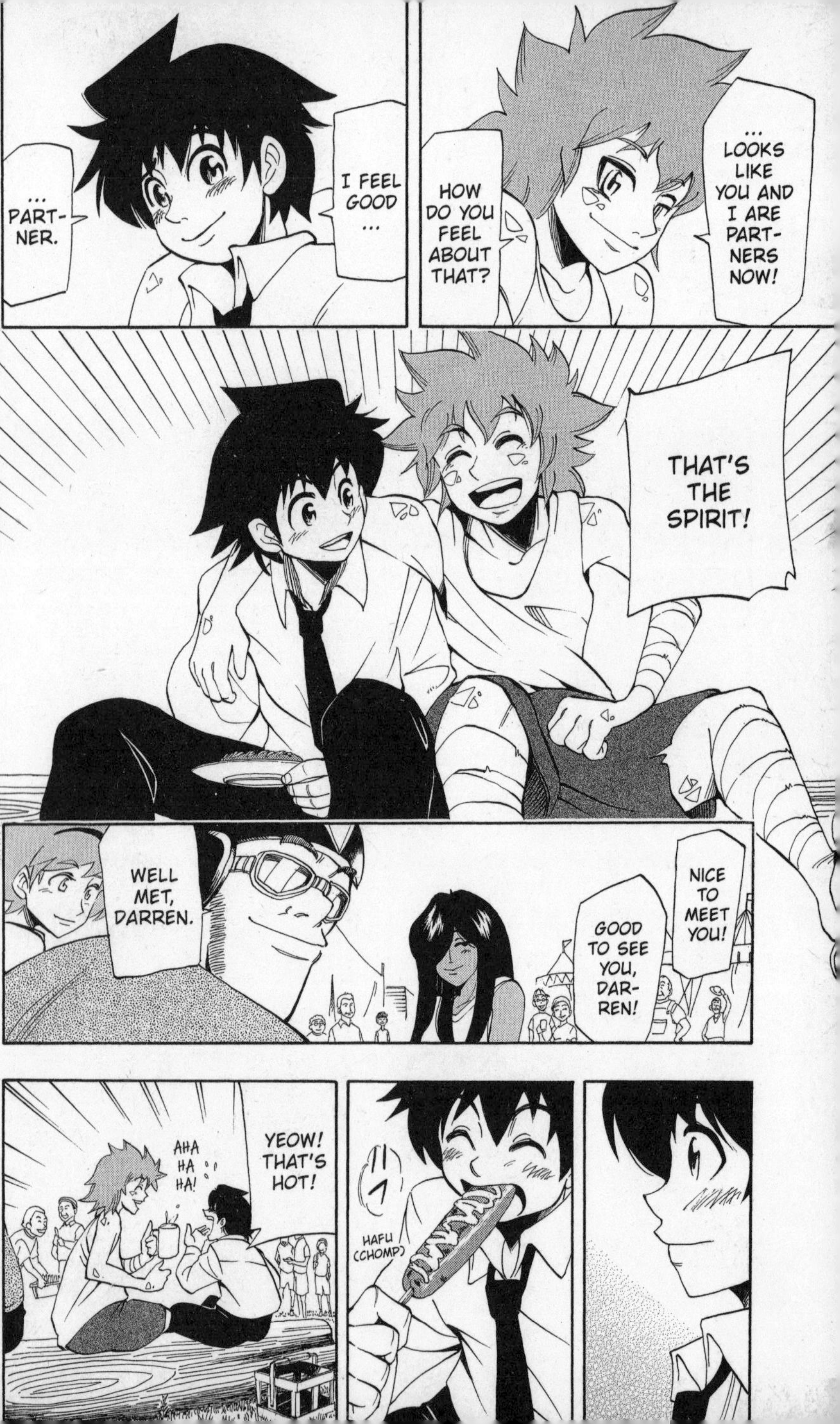
... LOOKS LIKE YOU AND I ARE PART-NERS NOW!
HOW DO YOU FEEL ABOUT THAT?
I FEEL GOOD ...
... PART-NER.
THAT'S THE SPIRIT!
NICE TO MEET YOU!
GOOD TO SEE YOU, DAR-REN!
WELL MET, DARREN.
HAFU (CHOMP)
YEOW! THAT'S HOT!
AHA HA HA!

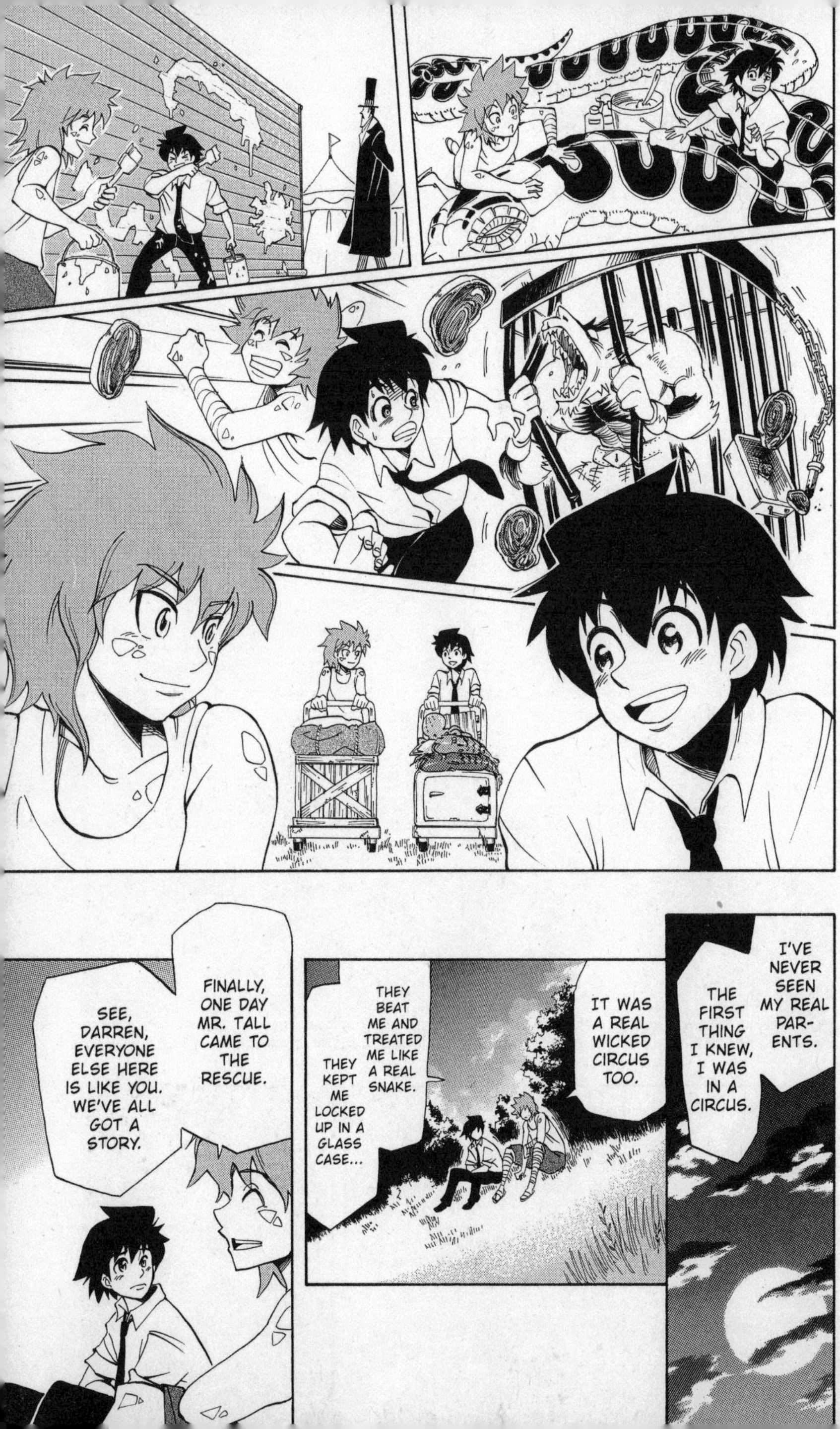
I'VE NEVER SEEN MY REAL PAR-ENTS.
THE FIRST THING I KNEW, I WAS IN A CIRCUS.
IT WAS A REAL WICKED CIRCUS TOO.
THEY BEAT ME AND TREATED ME LIKE A REAL SNAKE.
THEY KEPT ME LOCKED UP IN A GLASS CASE...
FINALLY, ONE DAY MR. TALL CAME TO THE RESCUE.
SEE, DARREN, EVERYONE ELSE HERE IS LIKE YOU. WE'VE ALL GOT A STORY.

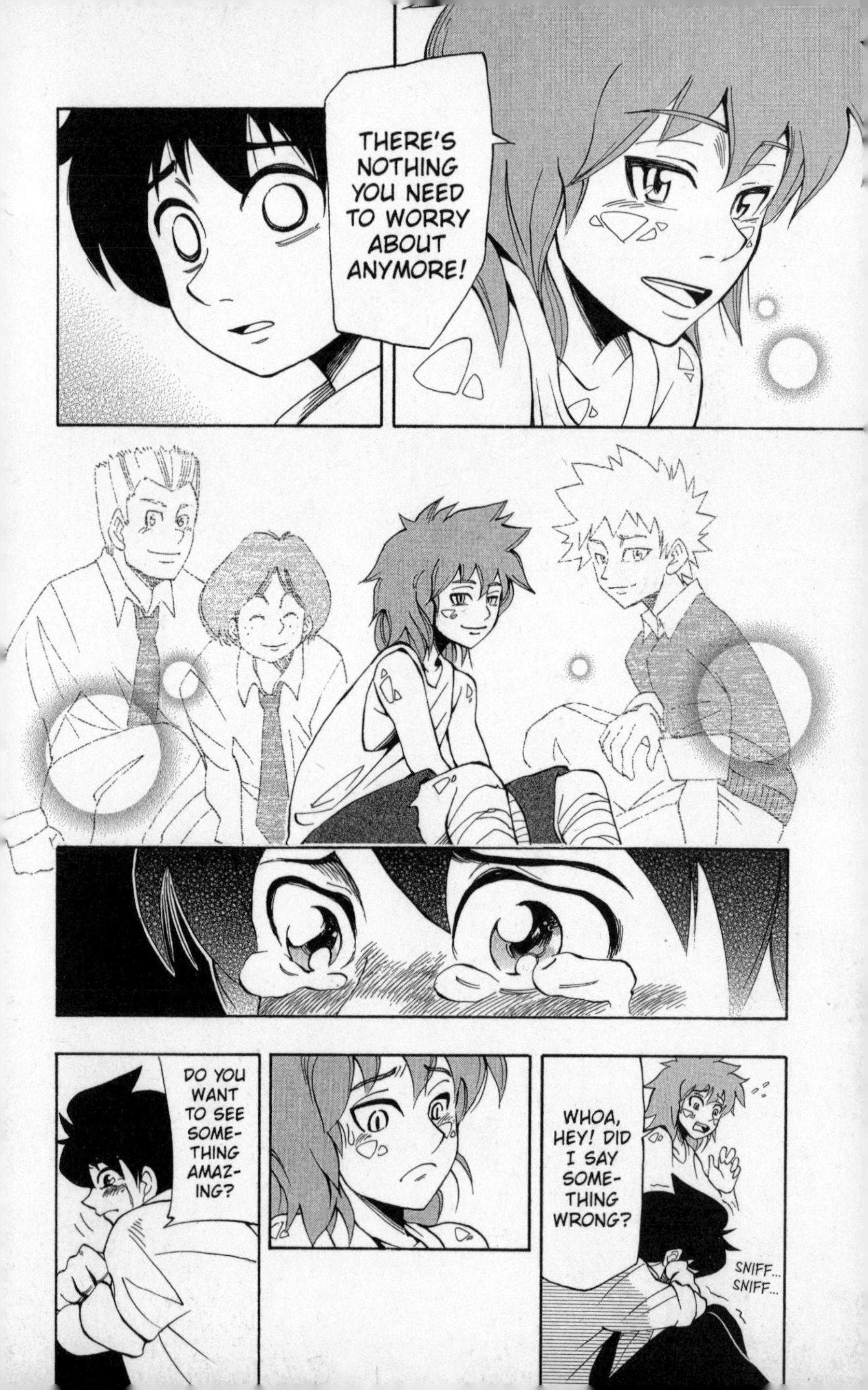
THERE'S NOTHING YOU NEED TO WORRY ABOUT ANYMORE!
WHOA, HEY! DID I SAY SOME-THING WRONG?
SNIFF... SNIFF...
DO YOU WANT TO SEE SOME-THING AMAZ-ING?

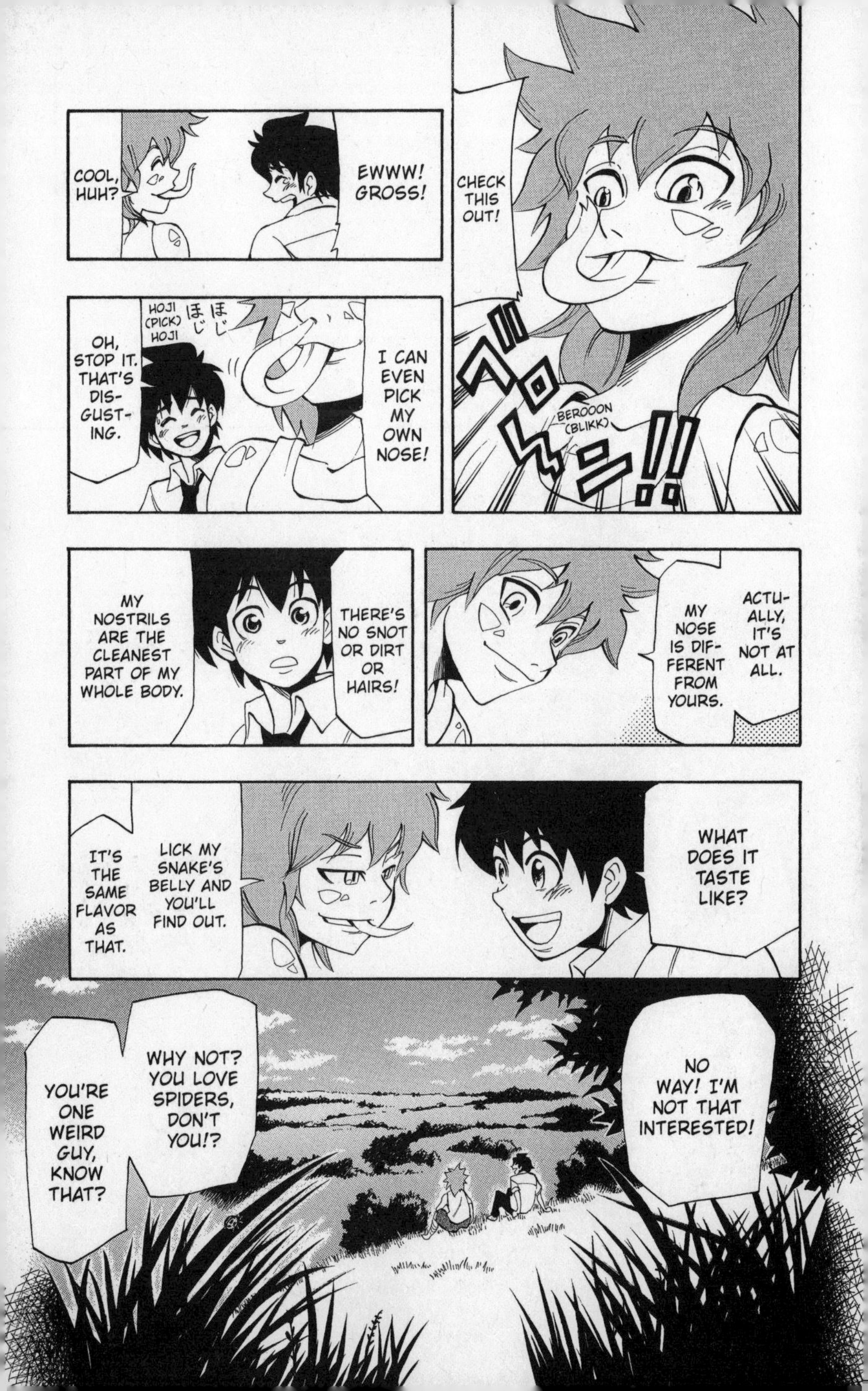
CHECK THIS OUT!
BEROOON (BLIKK)
EWWW! GROSS!
COOL, HUH?
I CAN EVEN PICK MY OWN NOSE!
ほじほじ
HOJI (PICK) HOJI
OH, STOP IT. THAT'S DISGUSTING.
ACTUALLY, IT'S NOT AT ALL.
MY NOSE IS DIFFERENT FROM YOURS.
THERE'S NO SNOT OR DIRT OR HAIRS!
MY NOSTRILS ARE THE CLEANEST PART OF MY WHOLE BODY.
WHAT DOES IT TASTE LIKE?
LICK MY SNAKE'S BELLY AND YOU'LL FIND OUT.
IT'S THE SAME FLAVOR AS THAT.
NO WAY! I'M NOT THAT INTERESTED!
WHY NOT? YOU LOVE SPIDERS, DON'T YOU!?
YOU'RE ONE WEIRD GUY, KNOW THAT?

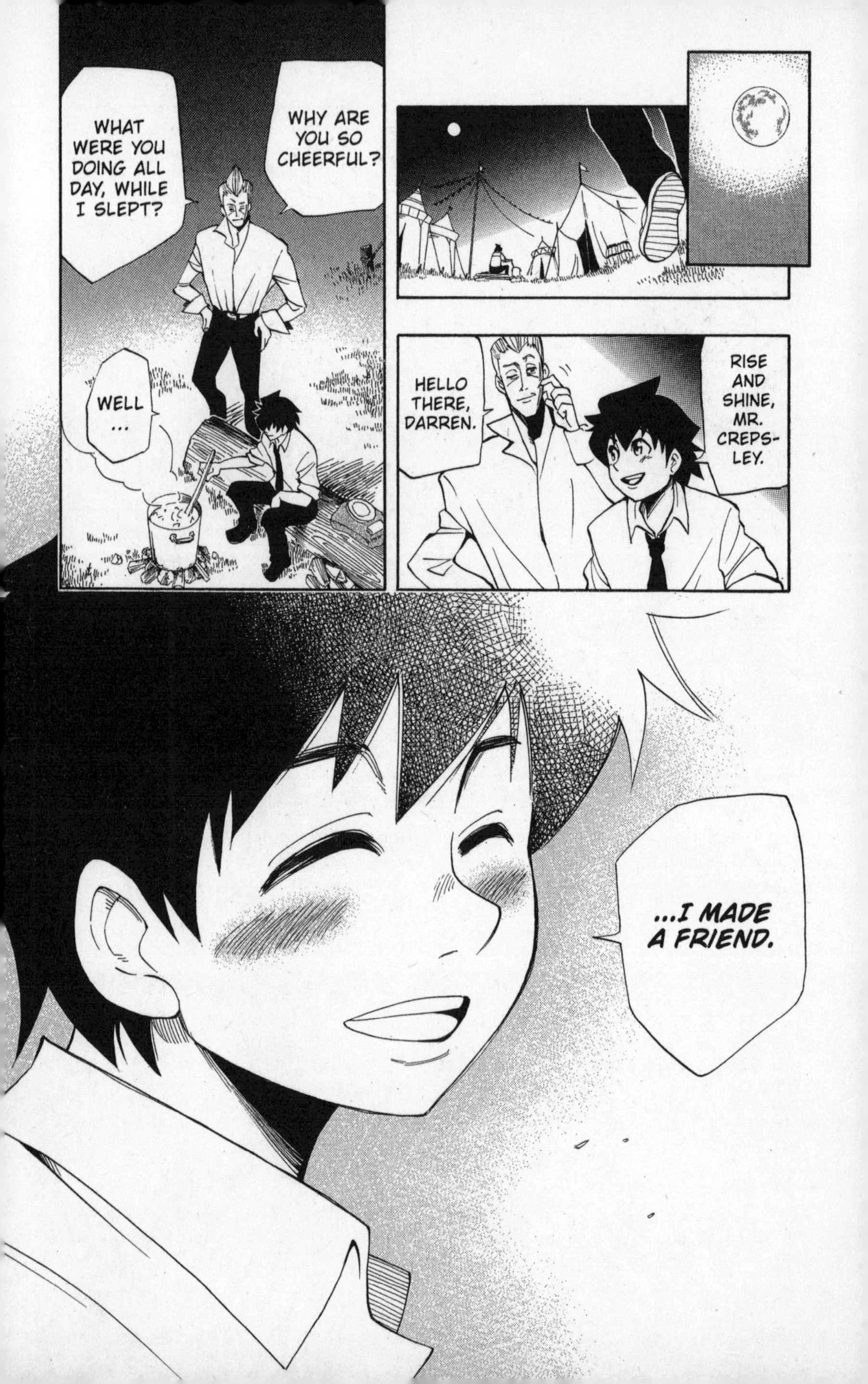
RISE AND SHINE, MR. CREPS-LEY.
HELLO THERE, DARREN.
WHY ARE YOU SO CHEERFUL?
WHAT WERE YOU DOING ALL DAY, WHILE I SLEPT?
WELL ...
...I MADE A FRIEND.

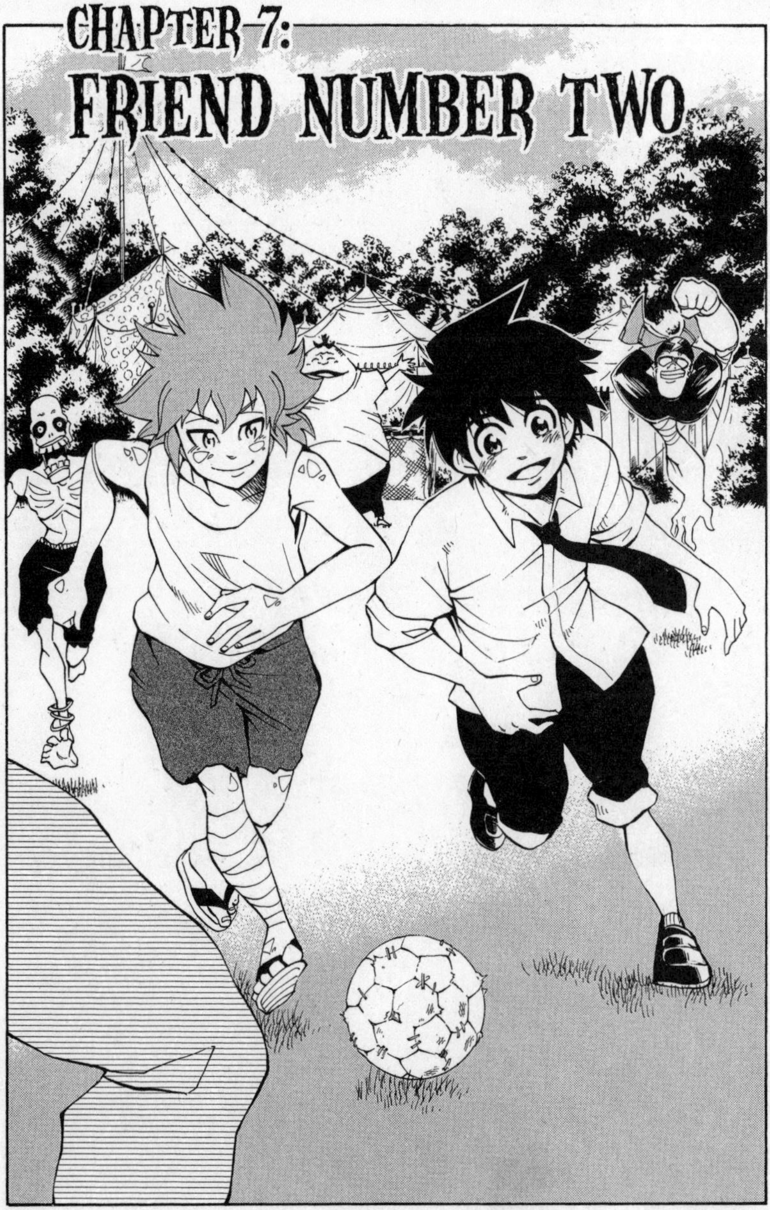
CHAPTER 7:
FRIEND NUMBER TWO

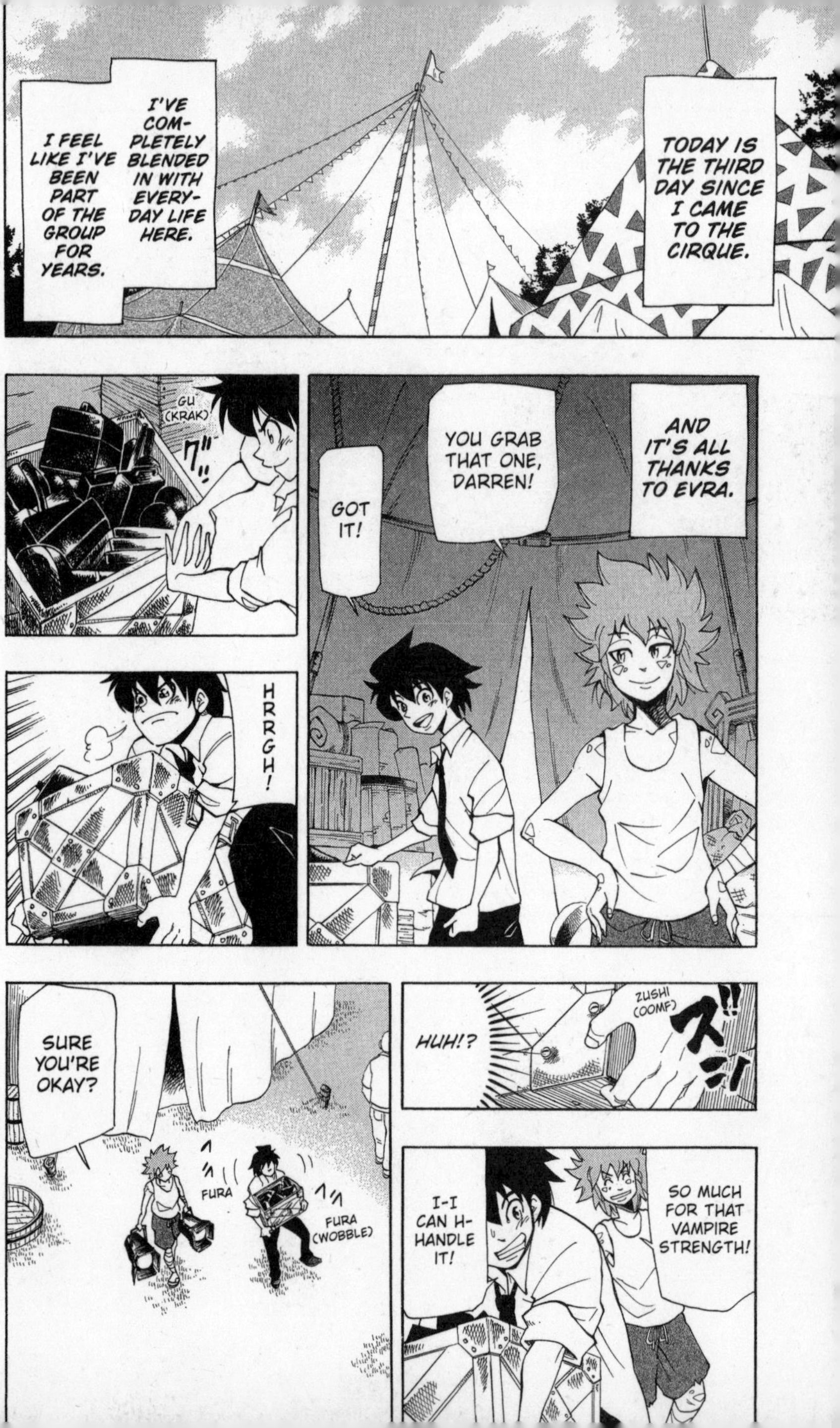

TODAY IS THE THIRD DAY SINCE I CAME TO THE CIRQUE.
I'VE COMPLETELY BLENDED IN WITH EVERYDAY LIFE HERE.
I FEEL LIKE I'VE BEEN PART OF THE GROUP FOR YEARS.
AND IT'S ALL THANKS TO EVRA.
YOU GRAB THAT ONE, DARREN!
GOT IT!
GU (KRAK)
HRRGH!
ZUSHI (OOMF)
HUH!?
SO MUCH FOR THAT VAMPIRE STRENGTH!
I-I CAN H-HANDLE IT!
SURE YOU'RE OKAY?
FURA
FURA (WOBBLE)

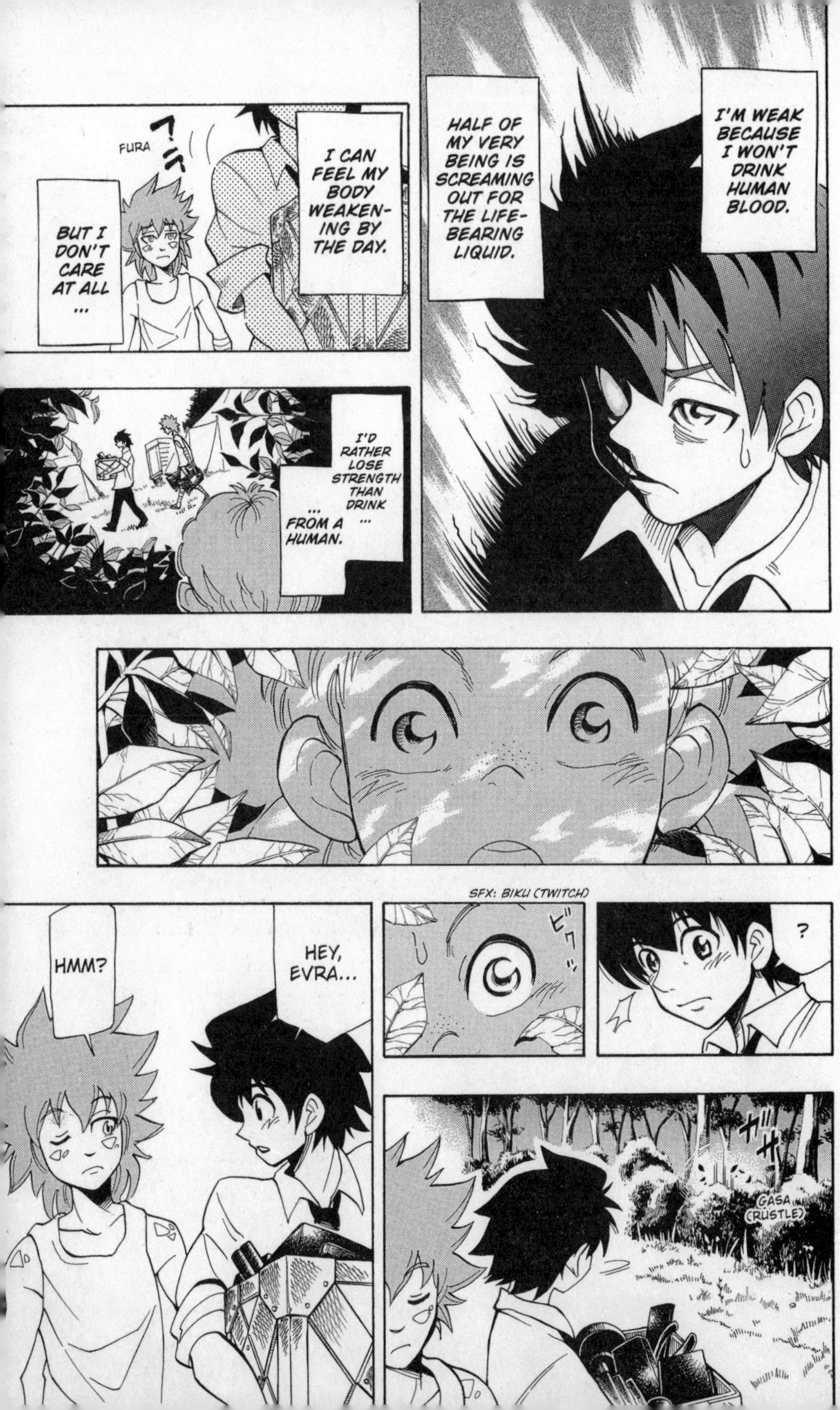
I'M WEAK BECAUSE I WON'T DRINK HUMAN BLOOD.
HALF OF MY VERY BEING IS SCREAMING OUT FOR THE LIFE-BEARING LIQUID.
I CAN FEEL MY BODY WEAKENING BY THE DAY.
FURA
BUT I DON'T CARE AT ALL ...
I'D RATHER LOSE STRENGTH THAN DRINK ...
... FROM A HUMAN.
?
SFX: BIKU (TWITCH)
GASA (RUSTLE)
HEY, EVRA...
HMM?

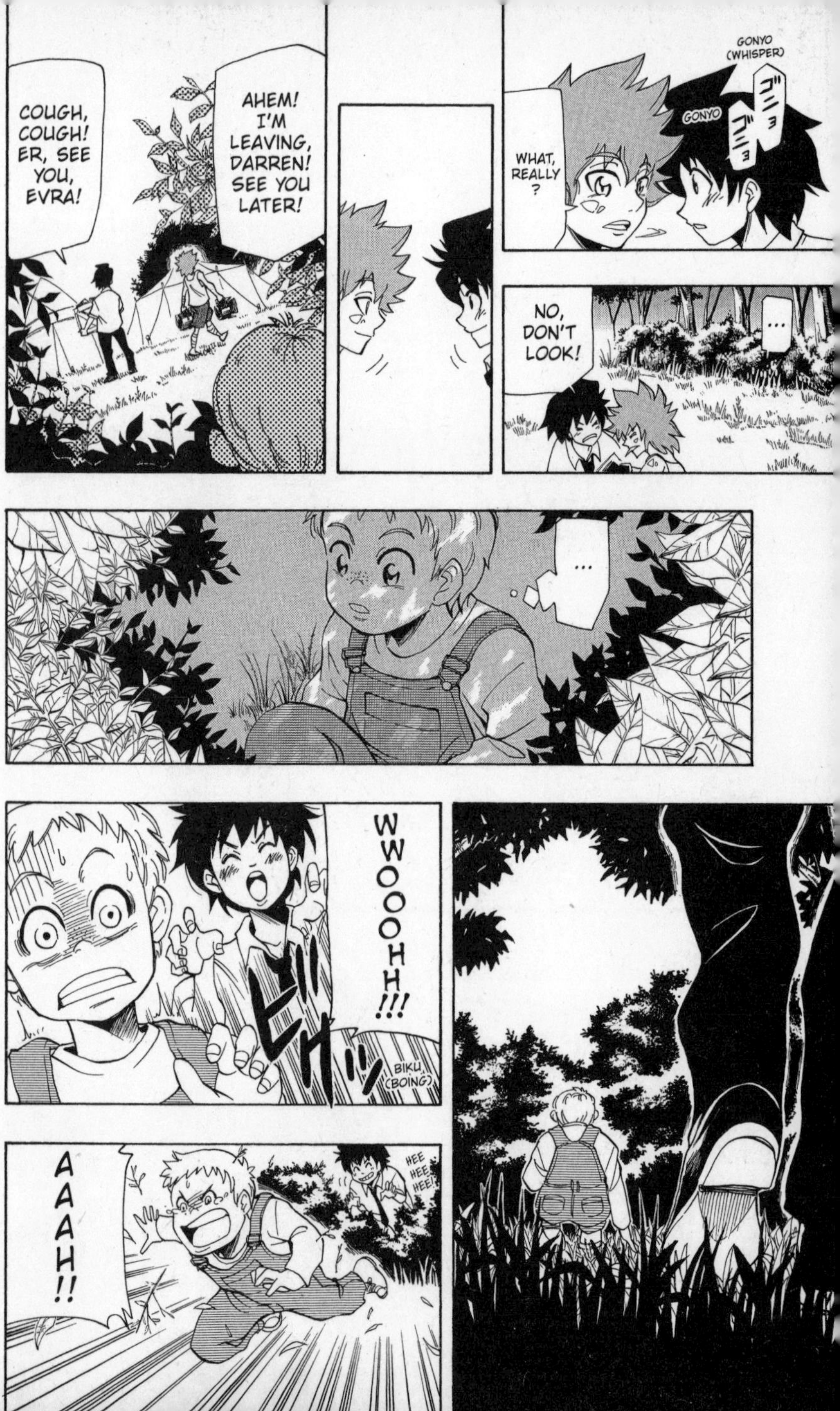
GONYO (WHISPER)
GONYO
WHAT, REALLY?
NO, DON'T LOOK!
...
AHEM! I'M LEAVING, DARREN! SEE YOU LATER!
COUGH, COUGH! ER, SEE YOU, EVRA!
...
WWOOOOHH!!!
BIKU (BOING)
HEE HEE HEE!
AAAAH!!

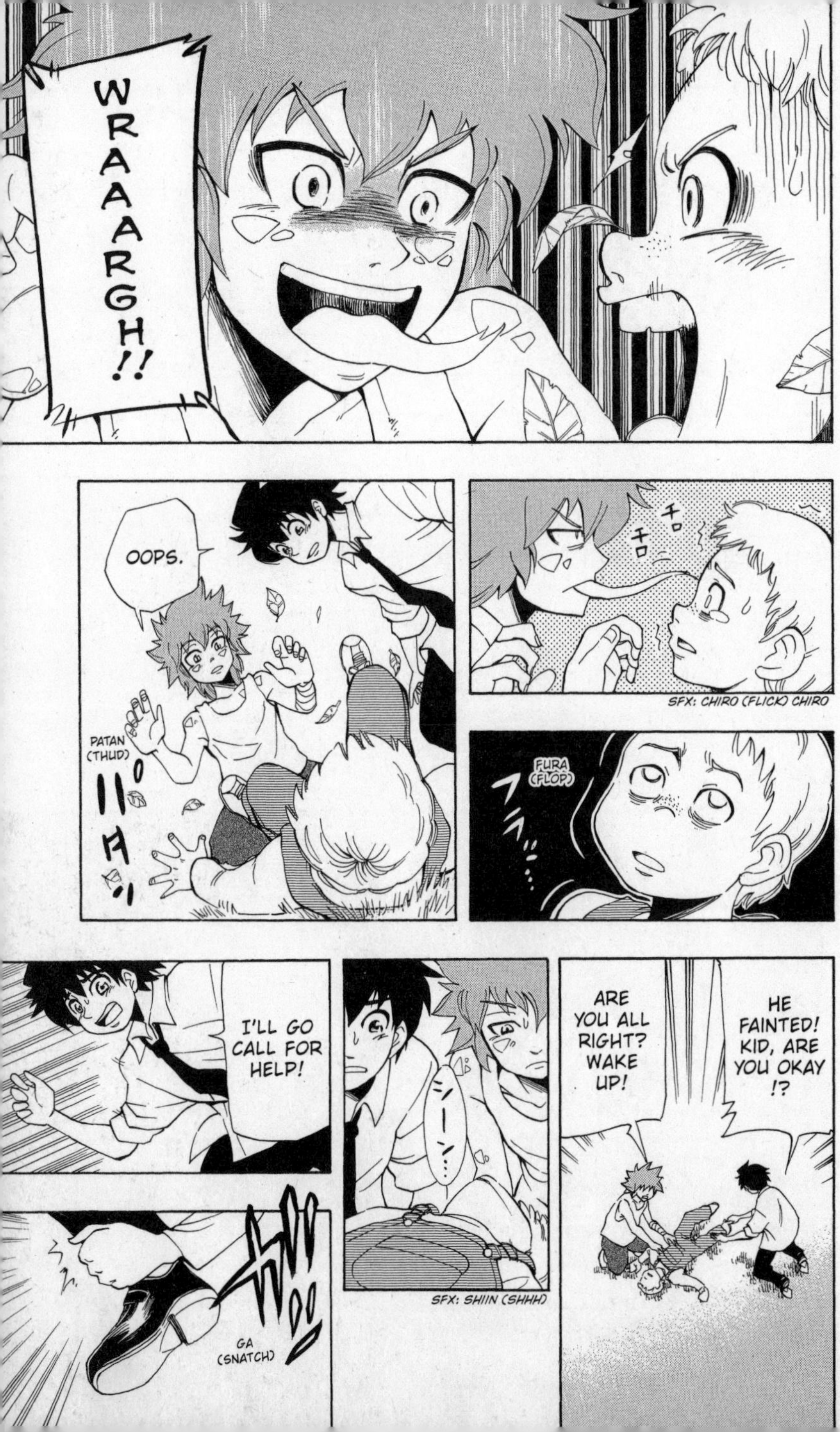
WRAAAARGH!!
SFX: CHIRO (FLICK) CHIRO
FURA (FLOP)
OOPS.
PATAN (THUD)
HE FAINTED! KID, ARE YOU OKAY!?
ARE YOU ALL RIGHT? WAKE UP!
SFX: SHIIN (SHHH)
I'LL GO CALL FOR HELP!
GA (SNATCH)

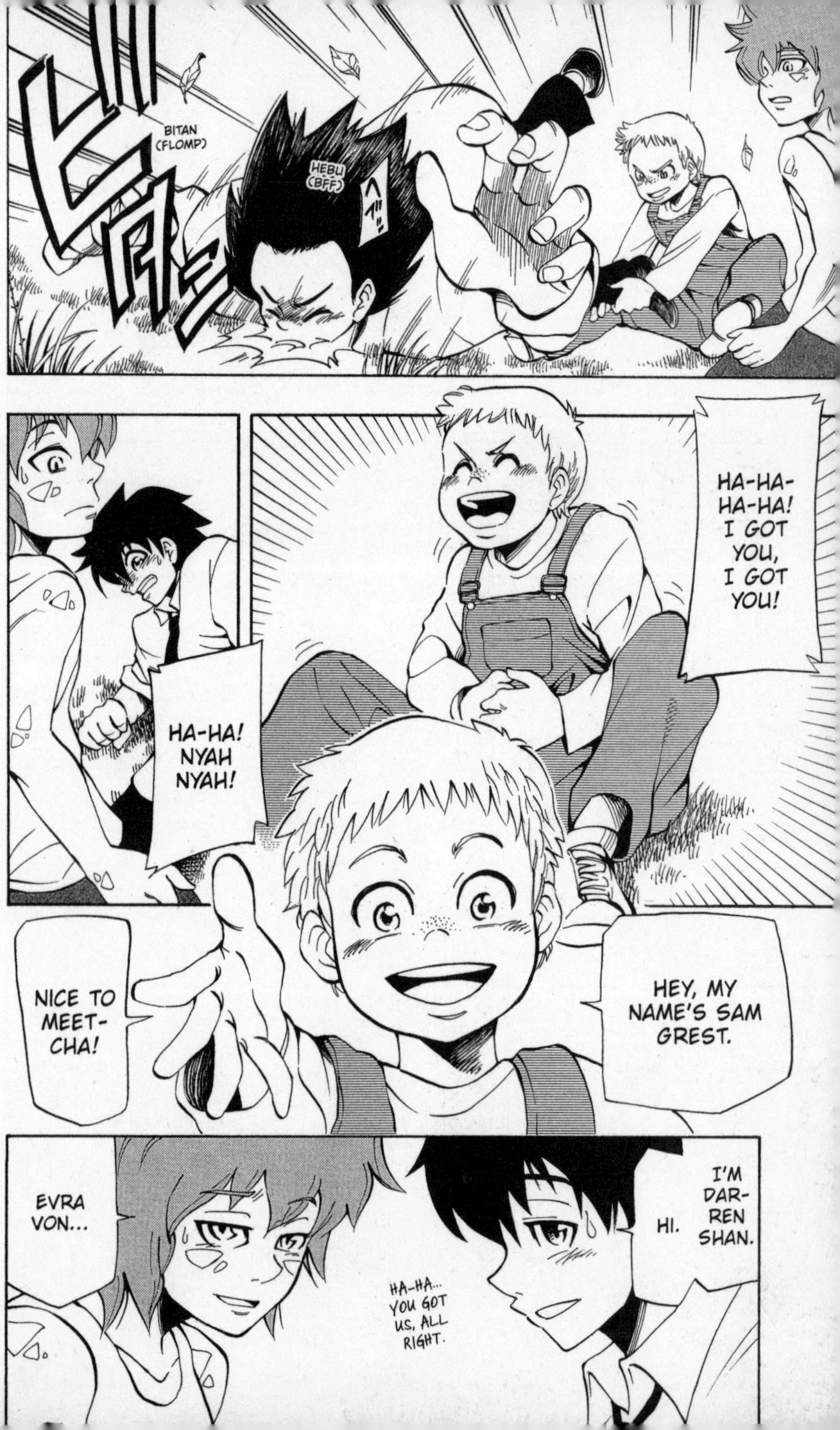
HEBU (BFF)
BITAN (FLOMP)
HA-HA-HA-HA! I GOT YOU, I GOT YOU!
HA-HA! NYAH NYAH!
HEY, MY NAME'S SAM GREST.
NICE TO MEET-CHA!
I'M DAR-REN SHAN.
HI.
HA-HA... YOU GOT US, ALL RIGHT.
EVRA VON...

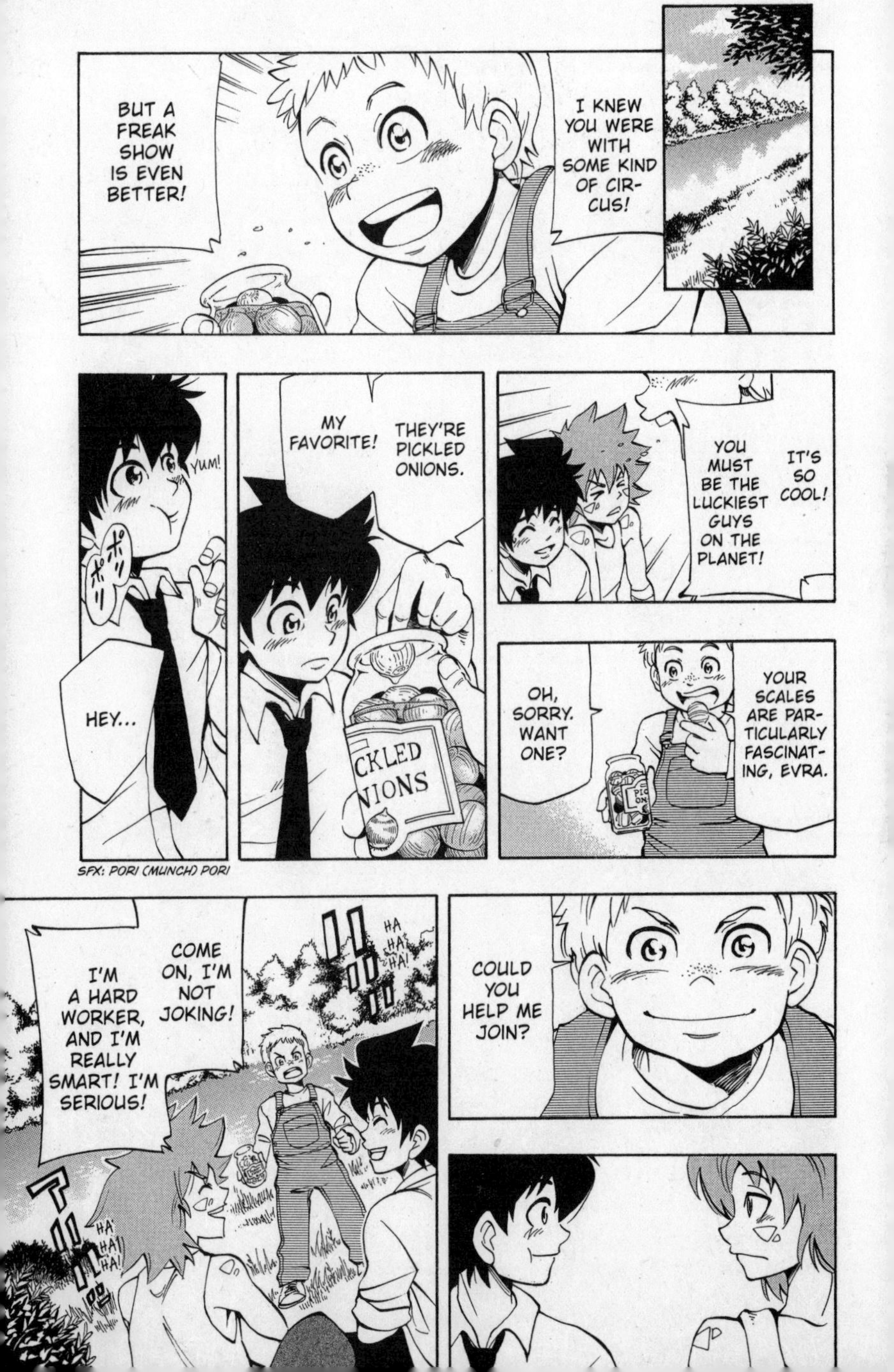
I KNEW YOU WERE WITH SOME KIND OF CIR-CUS!
BUT A FREAK SHOW IS EVEN BETTER!
IT'S SO COOL!
YOU MUST BE THE LUCKIEST GUYS ON THE PLANET!
YOUR SCALES ARE PAR-TICULARLY FASCINAT-ING, EVRA.
OH, SORRY. WANT ONE?
THEY'RE PICKLED ONIONS.
MY FAVORITE!
YUM!
ポリポリ
HEY...
SFX: PORI (MUNCH) PORI
COULD YOU HELP ME JOIN?
HA HA HA!
COME ON, I'M NOT JOKING!
I'M A HARD WORKER, AND I'M REALLY SMART! I'M SERIOUS!
HA HA HA!

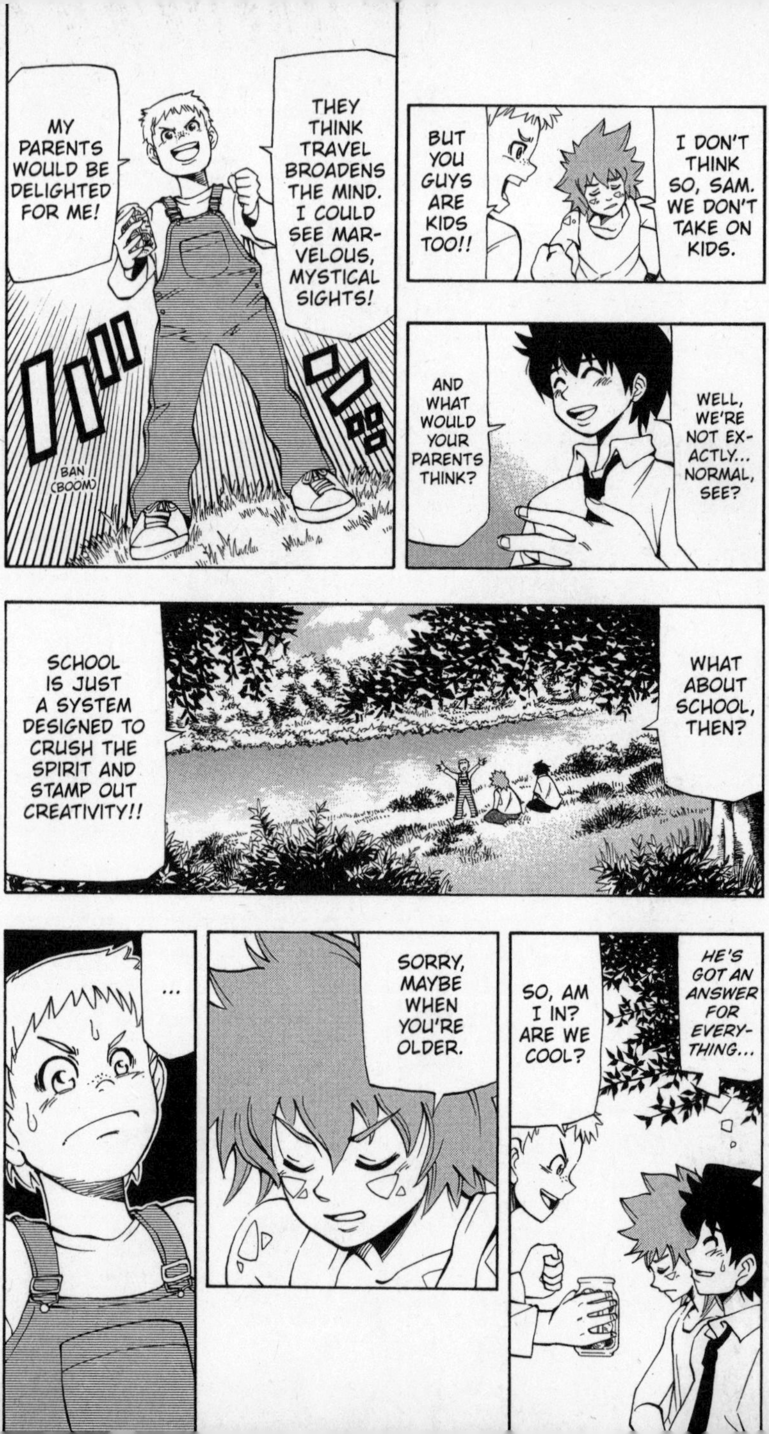
I DON'T THINK SO, SAM. WE DON'T TAKE ON KIDS.
BUT YOU GUYS ARE KIDS TOO!!
WELL, WE'RE NOT EXACTLY... NORMAL, SEE?
AND WHAT WOULD YOUR PARENTS THINK?
MY PARENTS WOULD BE DELIGHTED FOR ME!
THEY THINK TRAVEL BROADENS THE MIND. I COULD SEE MARVELOUS, MYSTICAL SIGHTS!
BAN (BOOM)
WHAT ABOUT SCHOOL, THEN?
SCHOOL IS JUST A SYSTEM DESIGNED TO CRUSH THE SPIRIT AND STAMP OUT CREATIVITY!!
HE'S GOT AN ANSWER FOR EVERYTHING...
SO, AM I IN? ARE WE COOL?
SORRY, MAYBE WHEN YOU'RE OLDER.
...

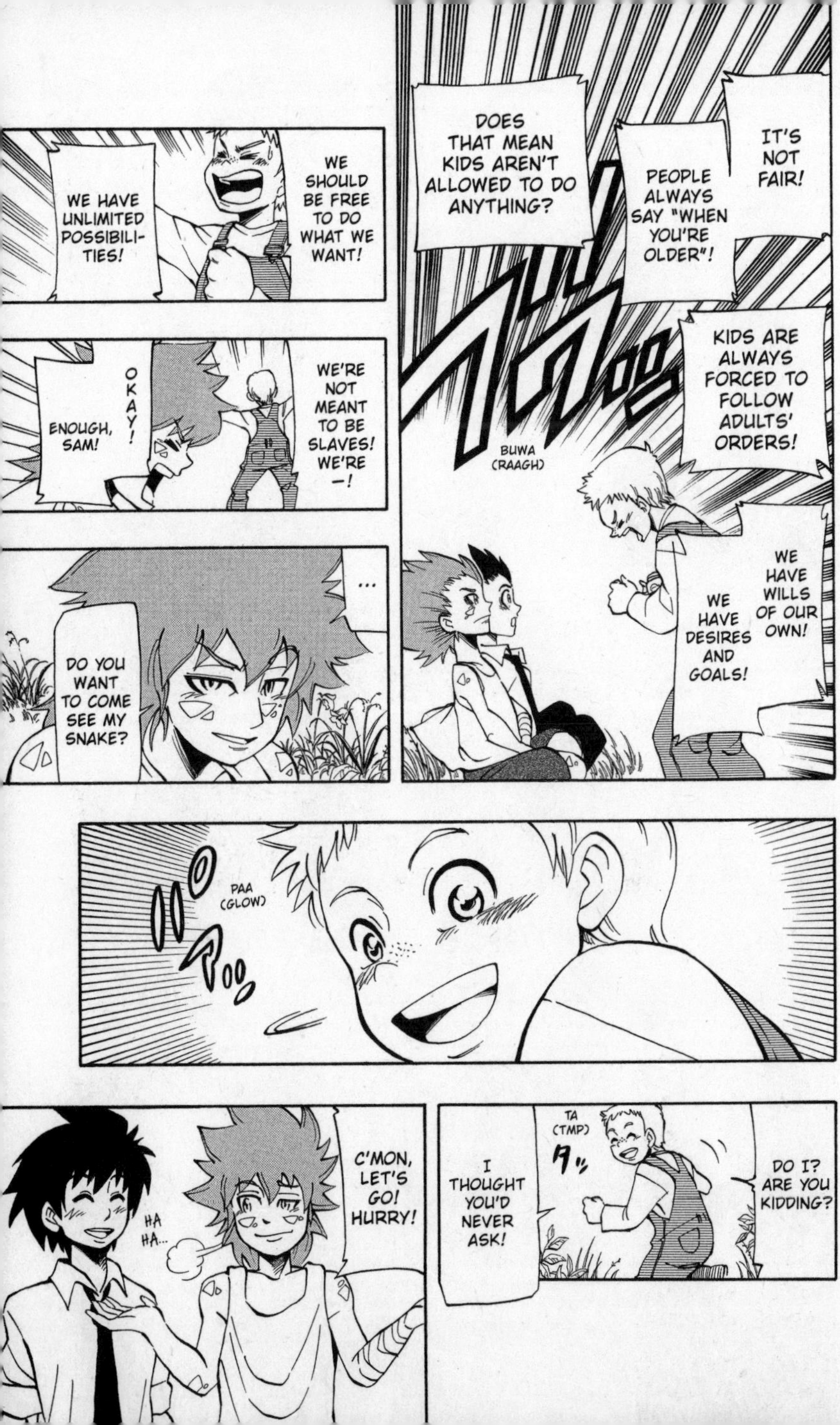
IT'S NOT FAIR!
PEOPLE ALWAYS SAY "WHEN YOU'RE OLDER"!
DOES THAT MEAN KIDS AREN'T ALLOWED TO DO ANYTHING?
KIDS ARE ALWAYS FORCED TO FOLLOW ADULTS' ORDERS!
BUWA (RAAGH)
WE HAVE WILLS OF OUR OWN!
WE HAVE DESIRES AND GOALS!
WE SHOULD BE FREE TO DO WHAT WE WANT!
WE HAVE UNLIMITED POSSIBILITIES!
WE'RE NOT MEANT TO BE SLAVES! WE'RE—!
OKAY!
ENOUGH, SAM!
...
DO YOU WANT TO COME SEE MY SNAKE?
PAA (GLOW)
DO I? ARE YOU KIDDING?
TA (TMP)
I THOUGHT YOU'D NEVER ASK!
C'MON, LET'S GO! HURRY!
HA HA...

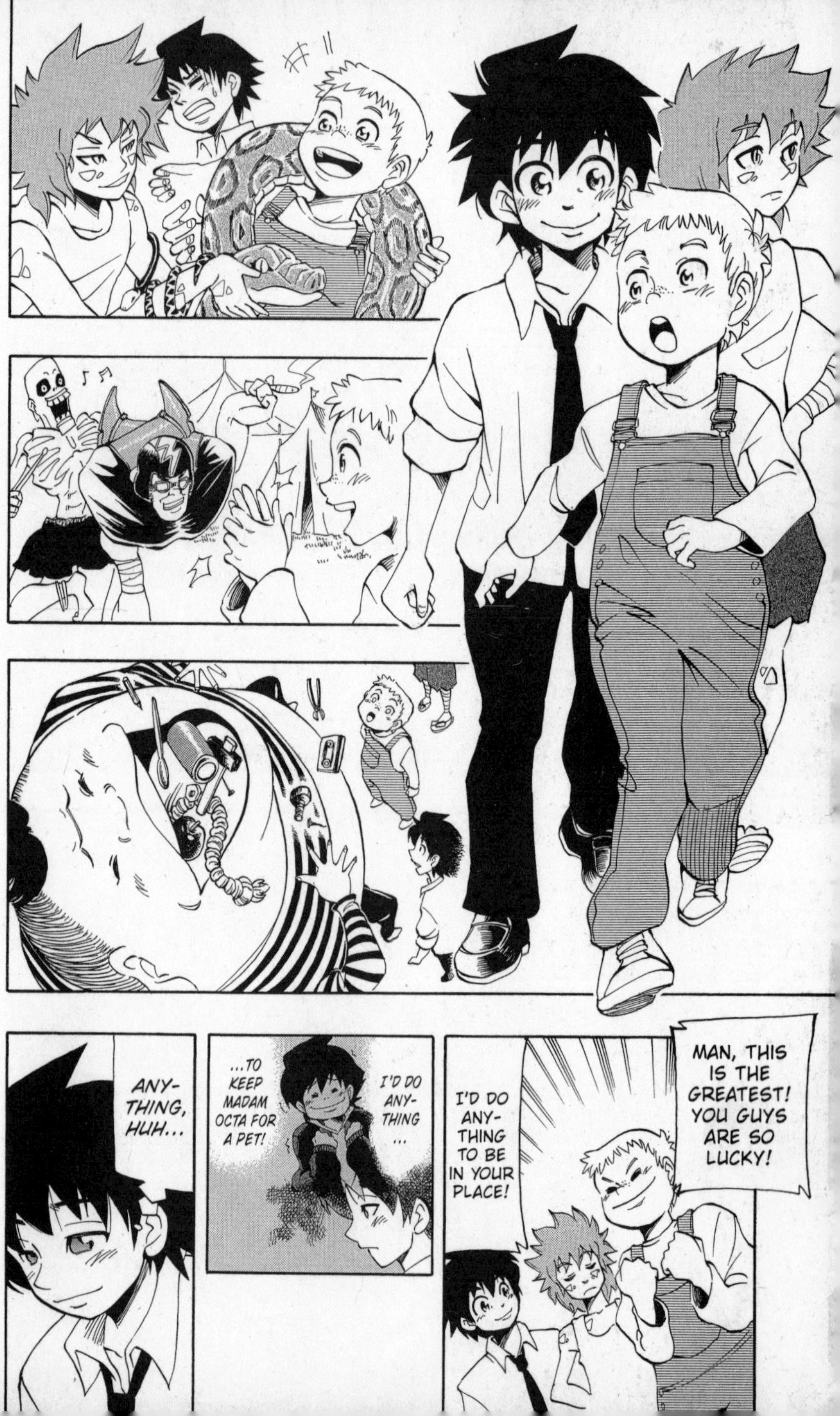
MAN, THIS IS THE GREATEST! YOU GUYS ARE SO LUCKY!
I'D DO ANY-THING TO BE IN YOUR PLACE!
I'D DO ANY-THING ...
...TO KEEP MADAM OCTA FOR A PET!
ANY-THING, HUH...

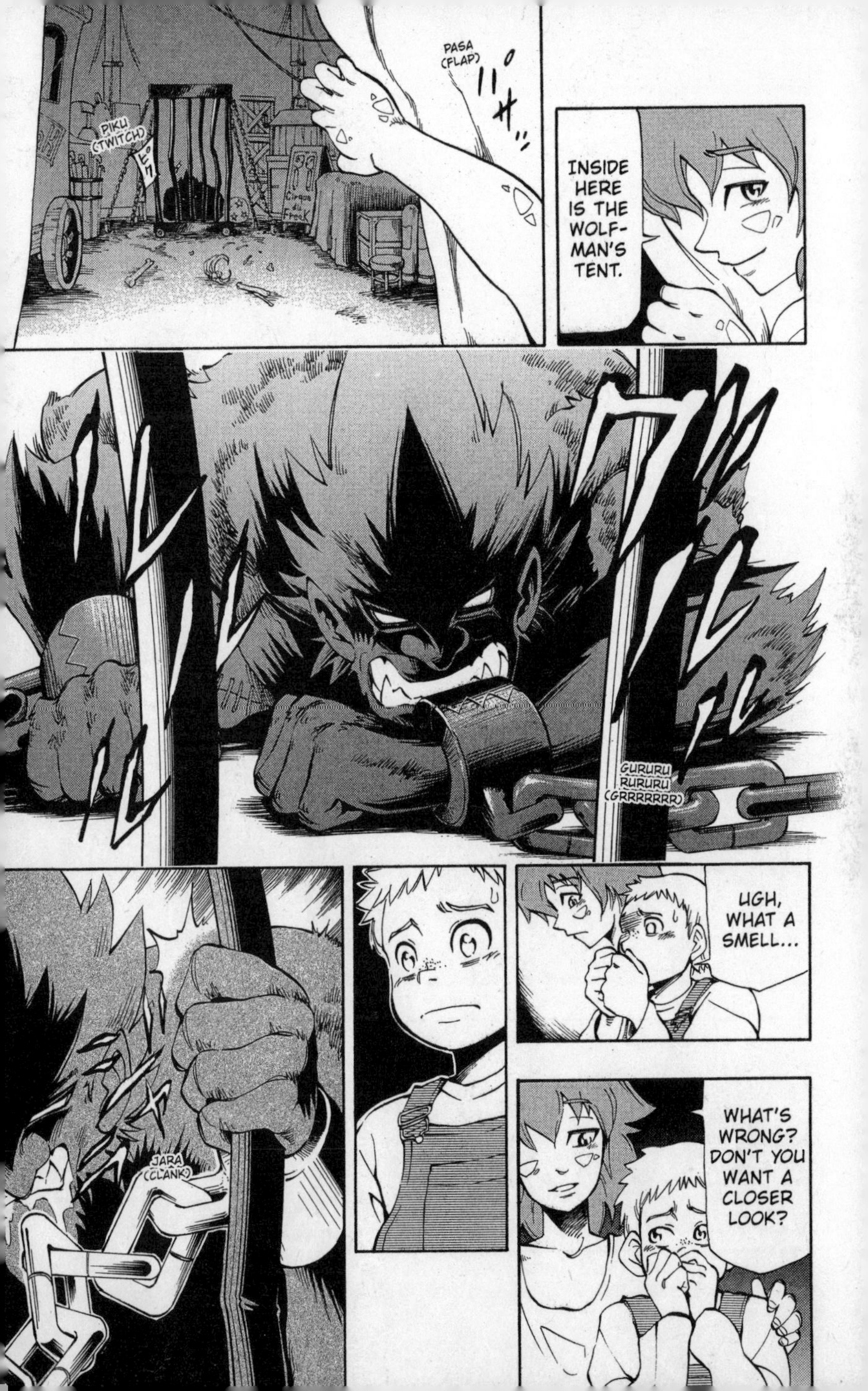
INSIDE HERE IS THE WOLF-MAN'S TENT.
PASA (FLAP)
PIKU (TWITCH)
Cirque du Freak
GURURU RURURU (GRRRRRRR)
UGH, WHAT A SMELL...
WHAT'S WRONG? DON'T YOU WANT A CLOSER LOOK?
JARA (CLANK)

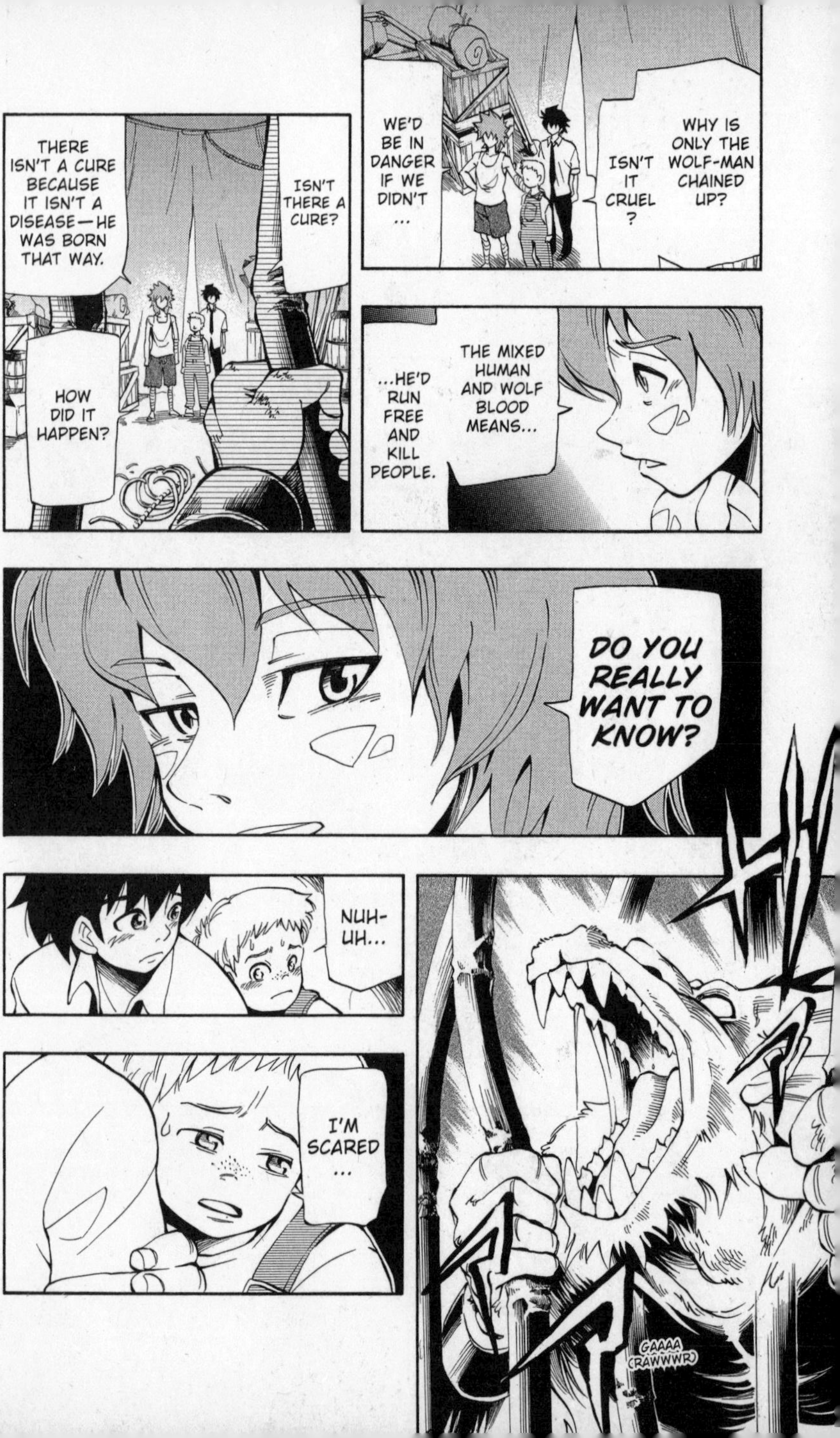
WHY IS ONLY THE WOLF-MAN CHAINED UP?
ISN'T IT CRUEL?
WE'D BE IN DANGER IF WE DIDN'T...
THE MIXED HUMAN AND WOLF BLOOD MEANS...
...HE'D RUN FREE AND KILL PEOPLE.
ISN'T THERE A CURE?
THERE ISN'T A CURE BECAUSE IT ISN'T A DISEASE—HE WAS BORN THAT WAY.
HOW DID IT HAPPEN?
DO YOU REALLY WANT TO KNOW?
GAAAA CRAWWWR
NUH-UH...
I'M SCARED...

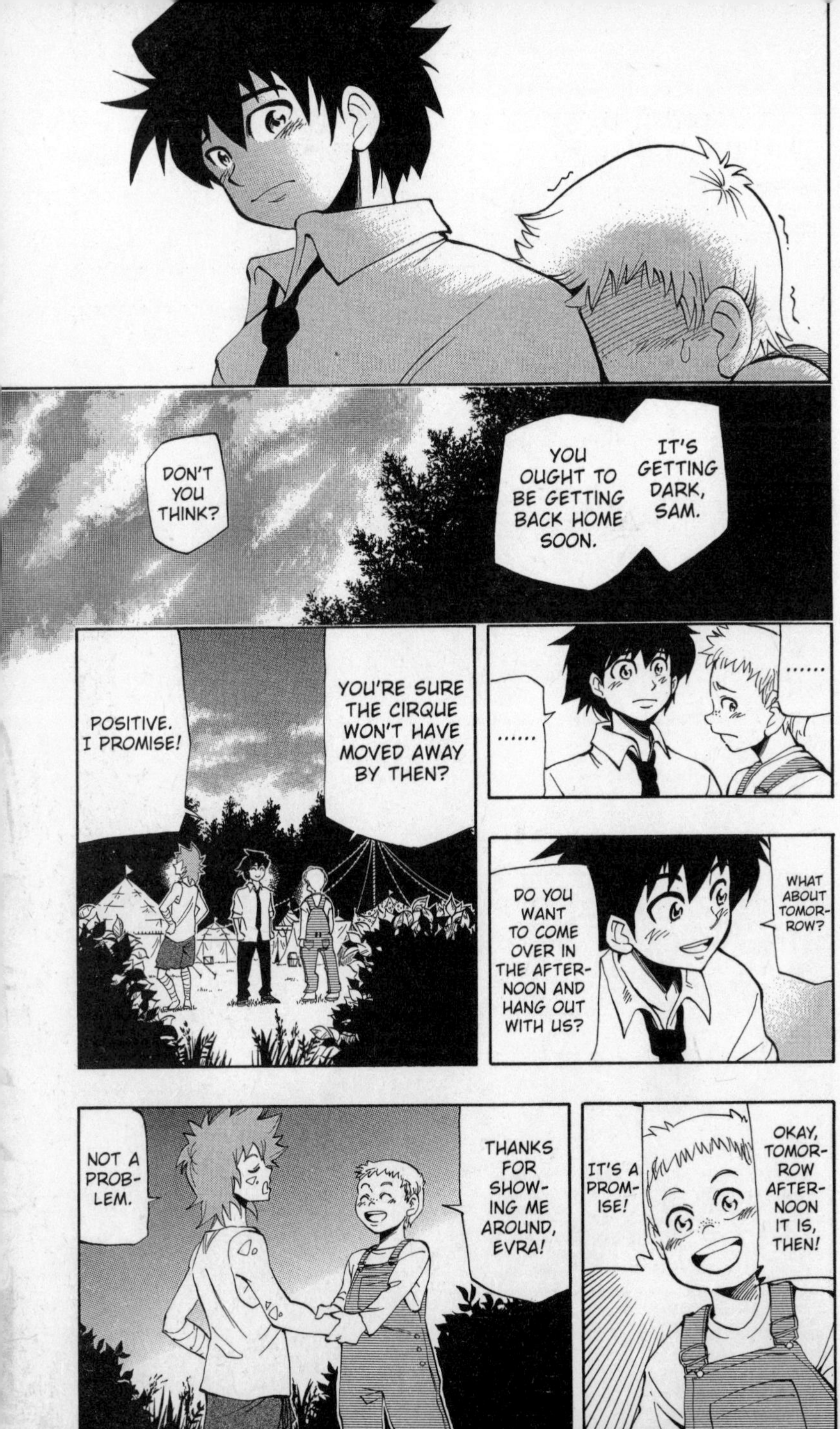
IT'S GETTING DARK, SAM.
YOU OUGHT TO BE GETTING BACK HOME SOON.
DON'T YOU THINK?
......
......
WHAT ABOUT TOMORROW?
DO YOU WANT TO COME OVER IN THE AFTERNOON AND HANG OUT WITH US?
YOU'RE SURE THE CIRQUE WON'T HAVE MOVED AWAY BY THEN?
POSITIVE. I PROMISE!
OKAY, TOMORROW AFTERNOON IT IS, THEN!
IT'S A PROMISE!
THANKS FOR SHOWING ME AROUND, EVRA!
NOT A PROBLEM.

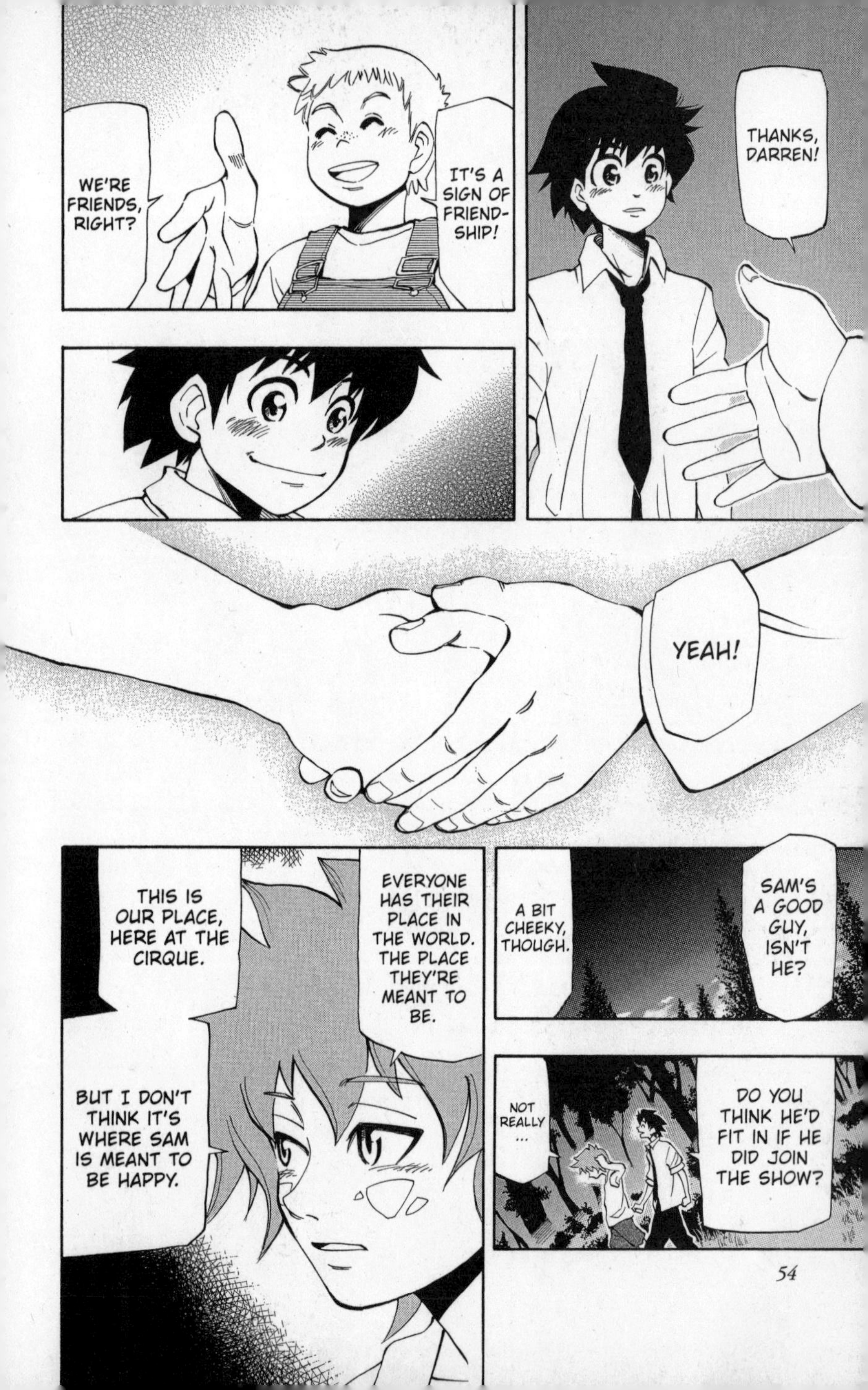
THANKS, DARREN!
IT'S A SIGN OF FRIEND-SHIP!
WE'RE FRIENDS, RIGHT?
YEAH!
SAM'S A GOOD GUY, ISN'T HE?
A BIT CHEEKY, THOUGH.
DO YOU THINK HE'D FIT IN IF HE DID JOIN THE SHOW?
NOT REALLY ...
EVERYONE HAS THEIR PLACE IN THE WORLD. THE PLACE THEY'RE MEANT TO BE.
THIS IS OUR PLACE, HERE AT THE CIRQUE.
BUT I DON'T THINK IT'S WHERE SAM IS MEANT TO BE HAPPY.

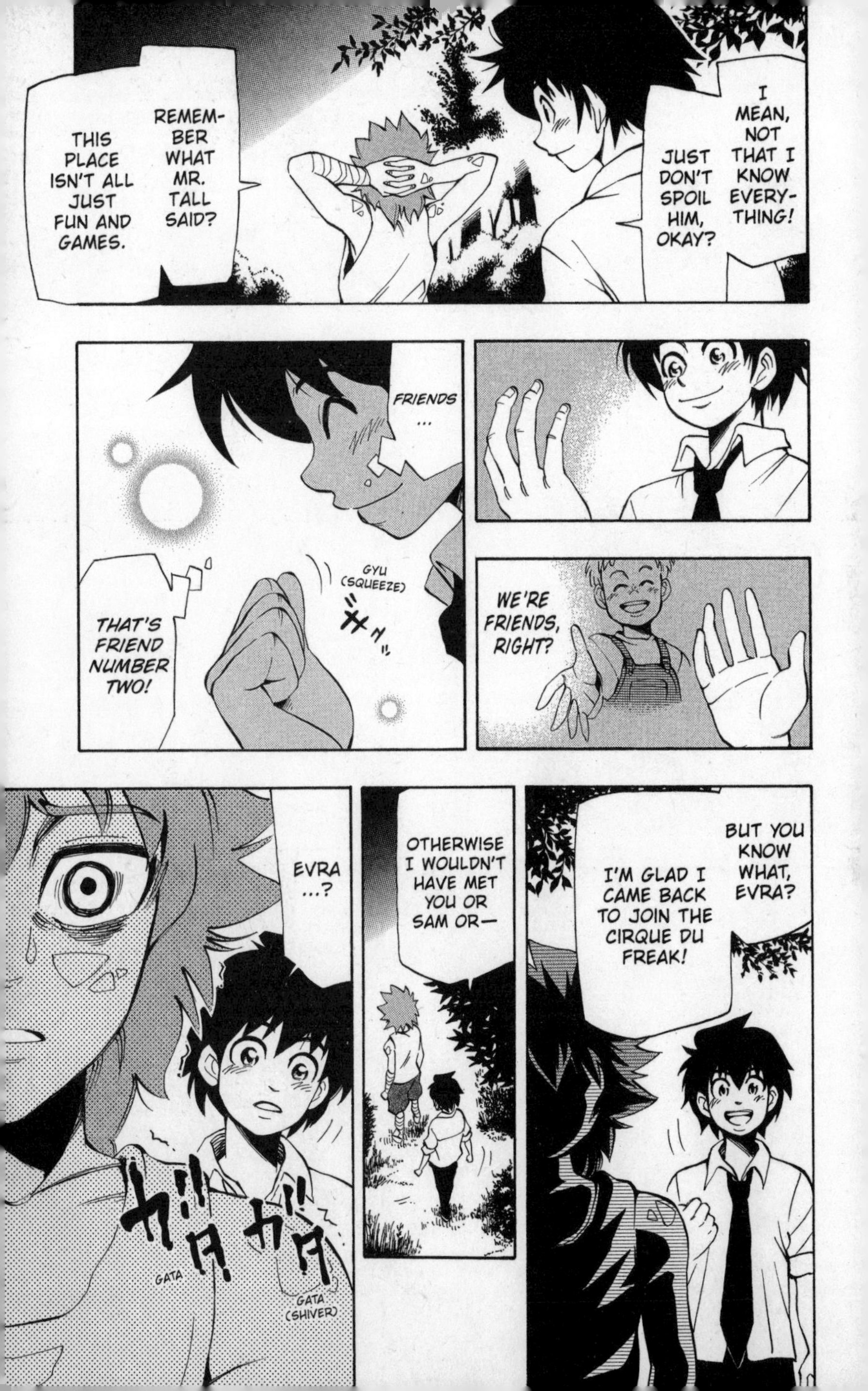
I MEAN, NOT THAT I KNOW EVERYTHING!
JUST DON'T SPOIL HIM, OKAY?
REMEMBER WHAT MR. TALL SAID?
THIS PLACE ISN'T ALL JUST FUN AND GAMES.
WE'RE FRIENDS, RIGHT?
FRIENDS ...
GYU (SQUEEZE)
THAT'S FRIEND NUMBER TWO!
BUT YOU KNOW WHAT, EVRA?
I'M GLAD I CAME BACK TO JOIN THE CIRQUE DU FREAK!
OTHERWISE I WOULDN'T HAVE MET YOU OR SAM OR—
EVRA ...?
GATA
GATA (SHIVER)

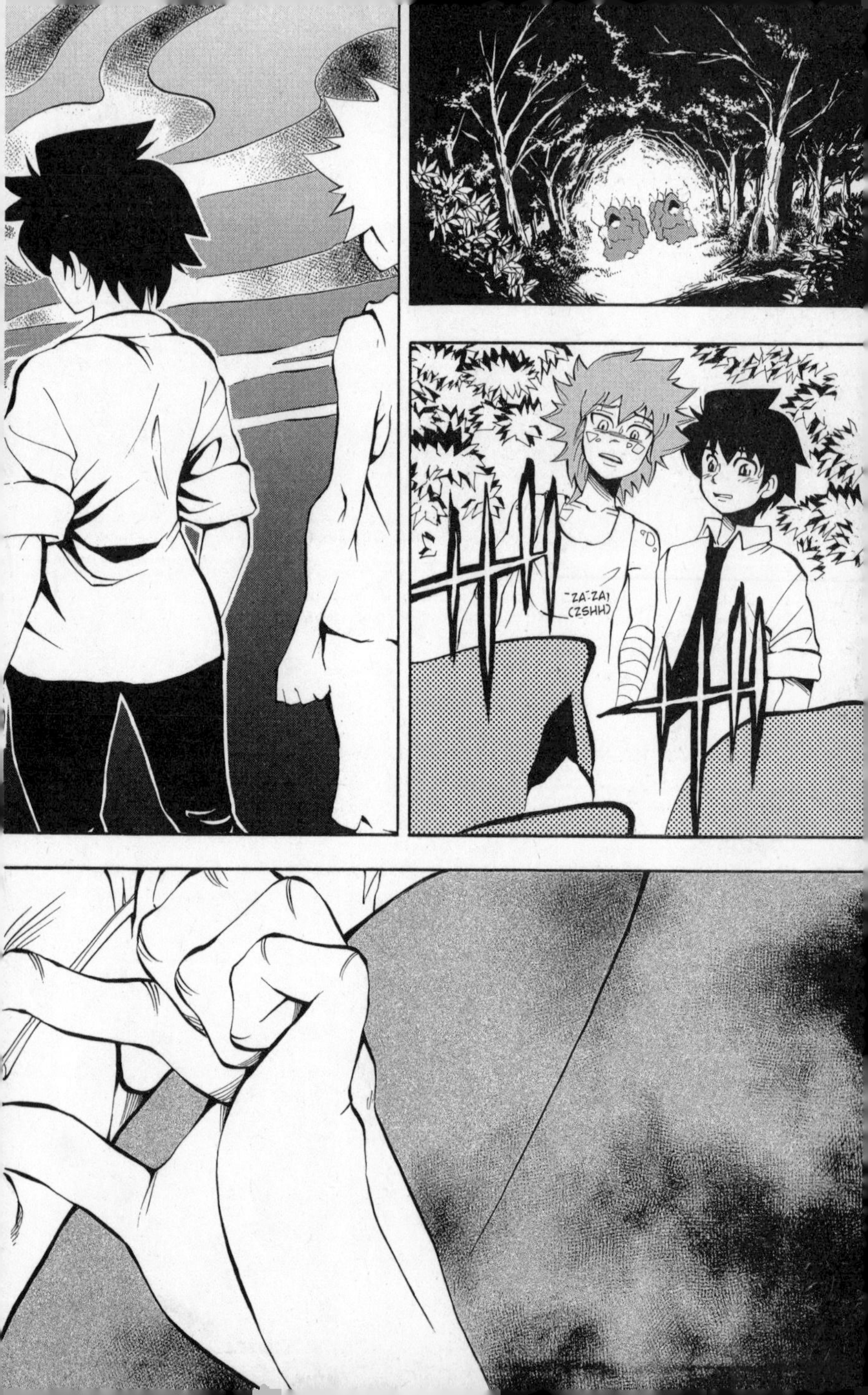
ZA ZA
(ZSHH)

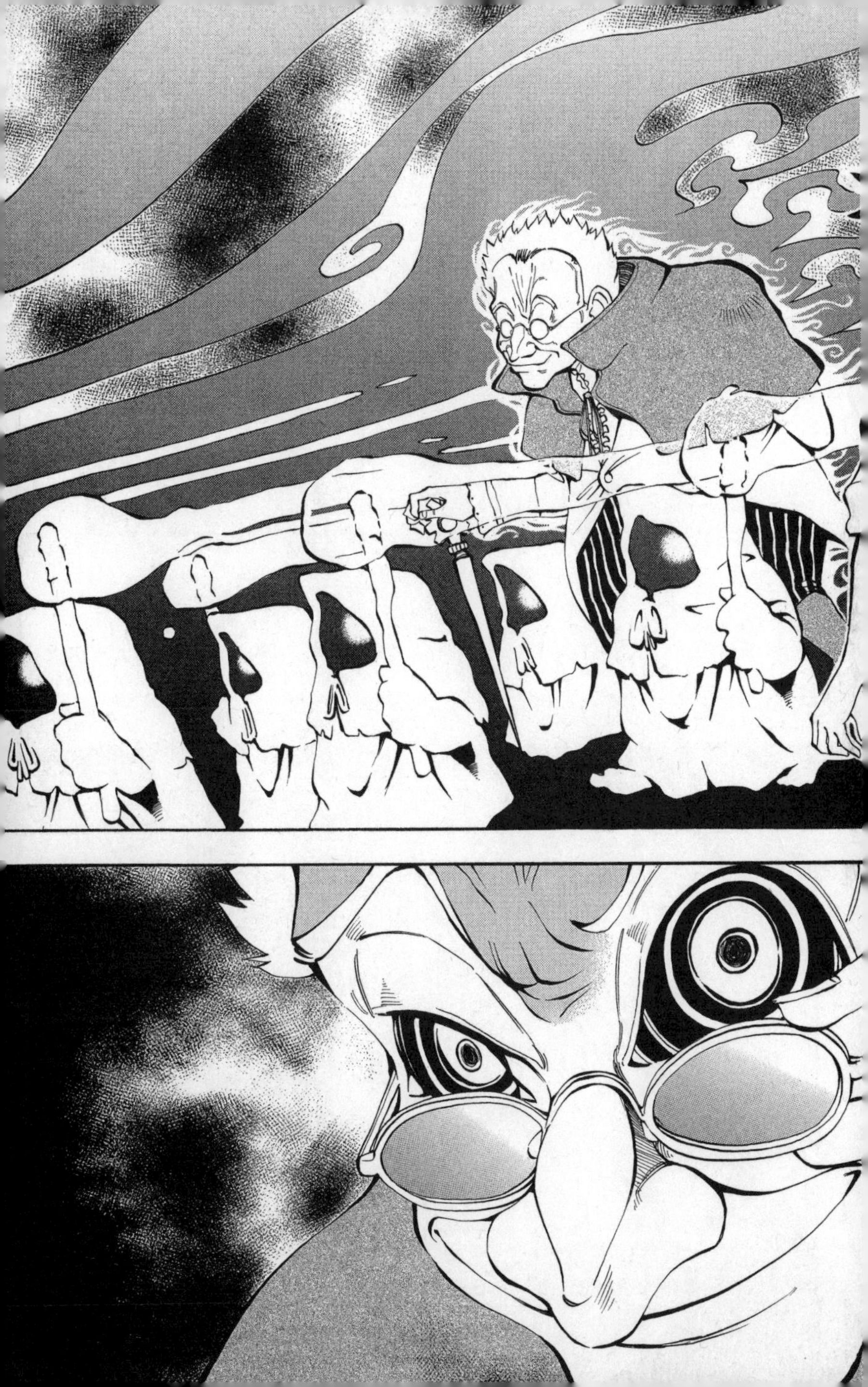

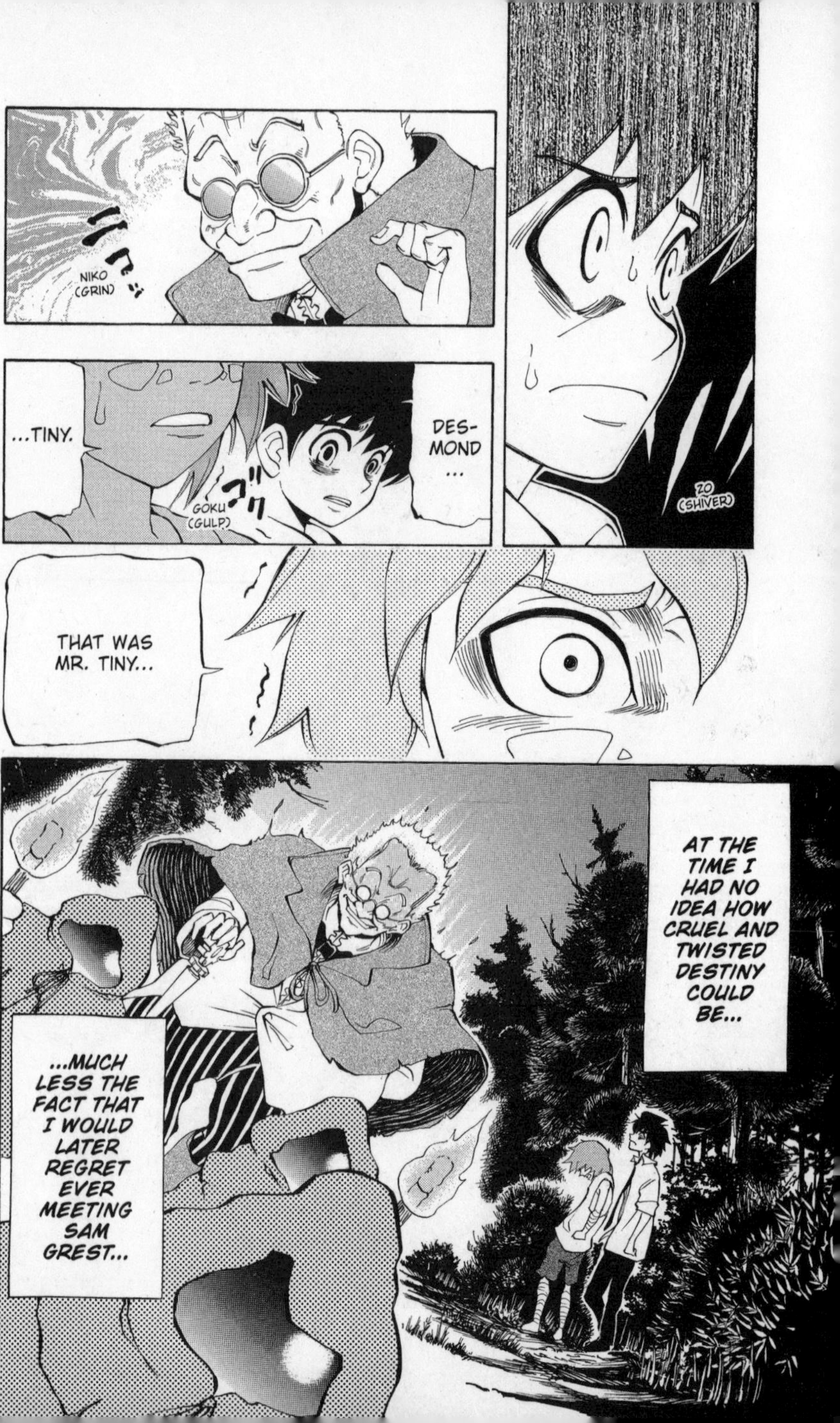
ZO (SHIVER)
NIKO (GRIN)
DES-MOND ...
...TINY.
GOKU (GULP)
THAT WAS MR. TINY...
AT THE TIME I HAD NO IDEA HOW CRUEL AND TWISTED DESTINY COULD BE...
...MUCH LESS THE FACT THAT I WOULD LATER REGRET EVER MEETING SAM GREST...

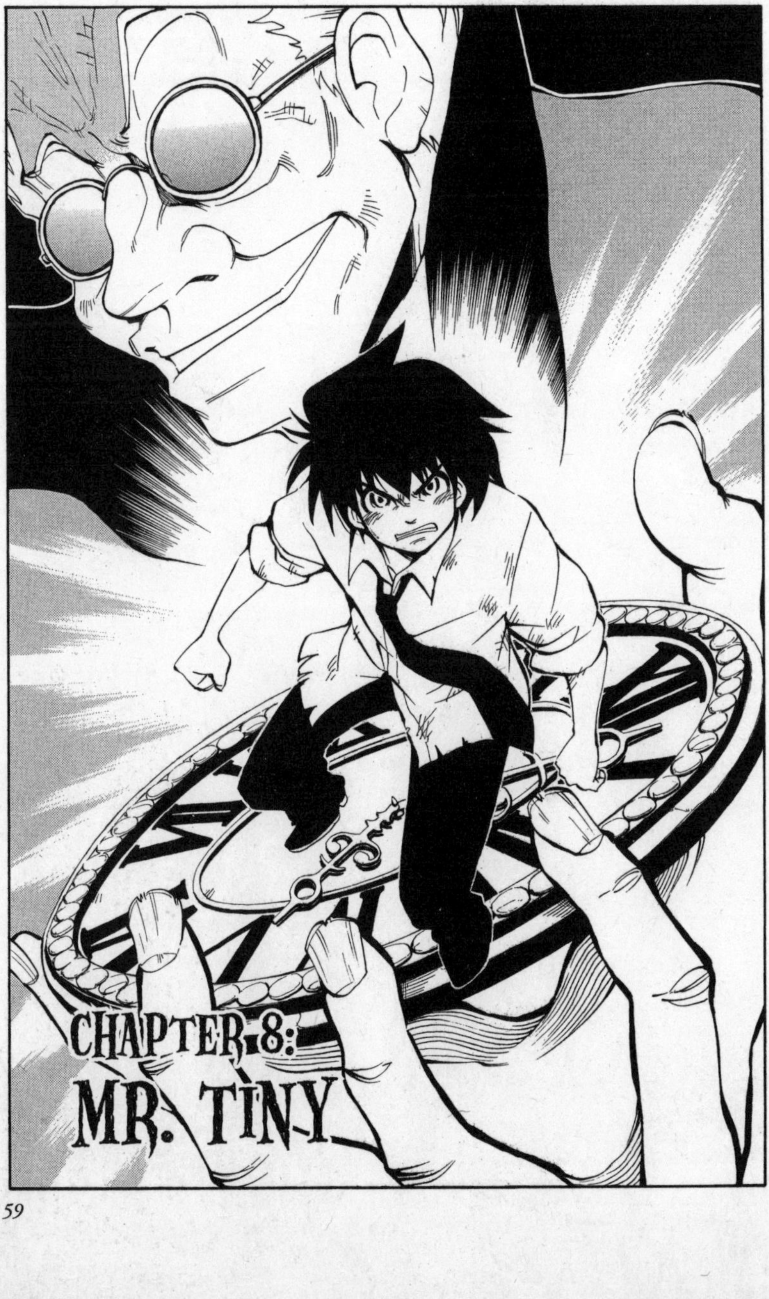
CHAPTER 8:
MR. TINY

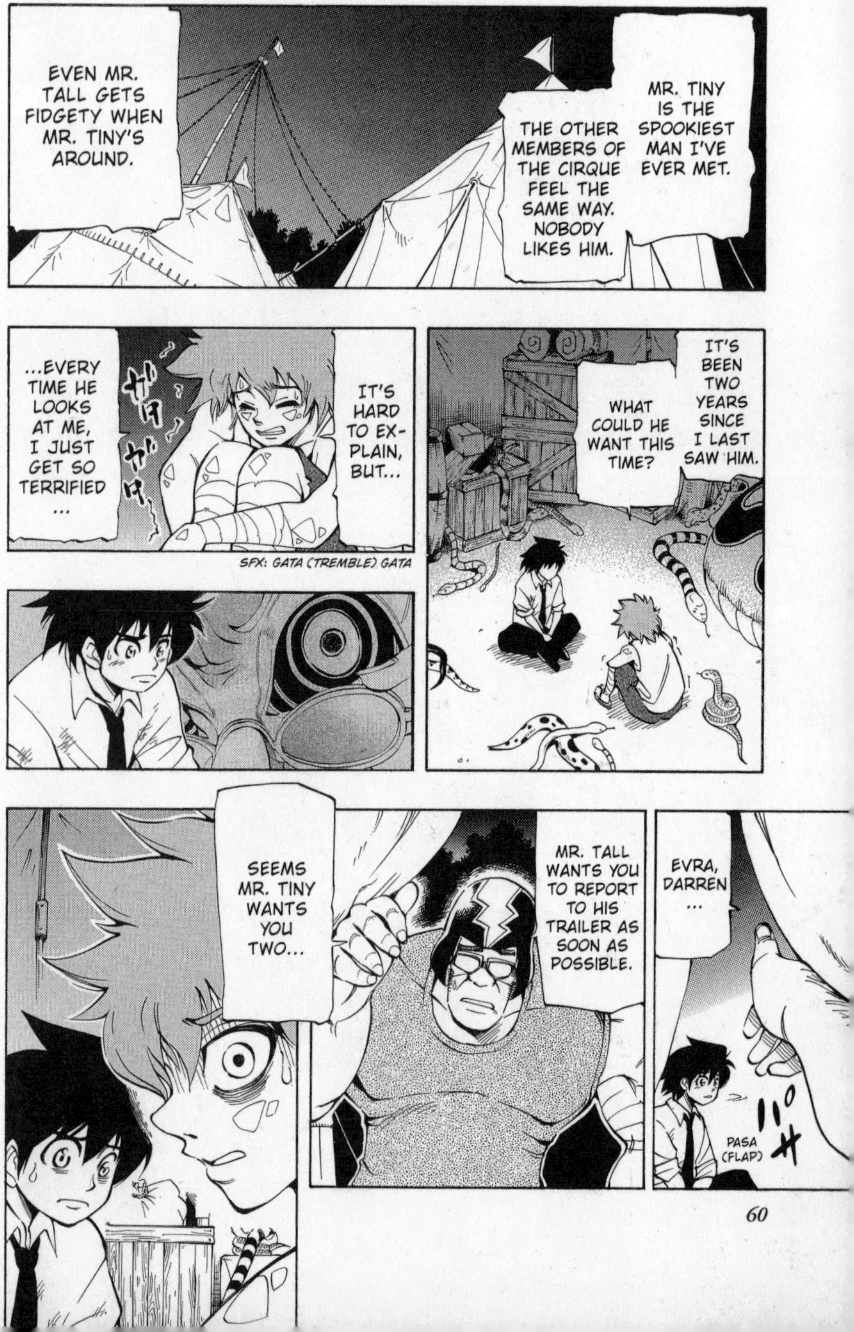

MR. TINY IS THE SPOOKIEST MAN I'VE EVER MET.
THE OTHER MEMBERS OF THE CIRQUE FEEL THE SAME WAY. NOBODY LIKES HIM.
EVEN MR. TALL GETS FIDGETY WHEN MR. TINY'S AROUND.
IT'S BEEN TWO YEARS SINCE I LAST SAW HIM.
WHAT COULD HE WANT THIS TIME?
IT'S HARD TO EX-PLAIN, BUT...
...EVERY TIME HE LOOKS AT ME, I JUST GET SO TERRIFIED ...
SFX: GATA (TREMBLE) GATA
EVRA, DARREN ...
PASA (FLAP)
MR. TALL WANTS YOU TO REPORT TO HIS TRAILER AS SOON AS POSSIBLE.
SEEMS MR. TINY WANTS YOU TWO...

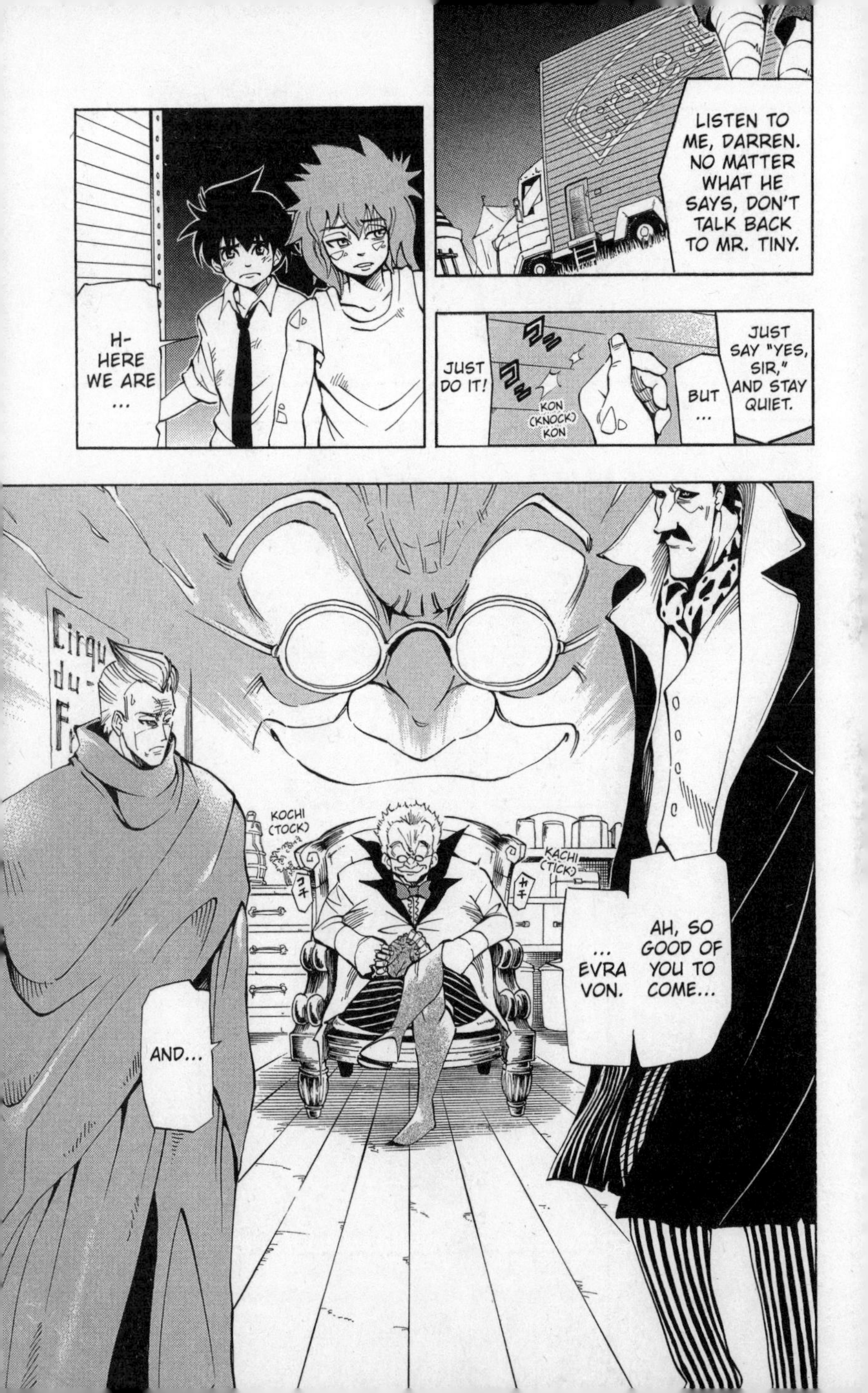
LISTEN TO ME, DARREN. NO MATTER WHAT HE SAYS, DON'T TALK BACK TO MR. TINY.
JUST SAY "YES, SIR," AND STAY QUIET.
BUT ...
KON (KNOCK) KON
JUST DO IT!
H-HERE WE ARE ...
AH, SO GOOD OF YOU TO COME...
... EVRA VON.
KACHI (TICK)
KOCHI (TOCK)
AND...

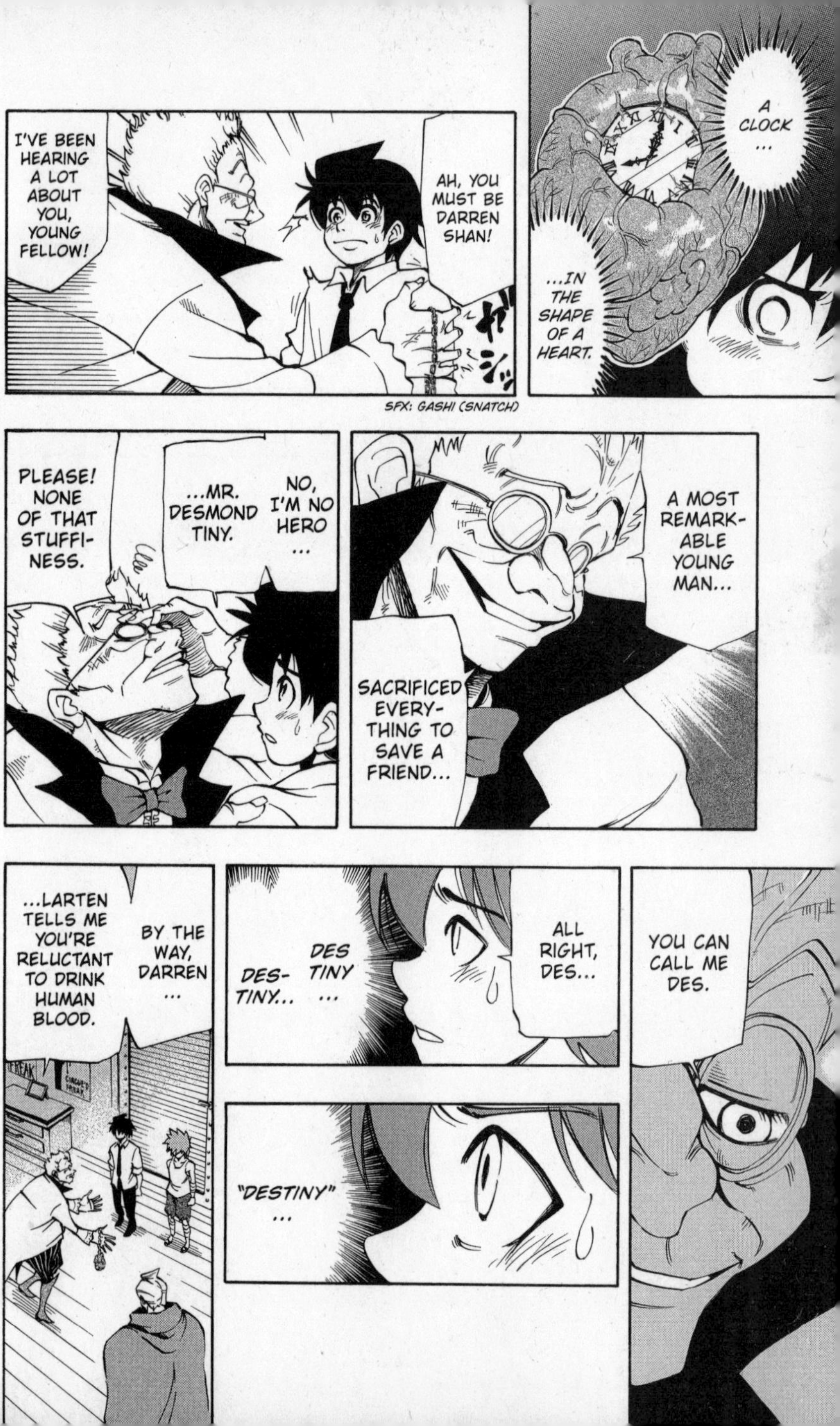
A CLOCK ...
...IN THE SHAPE OF A HEART.
AH, YOU MUST BE DARREN SHAN!
I'VE BEEN HEARING A LOT ABOUT YOU, YOUNG FELLOW!
ガシッ
SFX: GASHI (SNATCH)
A MOST REMARK-ABLE YOUNG MAN...
SACRIFICED EVERY-THING TO SAVE A FRIEND...
NO, I'M NO HERO ...
...MR. DESMOND TINY.
PLEASE! NONE OF THAT STUFFI-NESS.
YOU CAN CALL ME DES.
ALL RIGHT, DES...
DES TINY ...
DES-TINY...
"DESTINY" ...
BY THE WAY, DARREN ...
...LARTEN TELLS ME YOU'RE RELUCTANT TO DRINK HUMAN BLOOD.

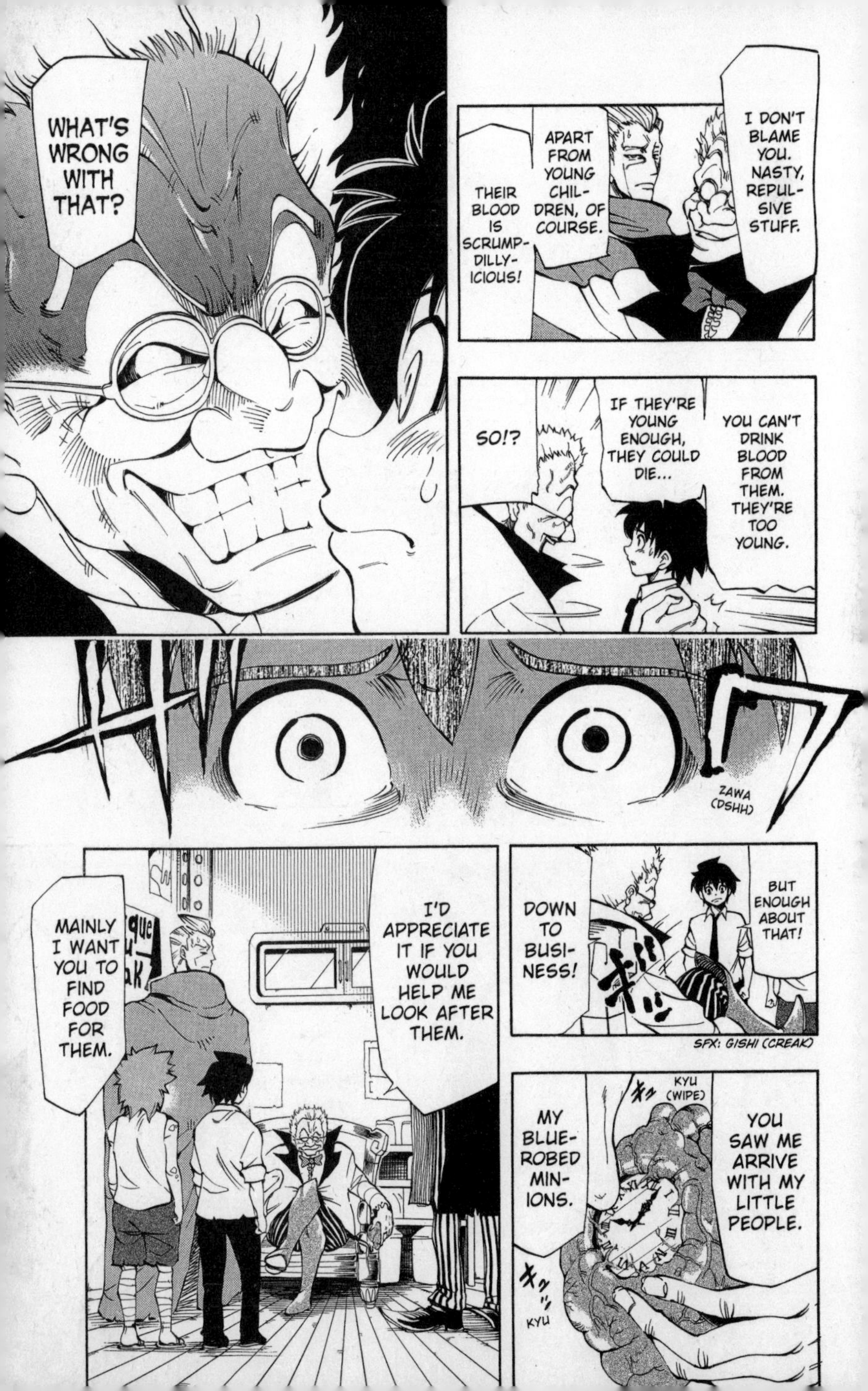
I DON'T BLAME YOU. NASTY, REPULSIVE STUFF.
APART FROM YOUNG CHILDREN, OF COURSE.
THEIR BLOOD IS SCRUMPDILLYICIOUS!
YOU CAN'T DRINK BLOOD FROM THEM. THEY'RE TOO YOUNG.
IF THEY'RE YOUNG ENOUGH, THEY COULD DIE...
SO!?
WHAT'S WRONG WITH THAT?
ZAWA (DSHH)
BUT ENOUGH ABOUT THAT!
DOWN TO BUSINESS!
SFX: GISHI (CREAK)
YOU SAW ME ARRIVE WITH MY LITTLE PEOPLE.
KYU (WIPE)
MY BLUE-ROBED MINIONS.
KYU
I'D APPRECIATE IT IF YOU WOULD HELP ME LOOK AFTER THEM.
MAINLY I WANT YOU TO FIND FOOD FOR THEM.

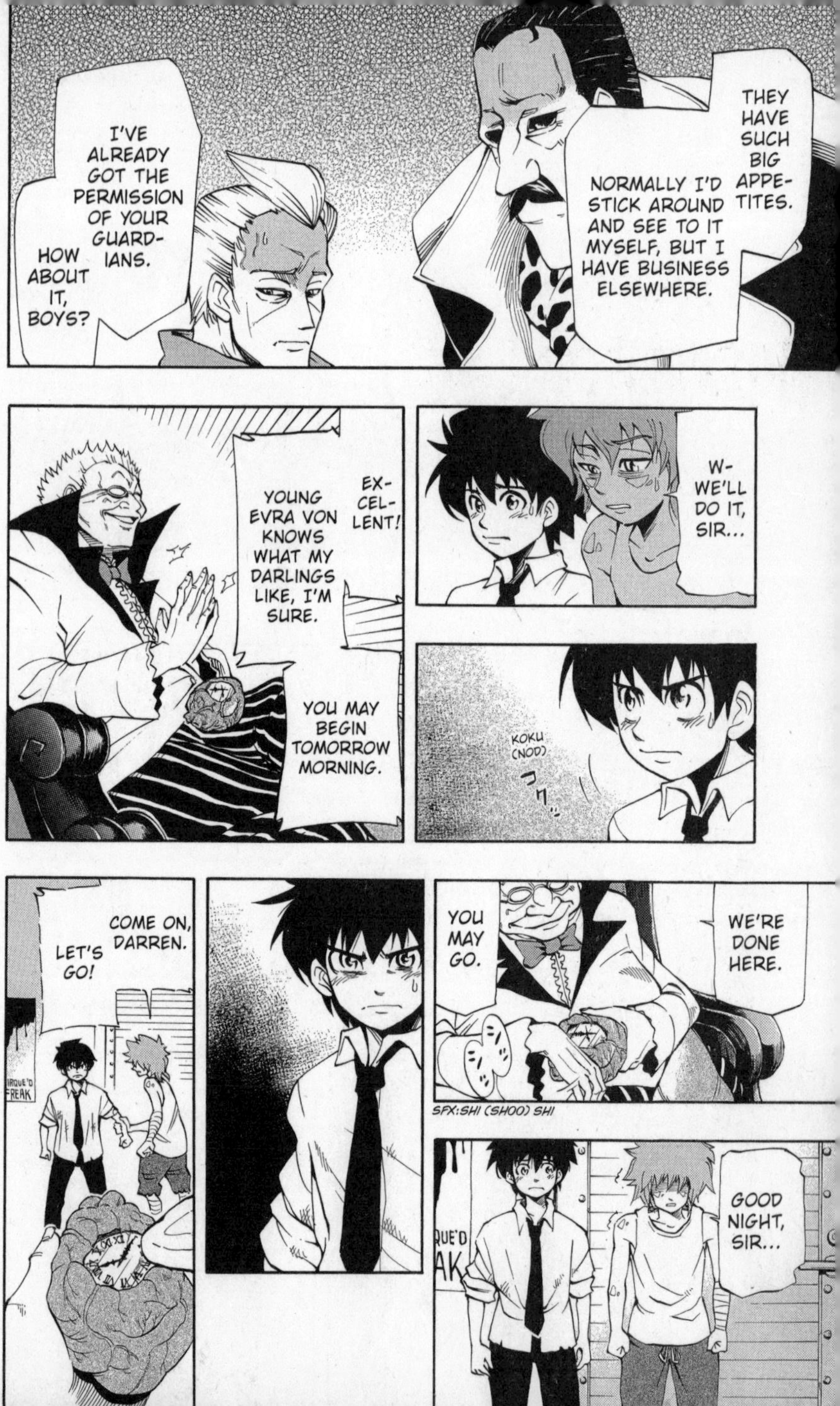
THEY HAVE SUCH BIG APPETITES.
NORMALLY I'D STICK AROUND AND SEE TO IT MYSELF, BUT I HAVE BUSINESS ELSEWHERE.
I'VE ALREADY GOT THE PERMISSION OF YOUR GUARDIANS.
HOW ABOUT IT, BOYS?
W-WE'LL DO IT, SIR...
KOKU (NOD)
EXCELLENT!
YOUNG EVRA VON KNOWS WHAT MY DARLINGS LIKE, I'M SURE.
YOU MAY BEGIN TOMORROW MORNING.
WE'RE DONE HERE.
YOU MAY GO.
SFX: SHI (SHOO) SHI
GOOD NIGHT, SIR...
COME ON, DARREN.
LET'S GO!
IRQUE'D FREAK

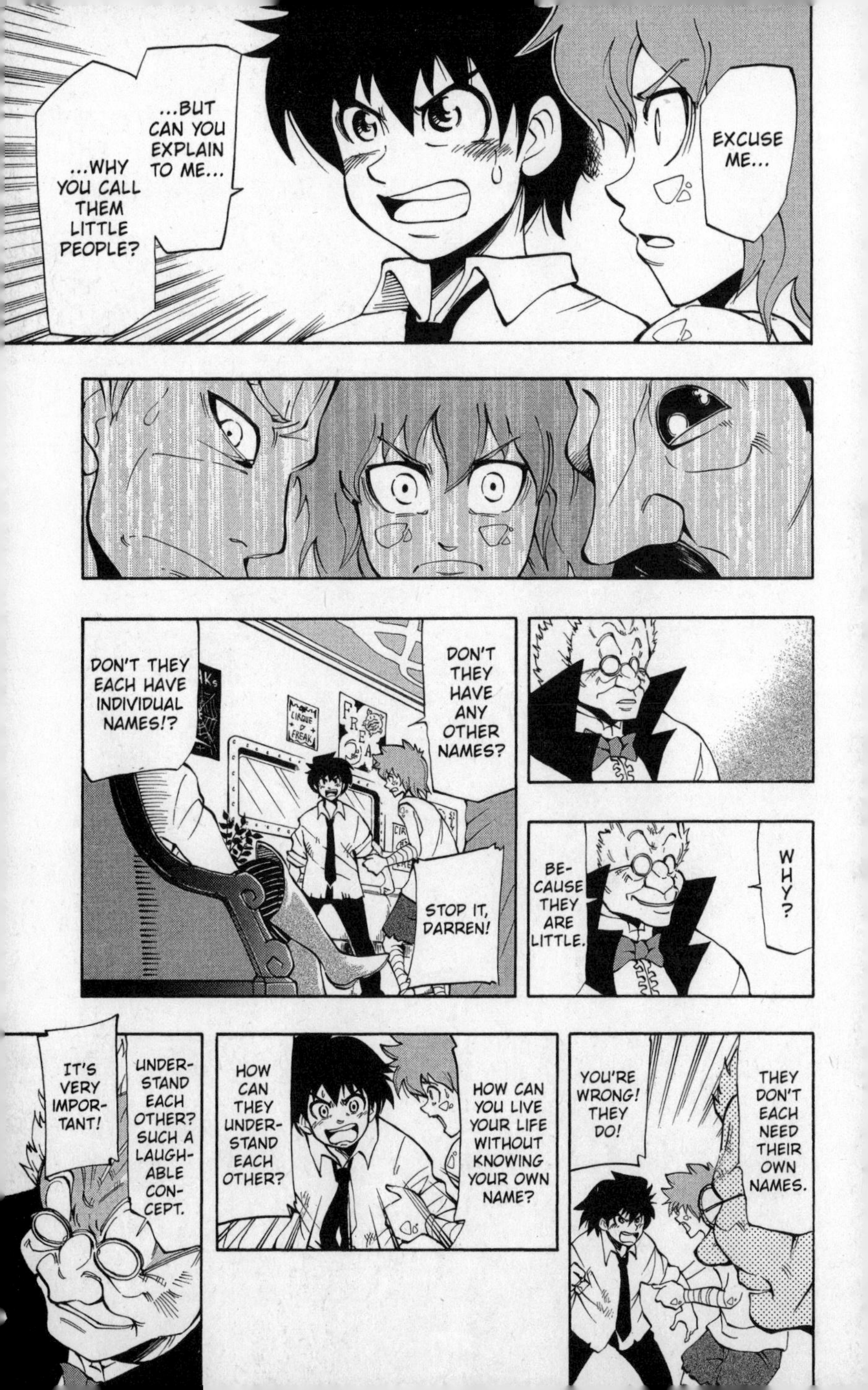
EXCUSE ME...
...BUT CAN YOU EXPLAIN TO ME...
...WHY YOU CALL THEM LITTLE PEOPLE?
WHY?
BE-CAUSE THEY ARE LITTLE.
DON'T THEY HAVE ANY OTHER NAMES?
DON'T THEY EACH HAVE INDIVIDUAL NAMES!?
CIRQUE DU FREAK
STOP IT, DARREN!
THEY DON'T EACH NEED THEIR OWN NAMES.
YOU'RE WRONG! THEY DO!
HOW CAN YOU LIVE YOUR LIFE WITHOUT KNOWING YOUR OWN NAME?
HOW CAN THEY UNDER-STAND EACH OTHER?
UNDER-STAND EACH OTHER? SUCH A LAUGH-ABLE CON-CEPT.
IT'S VERY IMPOR-TANT!

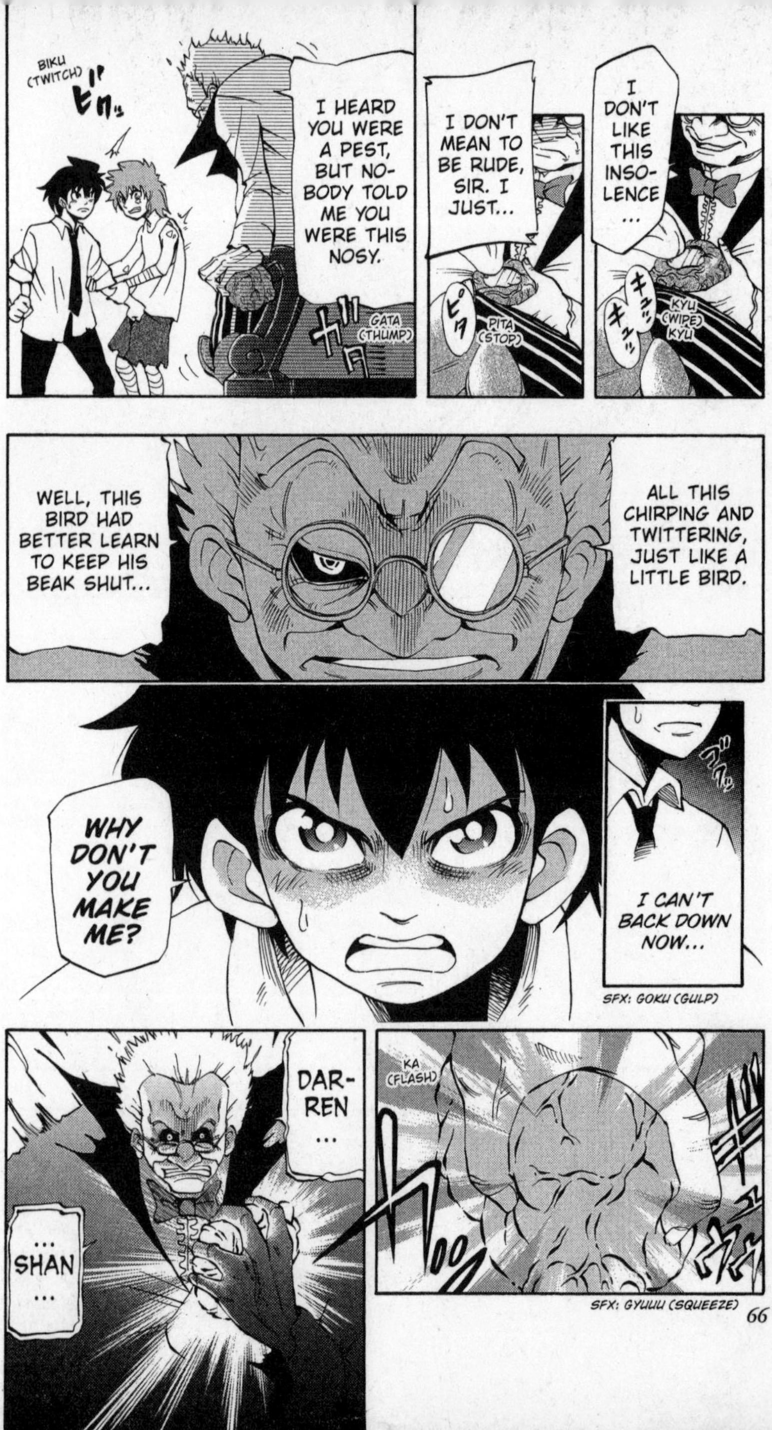
I DON'T LIKE THIS INSOLENCE...
KYU (WIPE) KYU
I DON'T MEAN TO BE RUDE, SIR. I JUST...
PITA (STOP)
I HEARD YOU WERE A PEST, BUT NOBODY TOLD ME YOU WERE THIS NOSY.
GATA (THUMP)
BIKU (TWITCH)
ALL THIS CHIRPING AND TWITTERING, JUST LIKE A LITTLE BIRD.
WELL, THIS BIRD HAD BETTER LEARN TO KEEP HIS BEAK SHUT...
I CAN'T BACK DOWN NOW...
SFX: GOKU (GULP)
WHY DON'T YOU MAKE ME?
KA (FLASH)
SFX: GYUUU (SQUEEZE)
DARREN...
...SHAN...

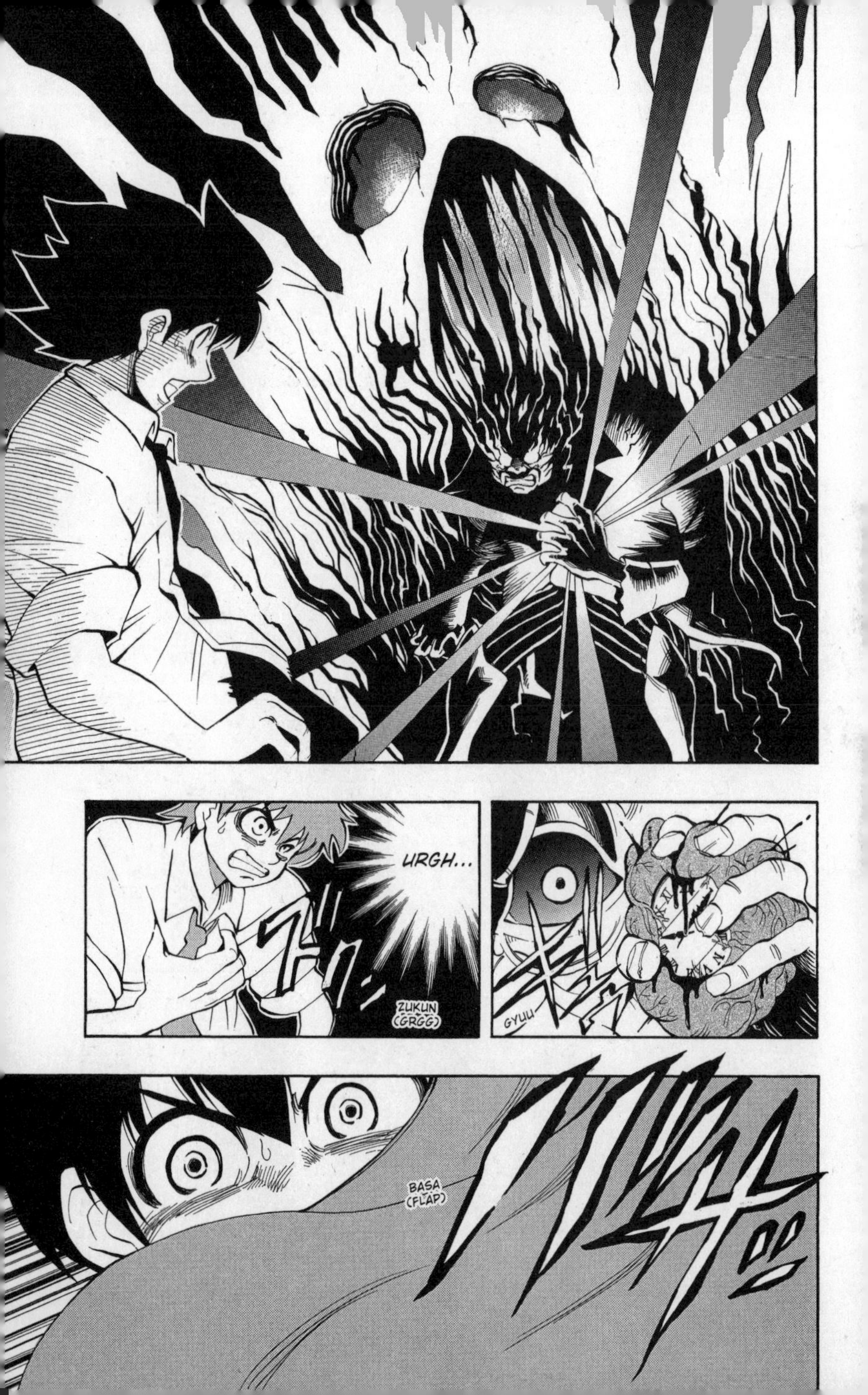
GYUU
URGH...
ZUKUN
(GRGG)
BASA
(FLAP)

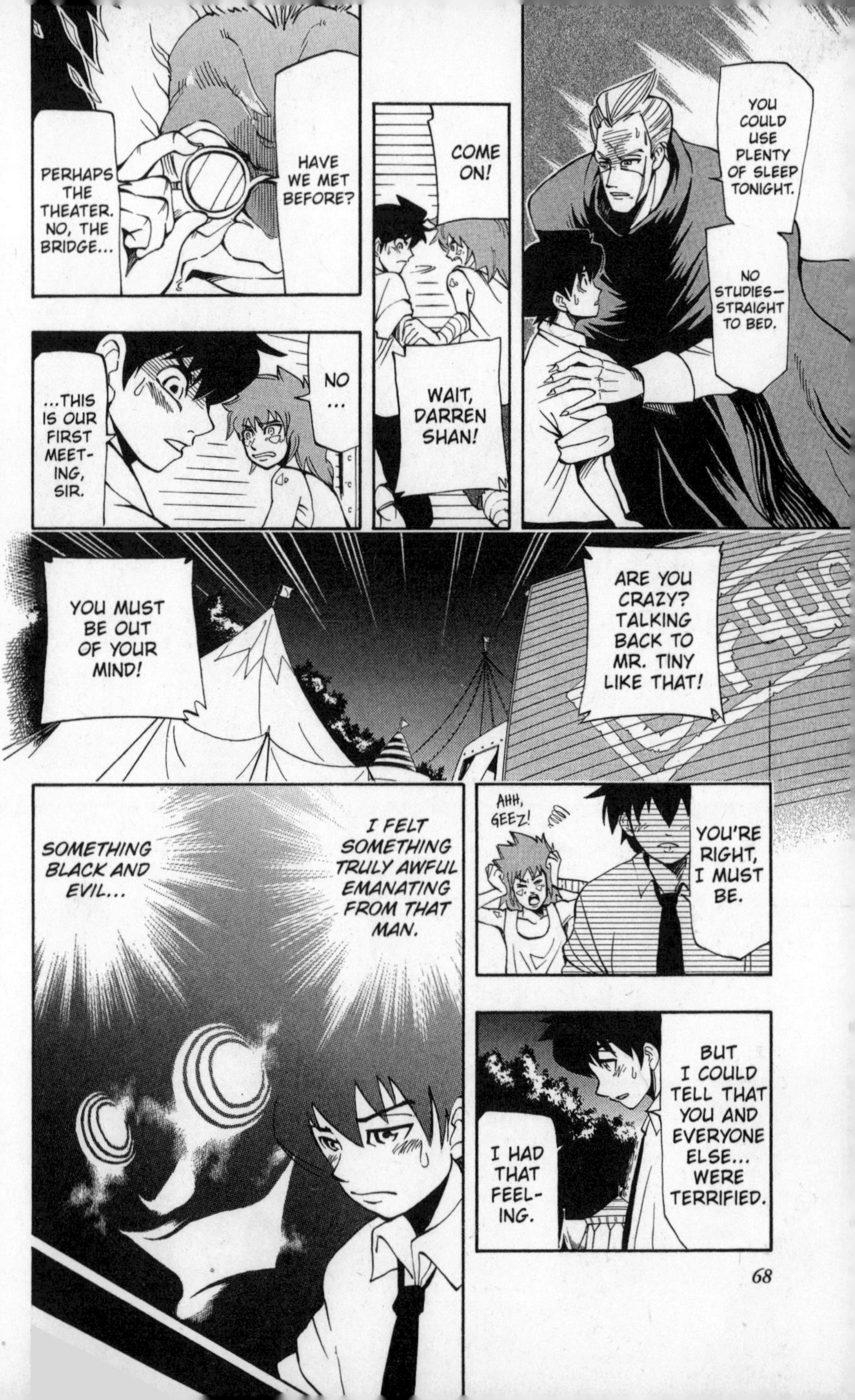

YOU COULD USE PLENTY OF SLEEP TONIGHT.
NO STUDIES— STRAIGHT TO BED.
COME ON!
WAIT, DARREN SHAN!
HAVE WE MET BEFORE?
PERHAPS THE THEATER. NO, THE BRIDGE...
NO ...
...THIS IS OUR FIRST MEET-ING, SIR.
ARE YOU CRAZY? TALKING BACK TO MR. TINY LIKE THAT!
YOU MUST BE OUT OF YOUR MIND!
YOU'RE RIGHT, I MUST BE.
AHH, GEEZ!
BUT I COULD TELL THAT YOU AND EVERYONE ELSE... WERE TERRIFIED.
I HAD THAT FEEL-ING.
I FELT SOMETHING TRULY AWFUL EMANATING FROM THAT MAN.
SOMETHING BLACK AND EVIL...

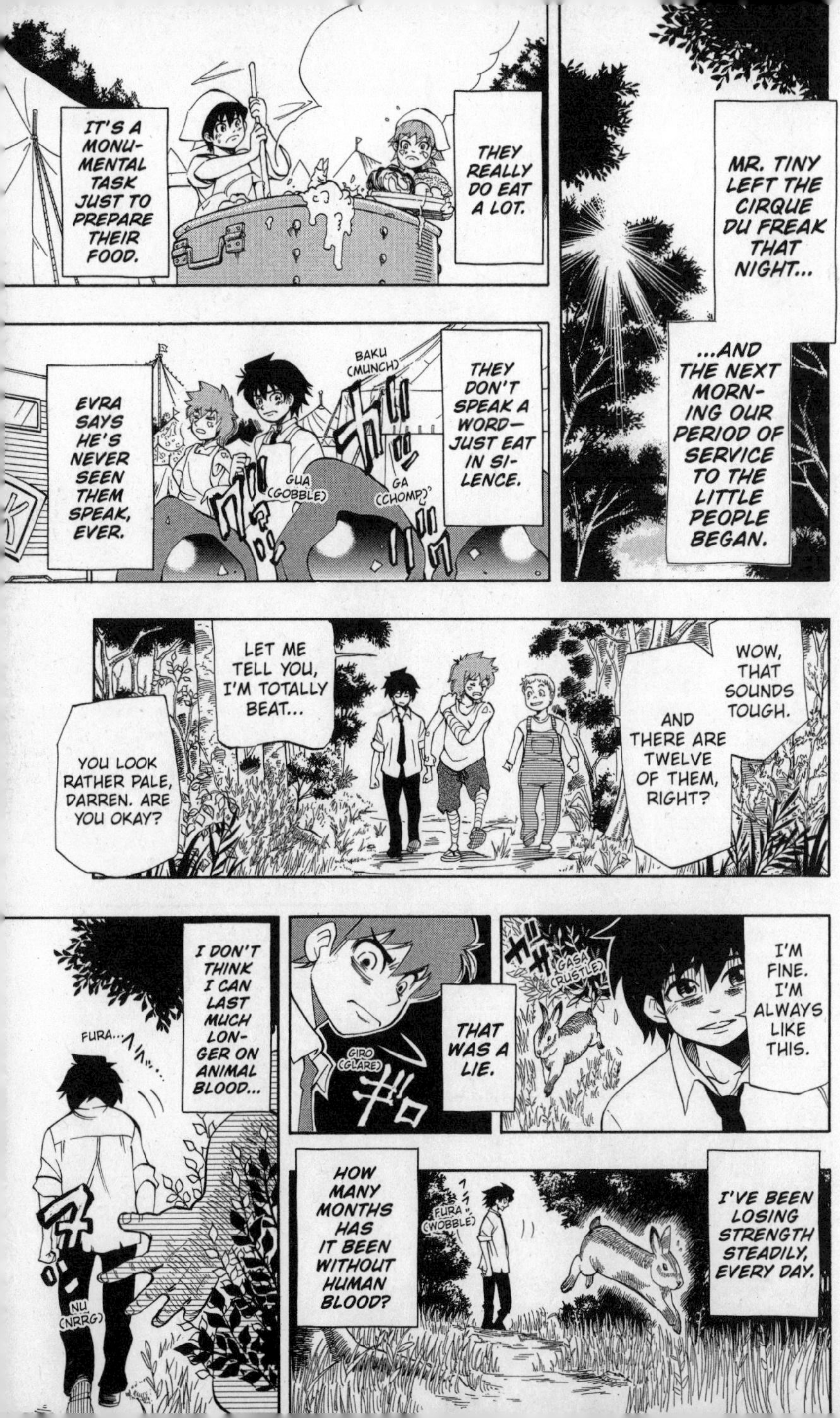
MR. TINY LEFT THE CIRQUE DU FREAK THAT NIGHT...
...AND THE NEXT MORNING OUR PERIOD OF SERVICE TO THE LITTLE PEOPLE BEGAN.
THEY REALLY DO EAT A LOT.
IT'S A MONUMENTAL TASK JUST TO PREPARE THEIR FOOD.
THEY DON'T SPEAK A WORD—JUST EAT IN SILENCE.
BAKU (MUNCH)
GA (CHOMP)
GUA (GOBBLE)
EVRA SAYS HE'S NEVER SEEN THEM SPEAK, EVER.
WOW, THAT SOUNDS TOUGH.
AND THERE ARE TWELVE OF THEM, RIGHT?
LET ME TELL YOU, I'M TOTALLY BEAT...
YOU LOOK RATHER PALE, DARREN. ARE YOU OKAY?
I'M FINE. I'M ALWAYS LIKE THIS.
GASA (RUSTLE)
THAT WAS A LIE.
GIRO (GLARE)
I'VE BEEN LOSING STRENGTH STEADILY, EVERY DAY.
FURA (WOBBLE)
HOW MANY MONTHS HAS IT BEEN WITHOUT HUMAN BLOOD?
I DON'T THINK I CAN LAST MUCH LONGER ON ANIMAL BLOOD...
FURA...
NU (NRRG)

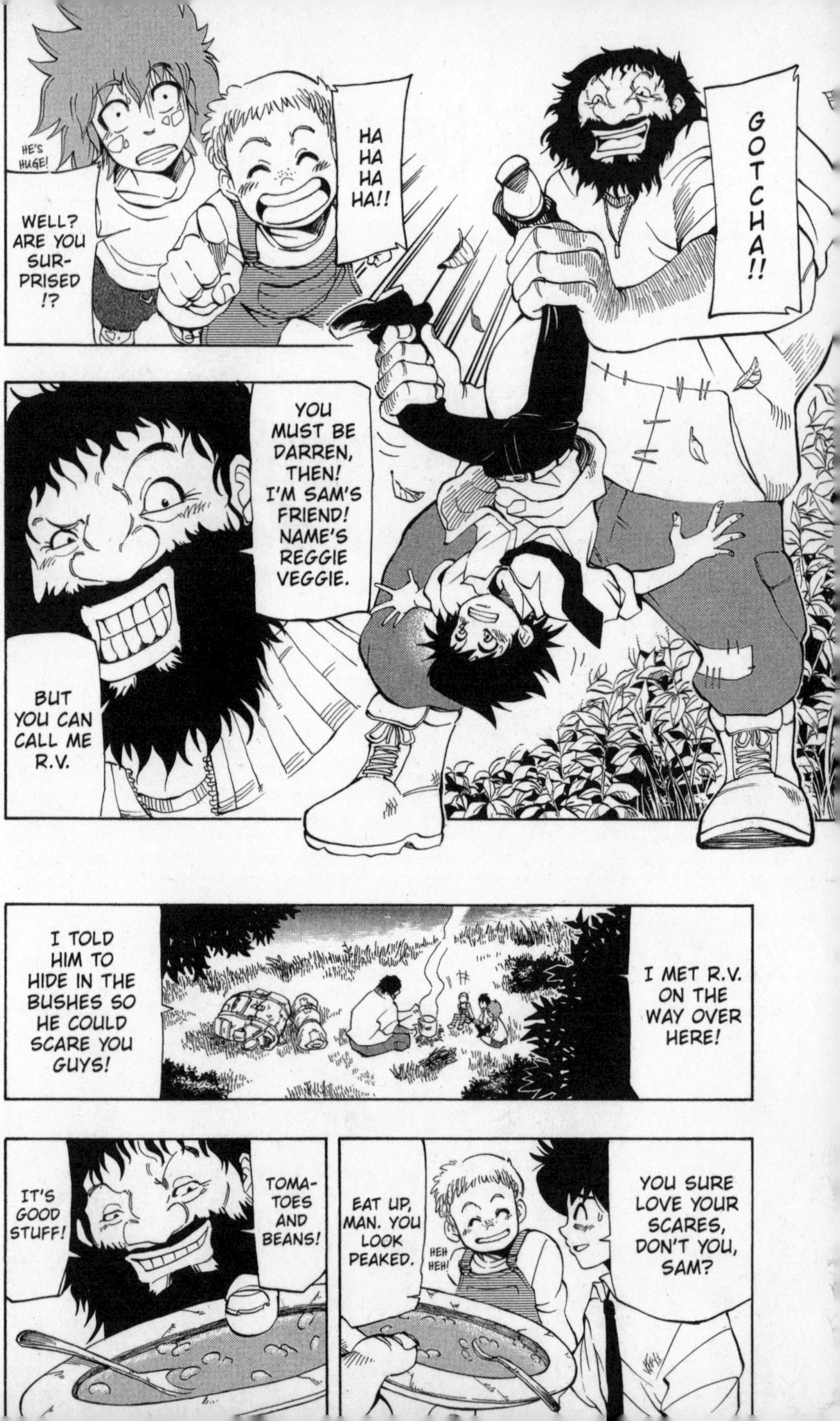
GOTCHA!!
HA HA HA HA!!
HE'S HUGE!
WELL? ARE YOU SUR-PRISED!?
YOU MUST BE DARREN, THEN! I'M SAM'S FRIEND! NAME'S REGGIE VEGGIE.
BUT YOU CAN CALL ME R.V.
I MET R.V. ON THE WAY OVER HERE!
I TOLD HIM TO HIDE IN THE BUSHES SO HE COULD SCARE YOU GUYS!
YOU SURE LOVE YOUR SCARES, DON'T YOU, SAM?
HEH HEH!
EAT UP, MAN. YOU LOOK PEAKED.
TOMA-TOES AND BEANS!
IT'S GOOD STUFF!

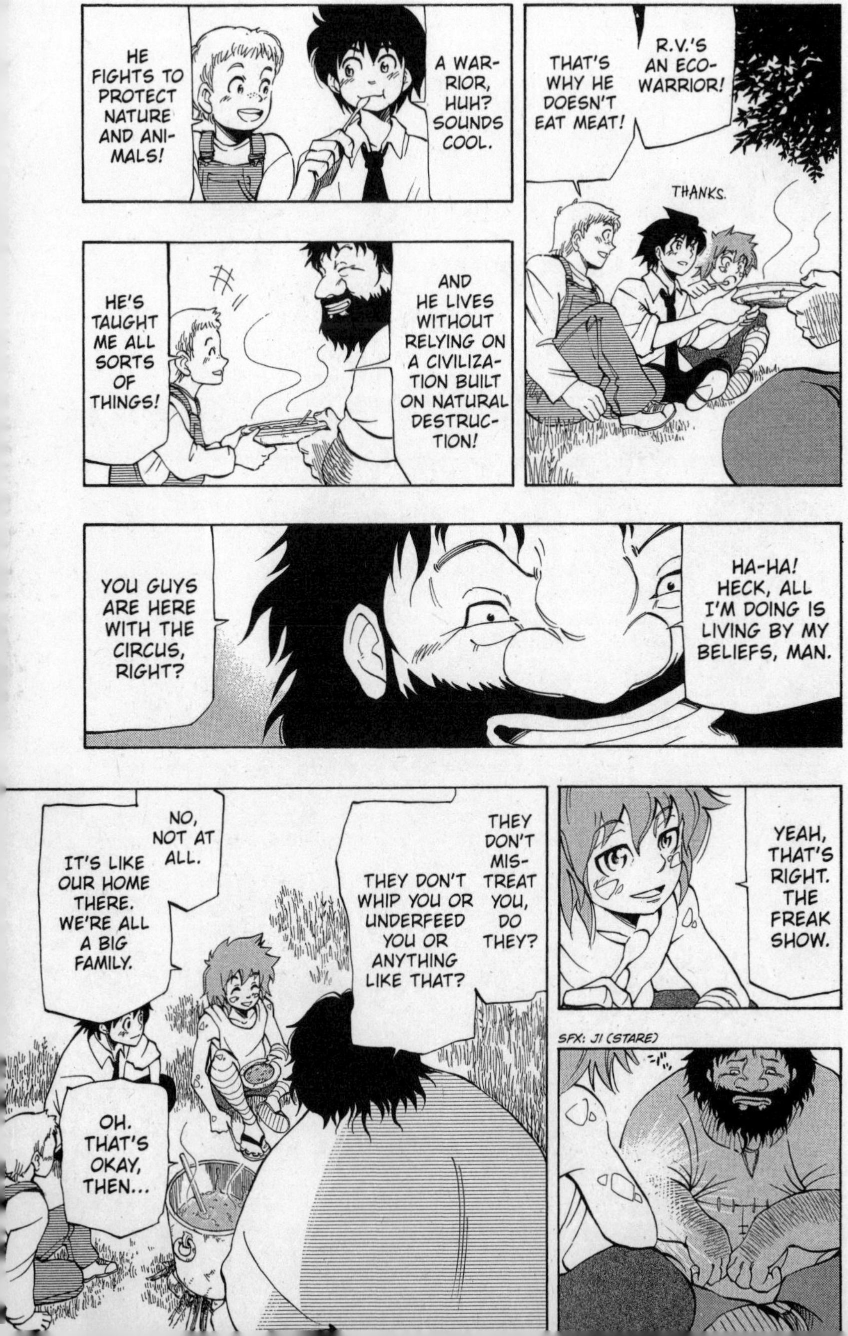
R.V.'S AN ECO-WARRIOR!
THAT'S WHY HE DOESN'T EAT MEAT!
THANKS.
A WAR-RIOR, HUH? SOUNDS COOL.
HE FIGHTS TO PROTECT NATURE AND ANI-MALS!
AND HE LIVES WITHOUT RELYING ON A CIVILIZA-TION BUILT ON NATURAL DESTRUC-TION!
HE'S TAUGHT ME ALL SORTS OF THINGS!
HA-HA! HECK, ALL I'M DOING IS LIVING BY MY BELIEFS, MAN.
YOU GUYS ARE HERE WITH THE CIRCUS, RIGHT?
YEAH, THAT'S RIGHT. THE FREAK SHOW.
SFX: JI (STARE)
THEY DON'T MIS-TREAT YOU, DO THEY?
THEY DON'T WHIP YOU OR UNDERFEED YOU OR ANYTHING LIKE THAT?
NO, NOT AT ALL.
IT'S LIKE OUR HOME THERE. WE'RE ALL A BIG FAMILY.
OH. THAT'S OKAY, THEN...

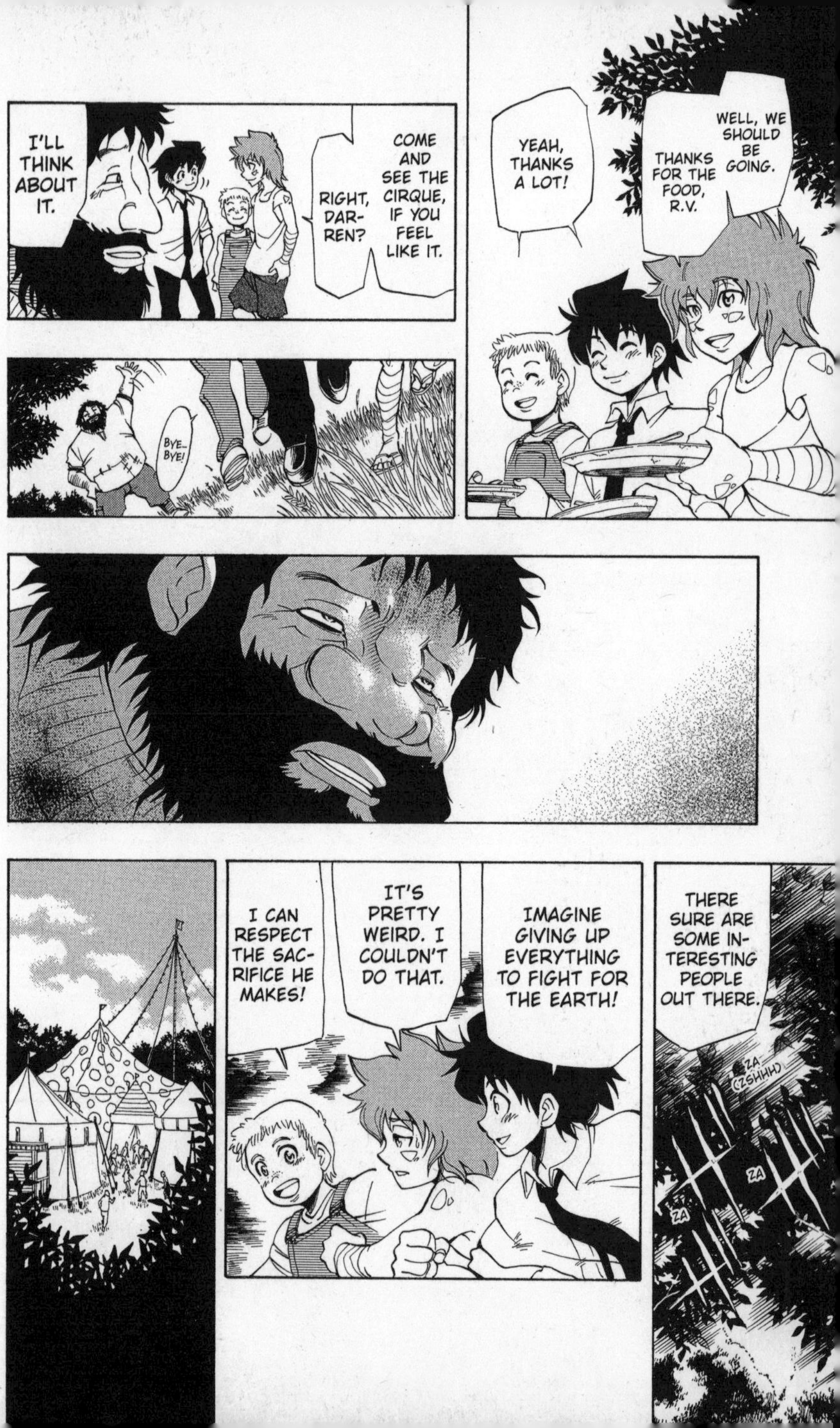
WELL, WE SHOULD BE GOING.
THANKS FOR THE FOOD, R.V.
YEAH, THANKS A LOT!
COME AND SEE THE CIRQUE, IF YOU FEEL LIKE IT.
RIGHT, DARREN?
I'LL THINK ABOUT IT.
BYE-BYE!
THERE SURE ARE SOME INTERESTING PEOPLE OUT THERE.
ZA (ZSHHH)
ZA
ZA
IMAGINE GIVING UP EVERYTHING TO FIGHT FOR THE EARTH!
IT'S PRETTY WEIRD. I COULDN'T DO THAT.
I CAN RESPECT THE SACRIFICE HE MAKES!

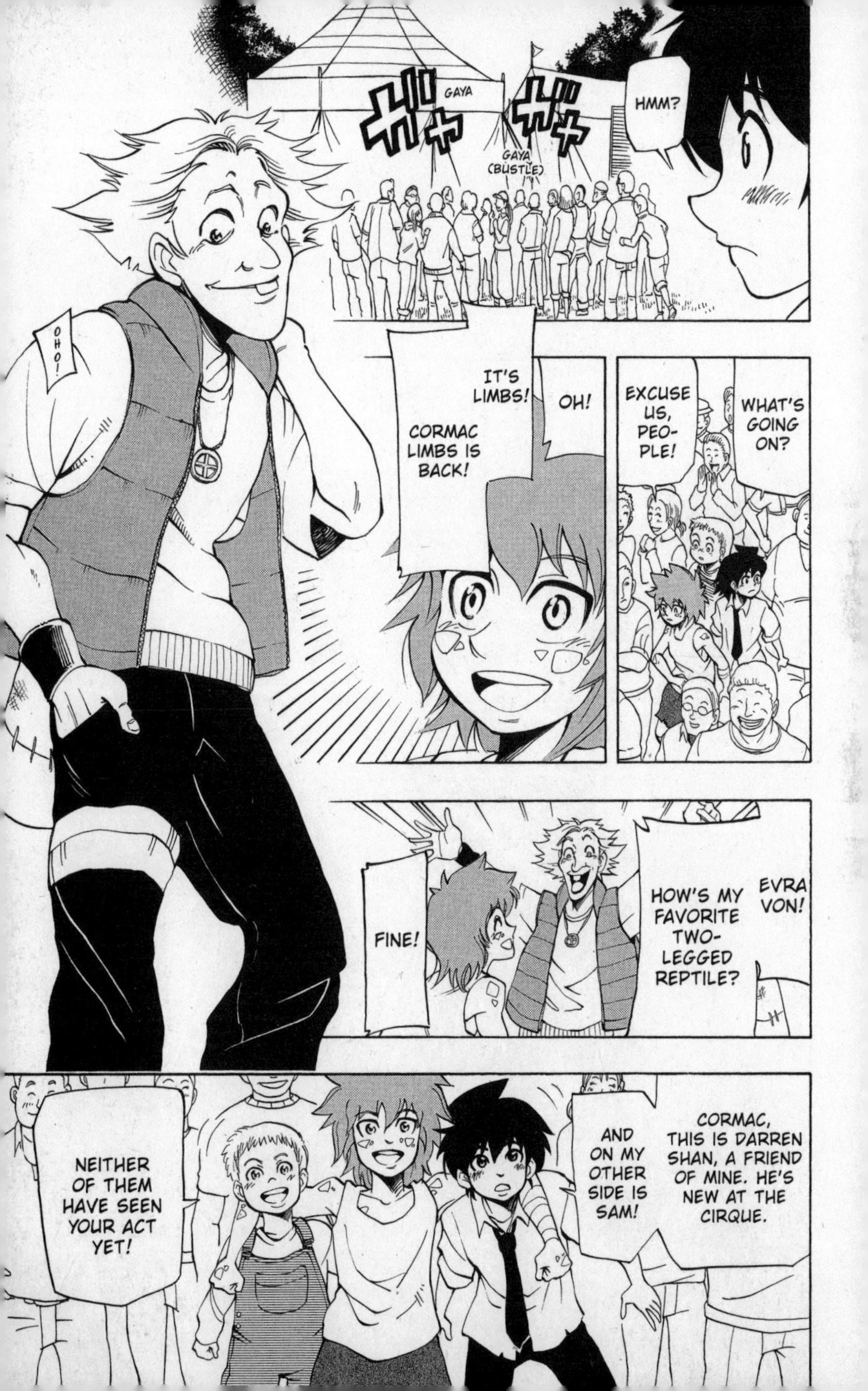
HMM?
GAYA
GAYA (BUSTLE)
WHAT'S GOING ON?
EXCUSE US, PEO-PLE!
OH!
IT'S LIMBS!
CORMAC LIMBS IS BACK!
EVRA VON!
HOW'S MY FAVORITE TWO-LEGGED REPTILE?
FINE!
OHO!
CORMAC, THIS IS DARREN SHAN, A FRIEND OF MINE. HE'S NEW AT THE CIRQUE.
AND ON MY OTHER SIDE IS SAM!
NEITHER OF THEM HAVE SEEN YOUR ACT YET!

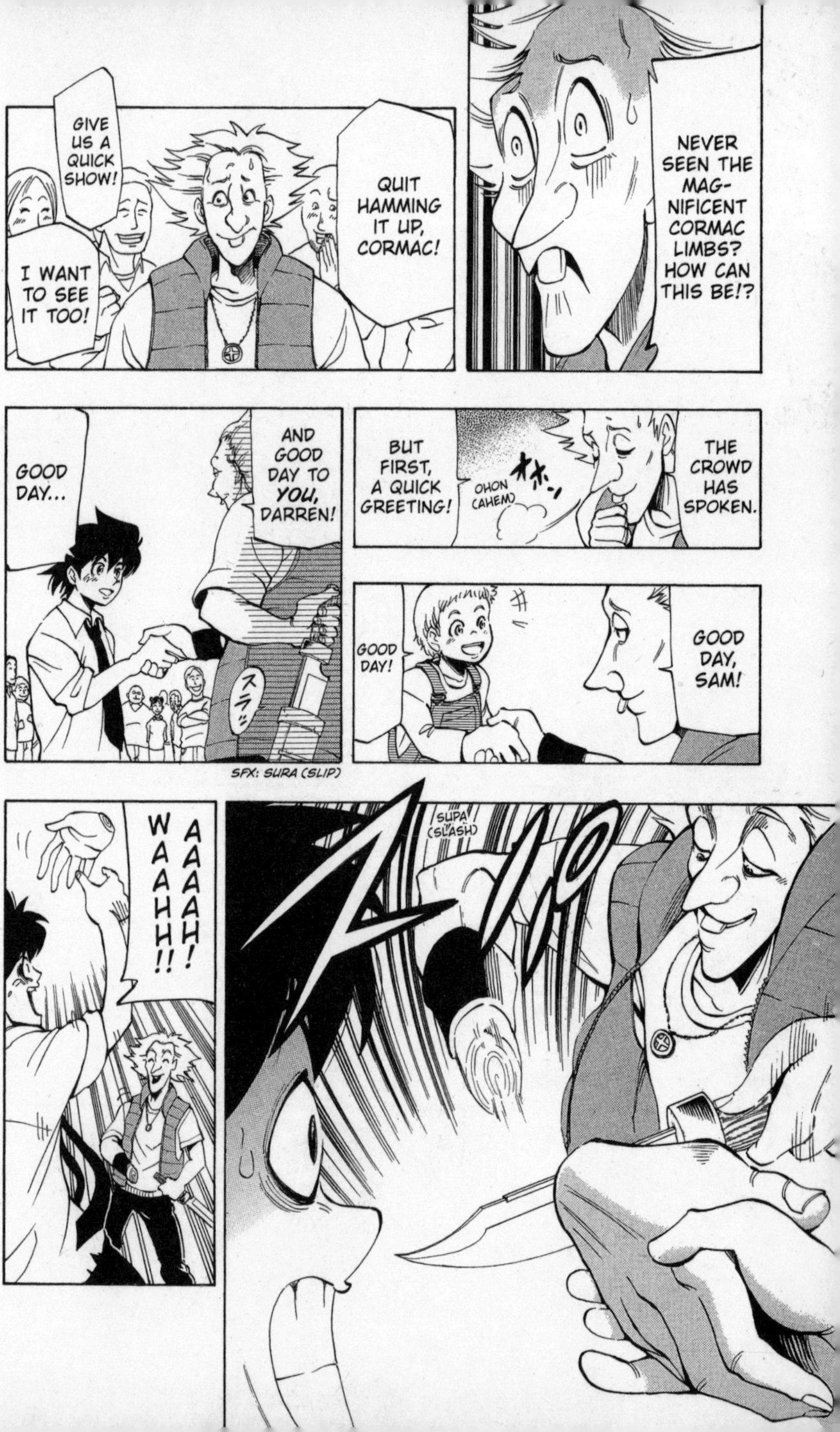
NEVER SEEN THE MAG-NIFICENT CORMAC LIMBS? HOW CAN THIS BE!?
QUIT HAMMING IT UP, CORMAC!
GIVE US A QUICK SHOW!
I WANT TO SEE IT TOO!
THE CROWD HAS SPOKEN.
OHON (AHEM)
BUT FIRST, A QUICK GREETING!
GOOD DAY, SAM!
GOOD DAY!
AND GOOD DAY TO YOU, DARREN!
GOOD DAY...
SFX: SURA (SLIP)
SUPA (SLASH)
AAAAAH!
WAAAHH!!

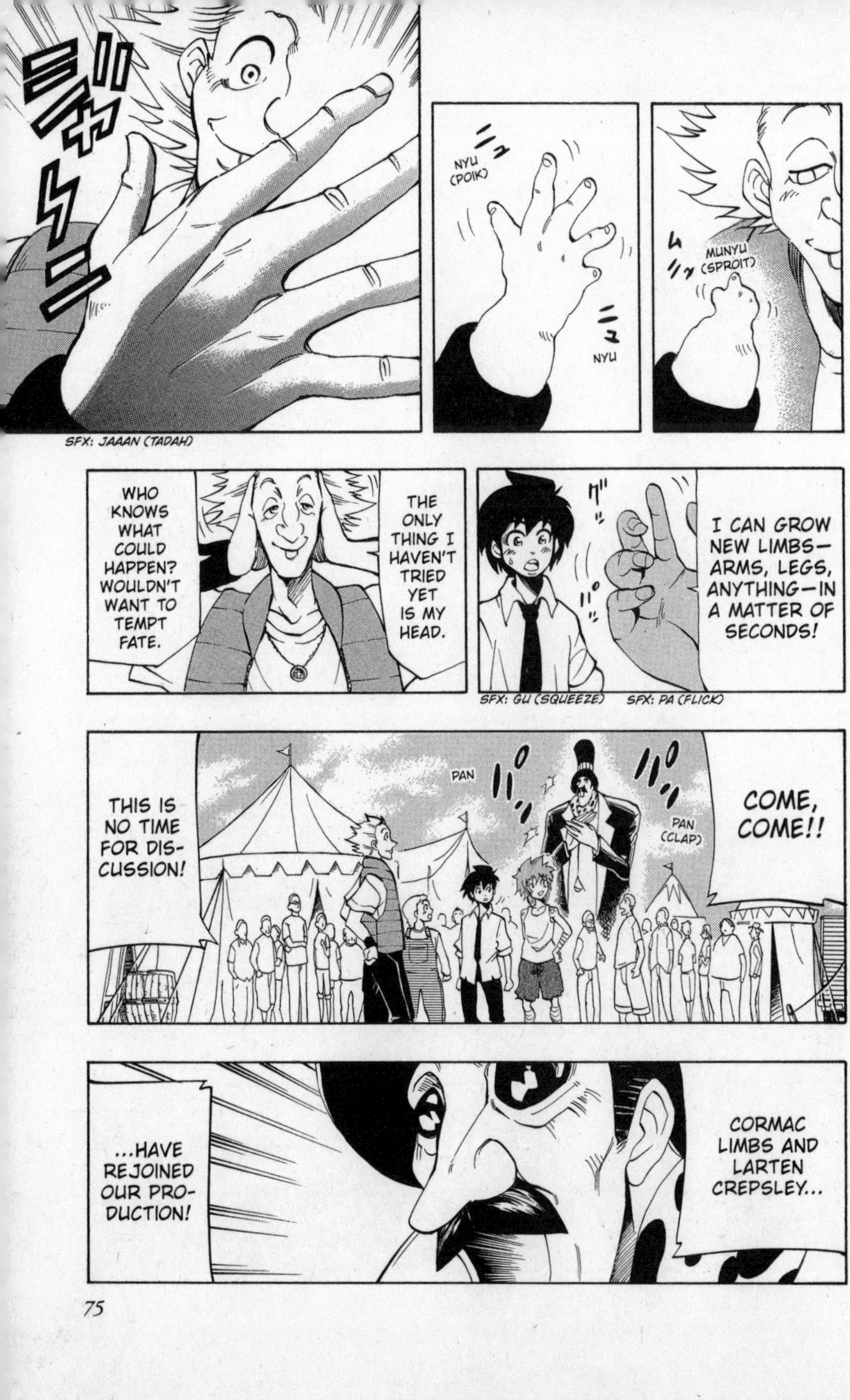
MUNYU (SPROIT)
NYU (POIK)
NYU
SFX: JAAAN (TADAH)
I CAN GROW NEW LIMBS—ARMS, LEGS, ANYTHING—IN A MATTER OF SECONDS!
SFX: PA (FLICK)
SFX: GU (SQUEEZE)
THE ONLY THING I HAVEN'T TRIED YET IS MY HEAD.
WHO KNOWS WHAT COULD HAPPEN? WOULDN'T WANT TO TEMPT FATE.
COME, COME!!
PAN (CLAP)
PAN
THIS IS NO TIME FOR DIS-CUSSION!
CORMAC LIMBS AND LARTEN CREPSLEY...
...HAVE REJOINED OUR PRO-DUCTION!

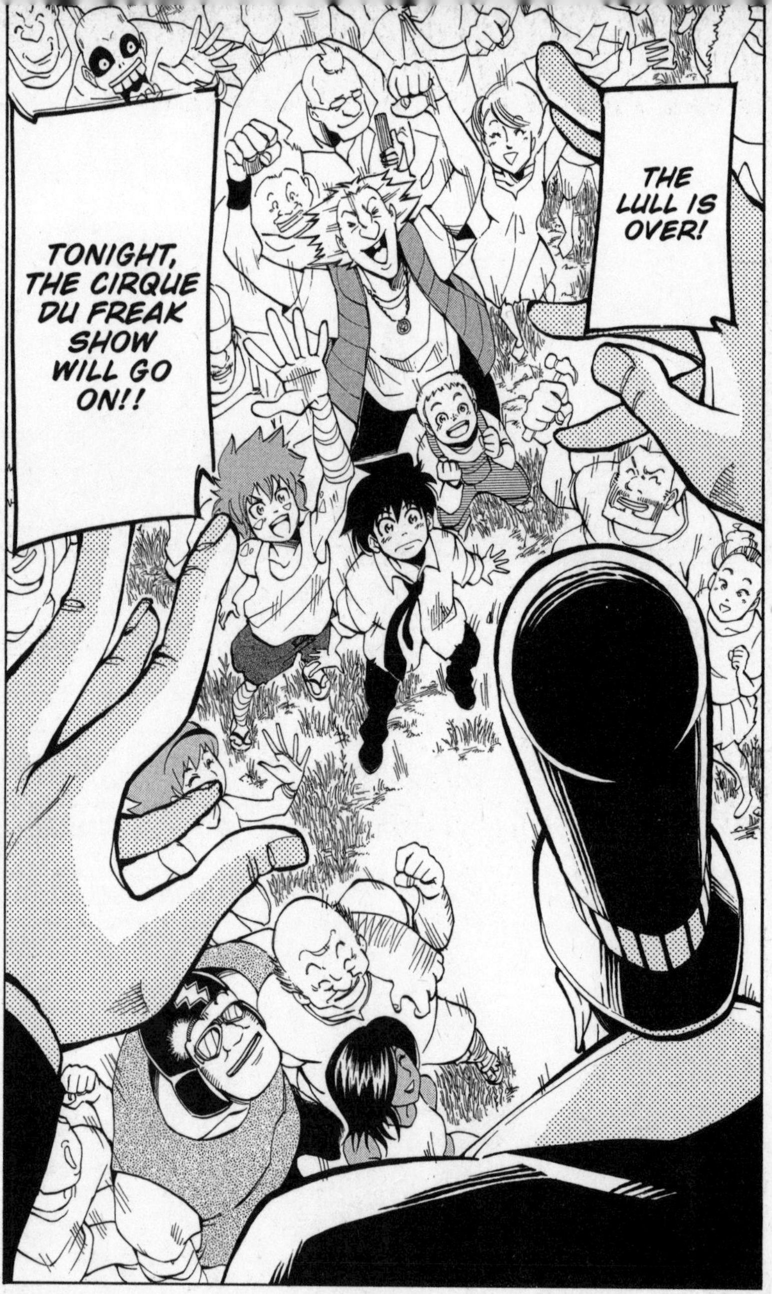
THE LULL IS OVER!
TONIGHT, THE CIRQUE DU FREAK SHOW WILL GO ON!!

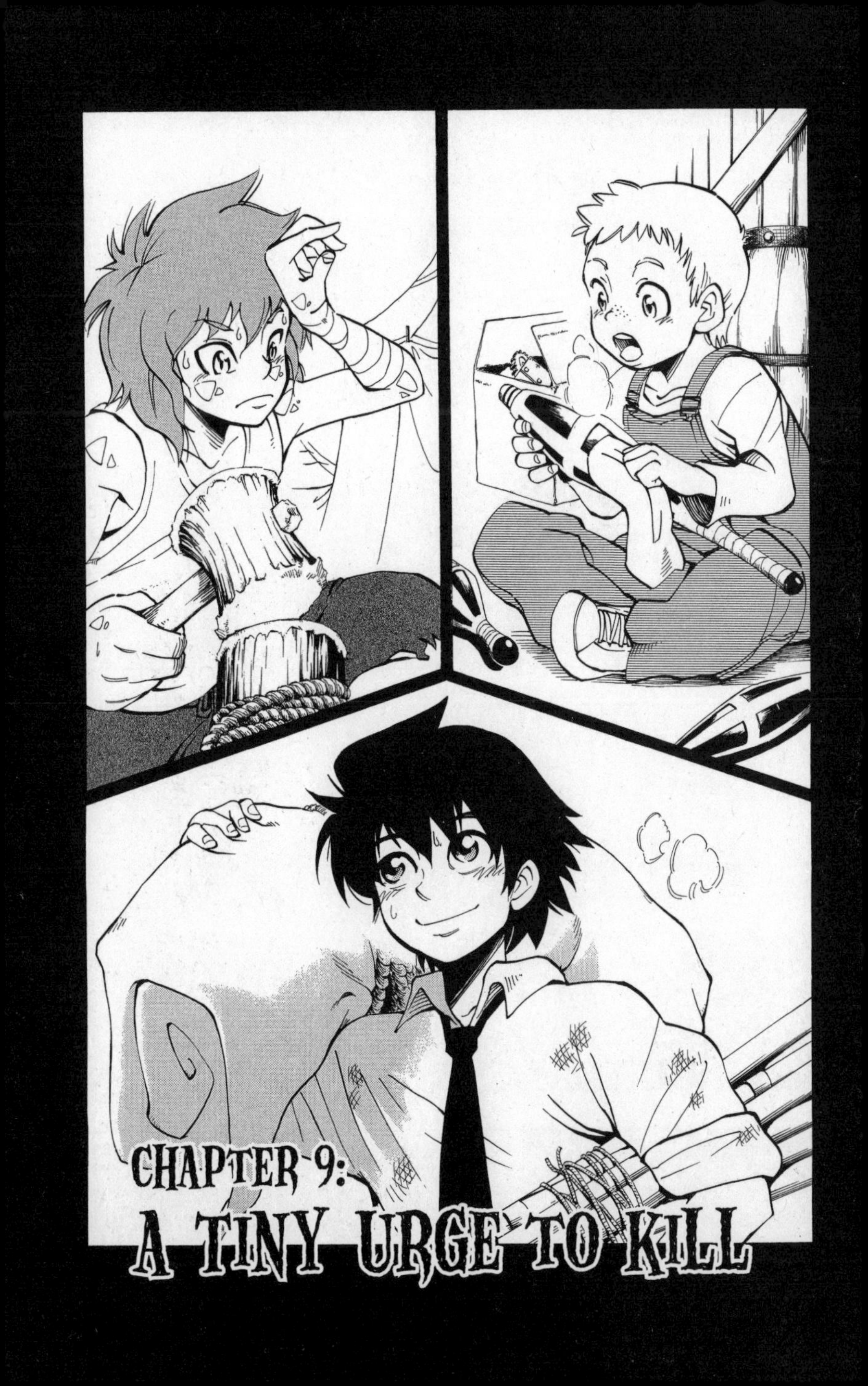
CHAPTER 9:
A TINY URGE TO KILL

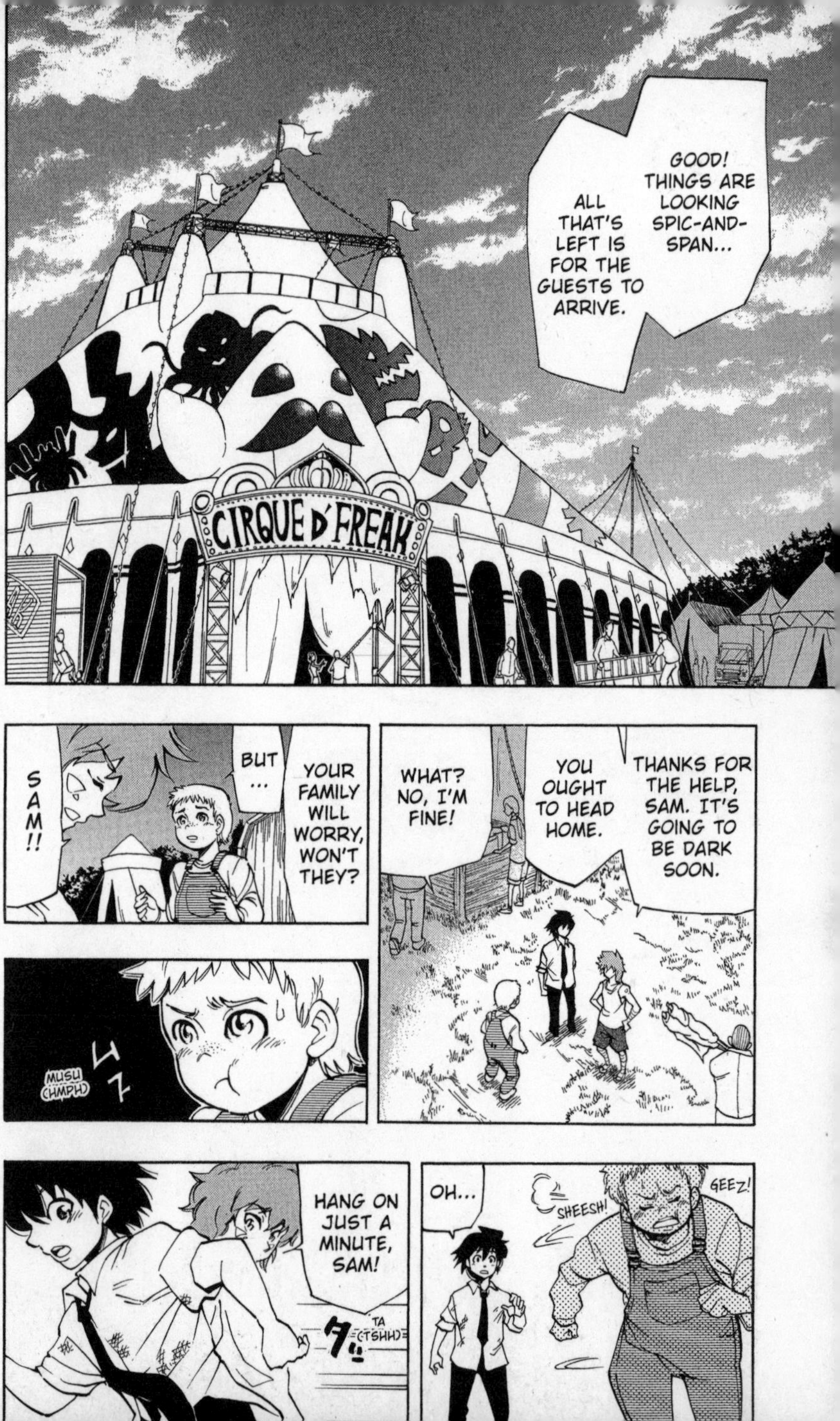
GOOD! THINGS ARE LOOKING SPIC-AND-SPAN...
ALL THAT'S LEFT IS FOR THE GUESTS TO ARRIVE.
CIRQUE D'FREAK
THANKS FOR THE HELP, SAM. IT'S GOING TO BE DARK SOON.
YOU OUGHT TO HEAD HOME.
WHAT? NO, I'M FINE!
YOUR FAMILY WILL WORRY, WON'T THEY?
BUT...
SAM!!
MUSU (HMPH)
GEEZ!
SHEESH!
OH...
HANG ON JUST A MINUTE, SAM!
TA (TSHH)

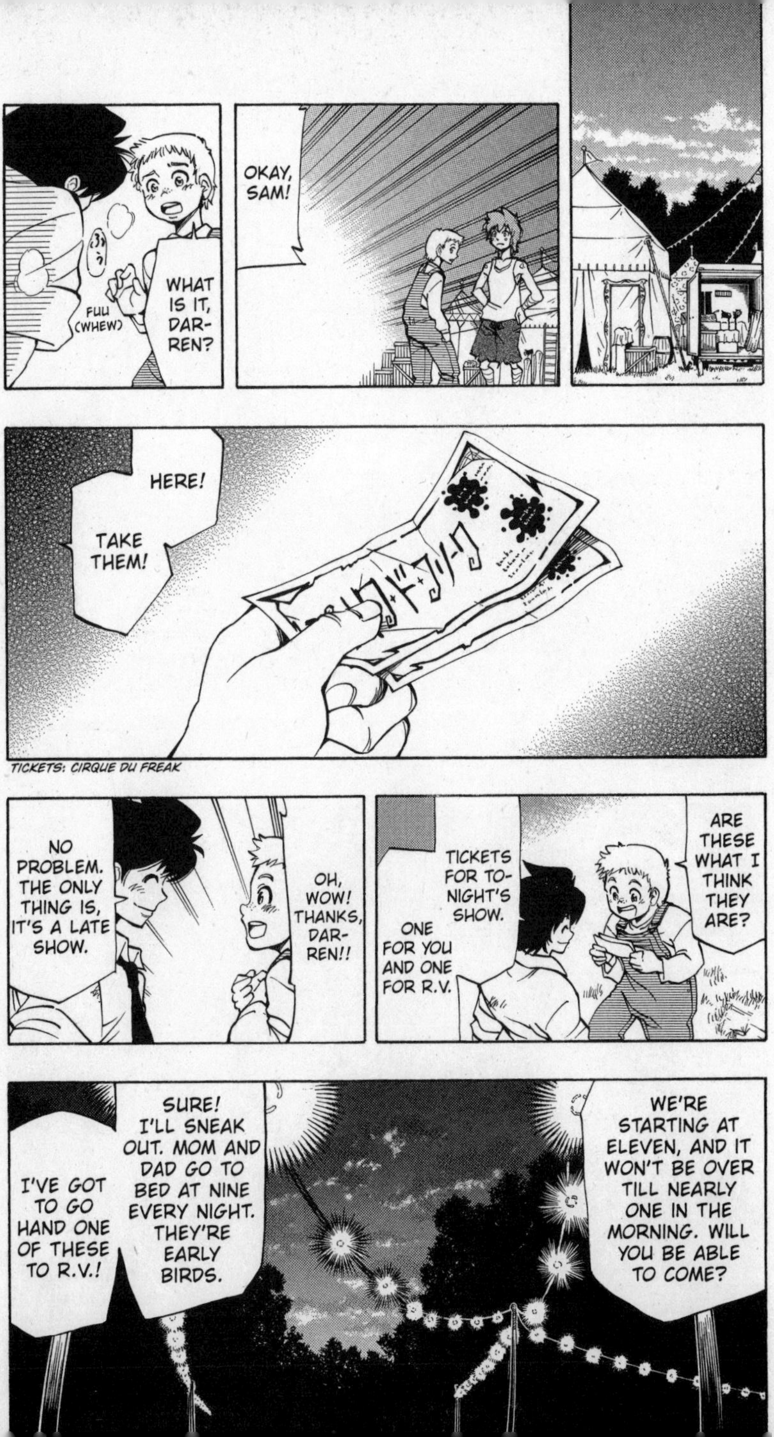
OKAY, SAM!
FUU (WHEW)
WHAT IS IT, DARREN?
HERE!
TAKE THEM!
TICKETS: CIRQUE DU FREAK
ARE THESE WHAT I THINK THEY ARE?
TICKETS FOR TONIGHT'S SHOW.
ONE FOR YOU AND ONE FOR R.V.
OH, WOW! THANKS, DARREN!!
NO PROBLEM. THE ONLY THING IS, IT'S A LATE SHOW.
WE'RE STARTING AT ELEVEN, AND IT WON'T BE OVER TILL NEARLY ONE IN THE MORNING. WILL YOU BE ABLE TO COME?
SURE! I'LL SNEAK OUT. MOM AND DAD GO TO BED AT NINE EVERY NIGHT. THEY'RE EARLY BIRDS.
I'VE GOT TO GO HAND ONE OF THESE TO R.V.!

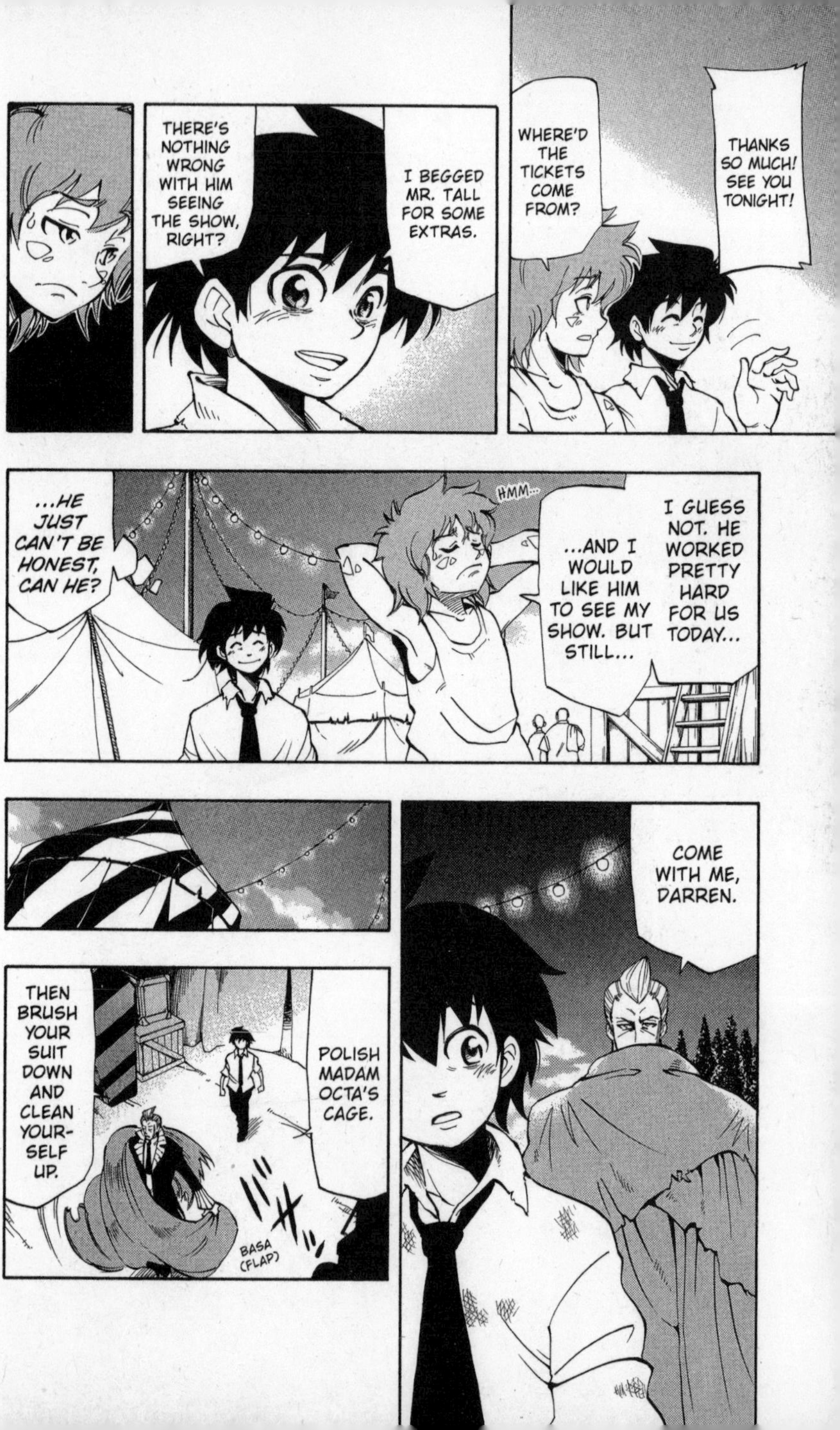
THANKS SO MUCH! SEE YOU TONIGHT!
WHERE'D THE TICKETS COME FROM?
I BEGGED MR. TALL FOR SOME EXTRAS.
THERE'S NOTHING WRONG WITH HIM SEEING THE SHOW, RIGHT?
HMM...
I GUESS NOT. HE WORKED PRETTY HARD FOR US TODAY...
...AND I WOULD LIKE HIM TO SEE MY SHOW. BUT STILL...
...HE JUST CAN'T BE HONEST, CAN HE?
COME WITH ME, DARREN.
POLISH MADAM OCTA'S CAGE.
THEN BRUSH YOUR SUIT DOWN AND CLEAN YOUR-SELF UP.
BASA (FLAP)

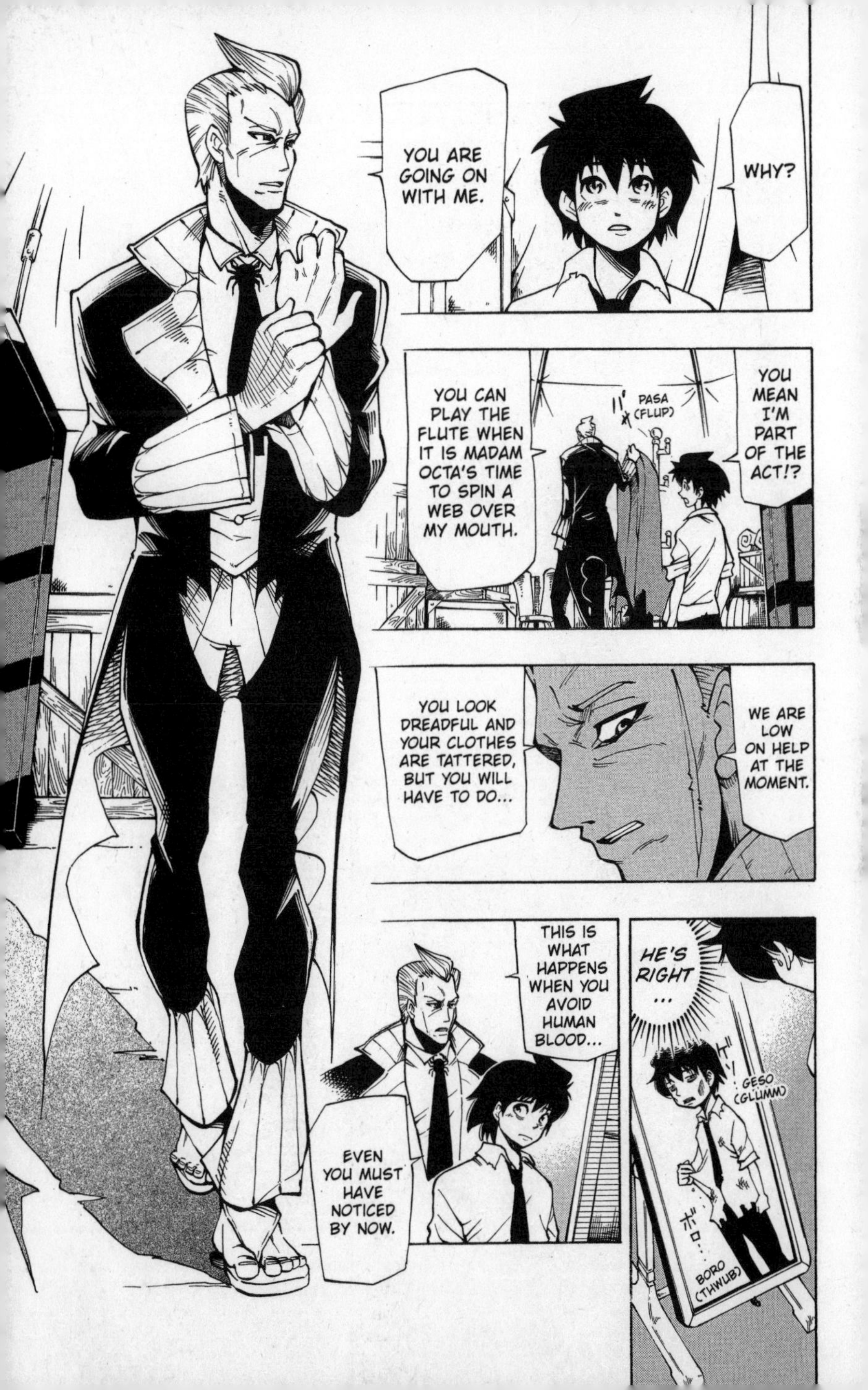
WHY?
YOU ARE GOING ON WITH ME.
YOU MEAN I'M PART OF THE ACT!?
PASA (FLUP)
YOU CAN PLAY THE FLUTE WHEN IT IS MADAM OCTA'S TIME TO SPIN A WEB OVER MY MOUTH.
WE ARE LOW ON HELP AT THE MOMENT.
YOU LOOK DREADFUL AND YOUR CLOTHES ARE TATTERED, BUT YOU WILL HAVE TO DO...
HE'S RIGHT...
GESO (GLUMM)
BORO (THWUB)
THIS IS WHAT HAPPENS WHEN YOU AVOID HUMAN BLOOD...
EVEN YOU MUST HAVE NOTICED BY NOW.

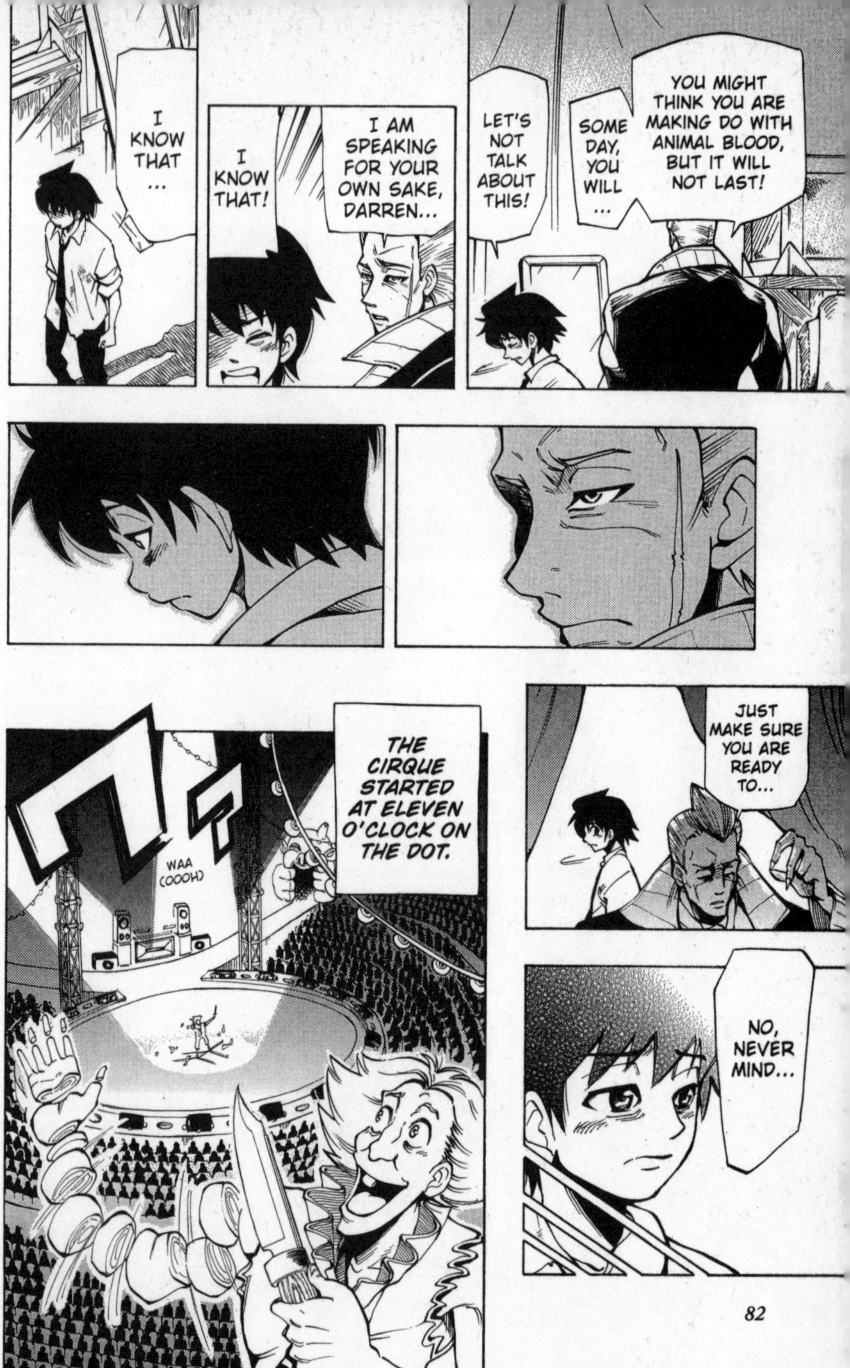
YOU MIGHT THINK YOU ARE MAKING DO WITH ANIMAL BLOOD, BUT IT WILL NOT LAST!
SOME DAY, YOU WILL ...
LET'S NOT TALK ABOUT THIS!
I AM SPEAKING FOR YOUR OWN SAKE, DARREN...
I KNOW THAT!
I KNOW THAT ...
JUST MAKE SURE YOU ARE READY TO...
NO, NEVER MIND...
THE CIRQUE STARTED AT ELEVEN O'CLOCK ON THE DOT.
WAA (OOOH)

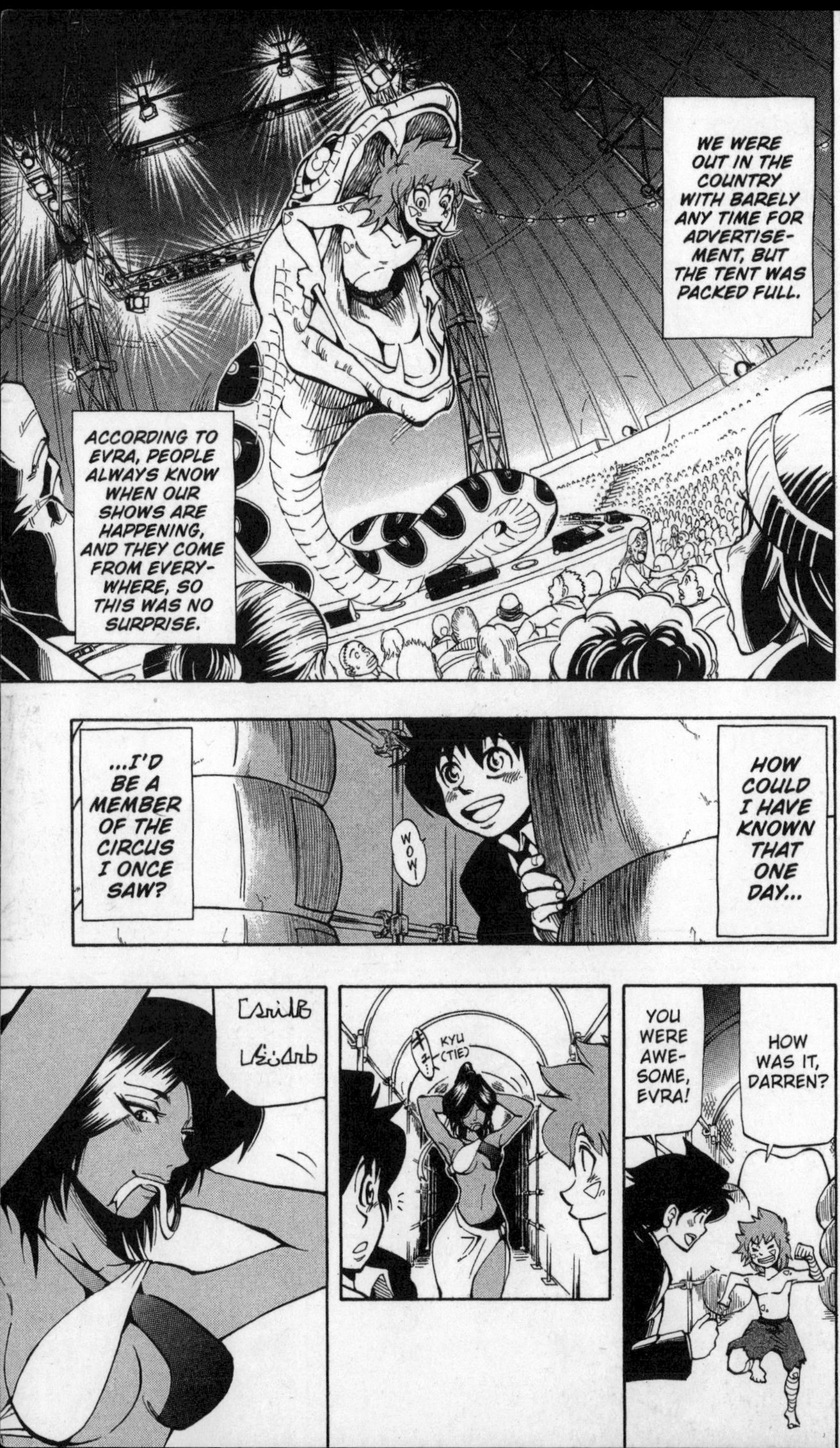
WE WERE OUT IN THE COUNTRY WITH BARELY ANY TIME FOR ADVERTISE-MENT, BUT THE TENT WAS PACKED FULL.
ACCORDING TO EVRA, PEOPLE ALWAYS KNOW WHEN OUR SHOWS ARE HAPPENING, AND THEY COME FROM EVERY-WHERE, SO THIS WAS NO SURPRISE.
HOW COULD I HAVE KNOWN THAT ONE DAY...
WOW!
...I'D BE A MEMBER OF THE CIRCUS I ONCE SAW?
HOW WAS IT, DARREN?
YOU WERE AWE-SOME, EVRA!
KYU (TIE)

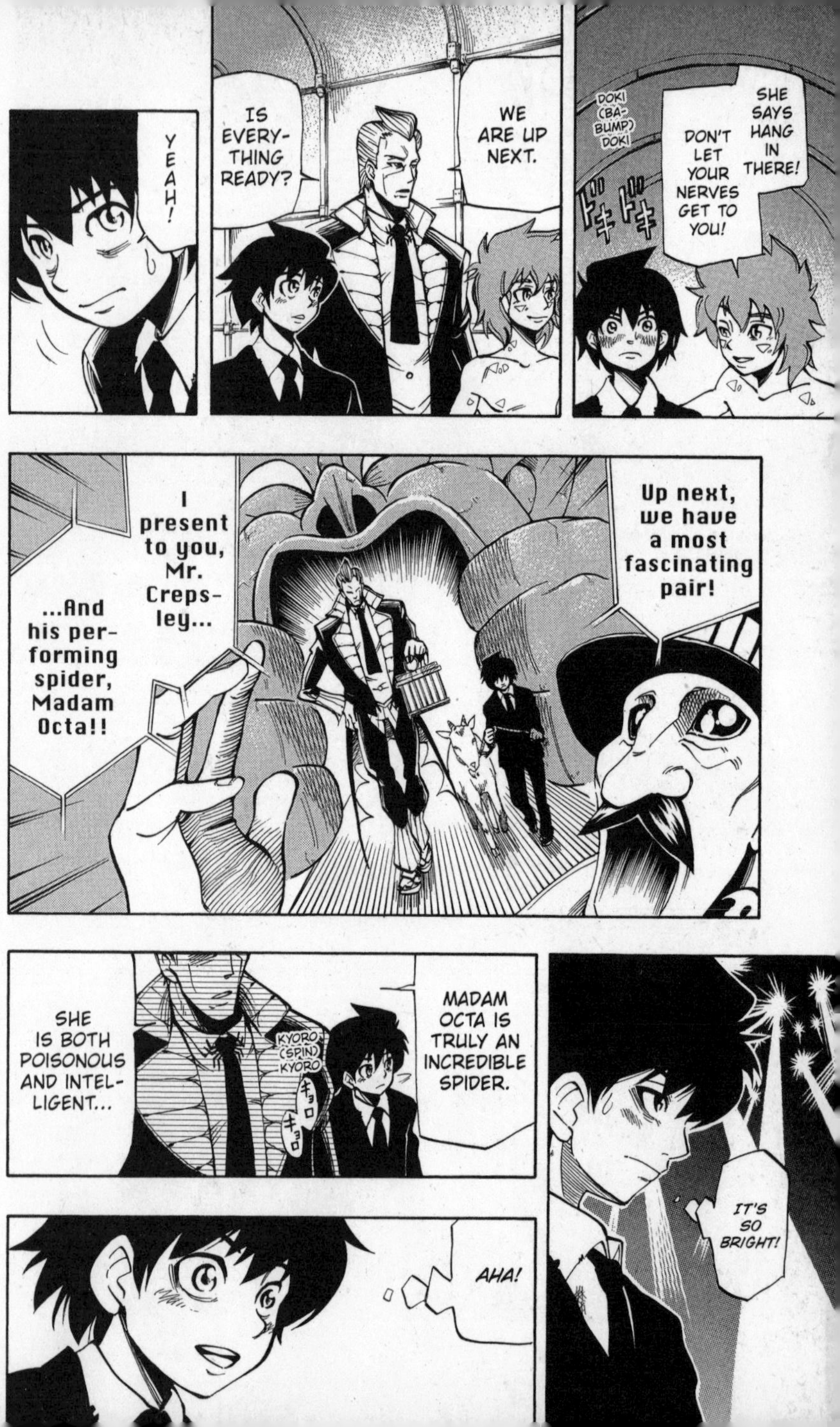
SHE SAYS HANG IN THERE!
DON'T LET YOUR NERVES GET TO YOU!
DOKI (BA-BUMP) DOKI
ドキドキ
WE ARE UP NEXT.
IS EVERY-THING READY?
YEAH!
Up next, we have a most fascinating pair!
I present to you, Mr. Creps-ley...
...And his per-forming spider, Madam Octa!!
IT'S SO BRIGHT!
MADAM OCTA IS TRULY AN INCREDIBLE SPIDER.
KYORO (SPIN) KYORO
キョロキョロ
SHE IS BOTH POISONOUS AND INTEL-LIGENT...
AHA!

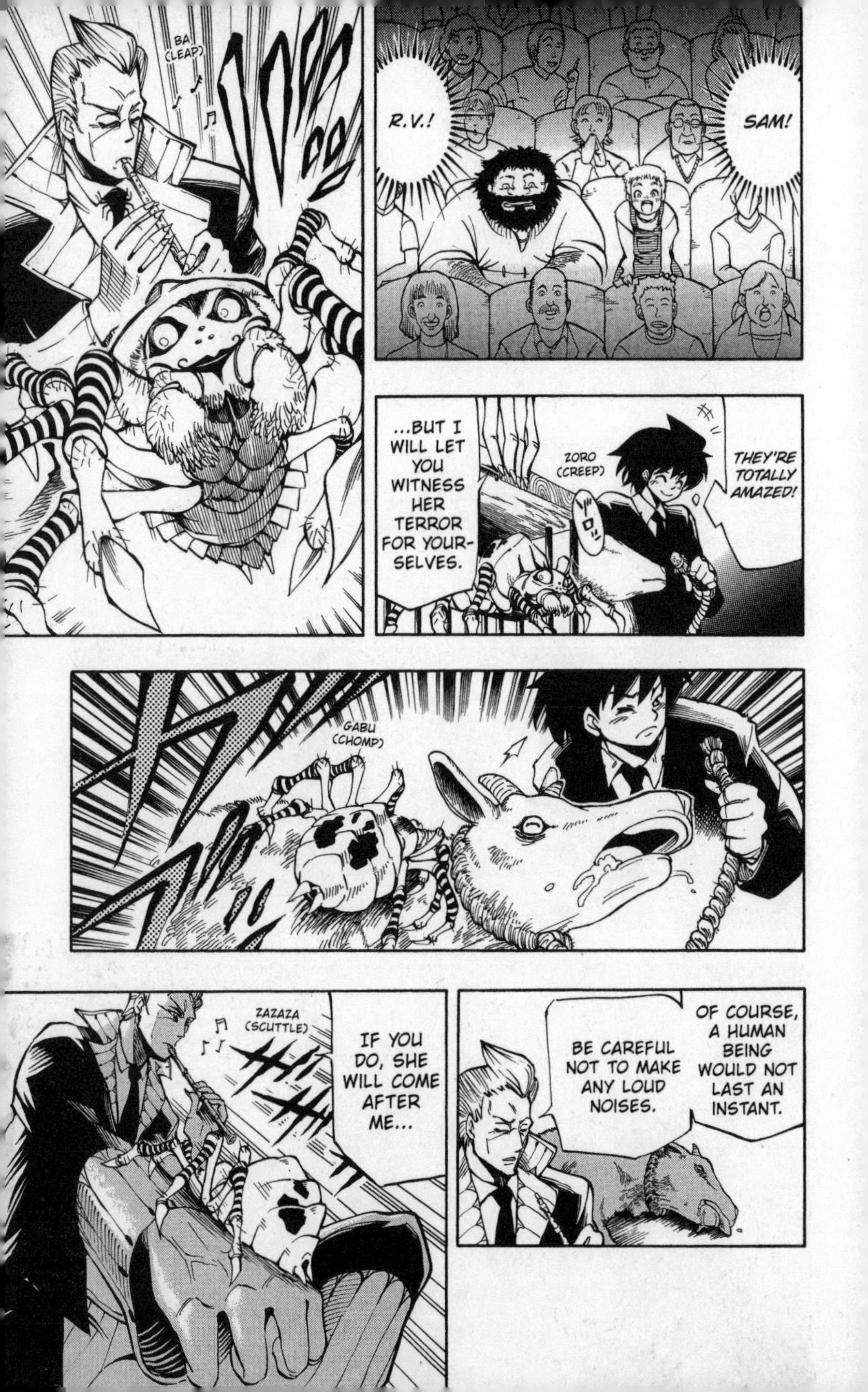
SAM!
R.V.!
THEY'RE TOTALLY AMAZED!
ZORO (CREEP)
...BUT I WILL LET YOU WITNESS HER TERROR FOR YOURSELVES.
BA (LEAP)
GABU (CHOMP)
OF COURSE, A HUMAN BEING WOULD NOT LAST AN INSTANT.
BE CAREFUL NOT TO MAKE ANY LOUD NOISES.
IF YOU DO, SHE WILL COME AFTER ME...
ZAZAZA (SCUTTLE)

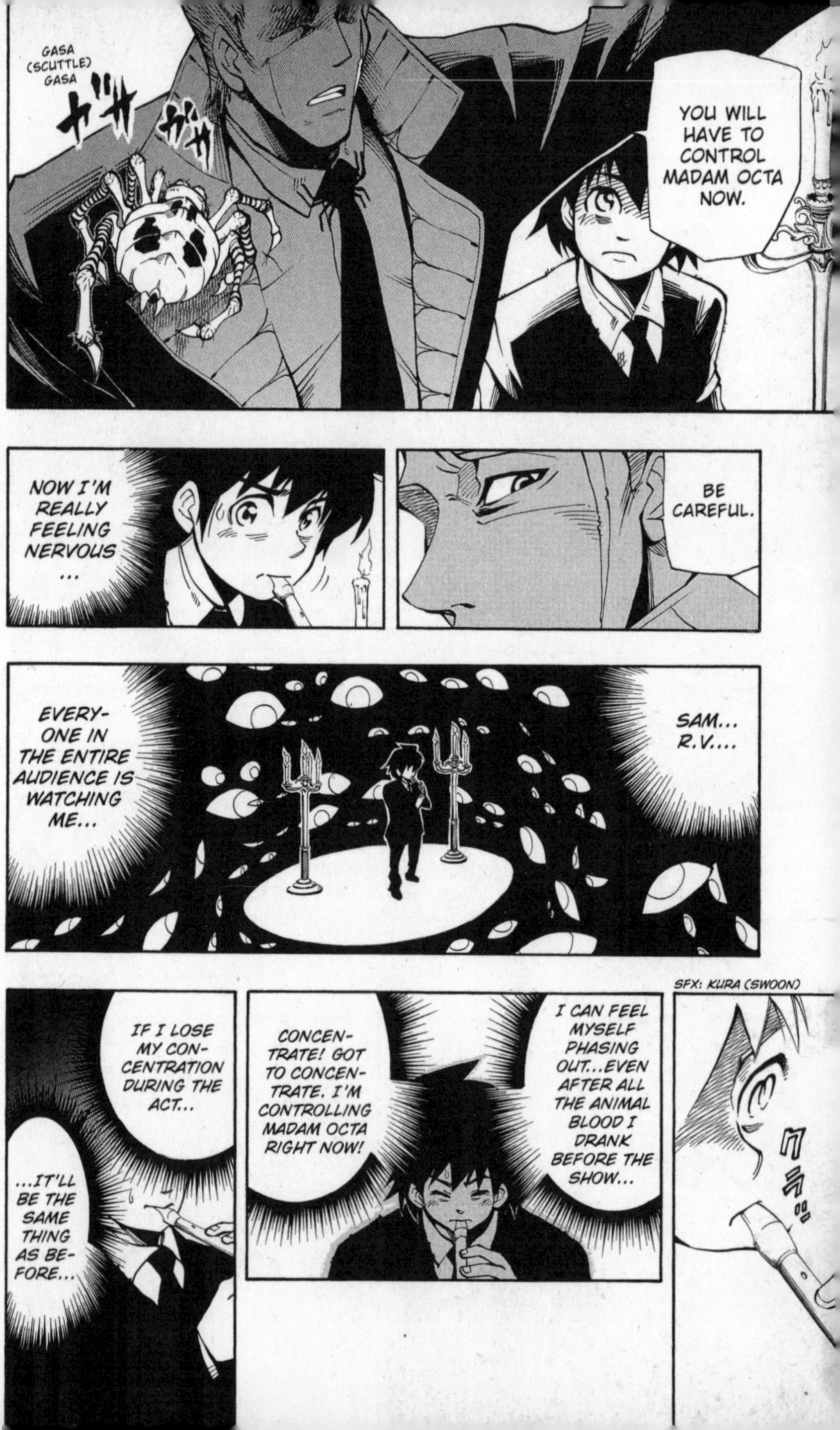
YOU WILL HAVE TO CONTROL MADAM OCTA NOW.
GASA (SCUTTLE) GASA
BE CAREFUL.
NOW I'M REALLY FEELING NERVOUS...
SAM... R.V....
EVERY-ONE IN THE ENTIRE AUDIENCE IS WATCHING ME...
SFX: KURA (SWOON)
I CAN FEEL MYSELF PHASING OUT...EVEN AFTER ALL THE ANIMAL BLOOD I DRANK BEFORE THE SHOW...
CONCEN-TRATE! GOT TO CONCEN-TRATE. I'M CONTROLLING MADAM OCTA RIGHT NOW!
IF I LOSE MY CON-CENTRATION DURING THE ACT...
...IT'LL BE THE SAME THING AS BE-FORE...

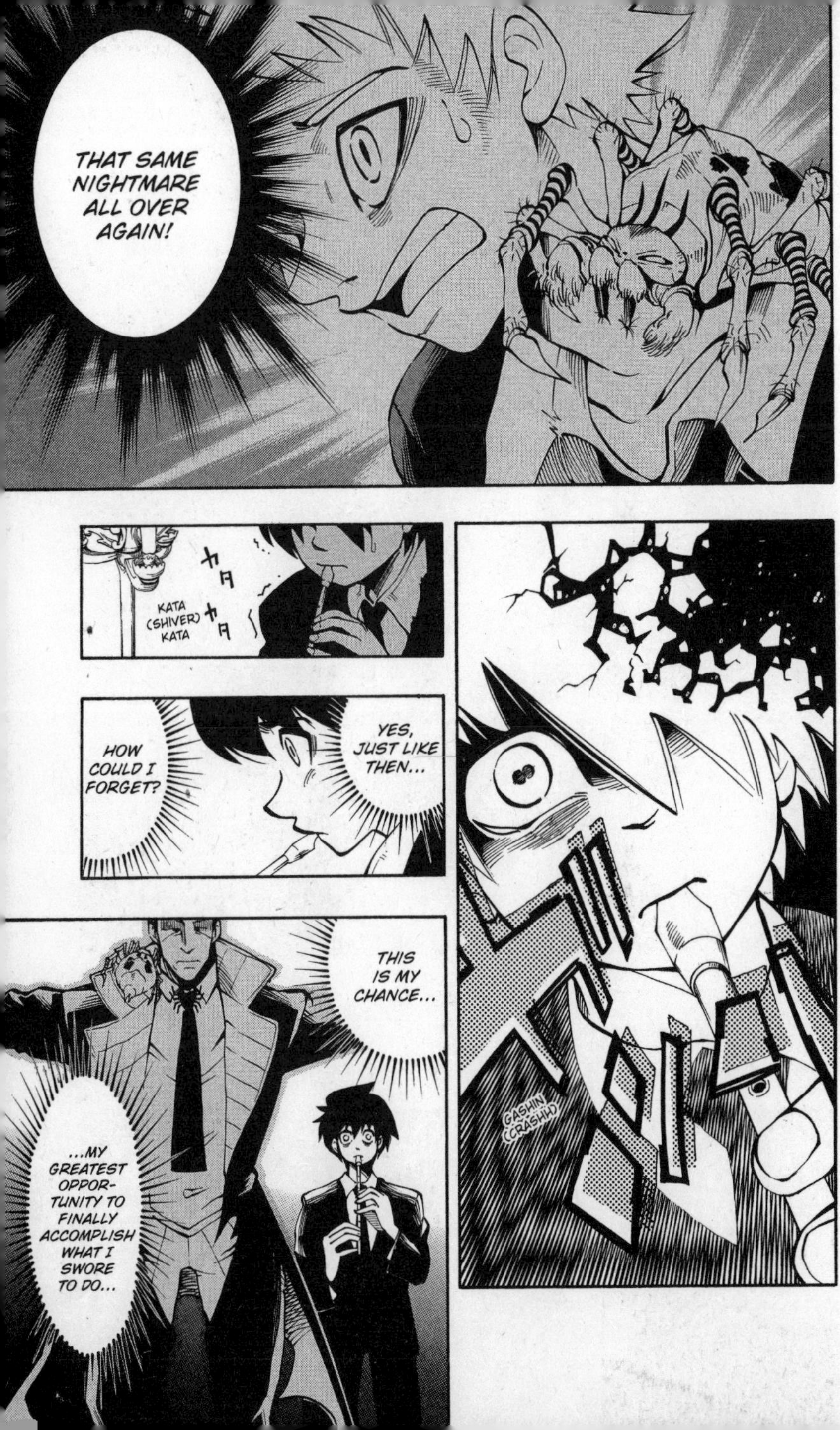
THAT SAME NIGHTMARE ALL OVER AGAIN!
GASHIN (CRASH)
KATA (SHIVER) KATA
YES, JUST LIKE THEN...
HOW COULD I FORGET?
THIS IS MY CHANCE...
...MY GREATEST OPPOR-TUNITY TO FINALLY ACCOMPLISH WHAT I SWORE TO DO...

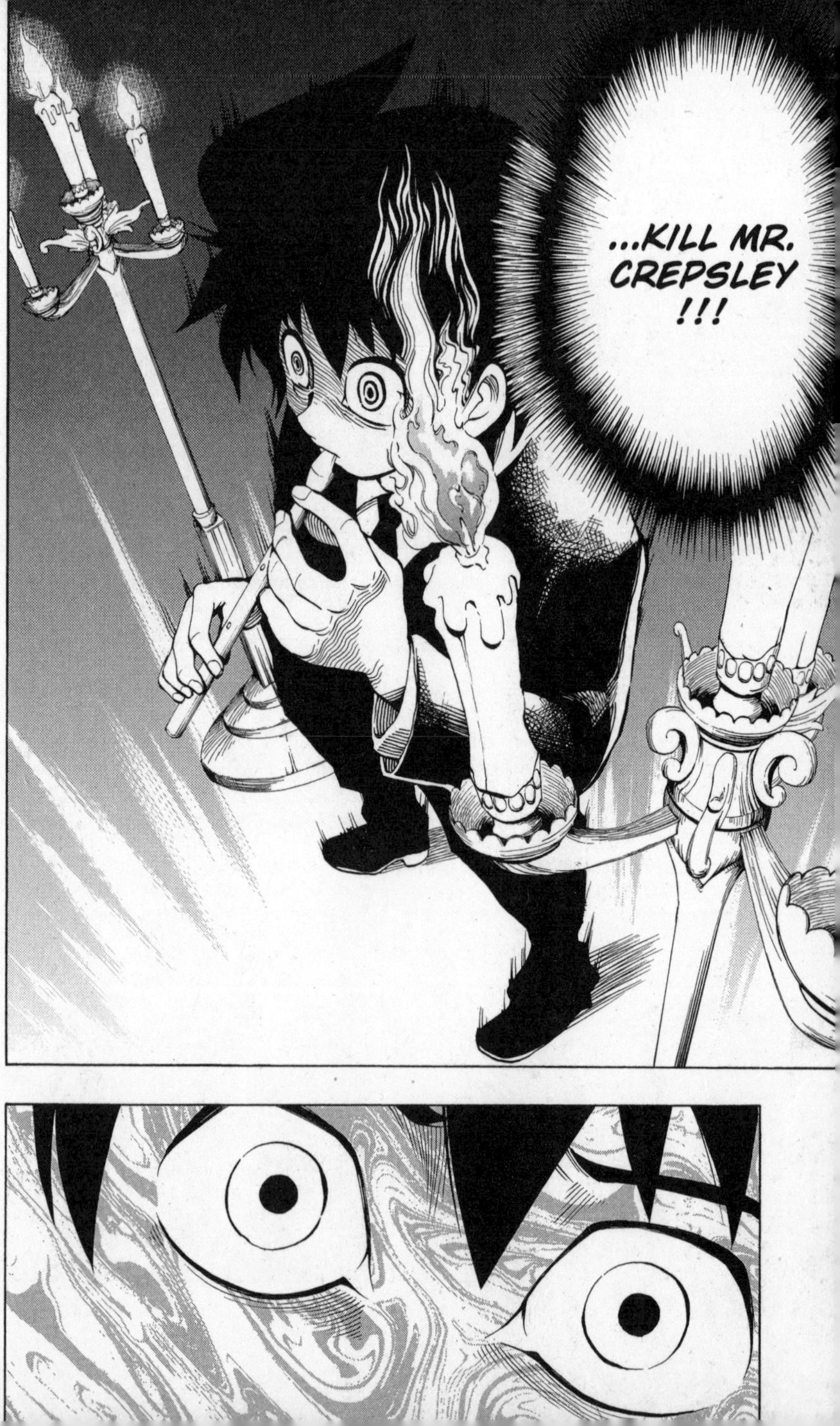
...KILL MR. CREPSLEY !!!

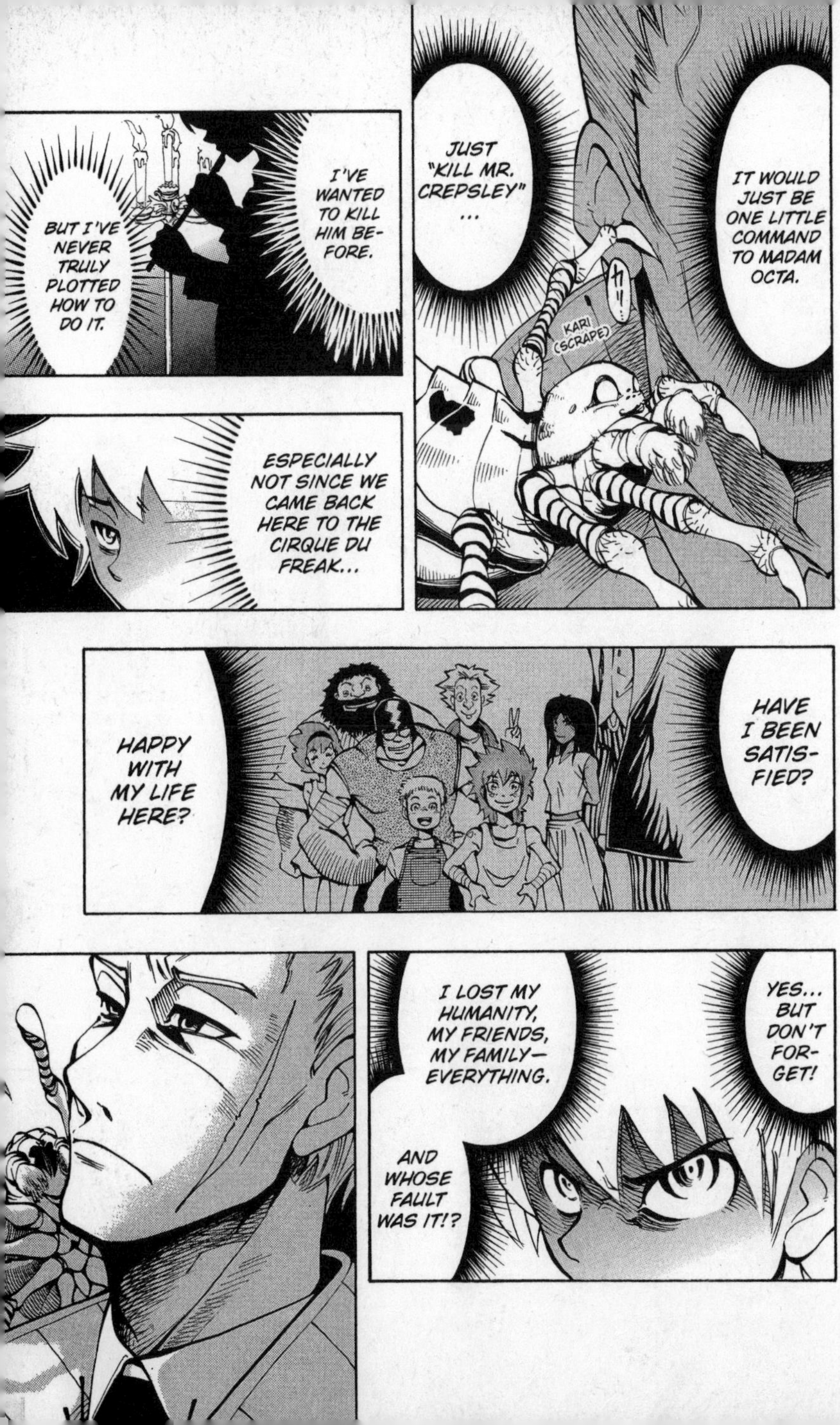
IT WOULD JUST BE ONE LITTLE COMMAND TO MADAM OCTA.
JUST "KILL MR. CREPSLEY" ...
カリ
KARI (SCRAPE)
I'VE WANTED TO KILL HIM BEFORE.
BUT I'VE NEVER TRULY PLOTTED HOW TO DO IT.
ESPECIALLY NOT SINCE WE CAME BACK HERE TO THE CIRQUE DU FREAK...
HAVE I BEEN SATISFIED?
HAPPY WITH MY LIFE HERE?
YES... BUT DON'T FORGET!
I LOST MY HUMANITY, MY FRIENDS, MY FAMILY—EVERYTHING.
AND WHOSE FAULT WAS IT!?

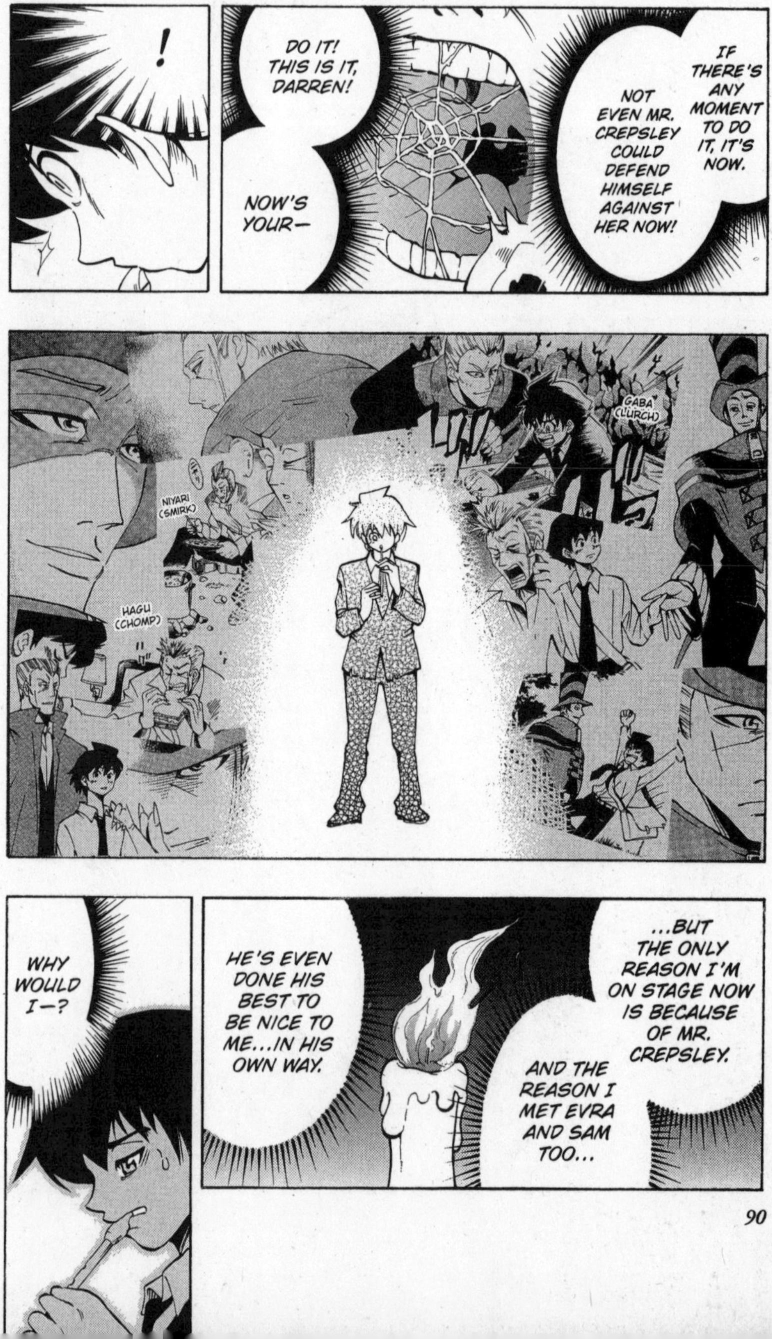
IF THERE'S ANY MOMENT TO DO IT, IT'S NOW.
NOT EVEN MR. CREPSLEY COULD DEFEND HIMSELF AGAINST HER NOW!
DO IT! THIS IS IT, DARREN!
NOW'S YOUR—
!
GABA (LURCH)
NIYARI (SMIRK)
HAGU (CHOMP)
...BUT THE ONLY REASON I'M ON STAGE NOW IS BECAUSE OF MR. CREPSLEY.
AND THE REASON I MET EVRA AND SAM TOO...
HE'S EVEN DONE HIS BEST TO BE NICE TO ME...IN HIS OWN WAY.
WHY WOULD I—?

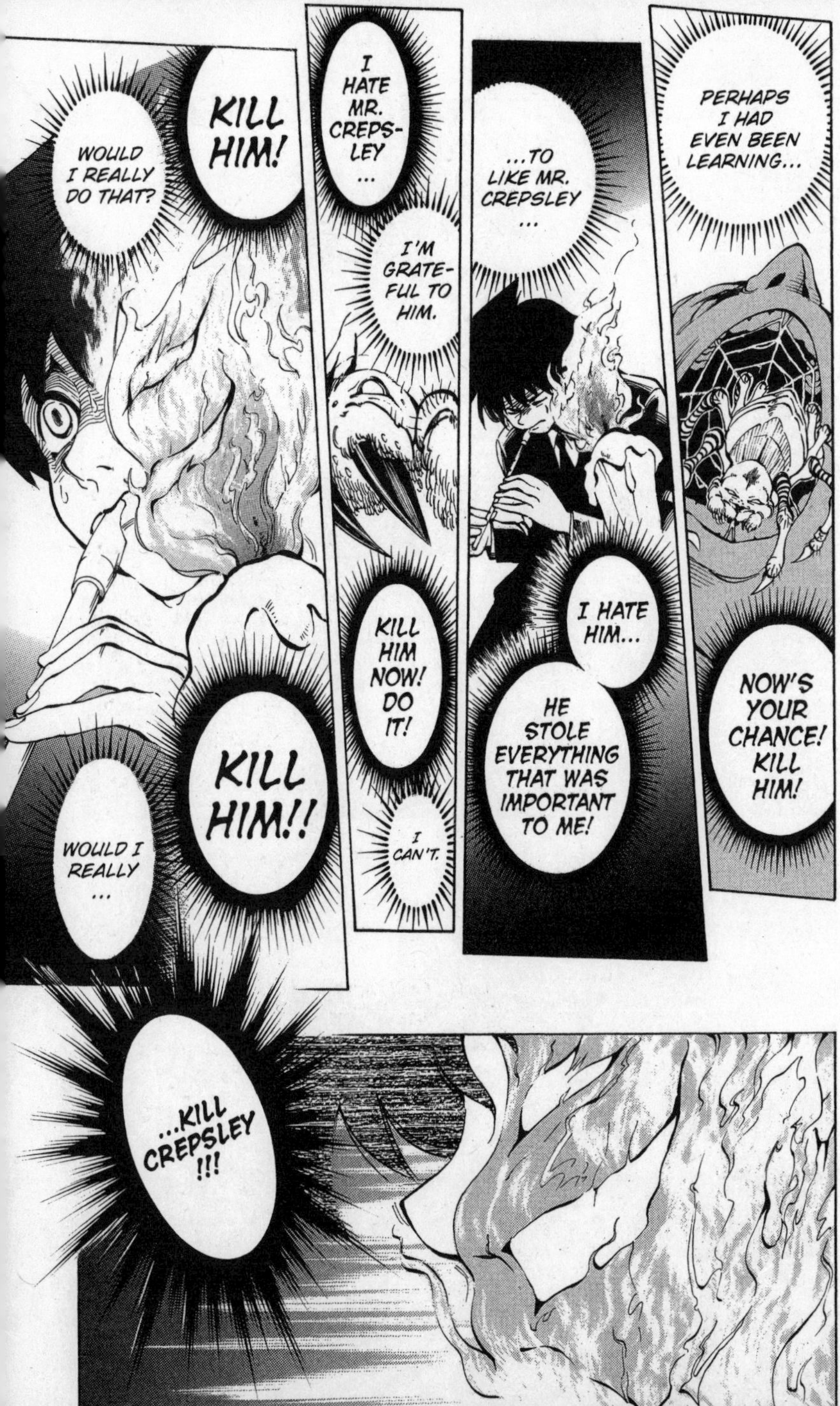
PERHAPS I HAD EVEN BEEN LEARNING...
NOW'S YOUR CHANCE! KILL HIM!
...TO LIKE MR. CREPSLEY ...
I HATE HIM...
HE STOLE EVERYTHING THAT WAS IMPORTANT TO ME!
I HATE MR. CREPSLEY ...
I'M GRATEFUL TO HIM.
KILL HIM NOW! DO IT!
I CAN'T.
KILL HIM!
WOULD I REALLY DO THAT?
KILL HIM!!
WOULD I REALLY ...
...KILL CREPSLEY !!!

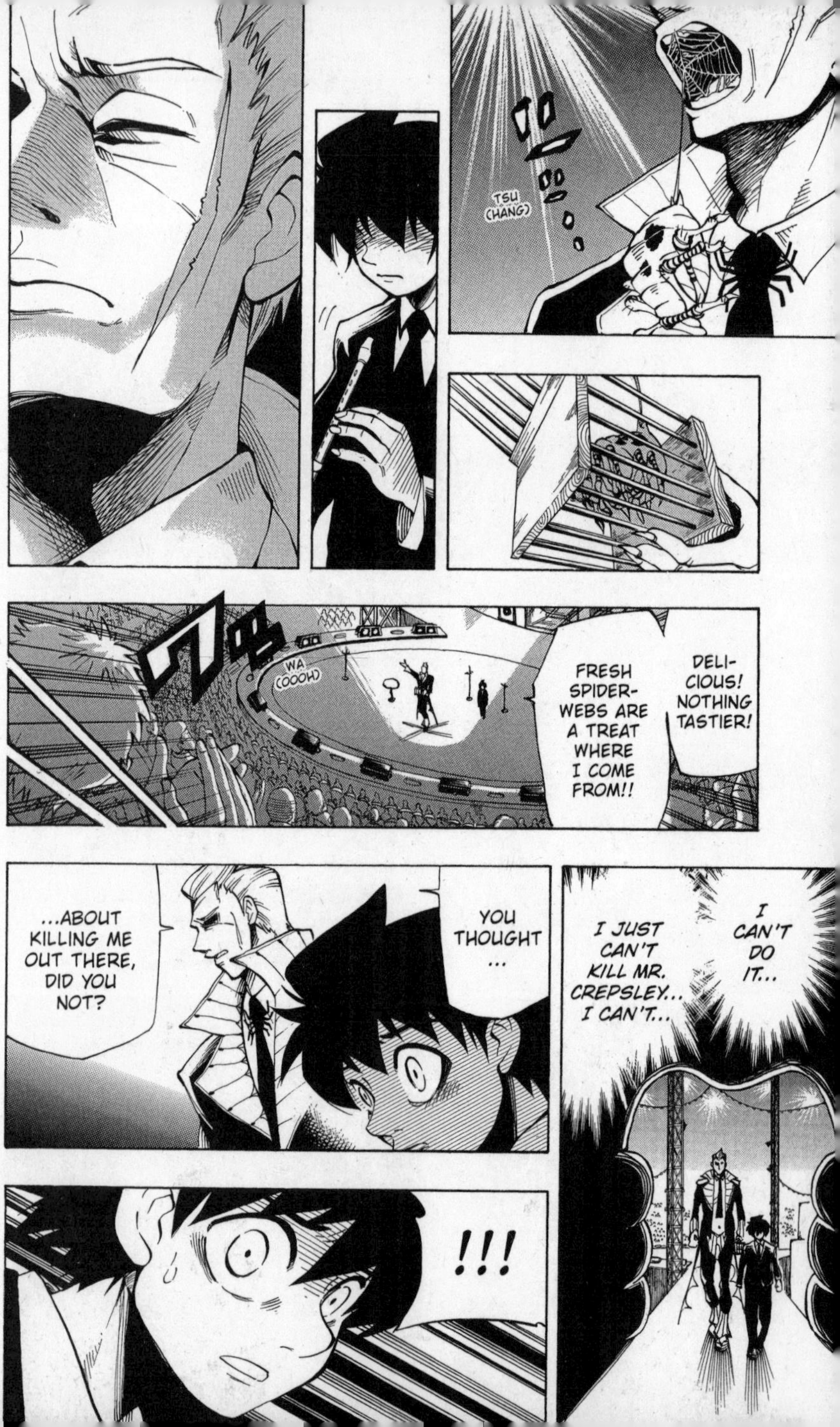
TSU (HANG)
DELI-CIOUS! NOTHING TASTIER!
FRESH SPIDER-WEBS ARE A TREAT WHERE I COME FROM!!
WA (OOOH)
I CAN'T DO IT...
I JUST CAN'T KILL MR. CREPSLEY... I CAN'T...
YOU THOUGHT...
...ABOUT KILLING ME OUT THERE, DID YOU NOT?
!!!

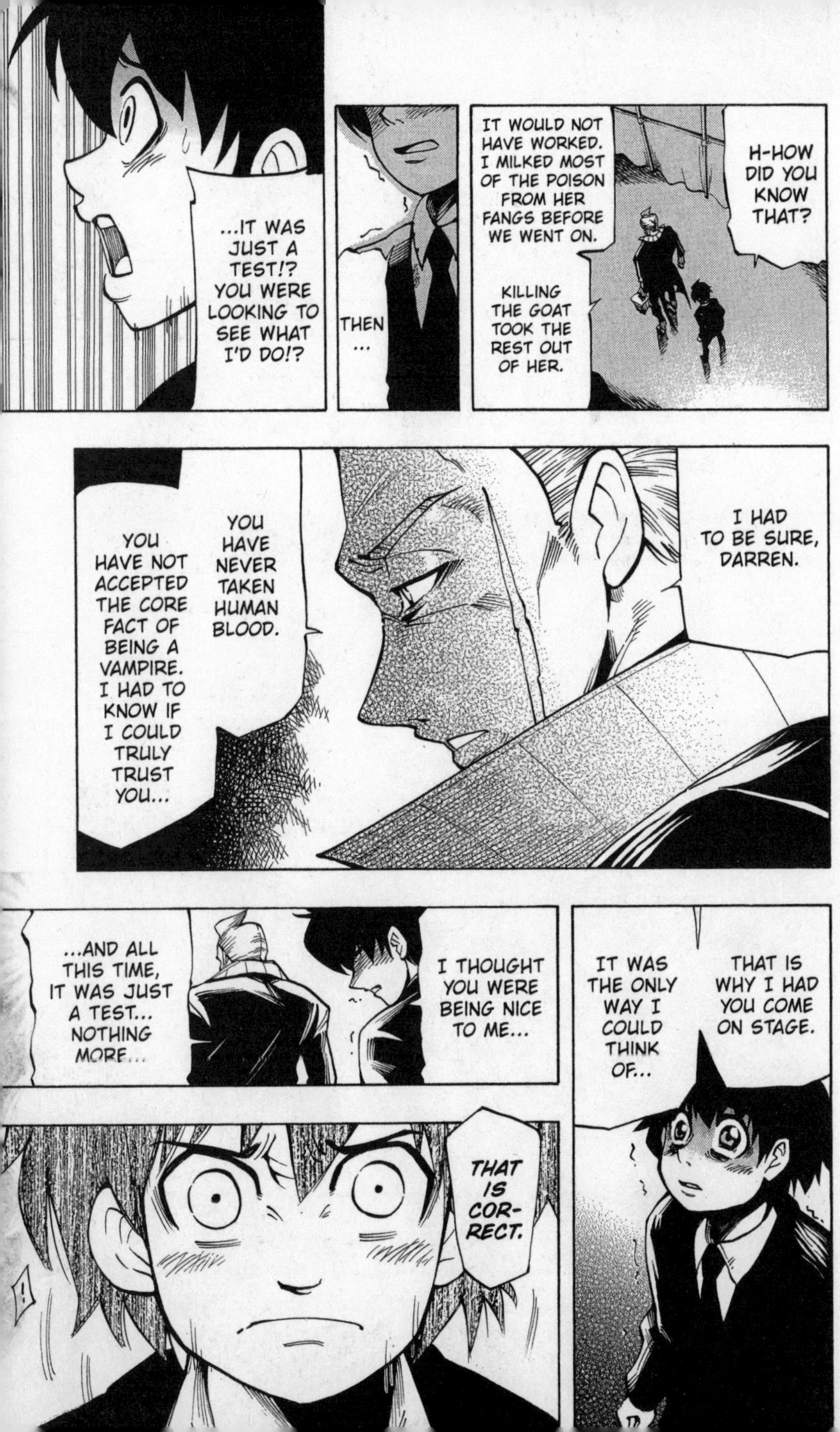
H-HOW DID YOU KNOW THAT?
IT WOULD NOT HAVE WORKED. I MILKED MOST OF THE POISON FROM HER FANGS BEFORE WE WENT ON.
KILLING THE GOAT TOOK THE REST OUT OF HER.
THEN ...
...IT WAS JUST A TEST!? YOU WERE LOOKING TO SEE WHAT I'D DO!?
I HAD TO BE SURE, DARREN.
YOU HAVE NEVER TAKEN HUMAN BLOOD.
YOU HAVE NOT ACCEPTED THE CORE FACT OF BEING A VAMPIRE. I HAD TO KNOW IF I COULD TRULY TRUST YOU...
THAT IS WHY I HAD YOU COME ON STAGE.
IT WAS THE ONLY WAY I COULD THINK OF...
I THOUGHT YOU WERE BEING NICE TO ME...
...AND ALL THIS TIME, IT WAS JUST A TEST... NOTHING MORE...
THAT IS COR-RECT.

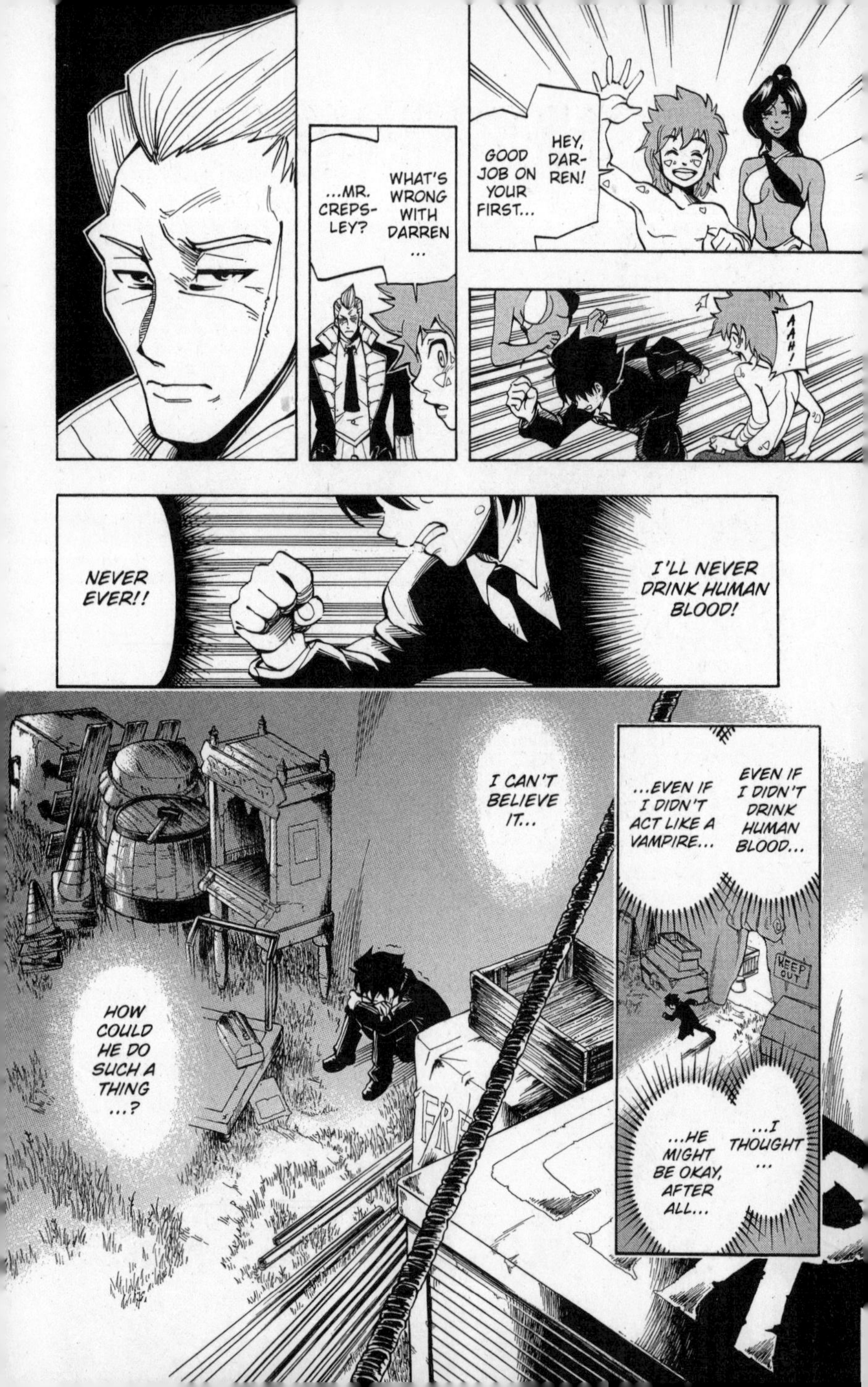
HEY, DARREN!
GOOD JOB ON YOUR FIRST...
AAH!
WHAT'S WRONG WITH DARREN...
...MR. CREPSLEY?
I'LL NEVER DRINK HUMAN BLOOD!
NEVER EVER!!
EVEN IF I DIDN'T DRINK HUMAN BLOOD...
...EVEN IF I DIDN'T ACT LIKE A VAMPIRE...
KEEP OUT
...I THOUGHT...
...HE MIGHT BE OKAY, AFTER ALL...
I CAN'T BELIEVE IT...
HOW COULD HE DO SUCH A THING...?

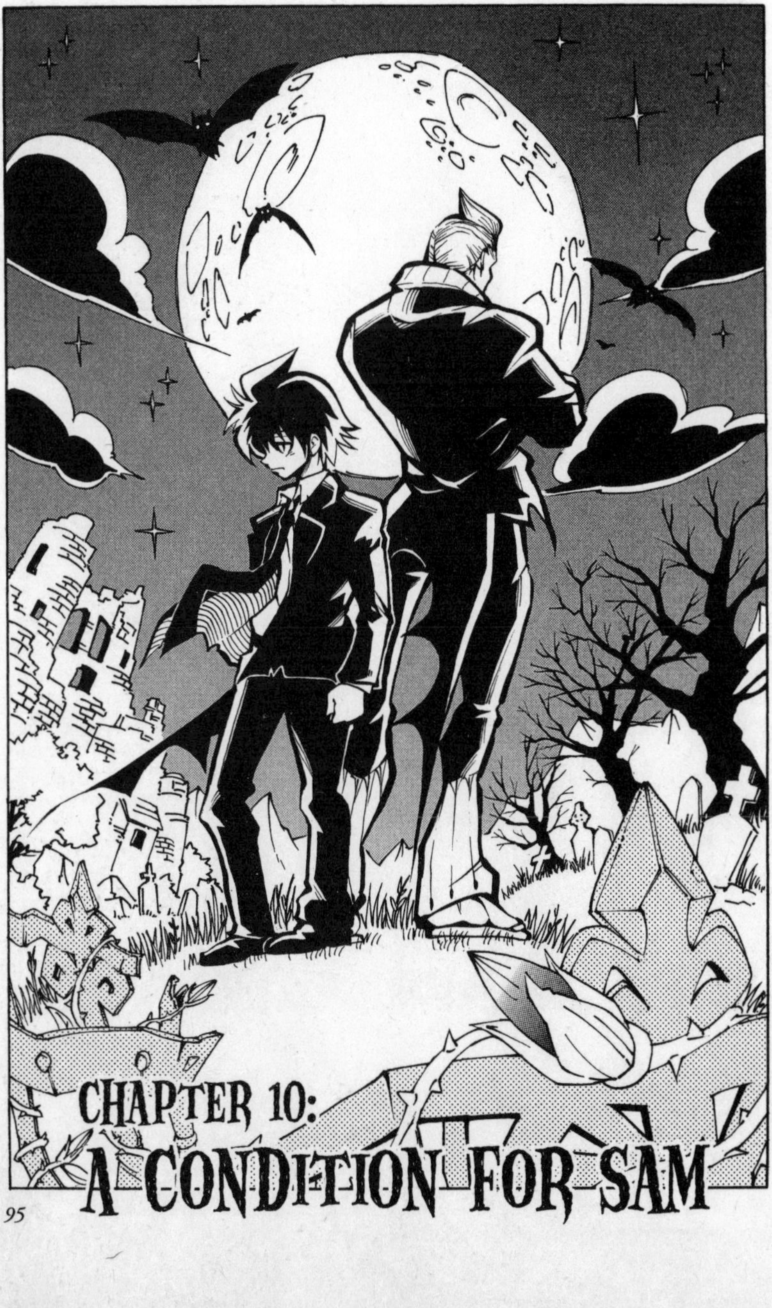
CHAPTER 10:
A CONDITION FOR SAM

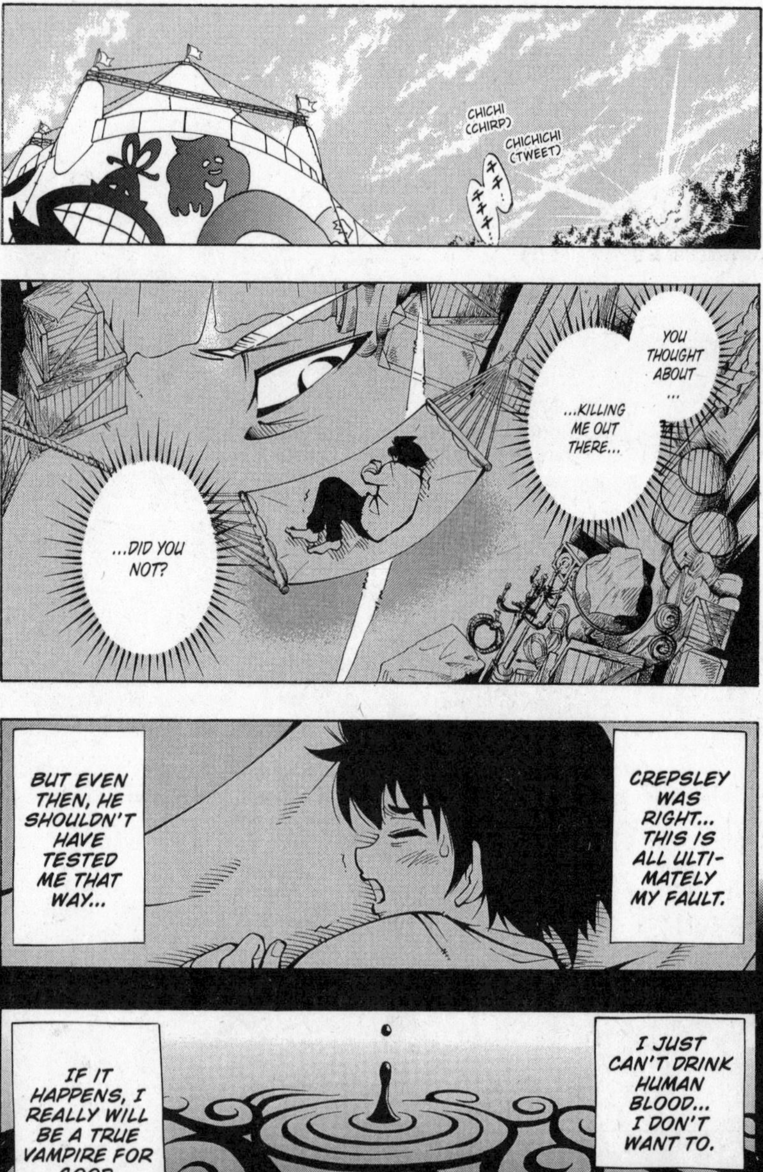
CHICHI (CHIRP)
CHICHICHI (TWEET)
チチ…
チチチ…
YOU THOUGHT ABOUT ...
...KILLING ME OUT THERE...
...DID YOU NOT?
CREPSLEY WAS RIGHT... THIS IS ALL ULTIMATELY MY FAULT.
BUT EVEN THEN, HE SHOULDN'T HAVE TESTED ME THAT WAY...
I JUST CAN'T DRINK HUMAN BLOOD... I DON'T WANT TO.
IF IT HAPPENS, I REALLY WILL BE A TRUE VAMPIRE FOR GOOD.

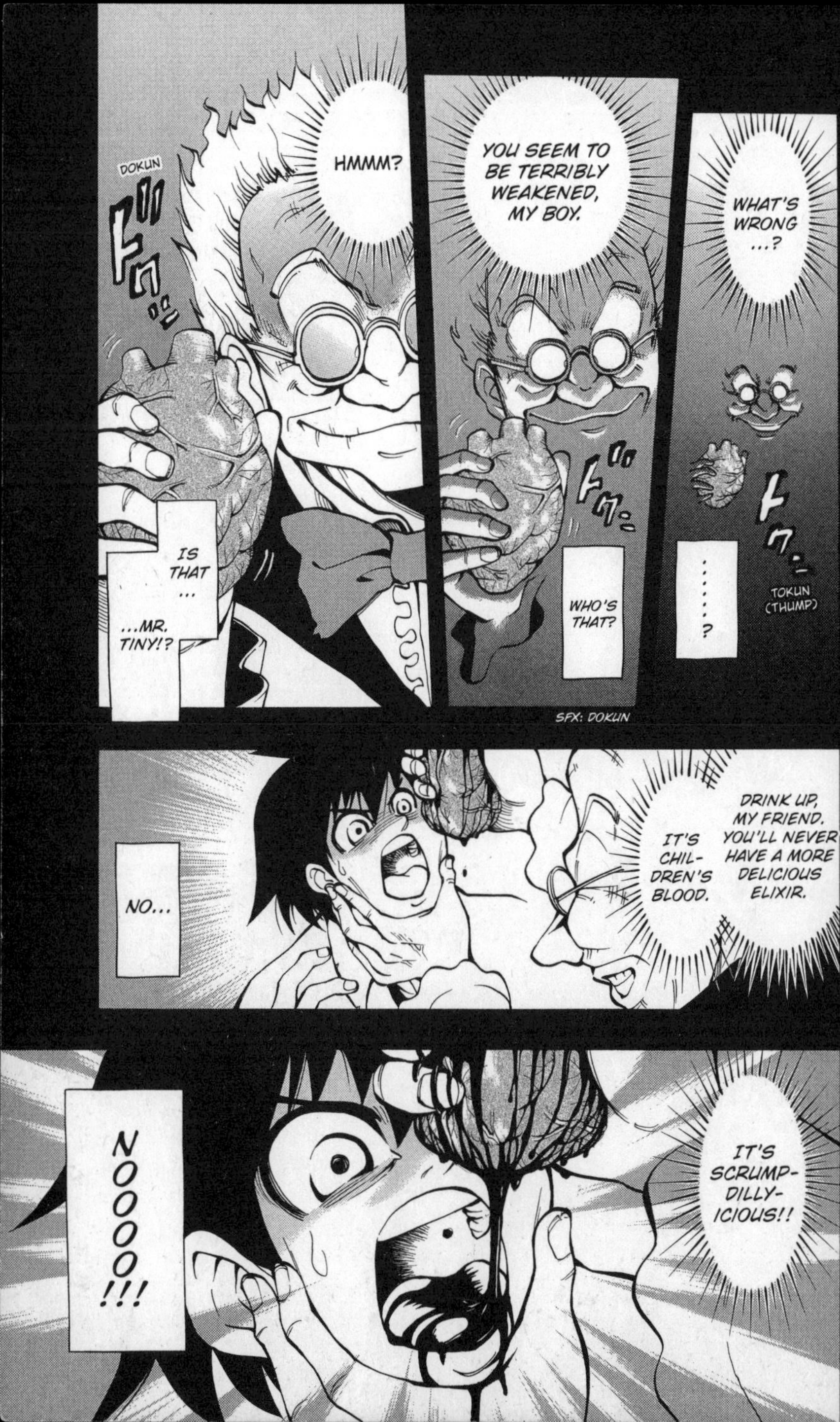
WHAT'S WRONG ...?
......?
TOKUN (THUMP)
YOU SEEM TO BE TERRIBLY WEAKENED, MY BOY.
WHO'S THAT?
HMMM?
DOKUN
IS THAT ...
...MR. TINY!?
SFX: DOKUN
DRINK UP, MY FRIEND. YOU'LL NEVER HAVE A MORE DELICIOUS ELIXIR.
IT'S CHILDREN'S BLOOD.
NO...
IT'S SCRUMP-DILLY-ICIOUS!!
NOOOOO!!!

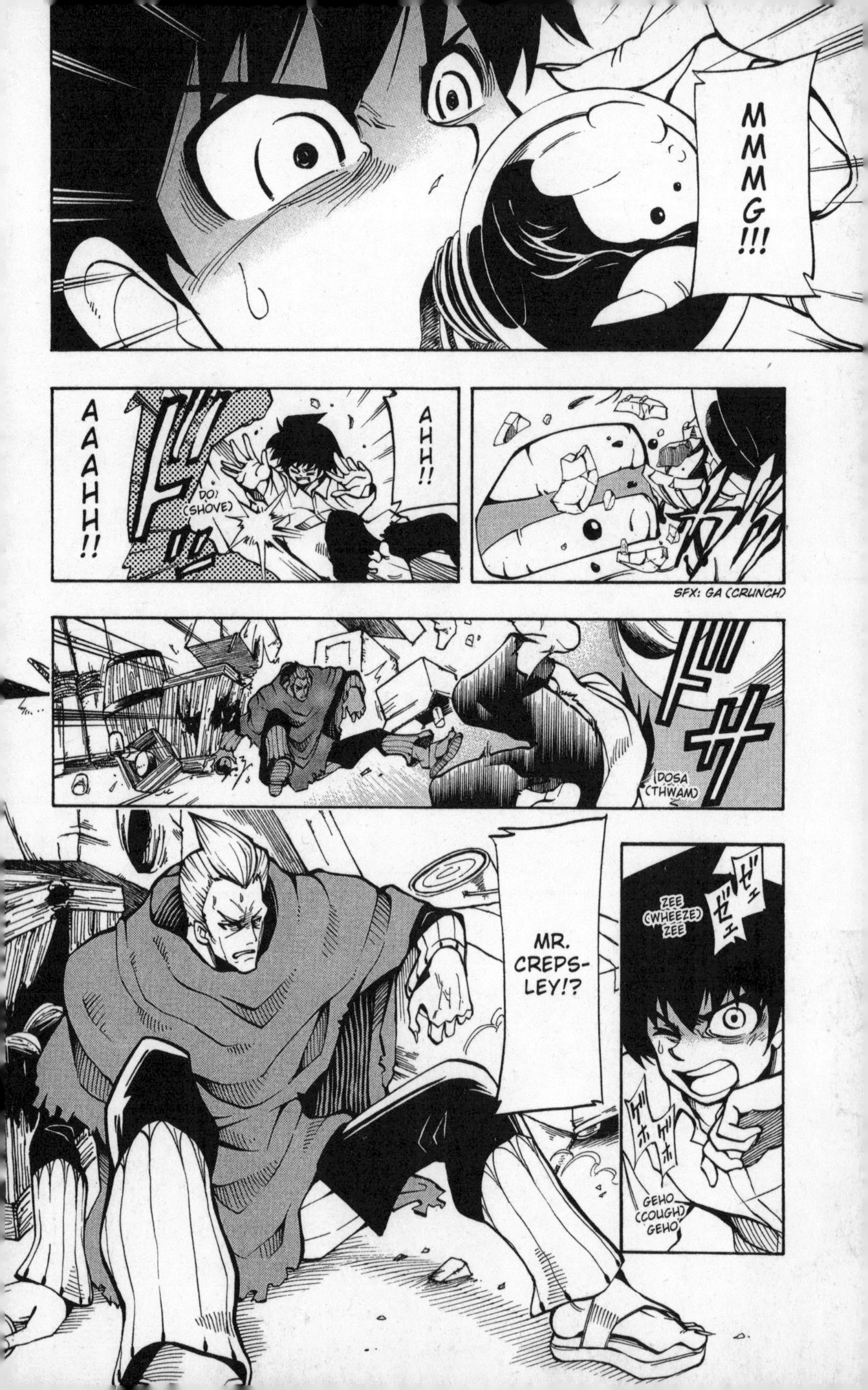
MMMG!!!
SFX: GA (CRUNCH)
AHH!!
DO (SHOVE)
AAAAHH!!
DOSA (THWAM)
ZEE (WHEEZE) ZEE
GEHO (COUGH) GEHO
MR. CREPSLEY!?

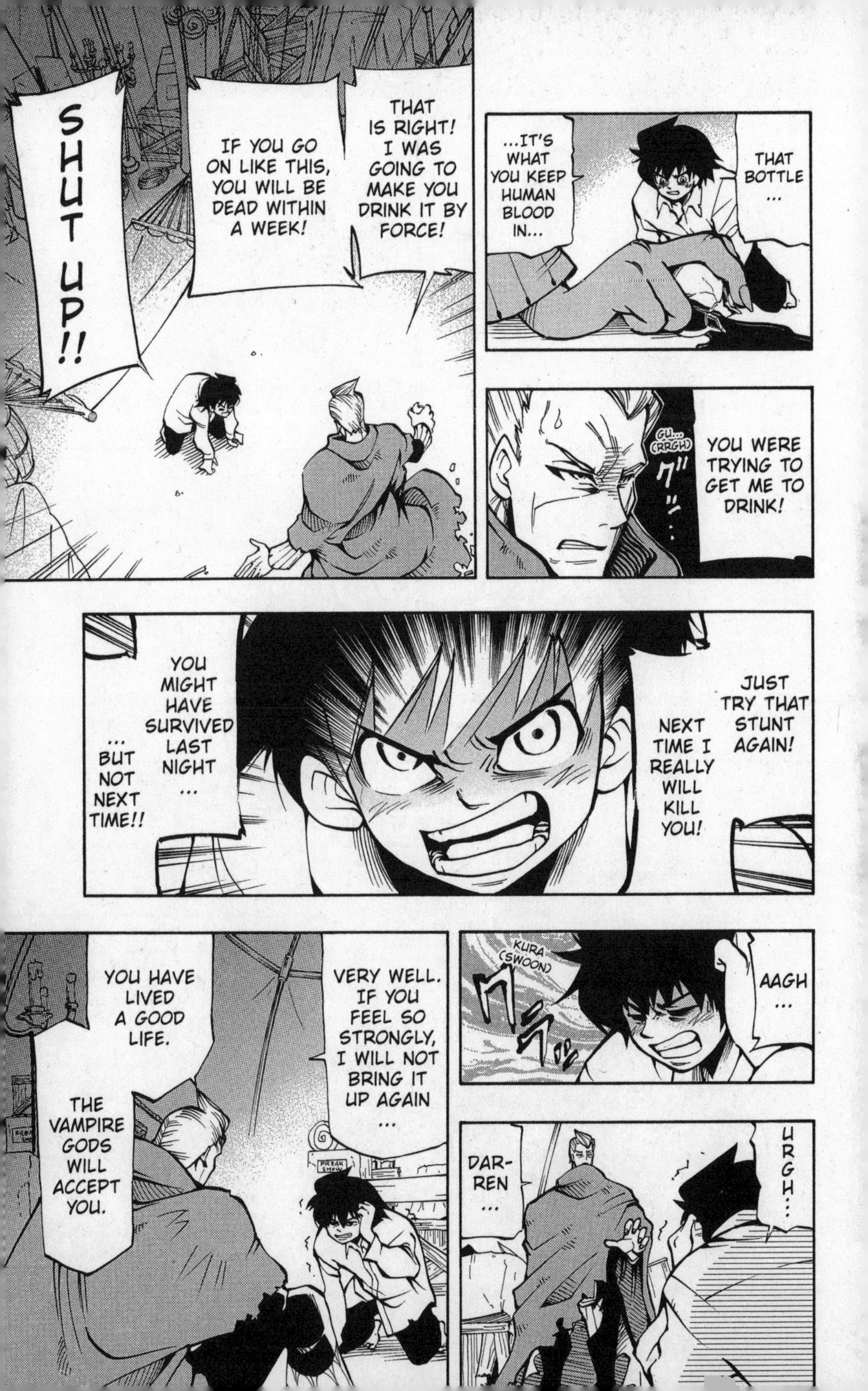
THAT BOTTLE...
...IT'S WHAT YOU KEEP HUMAN BLOOD IN...
GU... (RRGH)
YOU WERE TRYING TO GET ME TO DRINK!
THAT IS RIGHT! I WAS GOING TO MAKE YOU DRINK IT BY FORCE!
IF YOU GO ON LIKE THIS, YOU WILL BE DEAD WITHIN A WEEK!
SHUT UP!!
JUST TRY THAT STUNT AGAIN!
NEXT TIME I REALLY WILL KILL YOU!
YOU MIGHT HAVE SURVIVED LAST NIGHT...
...BUT NOT NEXT TIME!!
KURA (SWOON)
AAGH...
URGH...
DAR-REN...
VERY WELL. IF YOU FEEL SO STRONGLY, I WILL NOT BRING IT UP AGAIN...
FREAK SHOW
YOU HAVE LIVED A GOOD LIFE.
THE VAMPIRE GODS WILL ACCEPT YOU.

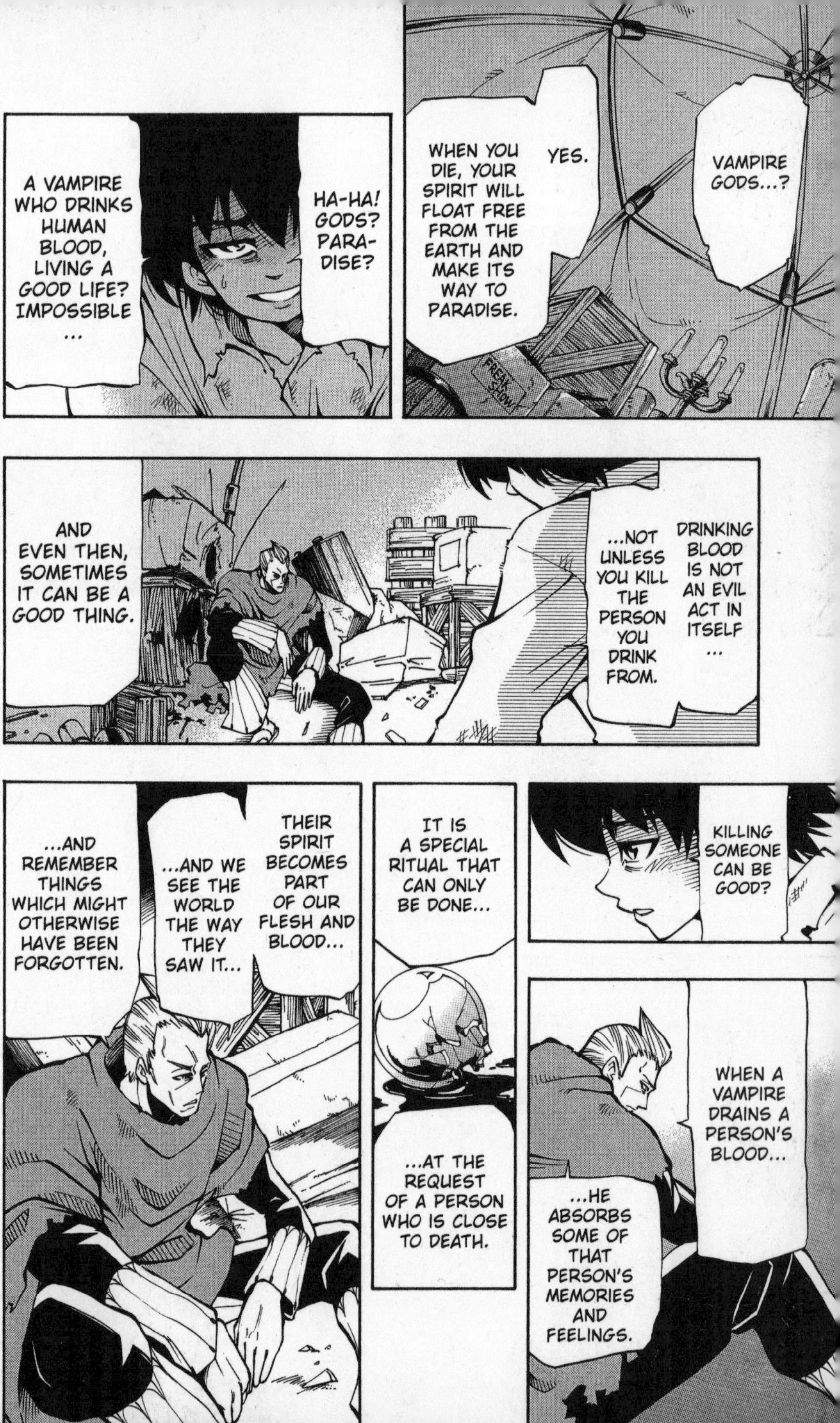
VAMPIRE GODS...?
YES.
WHEN YOU DIE, YOUR SPIRIT WILL FLOAT FREE FROM THE EARTH AND MAKE ITS WAY TO PARADISE.
FREAK SHOW
HA-HA! GODS? PARA-DISE?
A VAMPIRE WHO DRINKS HUMAN BLOOD, LIVING A GOOD LIFE? IMPOSSIBLE...
DRINKING BLOOD IS NOT AN EVIL ACT IN ITSELF...
...NOT UNLESS YOU KILL THE PERSON YOU DRINK FROM.
AND EVEN THEN, SOMETIMES IT CAN BE A GOOD THING.
KILLING SOMEONE CAN BE GOOD?
WHEN A VAMPIRE DRAINS A PERSON'S BLOOD...
...HE ABSORBS SOME OF THAT PERSON'S MEMORIES AND FEELINGS.
IT IS A SPECIAL RITUAL THAT CAN ONLY BE DONE...
...AT THE REQUEST OF A PERSON WHO IS CLOSE TO DEATH.
THEIR SPIRIT BECOMES PART OF OUR FLESH AND BLOOD...
...AND WE SEE THE WORLD THE WAY THEY SAW IT...
...AND REMEMBER THINGS WHICH MIGHT OTHERWISE HAVE BEEN FORGOTTEN.

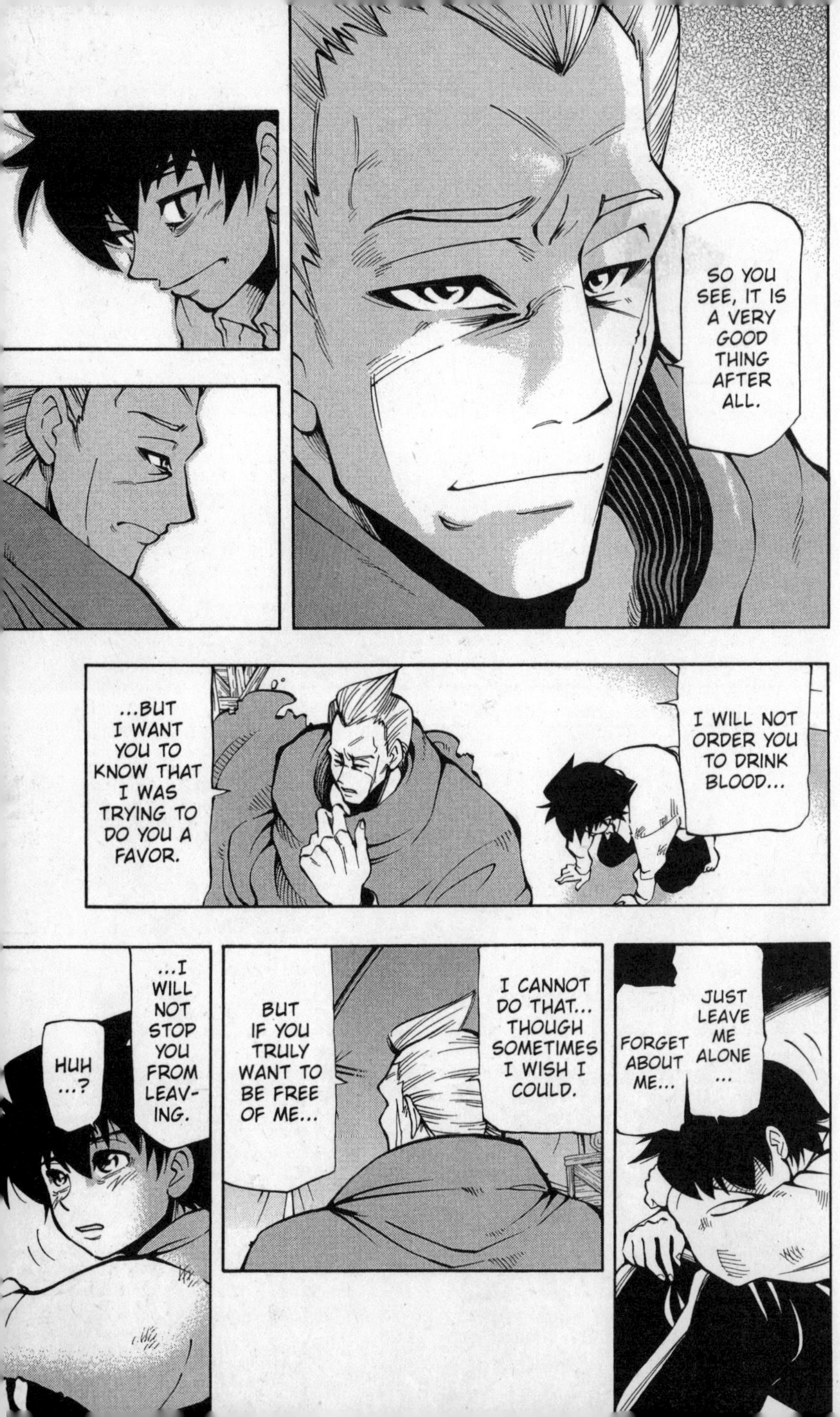
SO YOU SEE, IT IS A VERY GOOD THING AFTER ALL.
I WILL NOT ORDER YOU TO DRINK BLOOD...
...BUT I WANT YOU TO KNOW THAT I WAS TRYING TO DO YOU A FAVOR.
JUST LEAVE ME ALONE ...
FORGET ABOUT ME...
I CANNOT DO THAT... THOUGH SOMETIMES I WISH I COULD.
BUT IF YOU TRULY WANT TO BE FREE OF ME...
...I WILL NOT STOP YOU FROM LEAV-ING.
HUH ...?

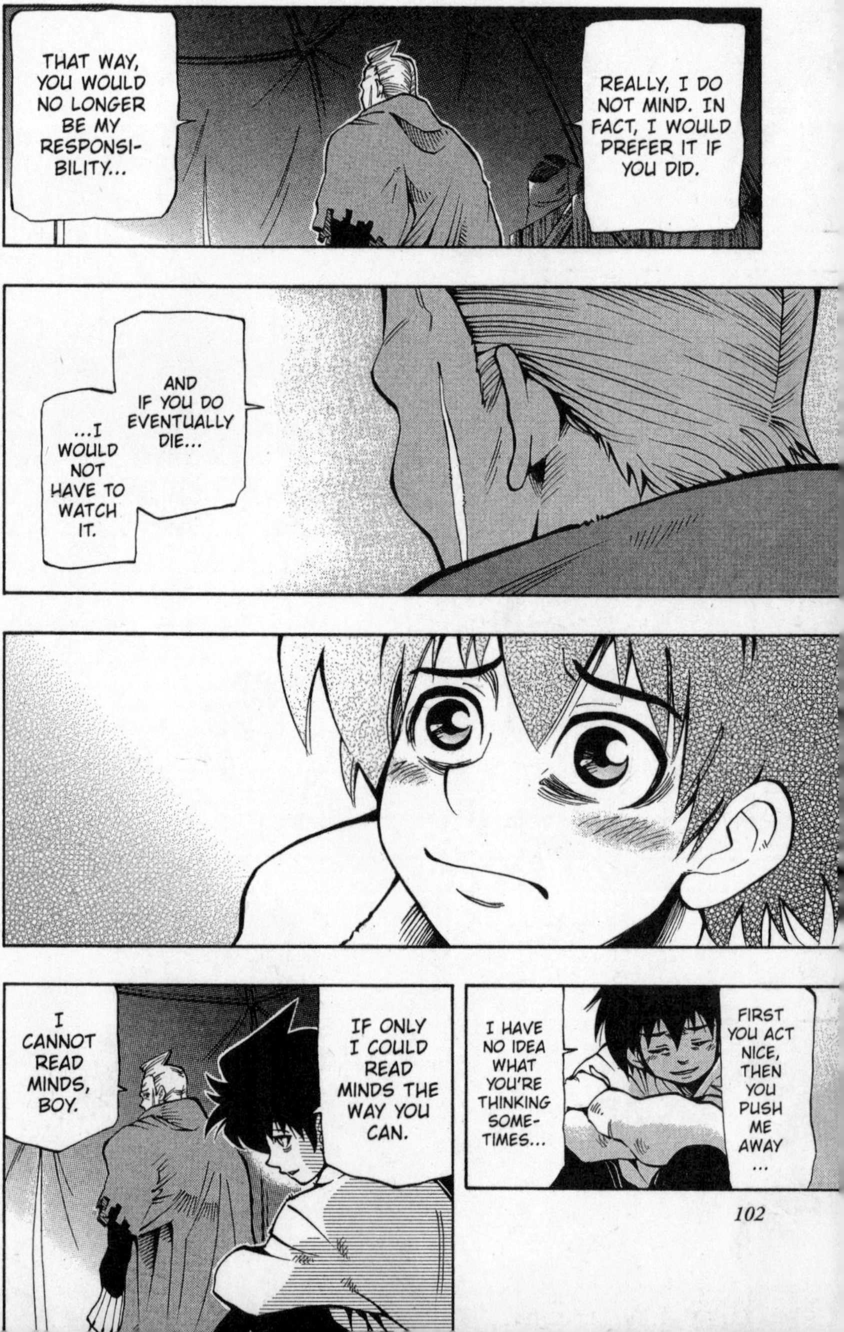
REALLY, I DO NOT MIND. IN FACT, I WOULD PREFER IT IF YOU DID.
THAT WAY, YOU WOULD NO LONGER BE MY RESPONSI-BILITY...
AND IF YOU DO EVENTUALLY DIE...
...I WOULD NOT HAVE TO WATCH IT.
FIRST YOU ACT NICE, THEN YOU PUSH ME AWAY...
I HAVE NO IDEA WHAT YOU'RE THINKING SOME-TIMES...
IF ONLY I COULD READ MINDS THE WAY YOU CAN.
I CANNOT READ MINDS, BOY.

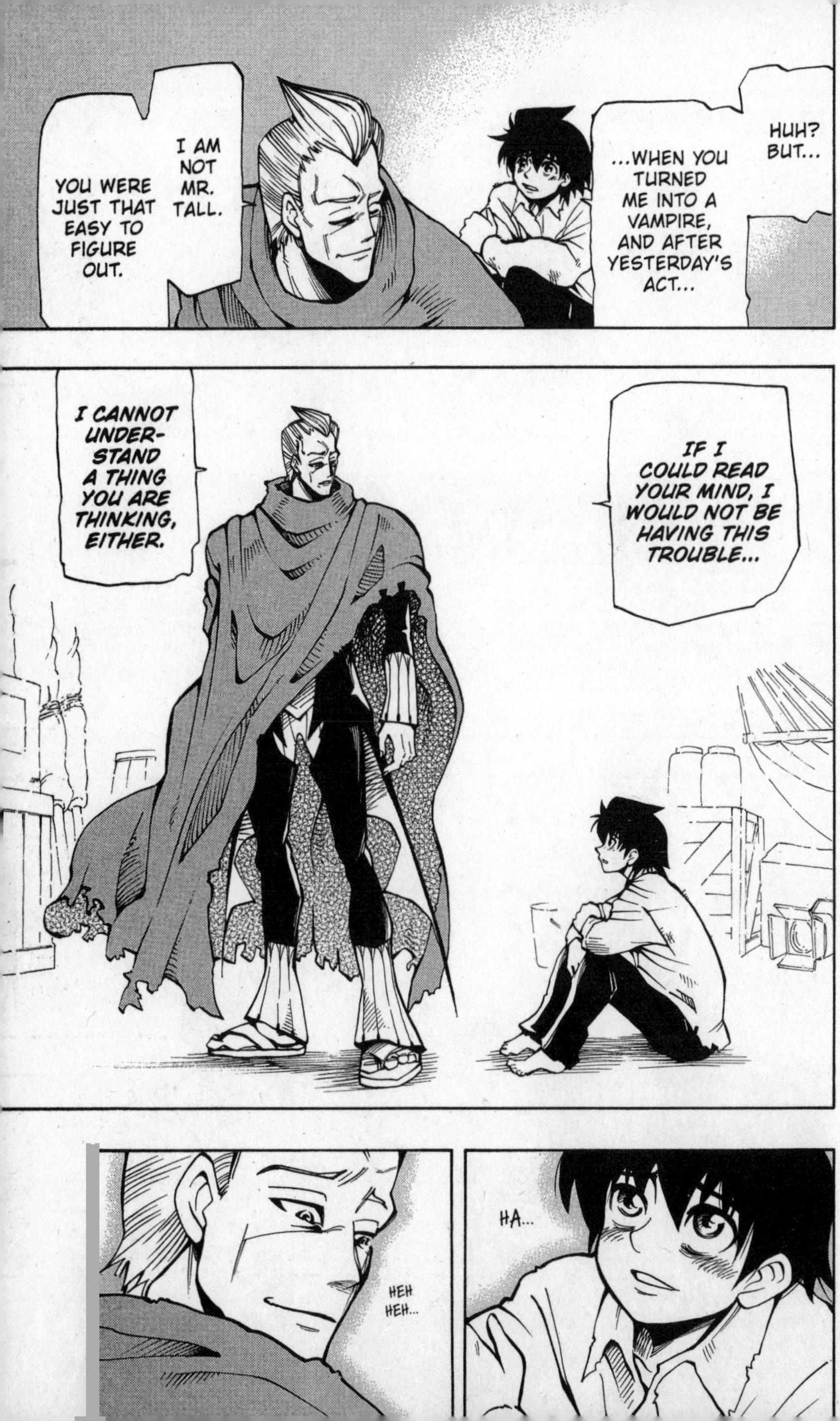
HUH? BUT...
...WHEN YOU TURNED ME INTO A VAMPIRE, AND AFTER YESTERDAY'S ACT...
I AM NOT MR. TALL.
YOU WERE JUST THAT EASY TO FIGURE OUT.
IF I COULD READ YOUR MIND, I WOULD NOT BE HAVING THIS TROUBLE...
I CANNOT UNDER-STAND A THING YOU ARE THINKING, EITHER.
HA...
HEH HEH...

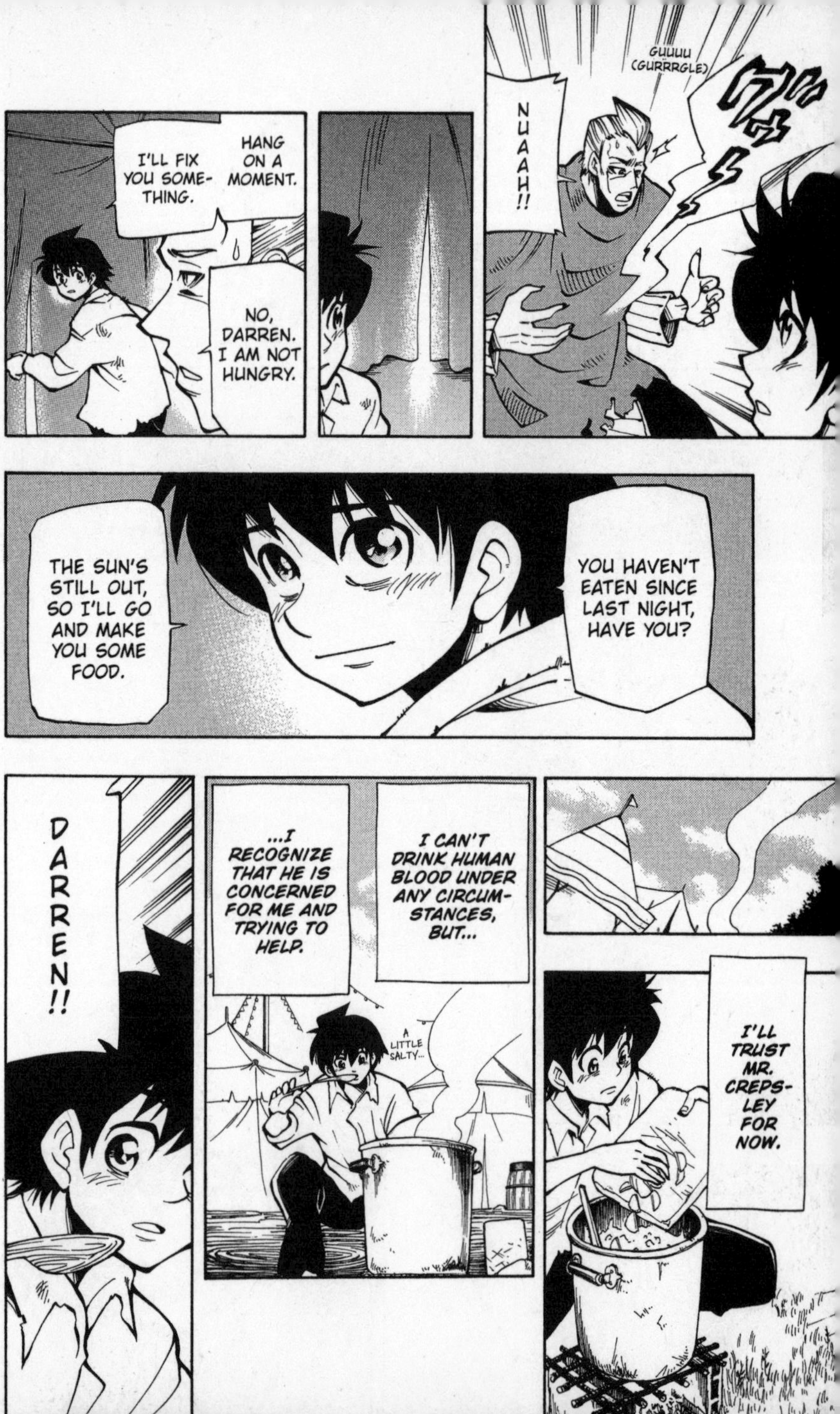
GUUUU (GURRRGLE)
NUAAAH!!
HANG ON A MOMENT.
I'LL FIX YOU SOME-THING.
NO, DARREN. I AM NOT HUNGRY.
YOU HAVEN'T EATEN SINCE LAST NIGHT, HAVE YOU?
THE SUN'S STILL OUT, SO I'LL GO AND MAKE YOU SOME FOOD.
I'LL TRUST MR. CREPS-LEY FOR NOW.
I CAN'T DRINK HUMAN BLOOD UNDER ANY CIRCUM-STANCES, BUT...
...I RECOGNIZE THAT HE IS CONCERNED FOR ME AND TRYING TO HELP.
A LITTLE SALTY...
DARREN!!

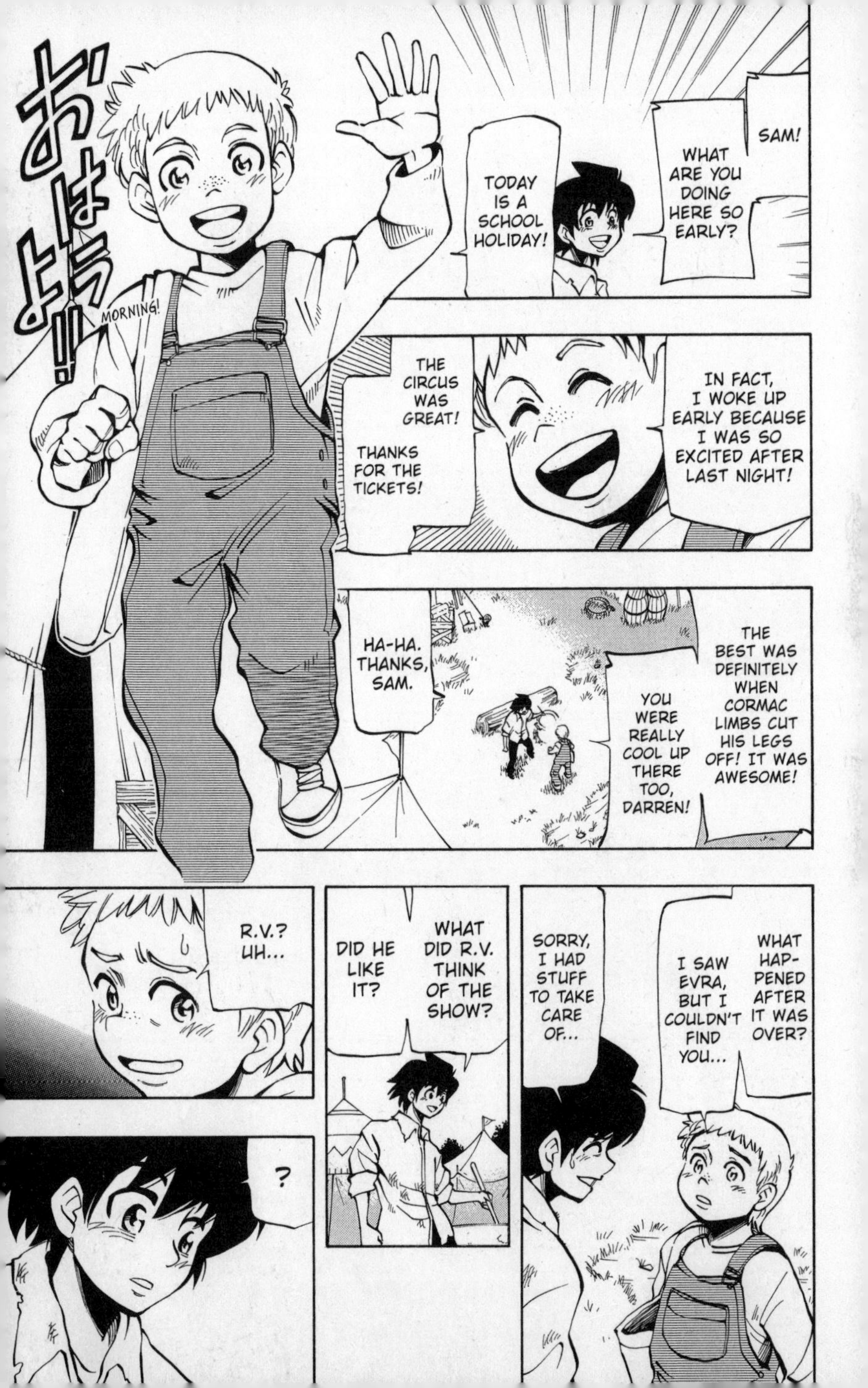
SAM!
WHAT ARE YOU DOING HERE SO EARLY?
TODAY IS A SCHOOL HOLIDAY!
IN FACT, I WOKE UP EARLY BECAUSE I WAS SO EXCITED AFTER LAST NIGHT!
THE CIRCUS WAS GREAT!
THANKS FOR THE TICKETS!
THE BEST WAS DEFINITELY WHEN CORMAC LIMBS CUT HIS LEGS OFF! IT WAS AWESOME!
YOU WERE REALLY COOL UP THERE TOO, DARREN!
HA-HA. THANKS, SAM.
おはよう!!
MORNING!
WHAT HAP-PENED AFTER IT WAS OVER?
I SAW EVRA, BUT I COULDN'T FIND YOU...
SORRY, I HAD STUFF TO TAKE CARE OF...
WHAT DID R.V. THINK OF THE SHOW?
DID HE LIKE IT?
R.V.? UH...
?

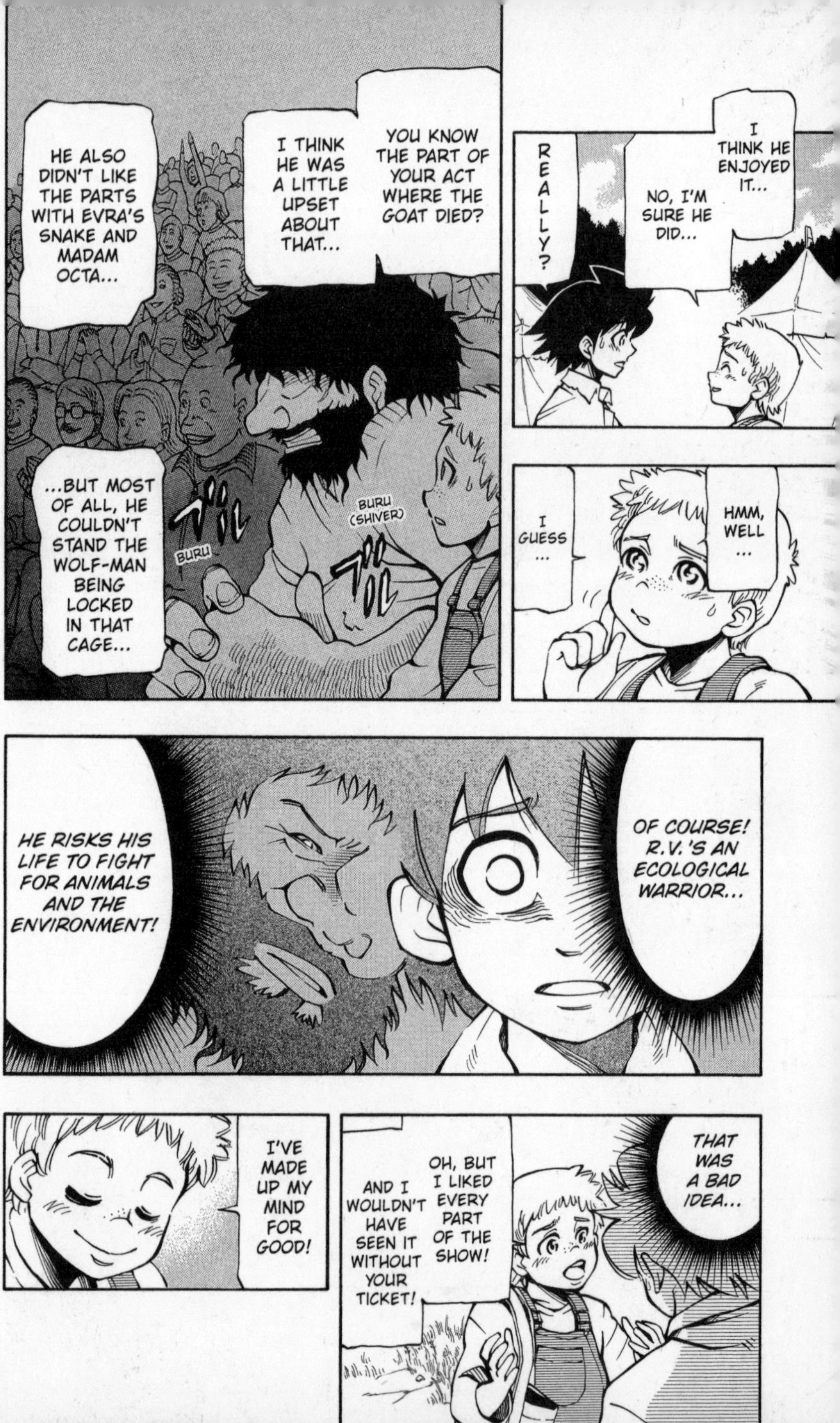
I THINK HE ENJOYED IT...
NO, I'M SURE HE DID...
REALLY?
HMM, WELL ...
I GUESS ...
YOU KNOW THE PART OF YOUR ACT WHERE THE GOAT DIED?
I THINK HE WAS A LITTLE UPSET ABOUT THAT...
HE ALSO DIDN'T LIKE THE PARTS WITH EVRA'S SNAKE AND MADAM OCTA...
ブル
BURU (SHIVER)
...BUT MOST OF ALL, HE COULDN'T STAND THE WOLF-MAN BEING LOCKED IN THAT CAGE...
ブル
BURU
OF COURSE! R.V.'S AN ECOLOGICAL WARRIOR...
HE RISKS HIS LIFE TO FIGHT FOR ANIMALS AND THE ENVIRONMENT!
THAT WAS A BAD IDEA...
OH, BUT I LIKED EVERY PART OF THE SHOW!
AND I WOULDN'T HAVE SEEN IT WITHOUT YOUR TICKET!
I'VE MADE UP MY MIND FOR GOOD!

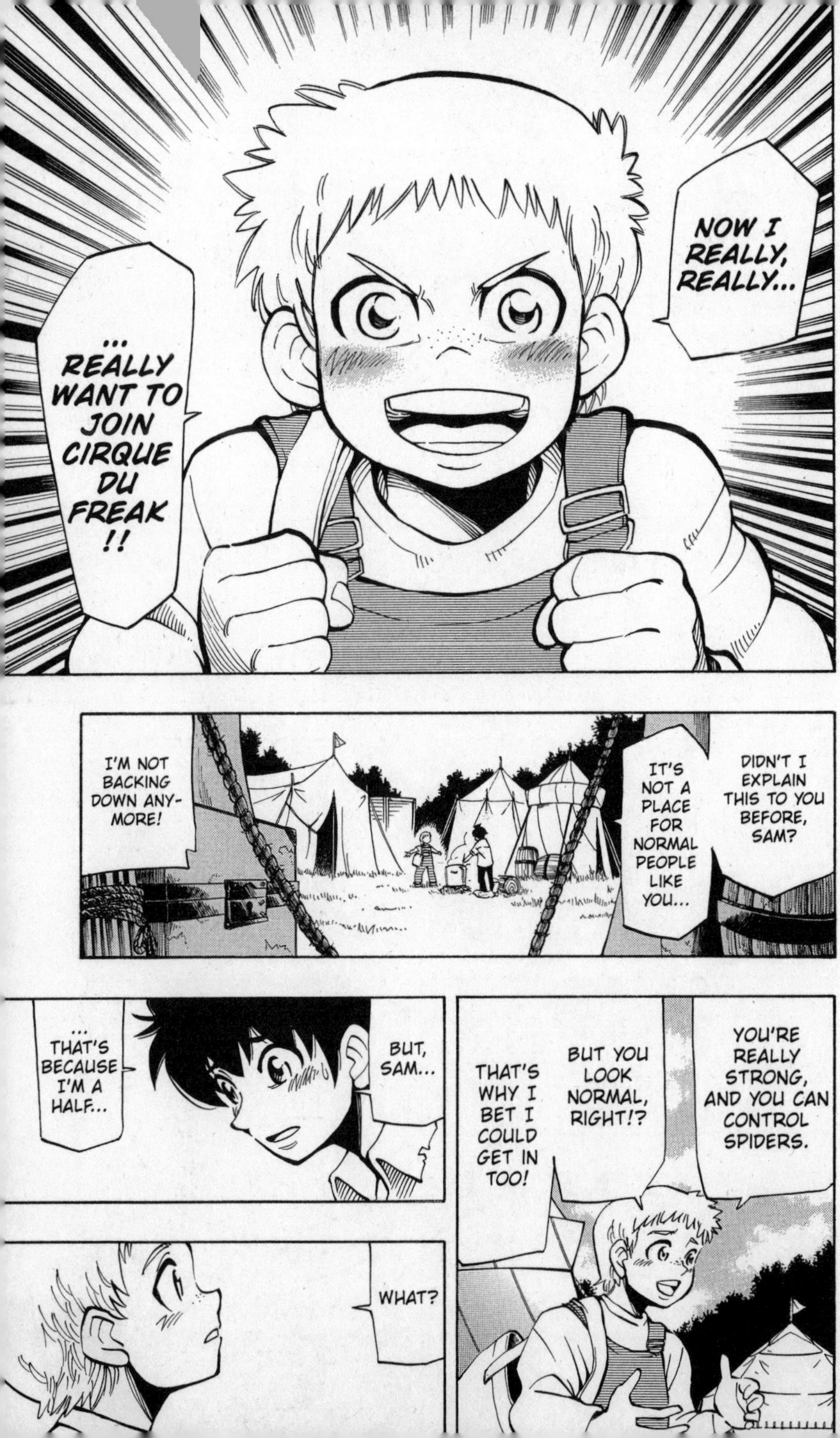
NOW I REALLY, REALLY...
...REALLY WANT TO JOIN CIRQUE DU FREAK!!
DIDN'T I EXPLAIN THIS TO YOU BEFORE, SAM?
IT'S NOT A PLACE FOR NORMAL PEOPLE LIKE YOU...
I'M NOT BACKING DOWN ANY-MORE!
YOU'RE REALLY STRONG, AND YOU CAN CONTROL SPIDERS.
BUT YOU LOOK NORMAL, RIGHT!?
THAT'S WHY I BET I COULD GET IN TOO!
BUT, SAM...
...THAT'S BECAUSE I'M A HALF...
WHAT?

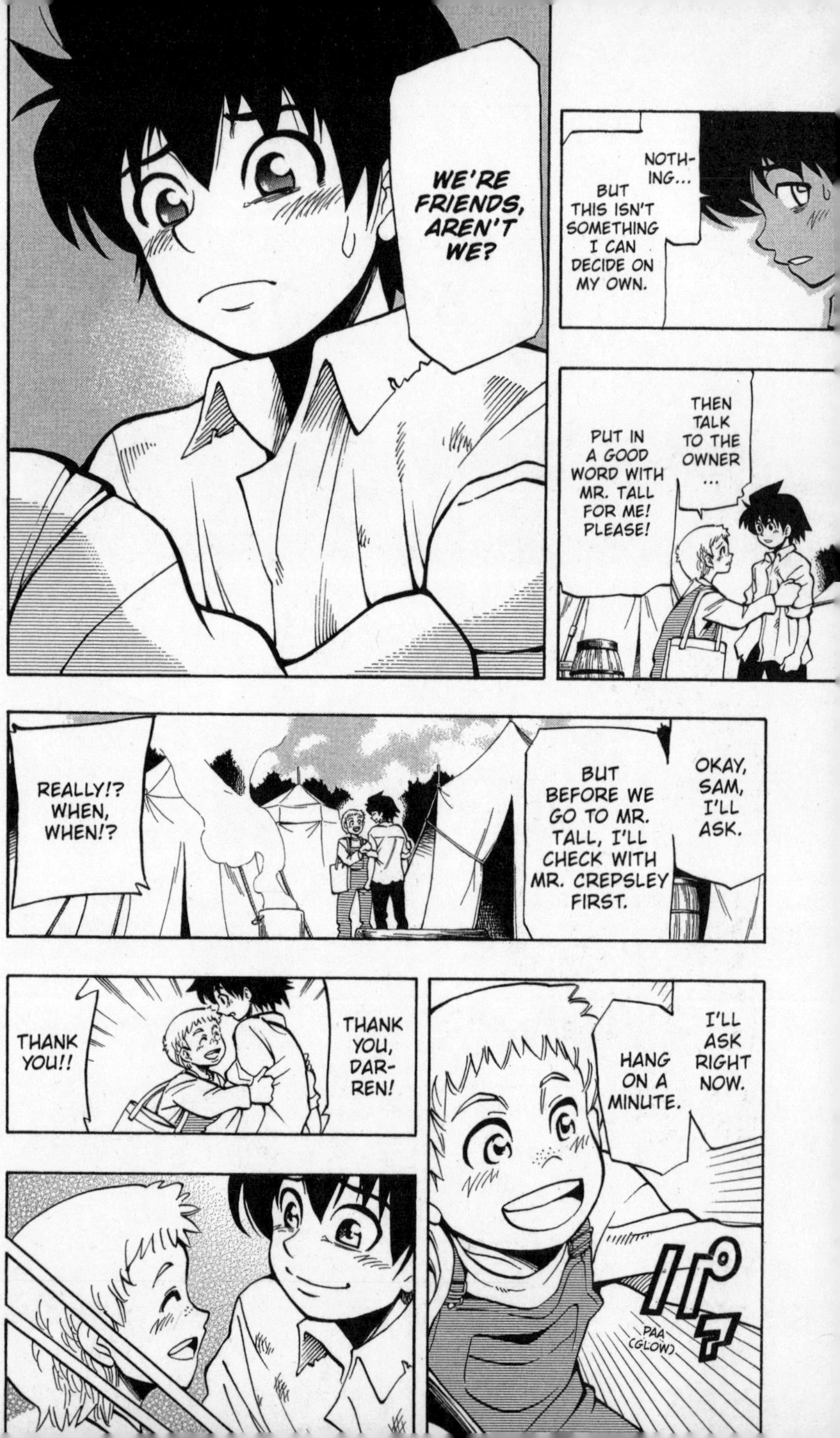
NOTHING...
BUT THIS ISN'T SOMETHING I CAN DECIDE ON MY OWN.
THEN TALK TO THE OWNER ...
PUT IN A GOOD WORD WITH MR. TALL FOR ME! PLEASE!
WE'RE FRIENDS, AREN'T WE?
OKAY, SAM, I'LL ASK.
BUT BEFORE WE GO TO MR. TALL, I'LL CHECK WITH MR. CREPSLEY FIRST.
REALLY!? WHEN, WHEN!?
I'LL ASK RIGHT NOW.
HANG ON A MINUTE.
PAA (GLOW)
THANK YOU, DARREN!
THANK YOU!!

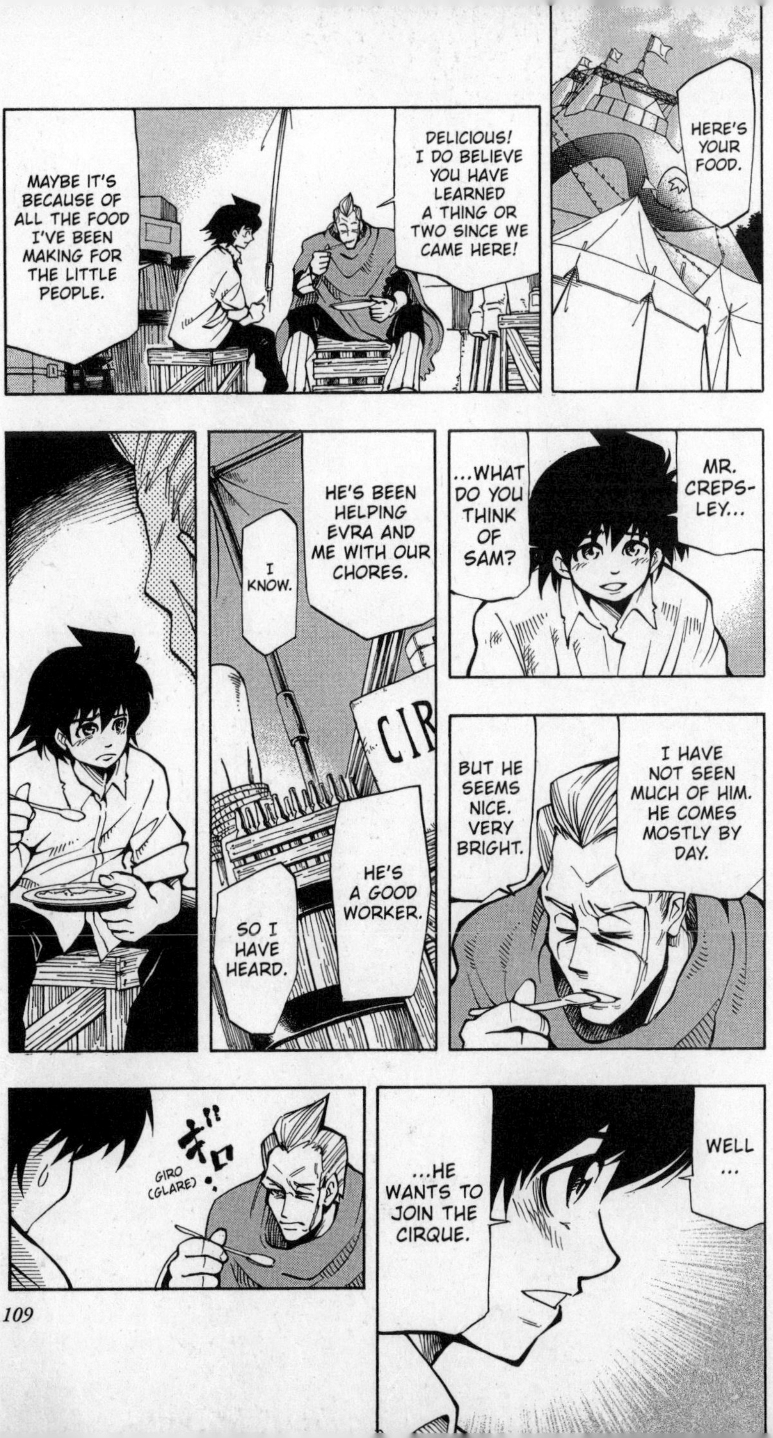

HERE'S YOUR FOOD.
DELICIOUS! I DO BELIEVE YOU HAVE LEARNED A THING OR TWO SINCE WE CAME HERE!
MAYBE IT'S BECAUSE OF ALL THE FOOD I'VE BEEN MAKING FOR THE LITTLE PEOPLE.
MR. CREPS-LEY...
...WHAT DO YOU THINK OF SAM?
I HAVE NOT SEEN MUCH OF HIM. HE COMES MOSTLY BY DAY.
BUT HE SEEMS NICE. VERY BRIGHT.
HE'S BEEN HELPING EVRA AND ME WITH OUR CHORES.
I KNOW.
CIR
HE'S A GOOD WORKER.
SO I HAVE HEARD.
WELL...
...HE WANTS TO JOIN THE CIRQUE.
GIRO (GLARE)

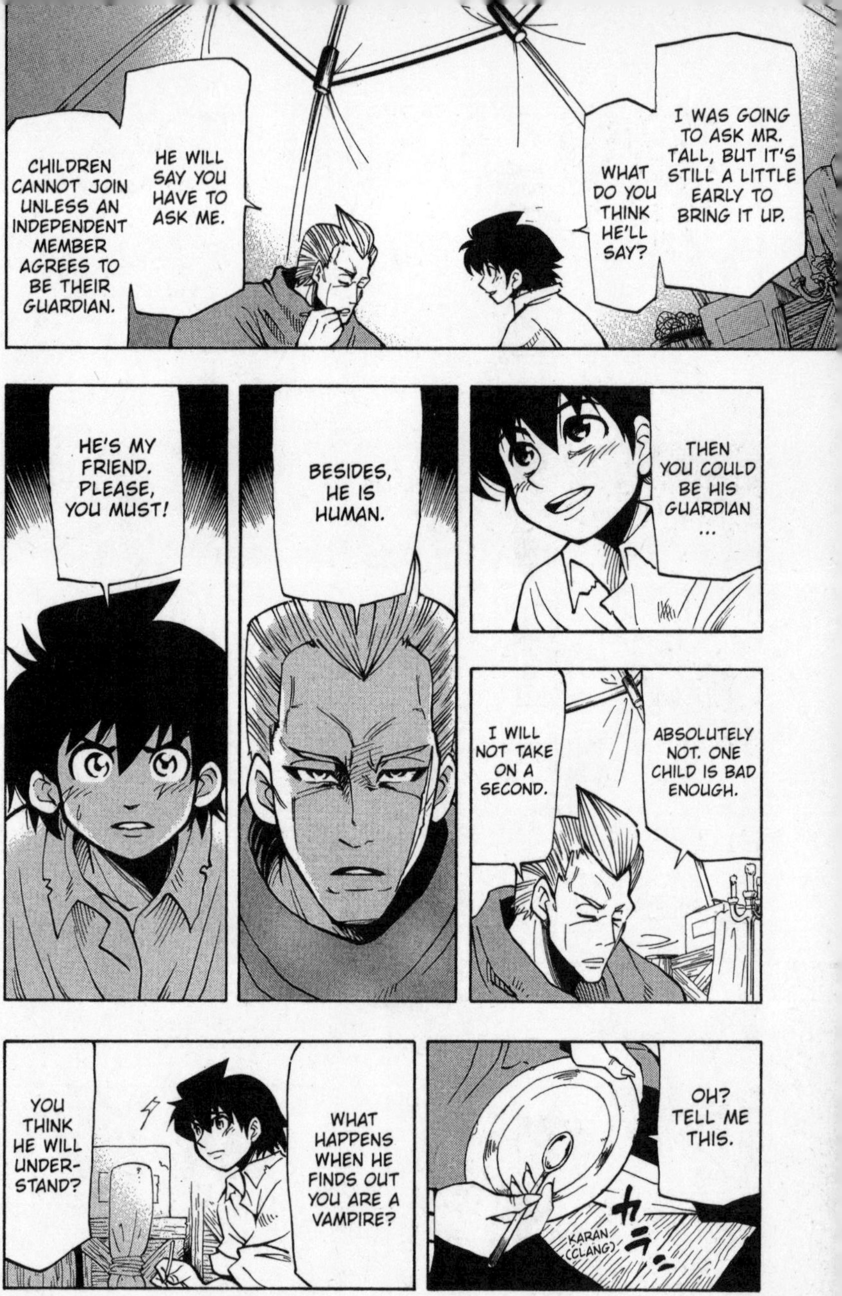
I WAS GOING TO ASK MR. TALL, BUT IT'S STILL A LITTLE EARLY TO BRING IT UP.
WHAT DO YOU THINK HE'LL SAY?
HE WILL SAY YOU HAVE TO ASK ME.
CHILDREN CANNOT JOIN UNLESS AN INDEPENDENT MEMBER AGREES TO BE THEIR GUARDIAN.
THEN YOU COULD BE HIS GUARDIAN ...
ABSOLUTELY NOT. ONE CHILD IS BAD ENOUGH.
I WILL NOT TAKE ON A SECOND.
BESIDES, HE IS HUMAN.
HE'S MY FRIEND. PLEASE, YOU MUST!
OH? TELL ME THIS.
カラン
KARAN (CLANG)
WHAT HAPPENS WHEN HE FINDS OUT YOU ARE A VAMPIRE?
YOU THINK HE WILL UNDER-STAND?

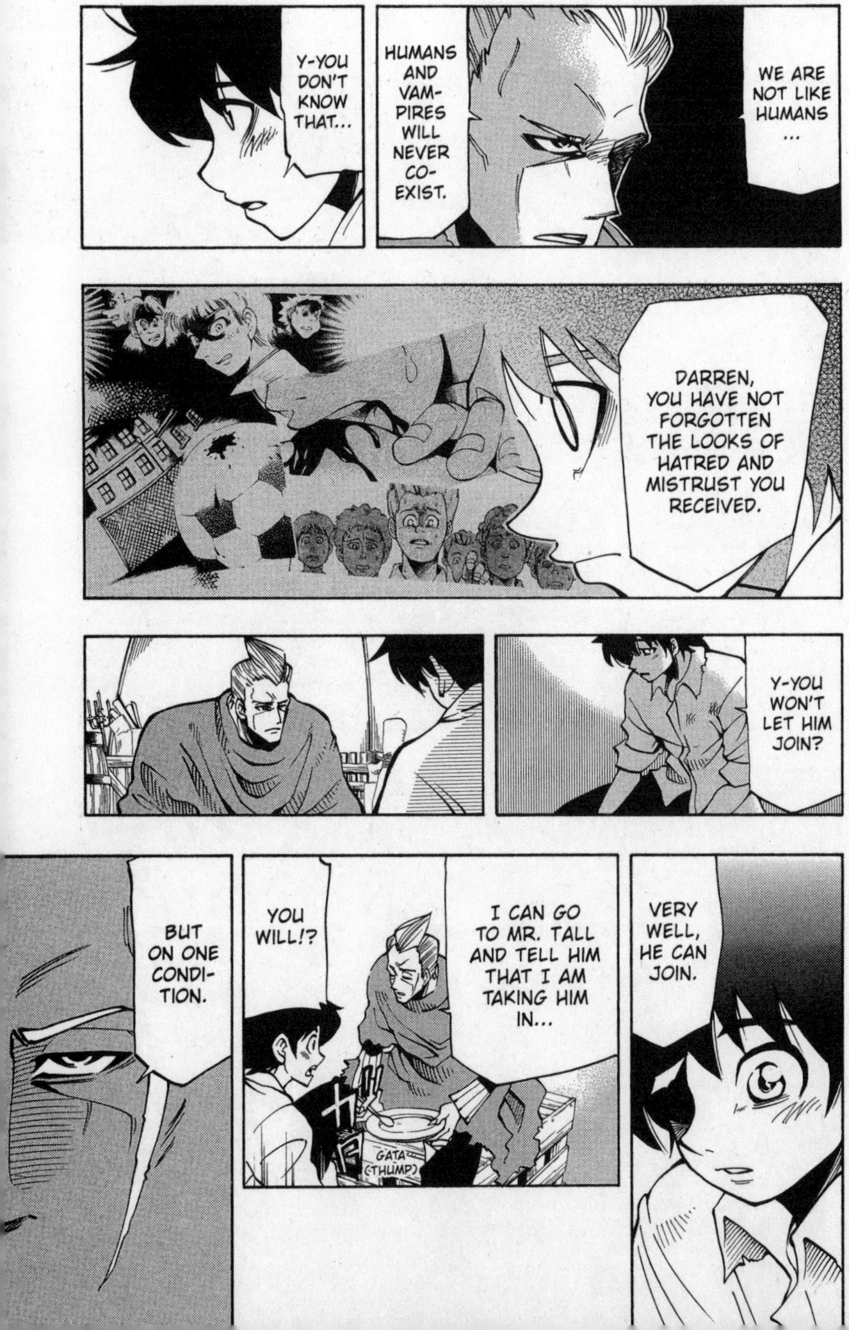
WE ARE NOT LIKE HUMANS ...
HUMANS AND VAMPIRES WILL NEVER CO-EXIST.
Y-YOU DON'T KNOW THAT...
DARREN, YOU HAVE NOT FORGOTTEN THE LOOKS OF HATRED AND MISTRUST YOU RECEIVED.
Y-YOU WON'T LET HIM JOIN?
VERY WELL, HE CAN JOIN.
I CAN GO TO MR. TALL AND TELL HIM THAT I AM TAKING HIM IN...
YOU WILL!?
GATA (THUMP)
BUT ON ONE CONDITION.

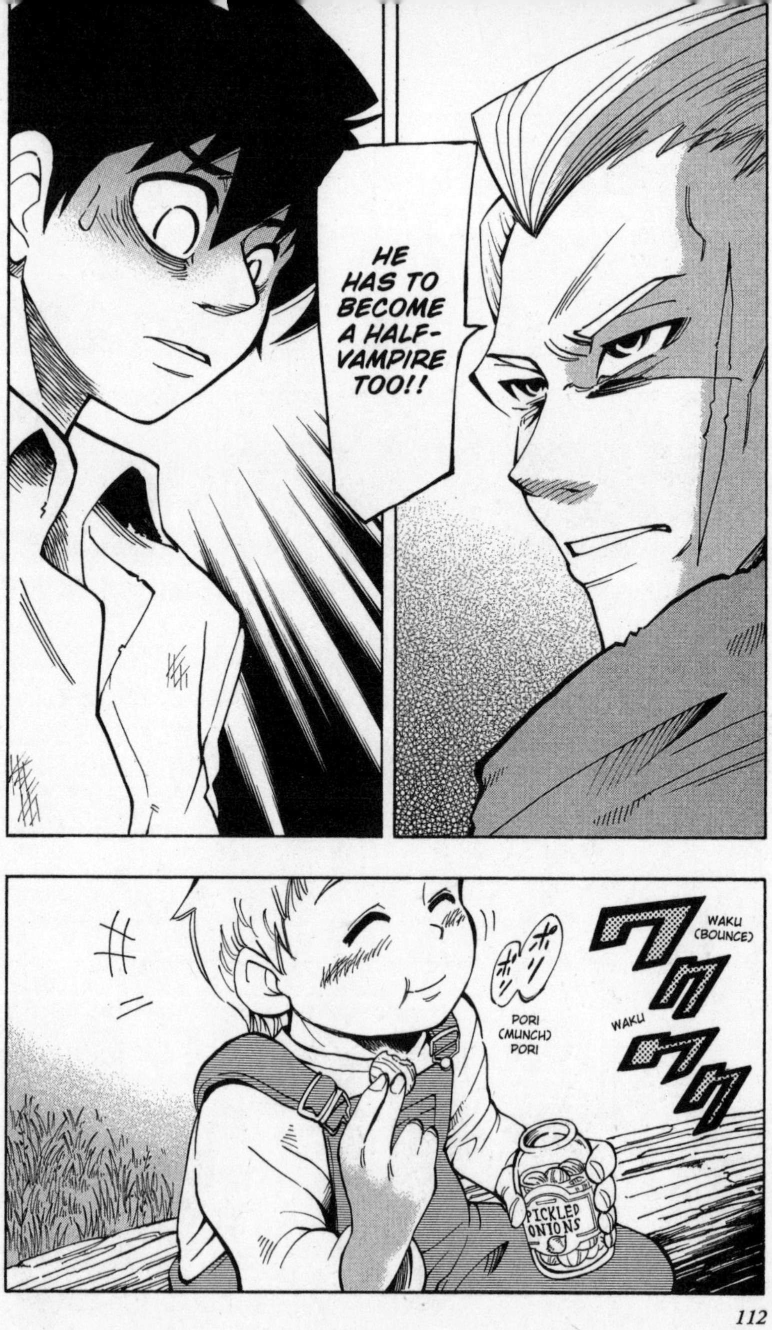
HE HAS TO BECOME A HALF-VAMPIRE TOO!!
ワクワク
WAKU (BOUNCE)
WAKU
ポリポリ
PORI (MUNCH) PORI
PICKLED ONIONS

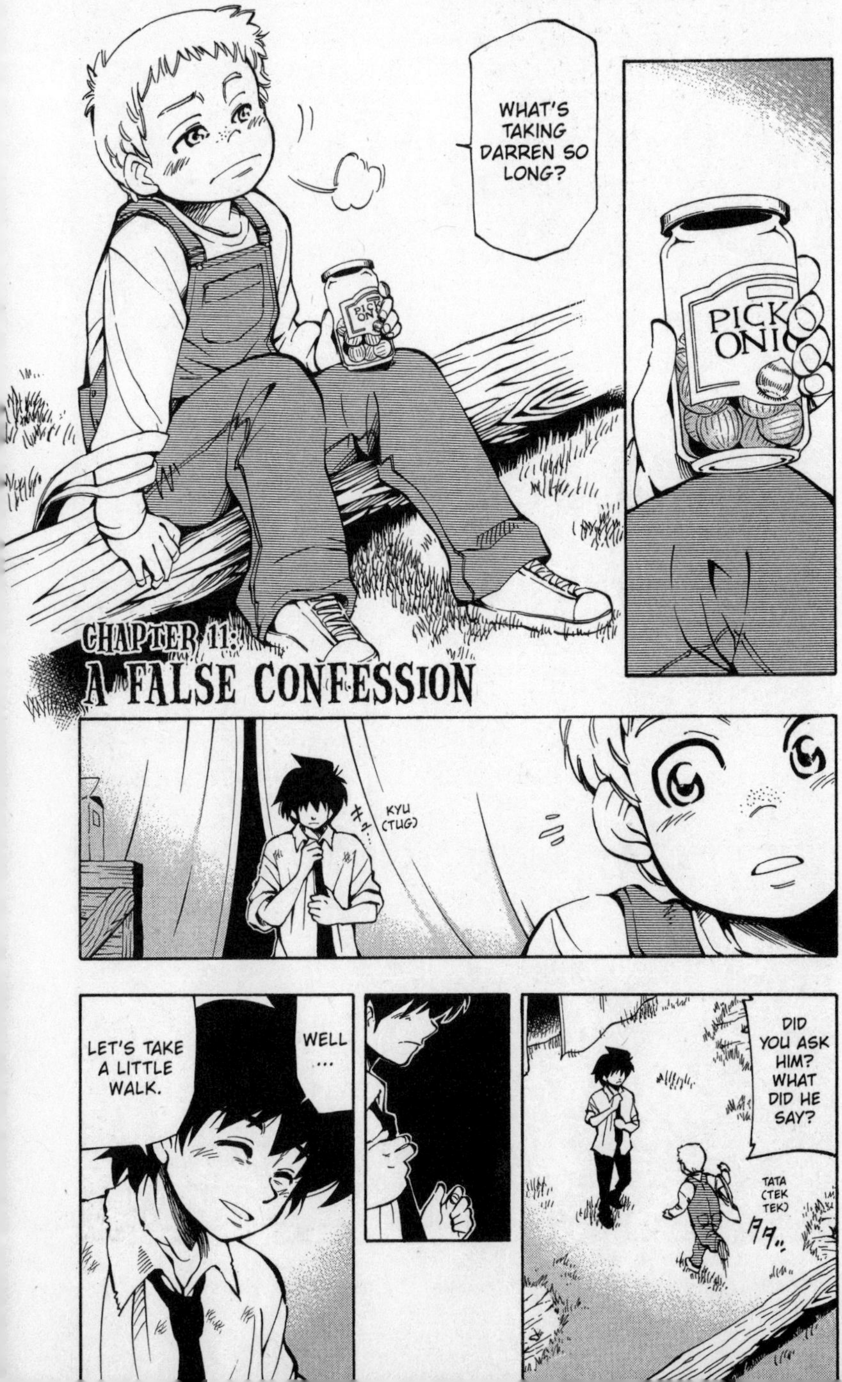
PICK ONIO
WHAT'S TAKING DARREN SO LONG?
CHAPTER 11:
A FALSE CONFESSION
KYU (TUG)
DID YOU ASK HIM? WHAT DID HE SAY?
TATA (TEK TEK)
WELL ...
LET'S TAKE A LITTLE WALK.

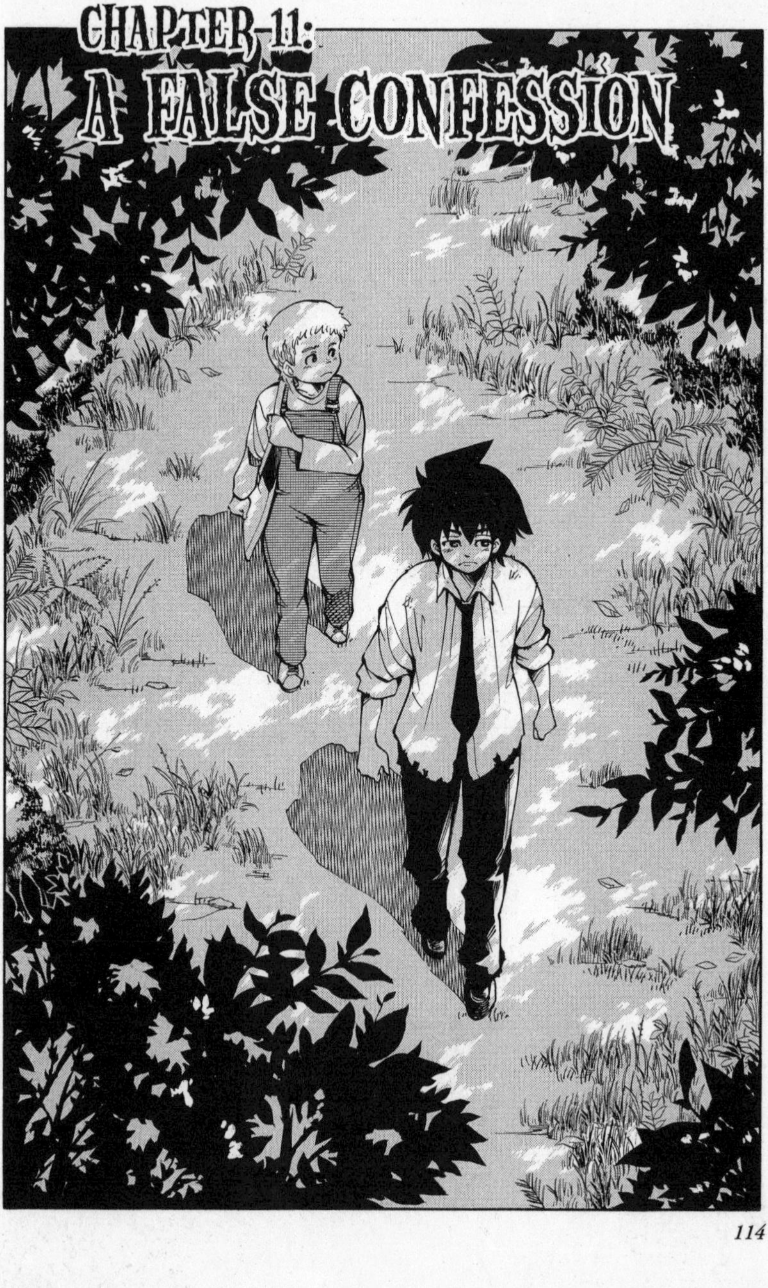
CHAPTER 11:
A FALSE CONFESSION

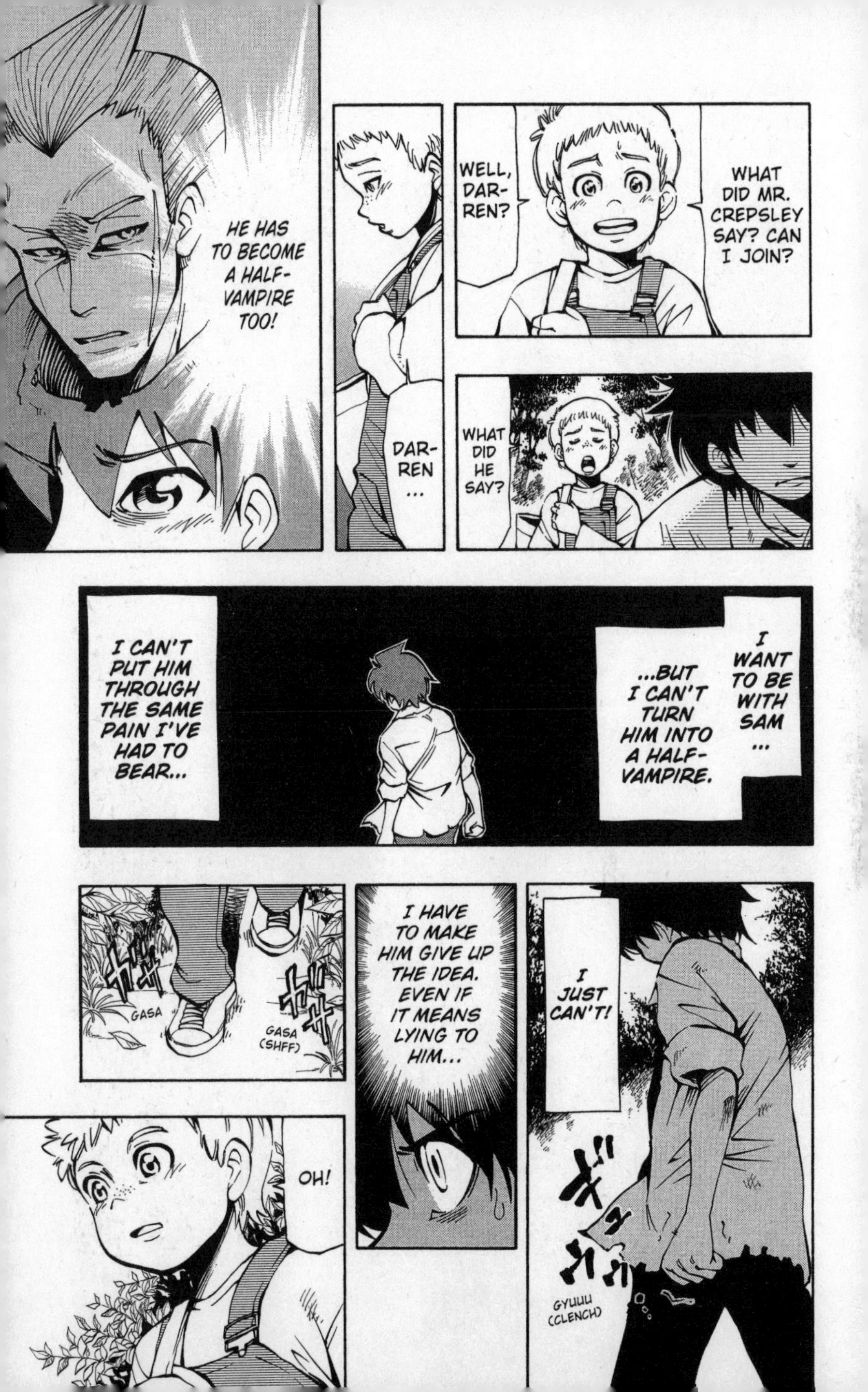
WHAT DID MR. CREPSLEY SAY? CAN I JOIN?
WELL, DAR-REN?
WHAT DID HE SAY?
DAR-REN ...
HE HAS TO BECOME A HALF-VAMPIRE TOO!
I WANT TO BE WITH SAM ...
...BUT I CAN'T TURN HIM INTO A HALF-VAMPIRE.
I CAN'T PUT HIM THROUGH THE SAME PAIN I'VE HAD TO BEAR...
I JUST CAN'T!
GYUUU (CLENCH)
I HAVE TO MAKE HIM GIVE UP THE IDEA. EVEN IF IT MEANS LYING TO HIM...
GASA
GASA (SHFF)
OH!

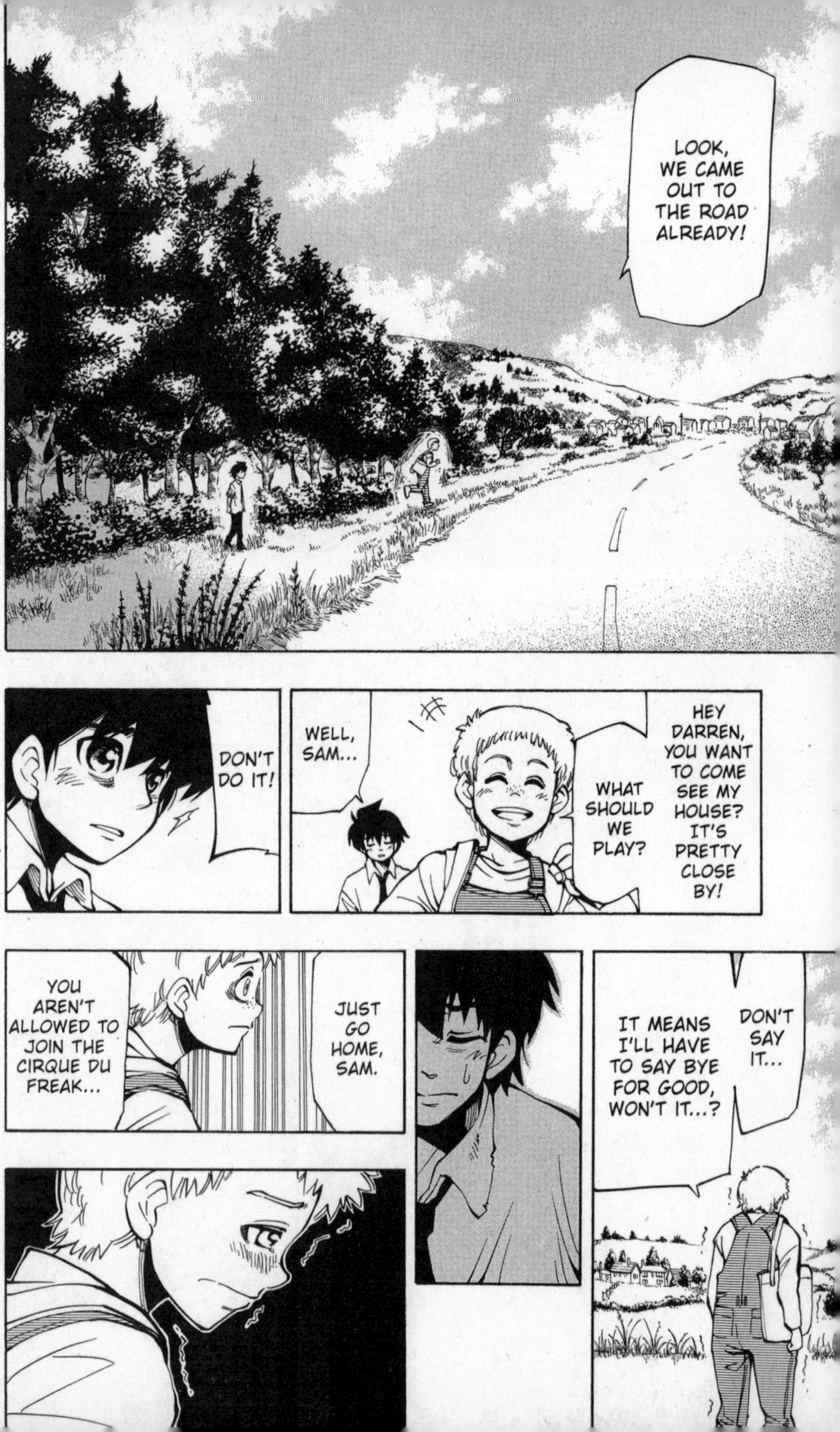
LOOK, WE CAME OUT TO THE ROAD ALREADY!
HEY DARREN, YOU WANT TO COME SEE MY HOUSE? IT'S PRETTY CLOSE BY!
WHAT SHOULD WE PLAY?
WELL, SAM...
DON'T DO IT!
DON'T SAY IT...
IT MEANS I'LL HAVE TO SAY BYE FOR GOOD, WON'T IT...?
JUST GO HOME, SAM.
YOU AREN'T ALLOWED TO JOIN THE CIRQUE DU FREAK...

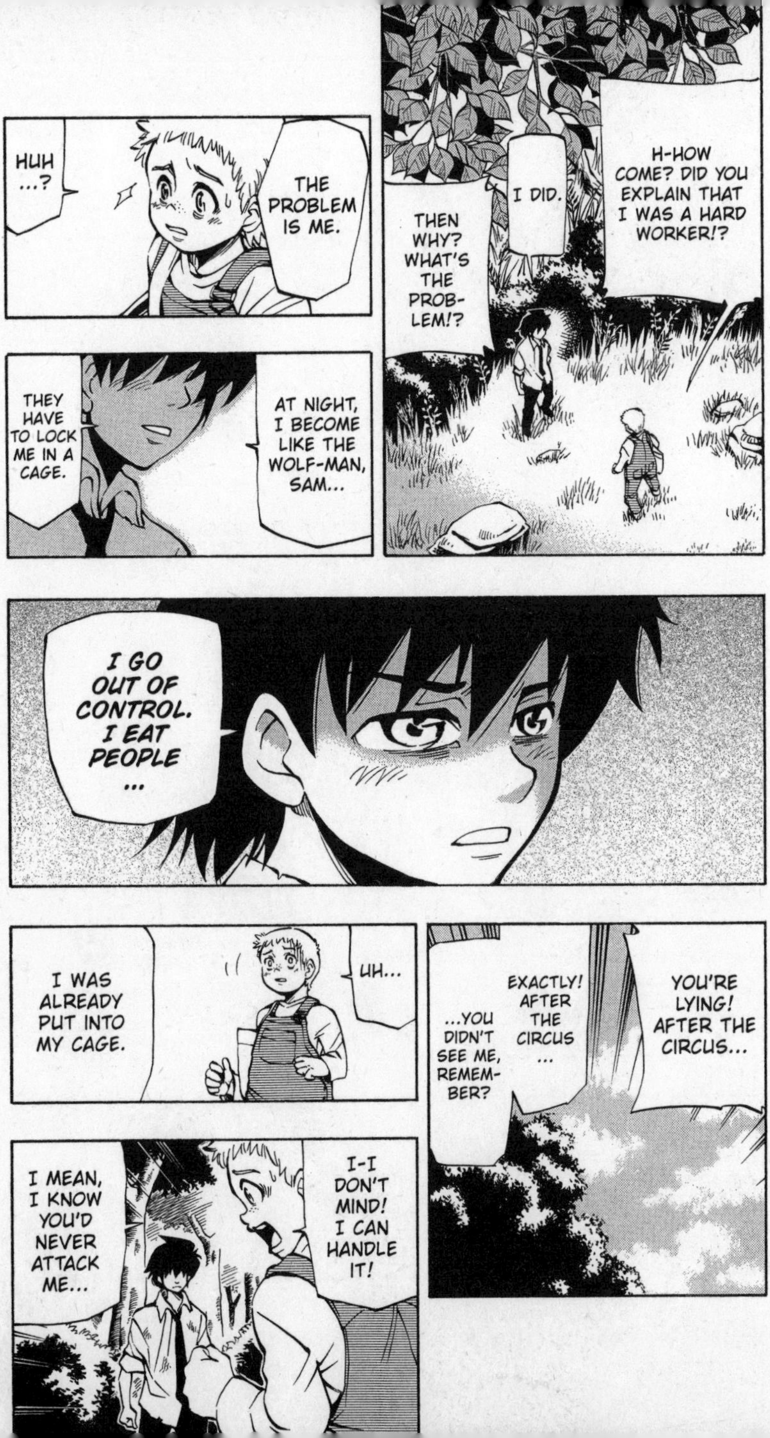
H-HOW COME? DID YOU EXPLAIN THAT I WAS A HARD WORKER!?
I DID.
THEN WHY? WHAT'S THE PROBLEM!?
THE PROBLEM IS ME.
HUH ...?
AT NIGHT, I BECOME LIKE THE WOLF-MAN, SAM...
THEY HAVE TO LOCK ME IN A CAGE.
I GO OUT OF CONTROL. I EAT PEOPLE ...
YOU'RE LYING! AFTER THE CIRCUS...
EXACTLY! AFTER THE CIRCUS ...
...YOU DIDN'T SEE ME, REMEMBER?
UH...
I WAS ALREADY PUT INTO MY CAGE.
I-I DON'T MIND! I CAN HANDLE IT!
I MEAN, I KNOW YOU'D NEVER ATTACK ME...

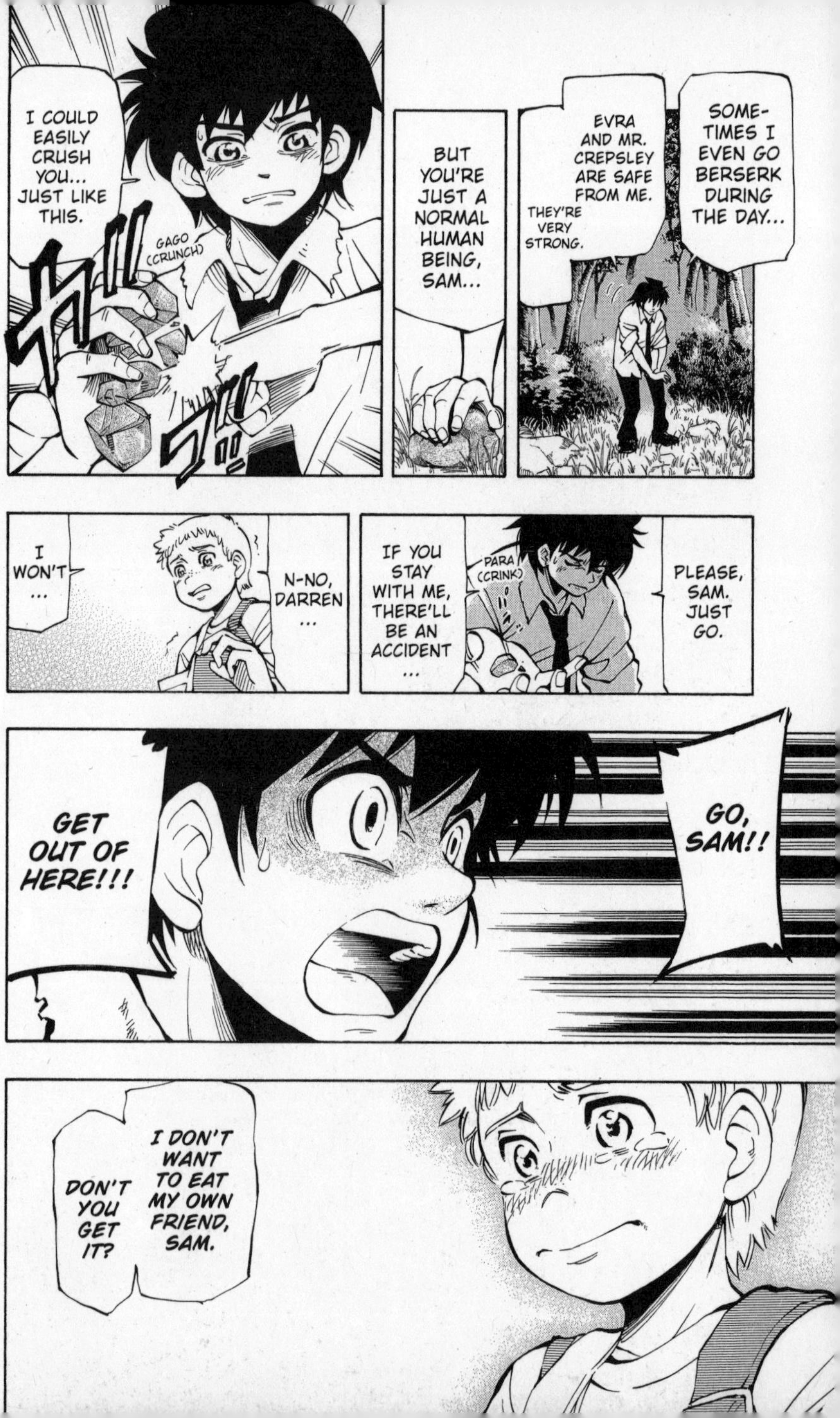
SOME-TIMES I EVEN GO BERSERK DURING THE DAY...
EVRA AND MR. CREPSLEY ARE SAFE FROM ME.
THEY'RE VERY STRONG.
BUT YOU'RE JUST A NORMAL HUMAN BEING, SAM...
I COULD EASILY CRUSH YOU... JUST LIKE THIS.
GAGO (CRUNCH)
PLEASE, SAM. JUST GO.
PARA (CRINK)
IF YOU STAY WITH ME, THERE'LL BE AN ACCIDENT...
N-NO, DARREN...
I WON'T...
GO, SAM!!
GET OUT OF HERE!!!
I DON'T WANT TO EAT MY OWN FRIEND, SAM.
DON'T YOU GET IT?

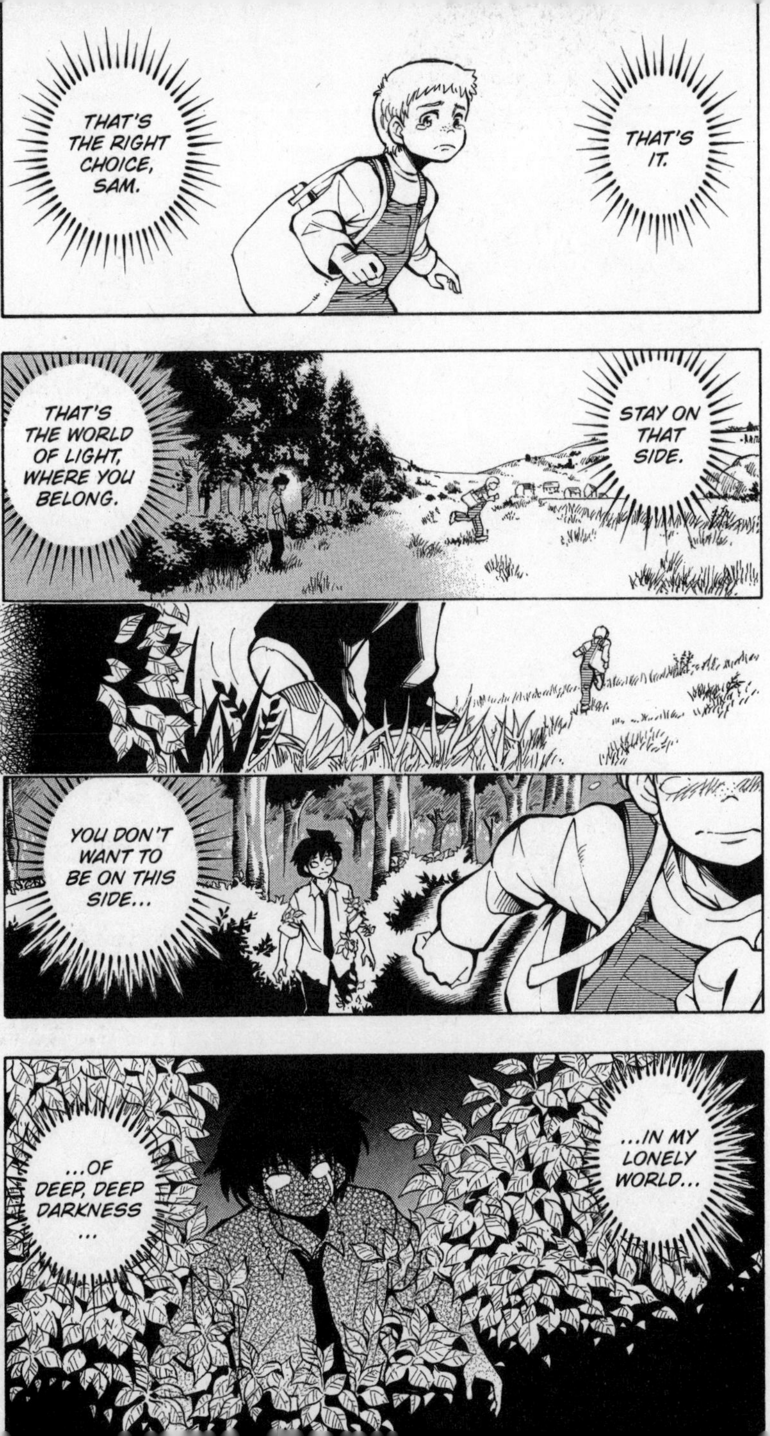
THAT'S IT.
THAT'S THE RIGHT CHOICE, SAM.
STAY ON THAT SIDE.
THAT'S THE WORLD OF LIGHT, WHERE YOU BELONG.
YOU DON'T WANT TO BE ON THIS SIDE...
...IN MY LONELY WORLD...
...OF DEEP, DEEP DARKNESS ...

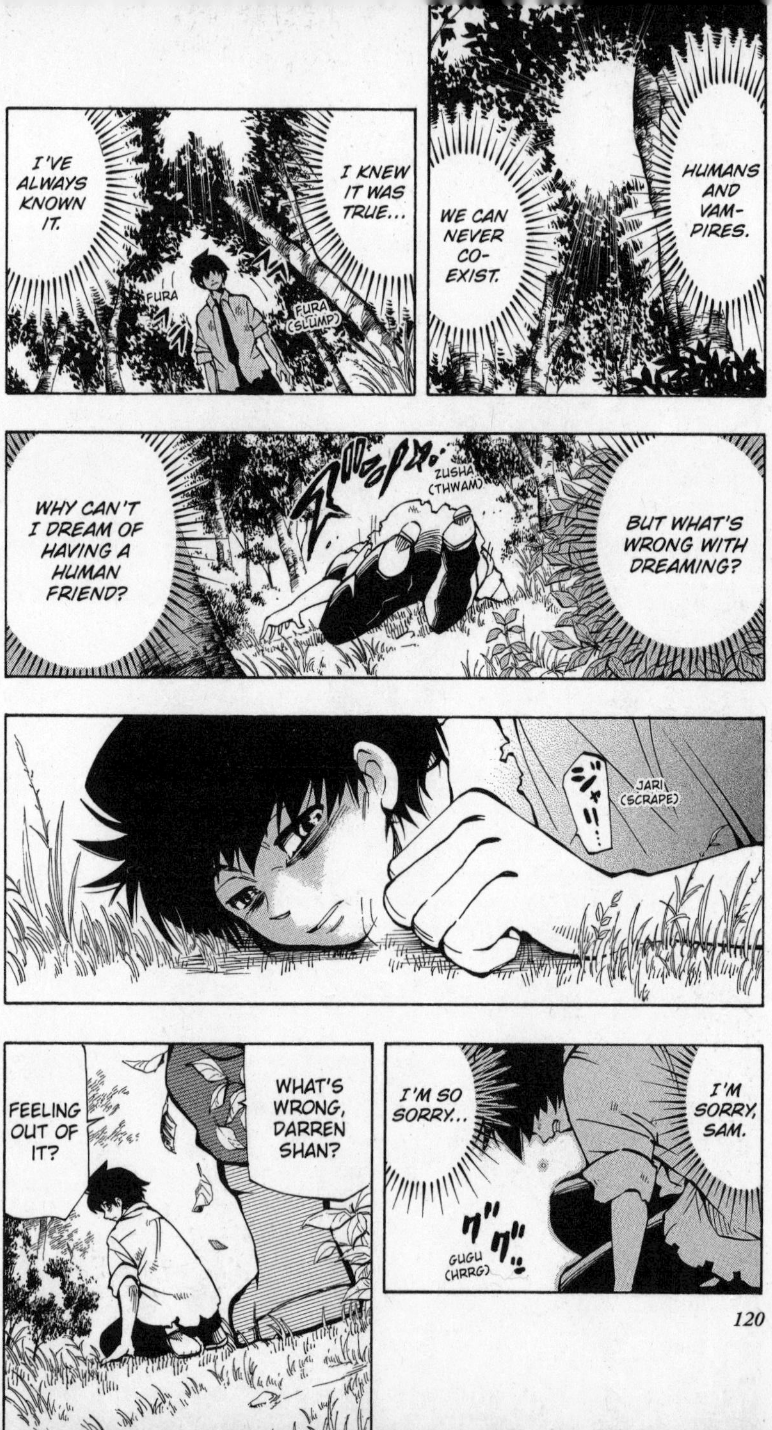
HUMANS AND VAMPIRES.
WE CAN NEVER CO-EXIST.
I KNEW IT WAS TRUE...
I'VE ALWAYS KNOWN IT.
FURA
FURA (SLUMP)
BUT WHAT'S WRONG WITH DREAMING?
ZUSHA (THWAM)
WHY CAN'T I DREAM OF HAVING A HUMAN FRIEND?
JARI (SCRAPE)
I'M SORRY, SAM.
I'M SO SORRY...
GUGU (HRRG)
WHAT'S WRONG, DARREN SHAN?
FEELING OUT OF IT?

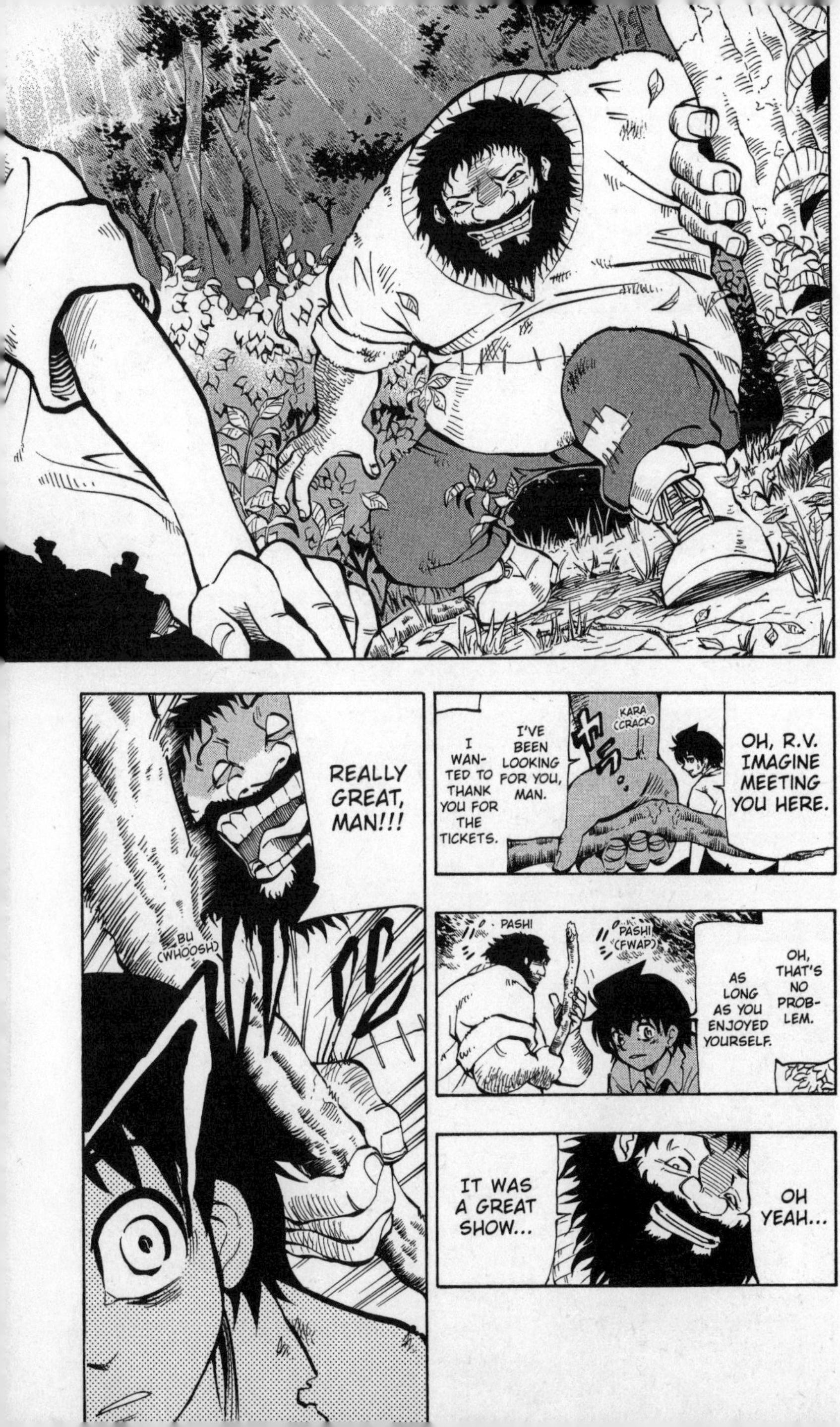
OH, R.V. IMAGINE MEETING YOU HERE.
KARA (CRACK)
I'VE BEEN LOOKING FOR YOU, MAN.
I WANTED TO THANK YOU FOR THE TICKETS.
PASHI (FWAP)
PASHI
OH, THAT'S NO PROBLEM.
AS LONG AS YOU ENJOYED YOURSELF.
OH YEAH...
IT WAS A GREAT SHOW...
REALLY GREAT, MAN!!!
BU (WHOOSH)

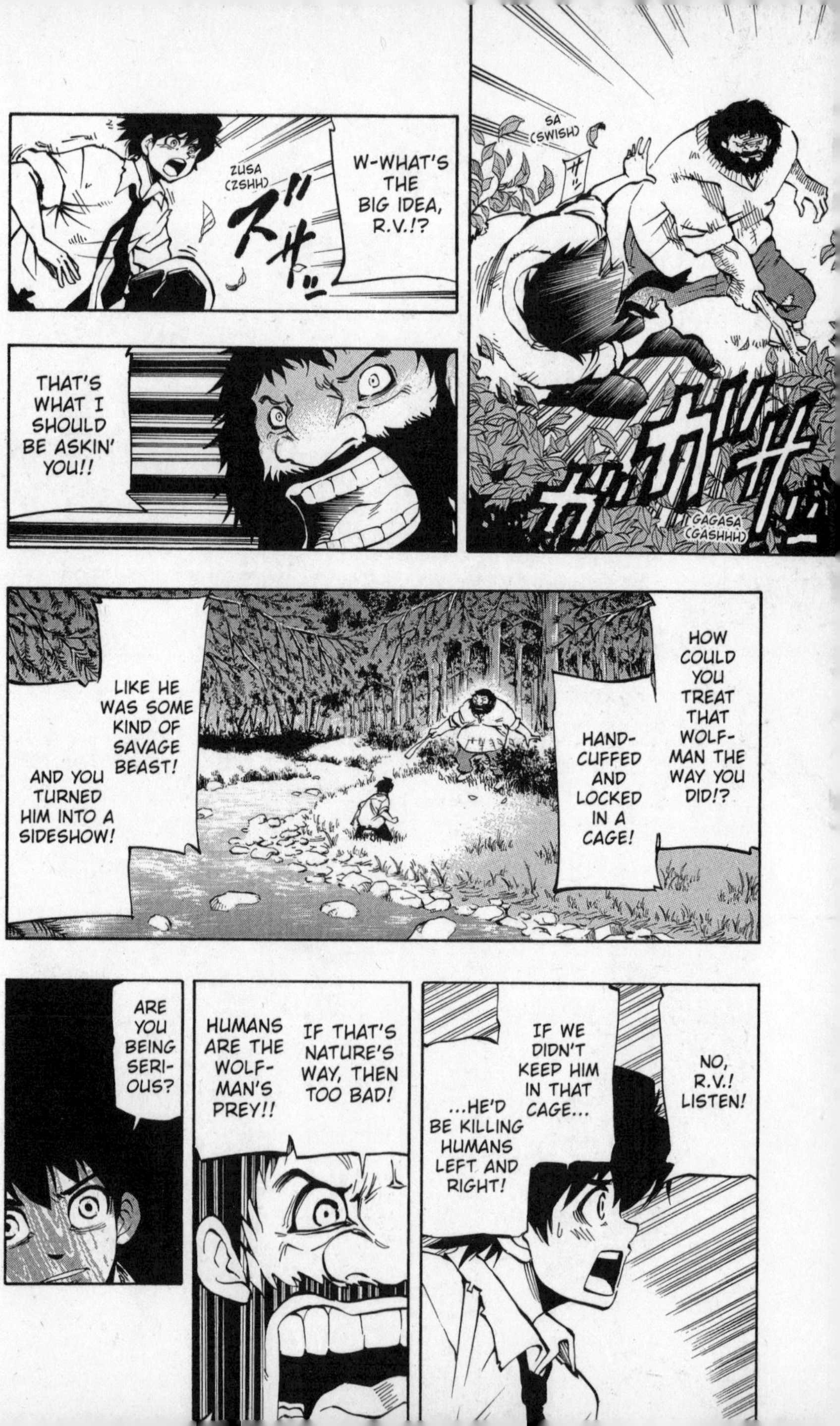
SA (SWISH)
GAGASA (GASHHH)
ZUSA (ZSHH)
W-WHAT'S THE BIG IDEA, R.V.!?
THAT'S WHAT I SHOULD BE ASKIN' YOU!!
HOW COULD YOU TREAT THAT WOLF-MAN THE WAY YOU DID!?
HAND-CUFFED AND LOCKED IN A CAGE!
LIKE HE WAS SOME KIND OF SAVAGE BEAST!
AND YOU TURNED HIM INTO A SIDESHOW!
NO, R.V.! LISTEN!
IF WE DIDN'T KEEP HIM IN THAT CAGE...
...HE'D BE KILLING HUMANS LEFT AND RIGHT!
IF THAT'S NATURE'S WAY, THEN TOO BAD!
HUMANS ARE THE WOLF-MAN'S PREY!!
ARE YOU BEING SERI-OUS?

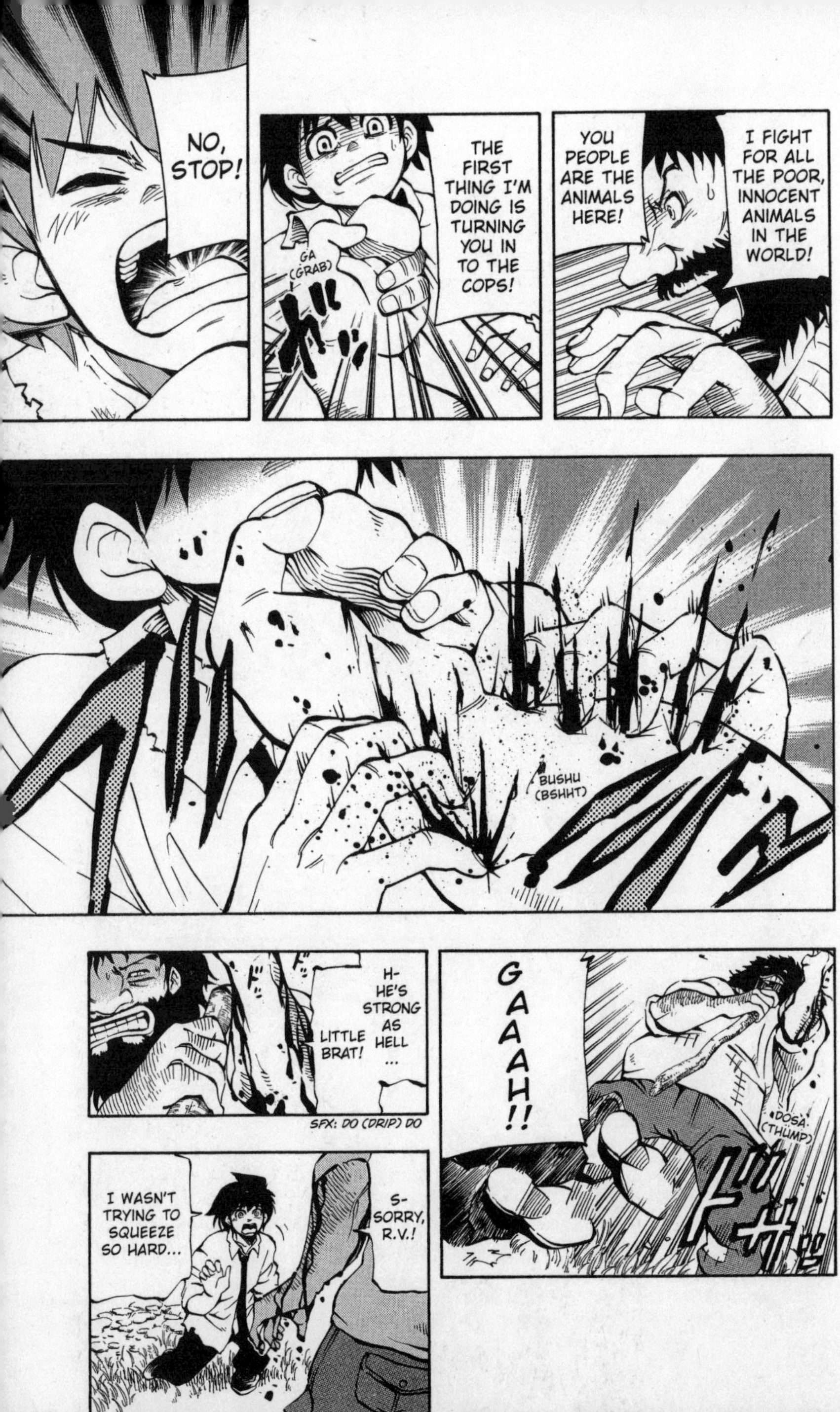
I FIGHT FOR ALL THE POOR, INNOCENT ANIMALS IN THE WORLD!
YOU PEOPLE ARE THE ANIMALS HERE!
THE FIRST THING I'M DOING IS TURNING YOU IN TO THE COPS!
GA (GRAB)
NO, STOP!
BUSHU (BSHHT)
GAAAH!!
DOSA (THUMP)
H- HE'S STRONG AS HELL ...
LITTLE BRAT!
SFX: DO (DRIP) DO
S- SORRY, R.V.!
I WASN'T TRYING TO SQUEEZE SO HARD...

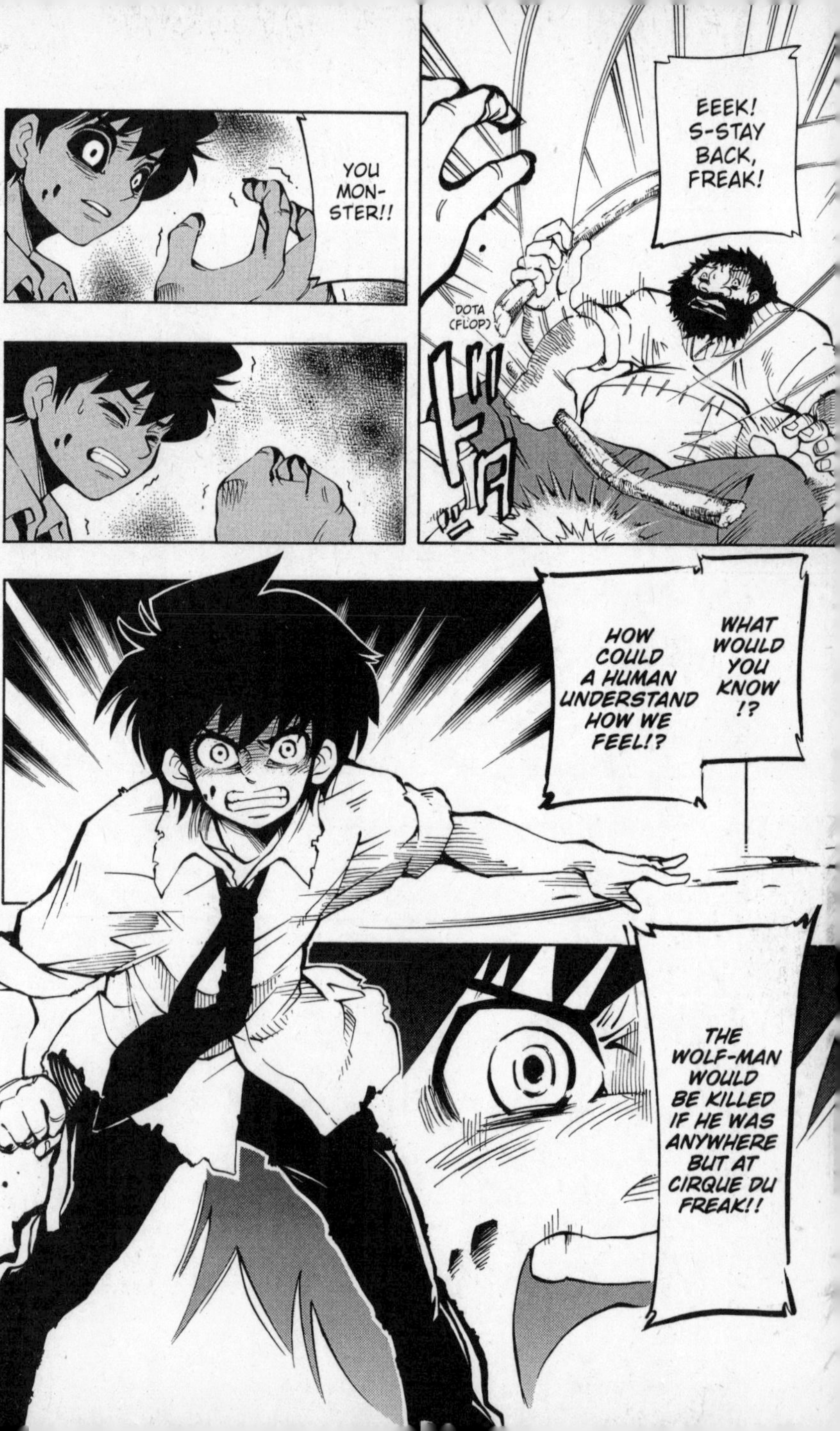
EEEK! S-STAY BACK, FREAK!
DOTA (FLOP)
YOU MON-STER!!
WHAT WOULD YOU KNOW!?
HOW COULD A HUMAN UNDERSTAND HOW WE FEEL!?
THE WOLF-MAN WOULD BE KILLED IF HE WAS ANYWHERE BUT AT CIRQUE DU FREAK!!

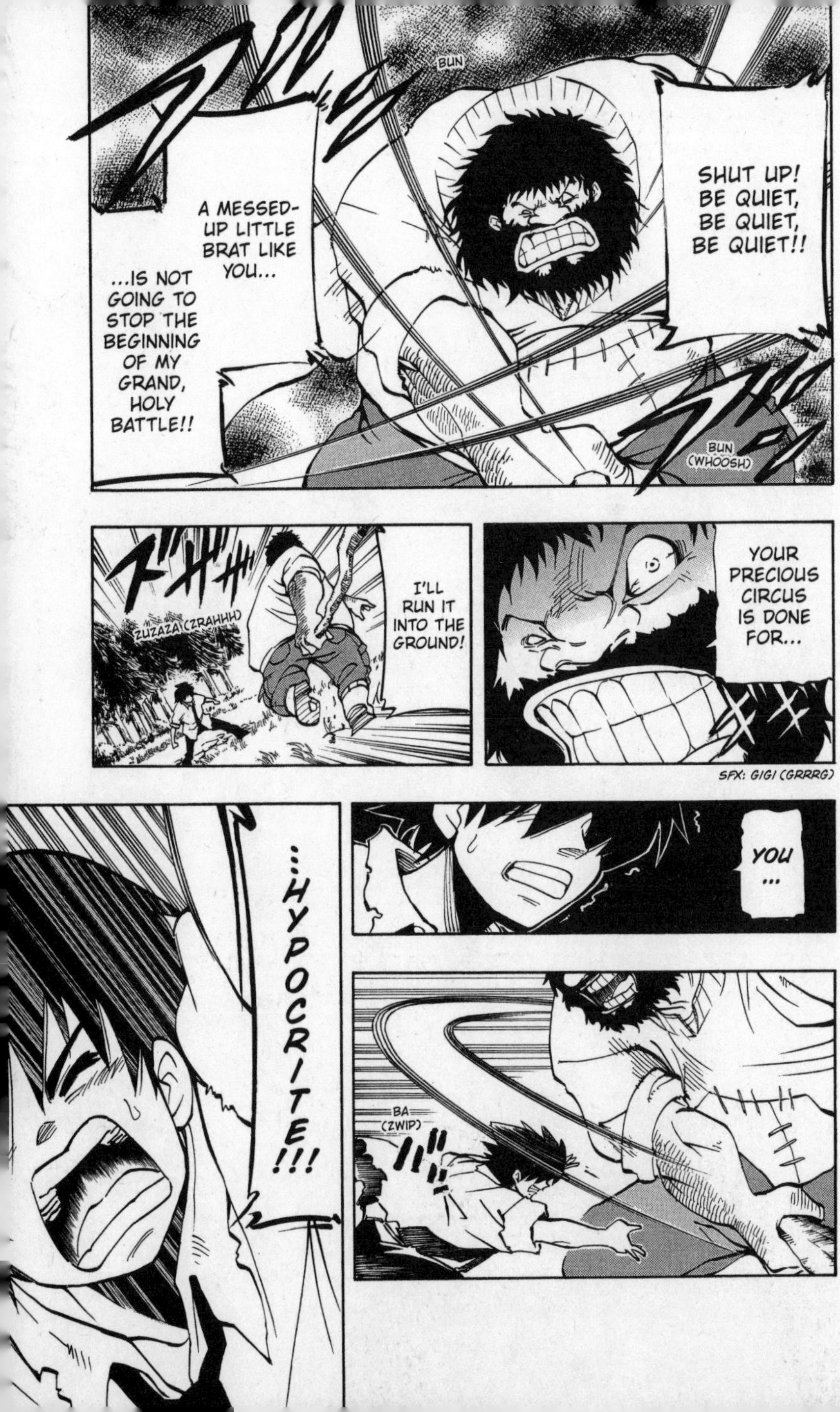
SHUT UP! BE QUIET, BE QUIET, BE QUIET!!
BUN
A MESSED-UP LITTLE BRAT LIKE YOU...
...IS NOT GOING TO STOP THE BEGINNING OF MY GRAND, HOLY BATTLE!!
BUN (WHOOSH)
YOUR PRECIOUS CIRCUS IS DONE FOR...
SFX: GIGI (GRRRG)
I'LL RUN IT INTO THE GROUND!
ZUZAZA (ZRAHHH)
YOU ...
BA (ZWIP)
...HYPOCRITE!!!

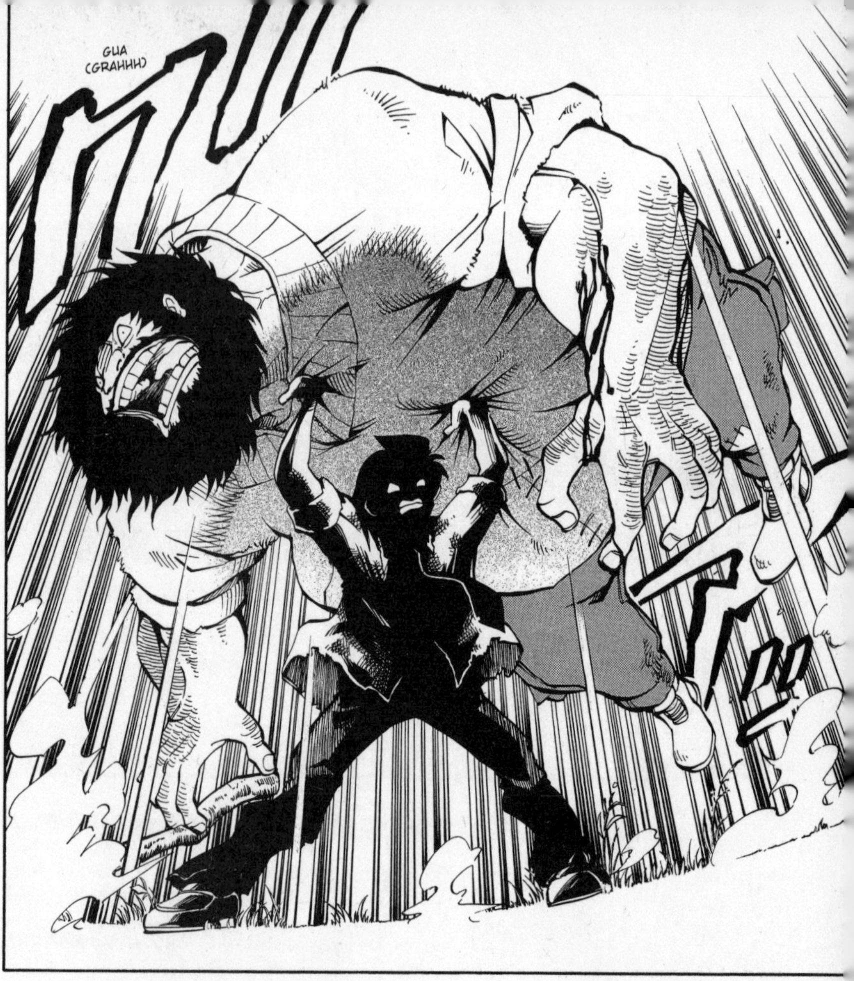
GUA
(GRAHHH)

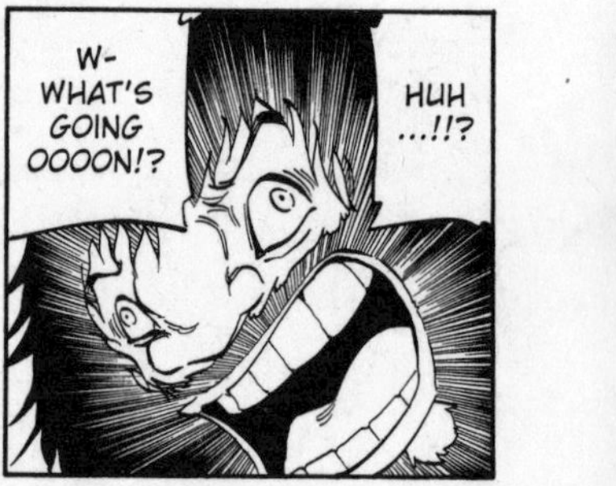
HUH
...!!?
W-
WHAT'S
GOING
OOOON!?

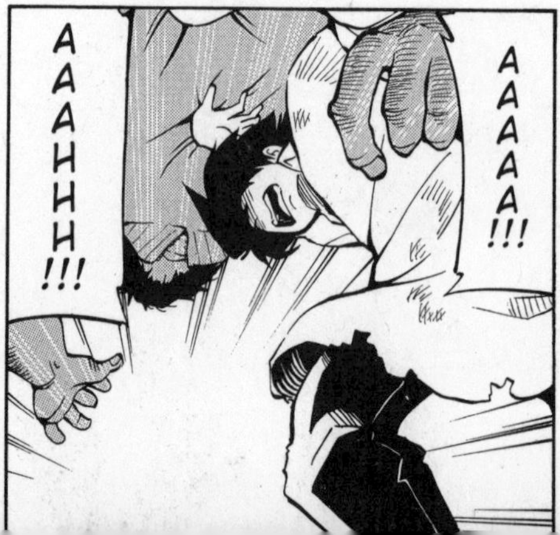
AAAAA!!!
AAAAHHH!!!

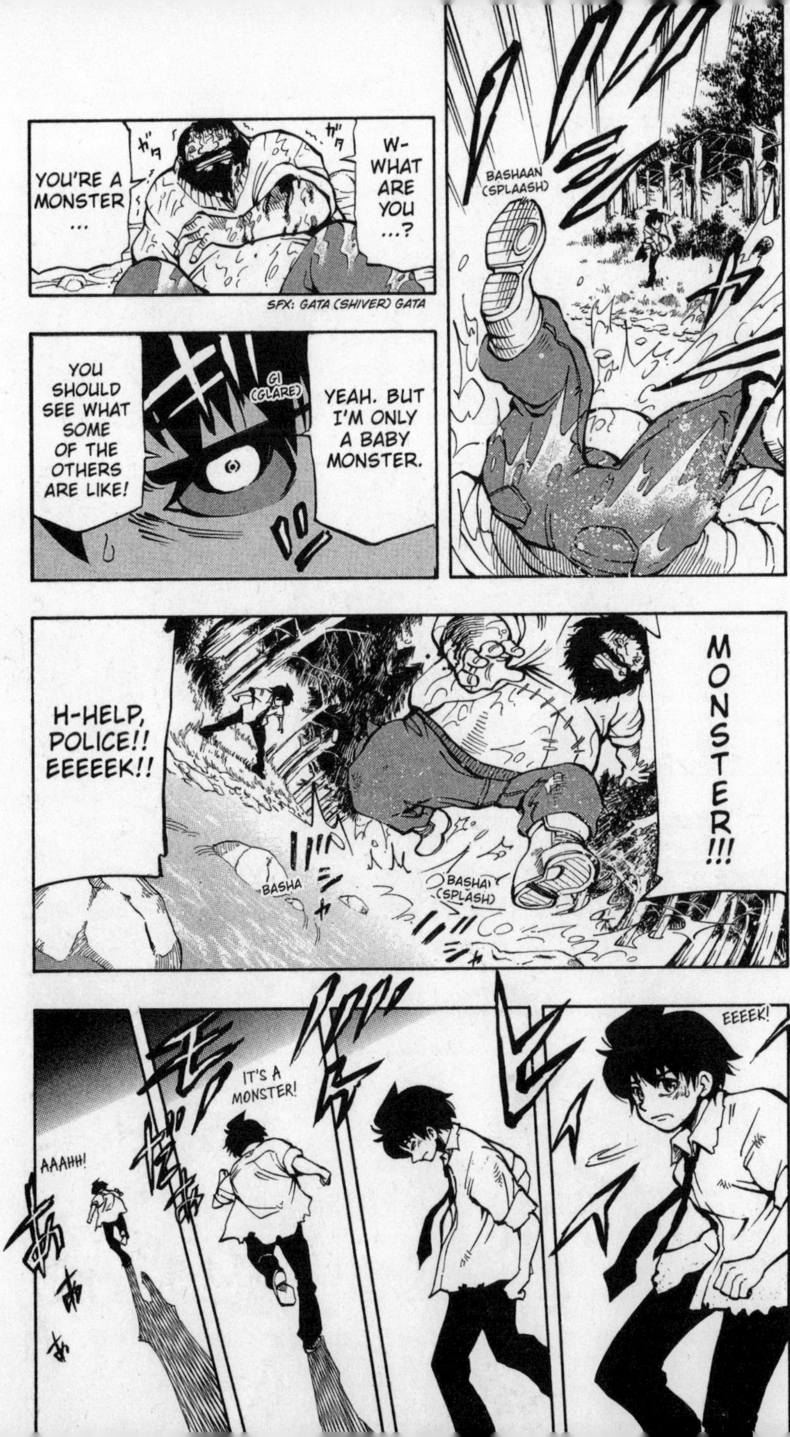
BASHAAN (SPLAASH)
W-WHAT ARE YOU ...?
YOU'RE A MONSTER ...
SFX: GATA (SHIVER) GATA
YEAH. BUT I'M ONLY A BABY MONSTER.
GI (GLARE)
YOU SHOULD SEE WHAT SOME OF THE OTHERS ARE LIKE!
MONSTER!!!
BASHA (SPLASH)
BASHA
H-HELP, POLICE!! EEEEEK!!
EEEEK!
IT'S A MONSTER!
AAAHH!

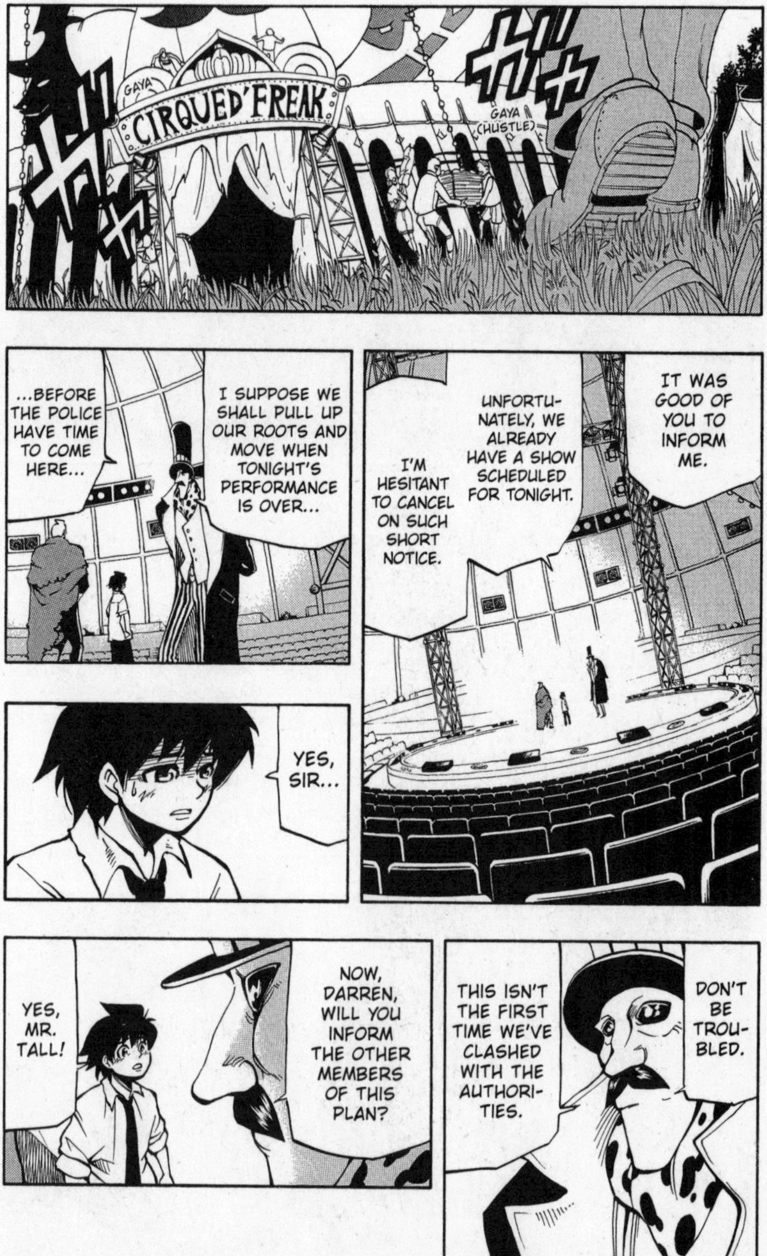
GAYA (HUSTLE)
GAYA
CIRQUE D'FREAK
IT WAS GOOD OF YOU TO INFORM ME.
UNFORTUNATELY, WE ALREADY HAVE A SHOW SCHEDULED FOR TONIGHT.
I'M HESITANT TO CANCEL ON SUCH SHORT NOTICE.
I SUPPOSE WE SHALL PULL UP OUR ROOTS AND MOVE WHEN TONIGHT'S PERFORMANCE IS OVER...
...BEFORE THE POLICE HAVE TIME TO COME HERE...
YES, SIR...
DON'T BE TROUBLED.
THIS ISN'T THE FIRST TIME WE'VE CLASHED WITH THE AUTHORITIES.
NOW, DARREN, WILL YOU INFORM THE OTHER MEMBERS OF THIS PLAN?
YES, MR. TALL!

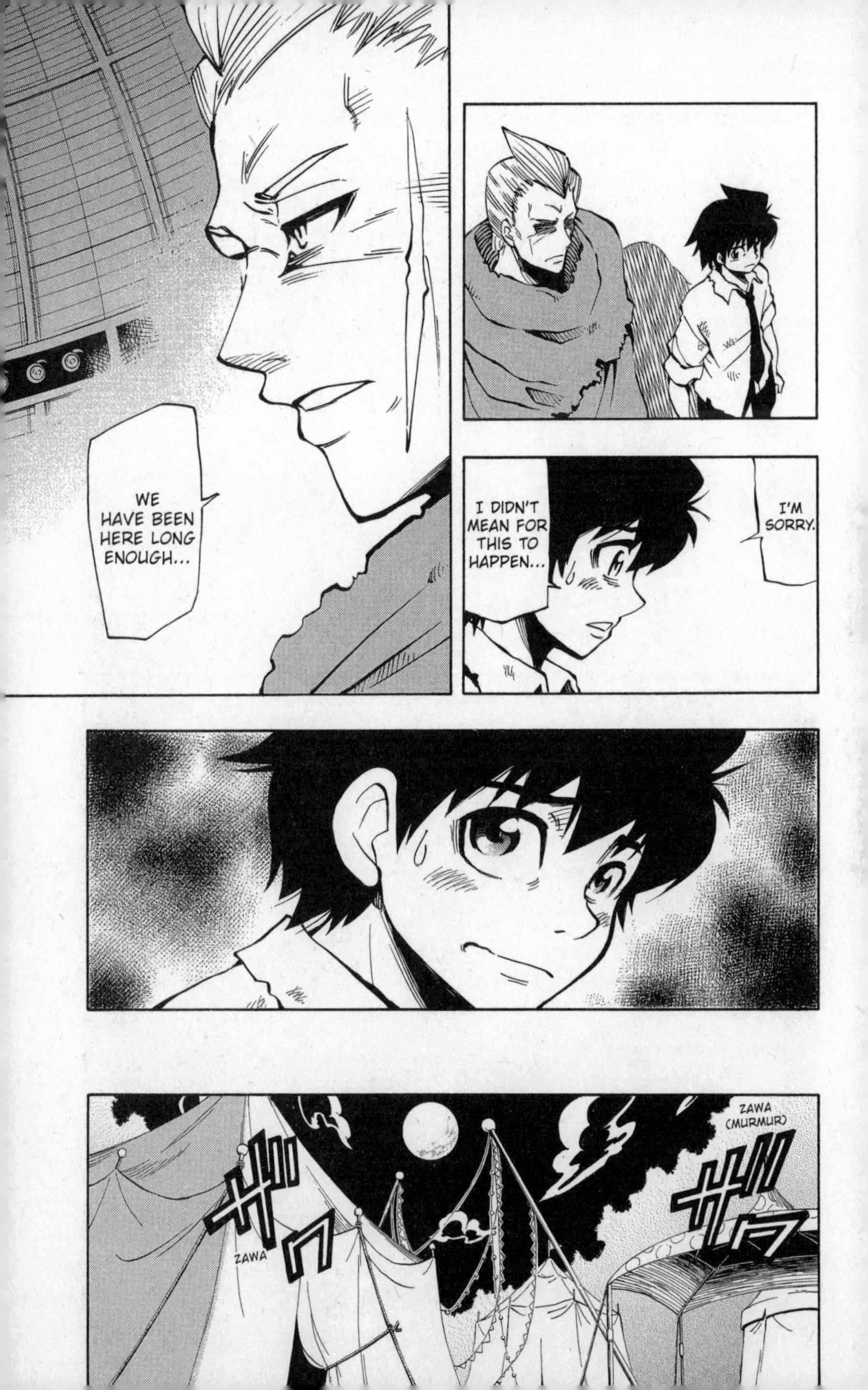
I'M SORRY.
I DIDN'T MEAN FOR THIS TO HAPPEN...
WE HAVE BEEN HERE LONG ENOUGH...
ZAWA (MURMUR)
ZAWA

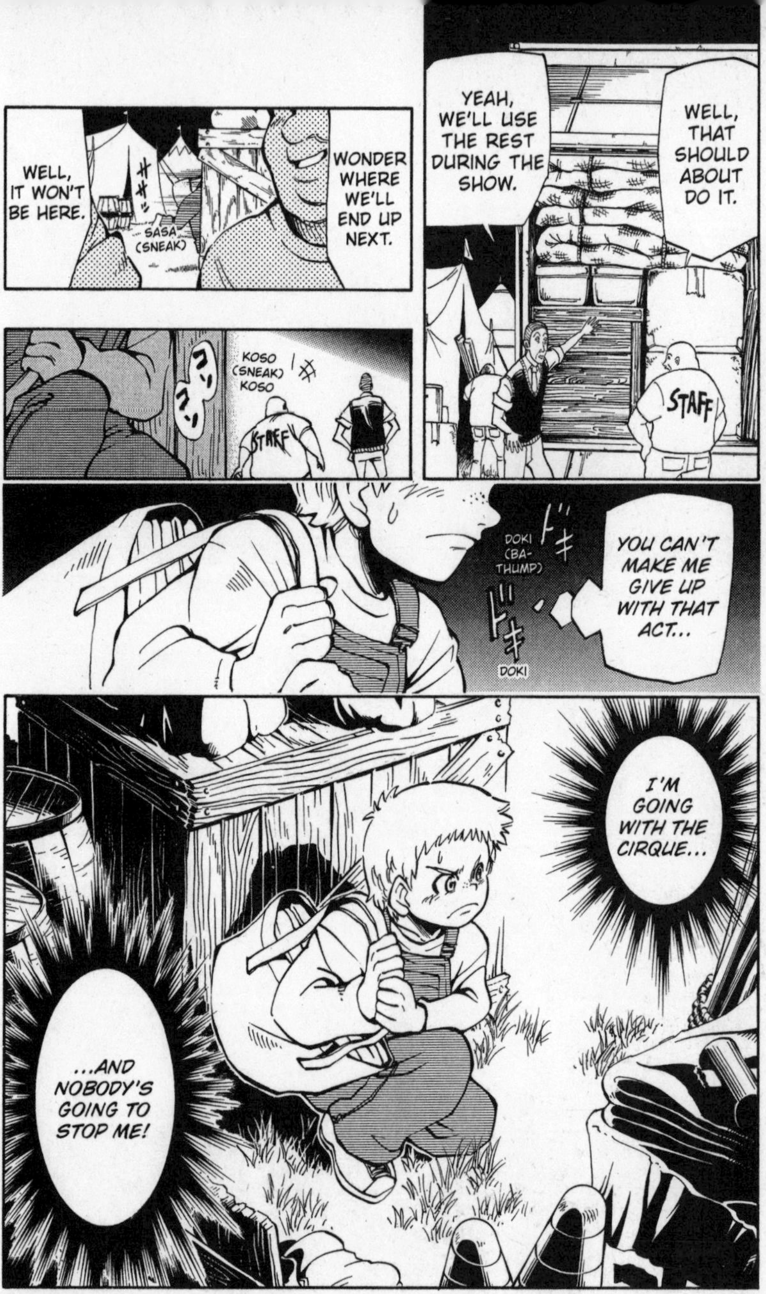
WELL, THAT SHOULD ABOUT DO IT.
YEAH, WE'LL USE THE REST DURING THE SHOW.
STAFF
WONDER WHERE WE'LL END UP NEXT.
WELL, IT WON'T BE HERE.
SASA (SNEAK)
KOSO (SNEAK) KOSO
STAFF
YOU CAN'T MAKE ME GIVE UP WITH THAT ACT...
DOKI (BA-THUMP)
DOKI
I'M GOING WITH THE CIRQUE...
...AND NOBODY'S GOING TO STOP ME!

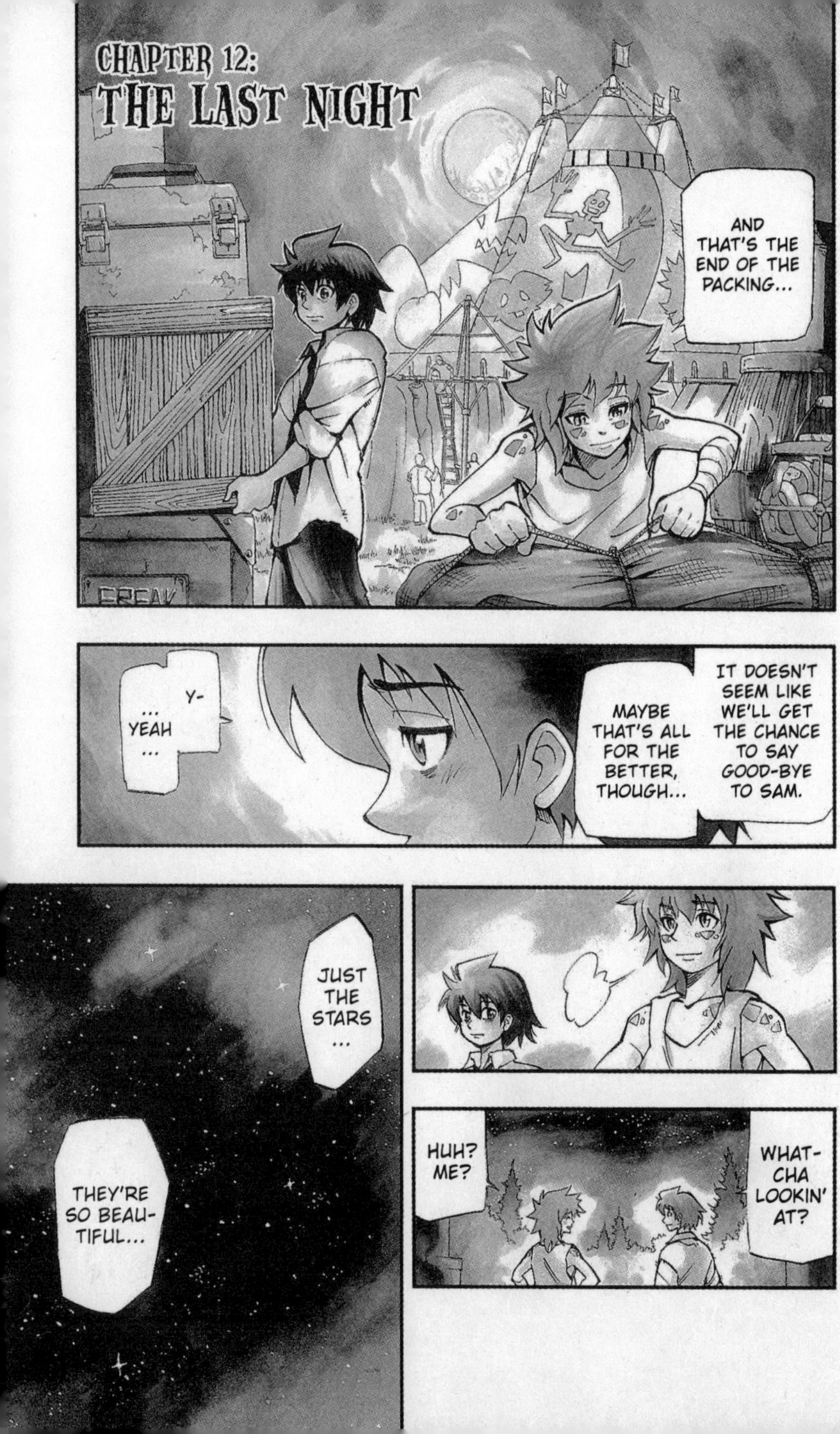
CHAPTER 12:
THE LAST NIGHT
AND THAT'S THE END OF THE PACKING...
IT DOESN'T SEEM LIKE WE'LL GET THE CHANCE TO SAY GOOD-BYE TO SAM.
MAYBE THAT'S ALL FOR THE BETTER, THOUGH...
Y- ... YEAH ...
WHAT-CHA LOOKIN' AT?
HUH? ME?
JUST THE STARS ...
THEY'RE SO BEAU-TIFUL...

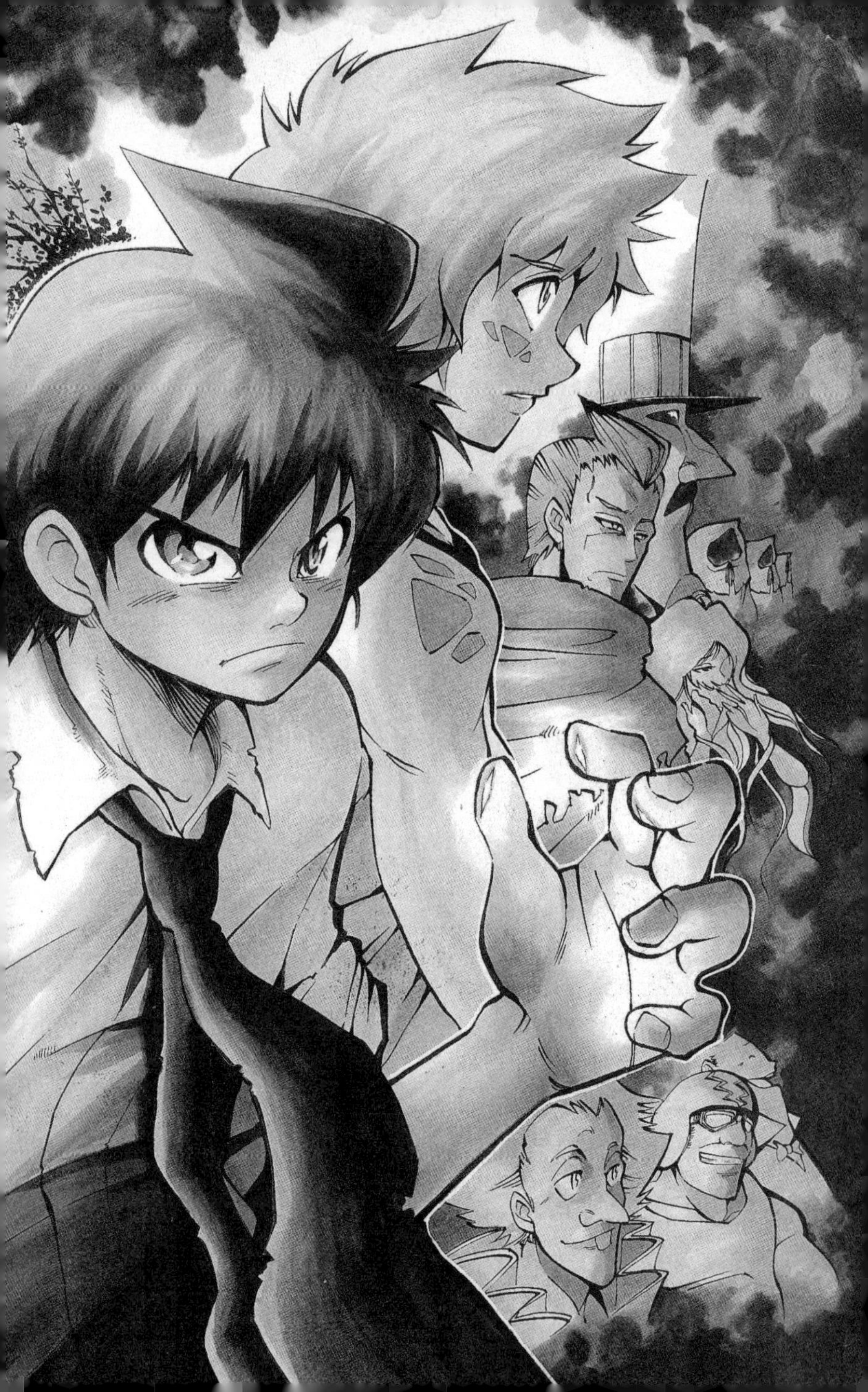

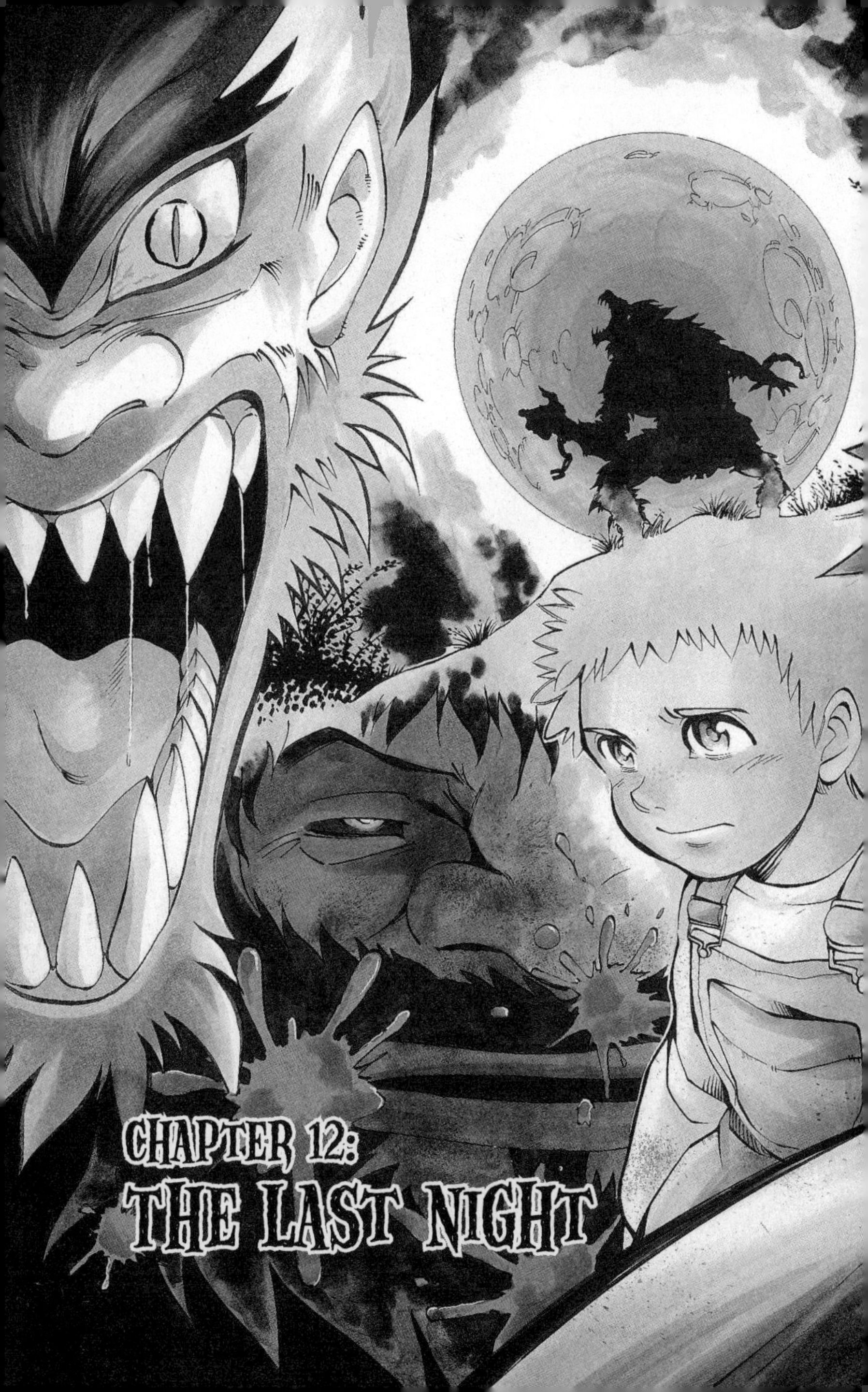
CHAPTER 12:
THE LAST NIGHT

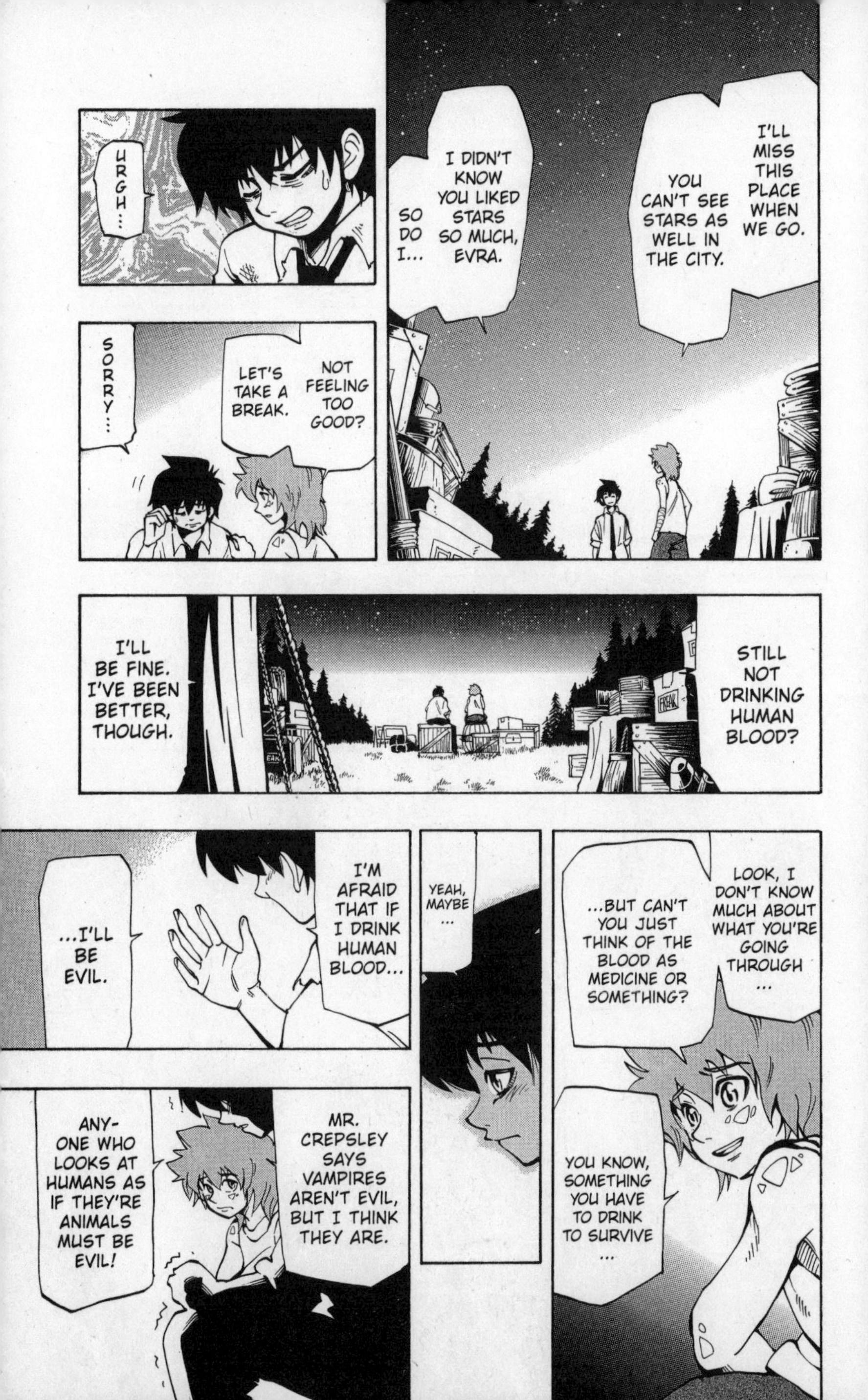
I'LL MISS THIS PLACE WHEN WE GO.
YOU CAN'T SEE STARS AS WELL IN THE CITY.
I DIDN'T KNOW YOU LIKED STARS SO MUCH, EVRA.
SO DO I...
URGH...
NOT FEELING TOO GOOD?
LET'S TAKE A BREAK.
SORRY...
STILL NOT DRINKING HUMAN BLOOD?
I'LL BE FINE. I'VE BEEN BETTER, THOUGH.
LOOK, I DON'T KNOW MUCH ABOUT WHAT YOU'RE GOING THROUGH...
...BUT CAN'T YOU JUST THINK OF THE BLOOD AS MEDICINE OR SOMETHING?
YOU KNOW, SOMETHING YOU HAVE TO DRINK TO SURVIVE...
YEAH, MAYBE...
I'M AFRAID THAT IF I DRINK HUMAN BLOOD...
...I'LL BE EVIL.
MR. CREPSLEY SAYS VAMPIRES AREN'T EVIL, BUT I THINK THEY ARE.
ANY-ONE WHO LOOKS AT HUMANS AS IF THEY'RE ANIMALS MUST BE EVIL!

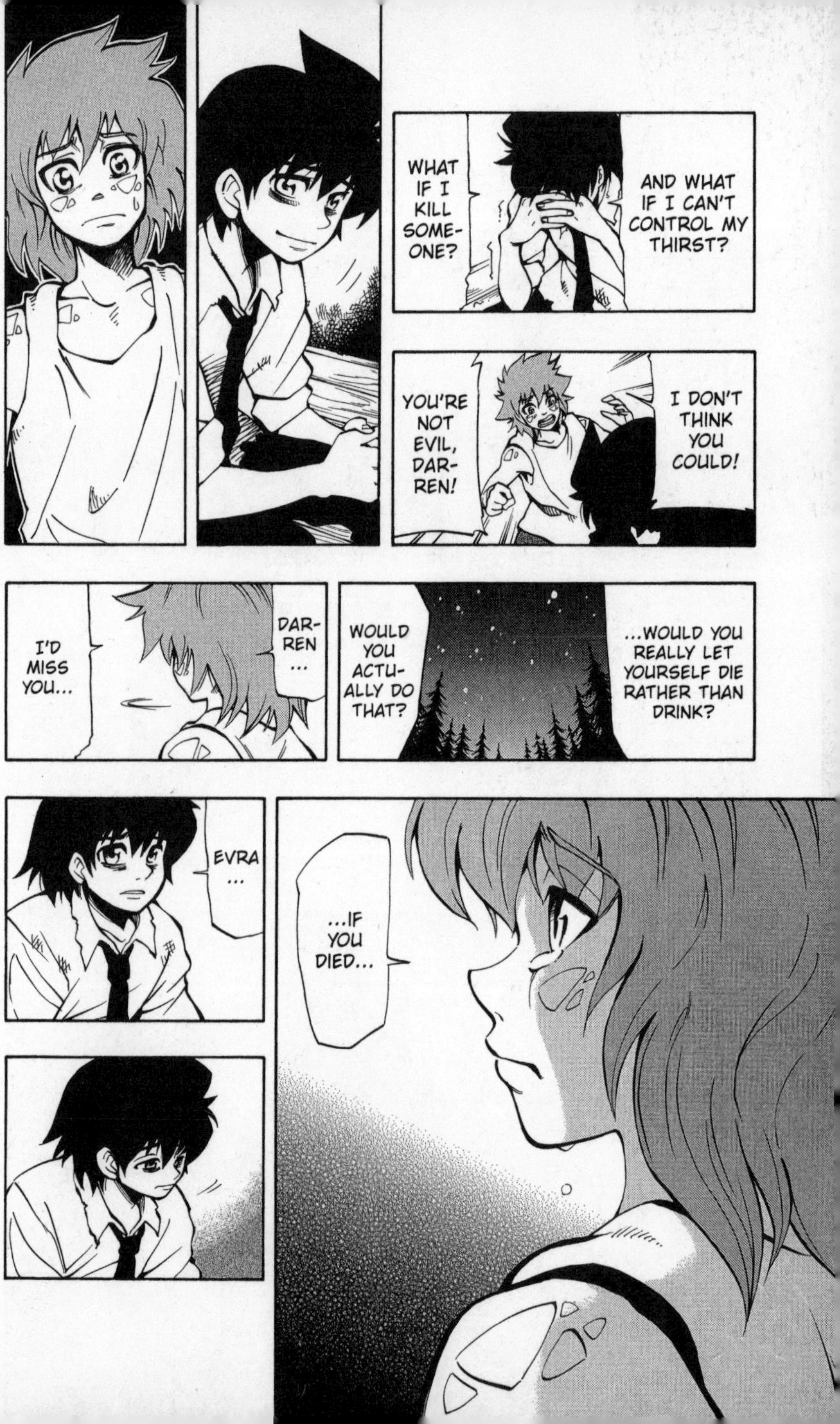
AND WHAT IF I CAN'T CONTROL MY THIRST?
WHAT IF I KILL SOMEONE?
I DON'T THINK YOU COULD!
YOU'RE NOT EVIL, DARREN!
...WOULD YOU REALLY LET YOURSELF DIE RATHER THAN DRINK?
WOULD YOU ACTUALLY DO THAT?
DARREN...
I'D MISS YOU...
...IF YOU DIED...
EVRA...

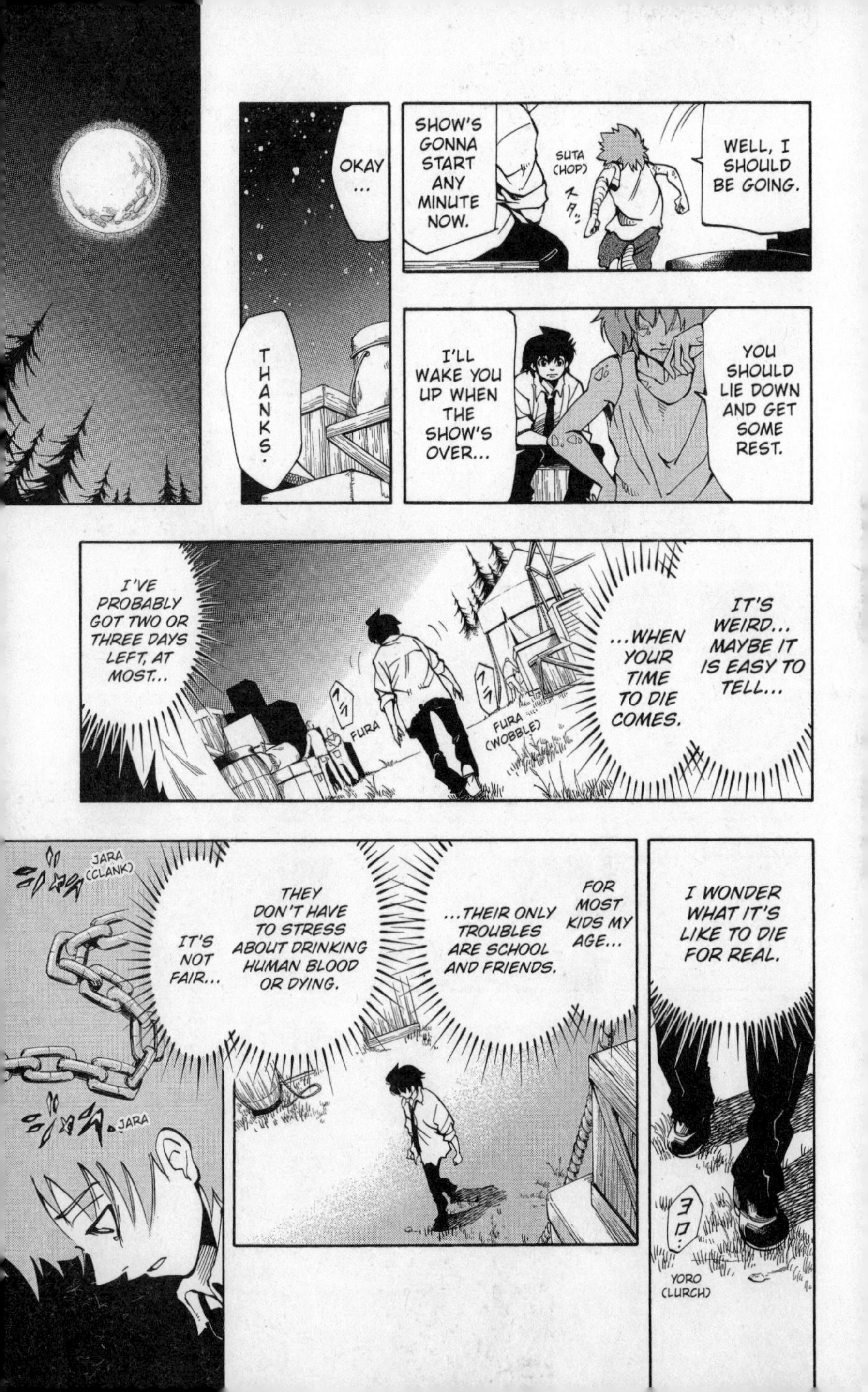
WELL, I SHOULD BE GOING.
SUTA (HOP)
SHOW'S GONNA START ANY MINUTE NOW.
YOU SHOULD LIE DOWN AND GET SOME REST.
I'LL WAKE YOU UP WHEN THE SHOW'S OVER...
OKAY...
THANKS.
IT'S WEIRD... MAYBE IT IS EASY TO TELL...
...WHEN YOUR TIME TO DIE COMES.
FURA (WOBBLE)
FURA
I'VE PROBABLY GOT TWO OR THREE DAYS LEFT, AT MOST...
I WONDER WHAT IT'S LIKE TO DIE FOR REAL.
YORO (LURCH)
FOR MOST KIDS MY AGE...
...THEIR ONLY TROUBLES ARE SCHOOL AND FRIENDS.
THEY DON'T HAVE TO STRESS ABOUT DRINKING HUMAN BLOOD OR DYING.
IT'S NOT FAIR...
JARA (CLANK)
JARA

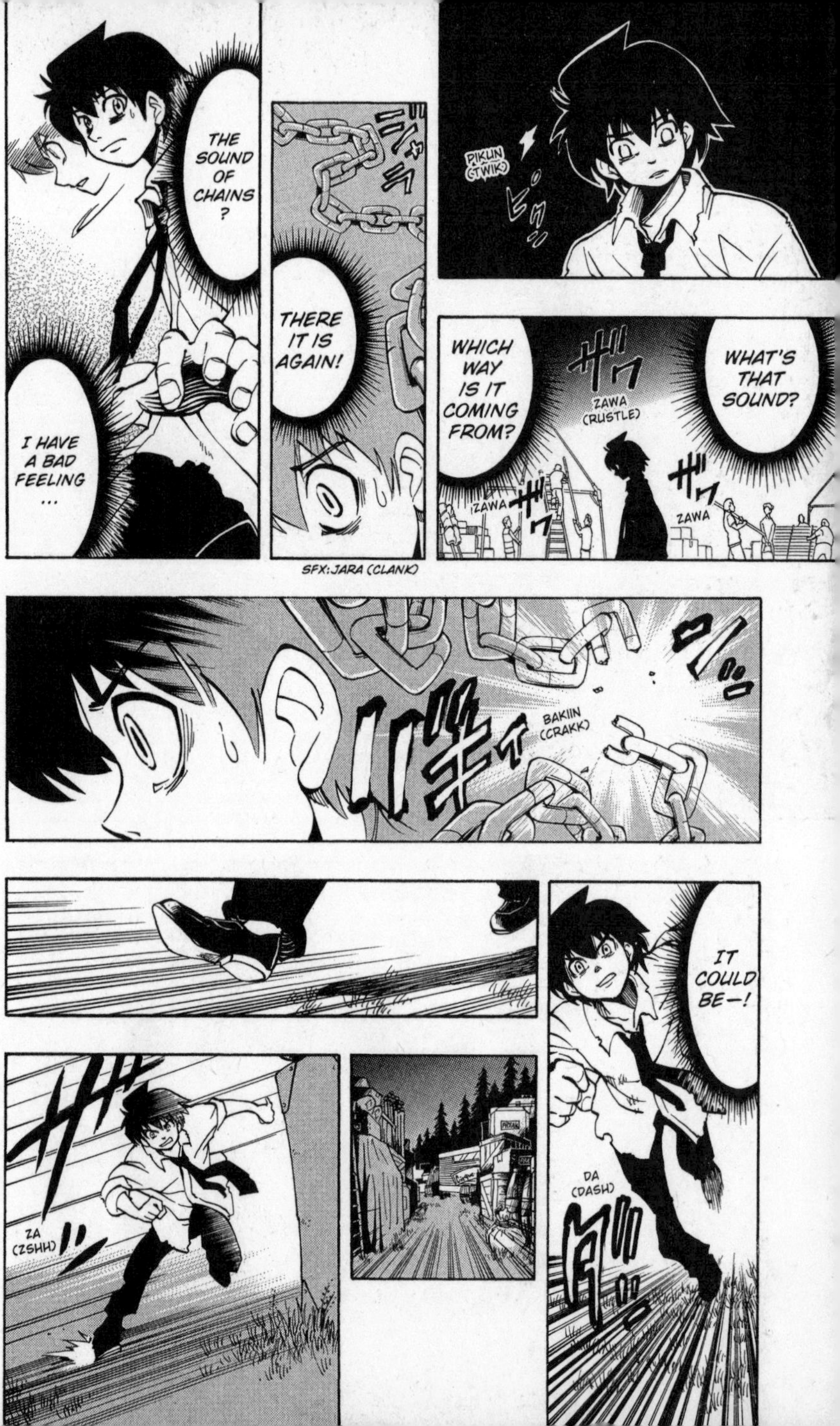
PIKUN (TWIK)
WHAT'S THAT SOUND?
ZAWA (RUSTLE)
WHICH WAY IS IT COMING FROM?
ZAWA
ZAWA
THERE IT IS AGAIN!
THE SOUND OF CHAINS?
I HAVE A BAD FEELING...
SFX: JARA (CLANK)
BAKIIN (CRAKK)
IT COULD BE—!
DA (DASH)
ZA (ZSHH)

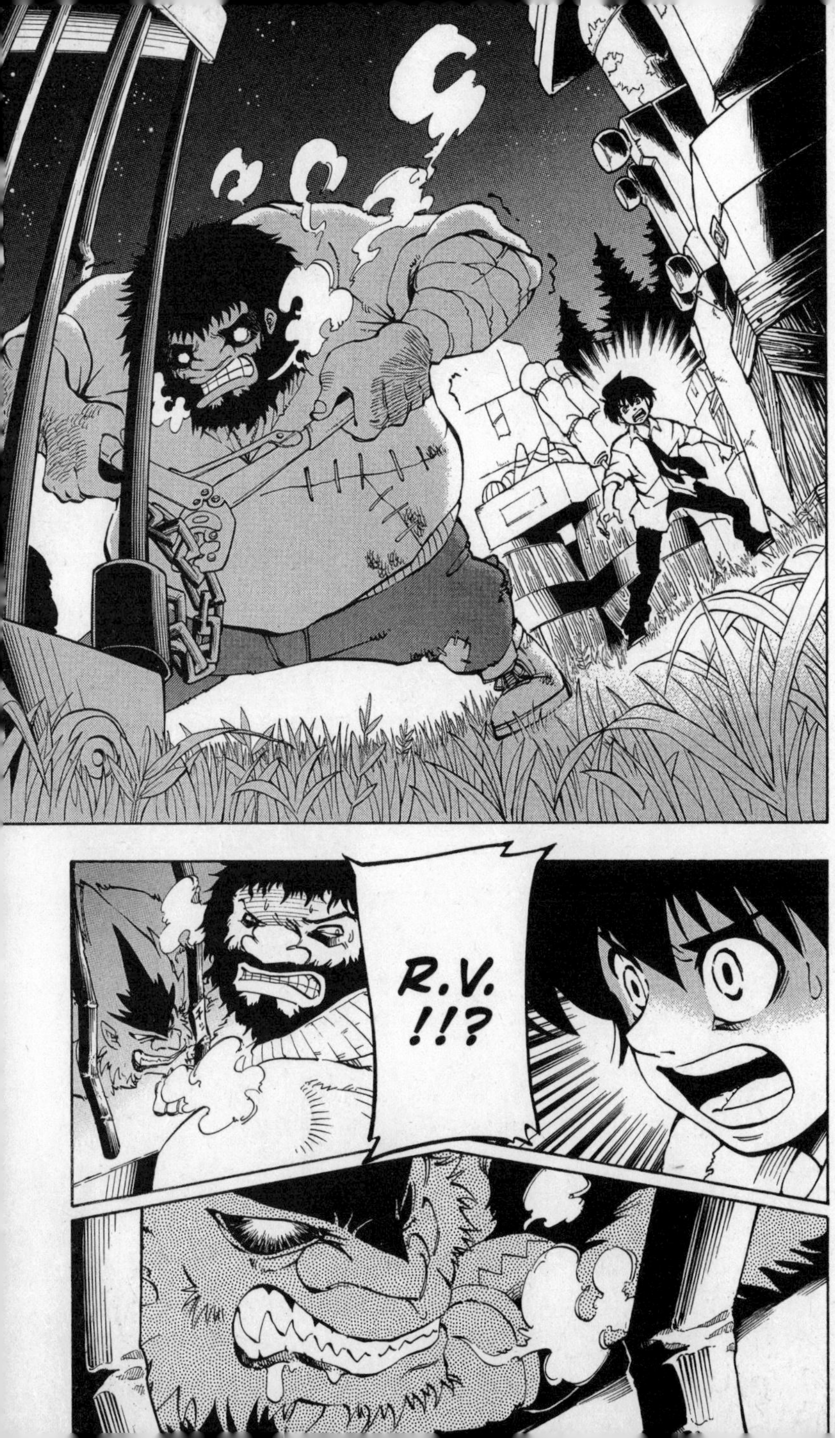
R.V. !!?

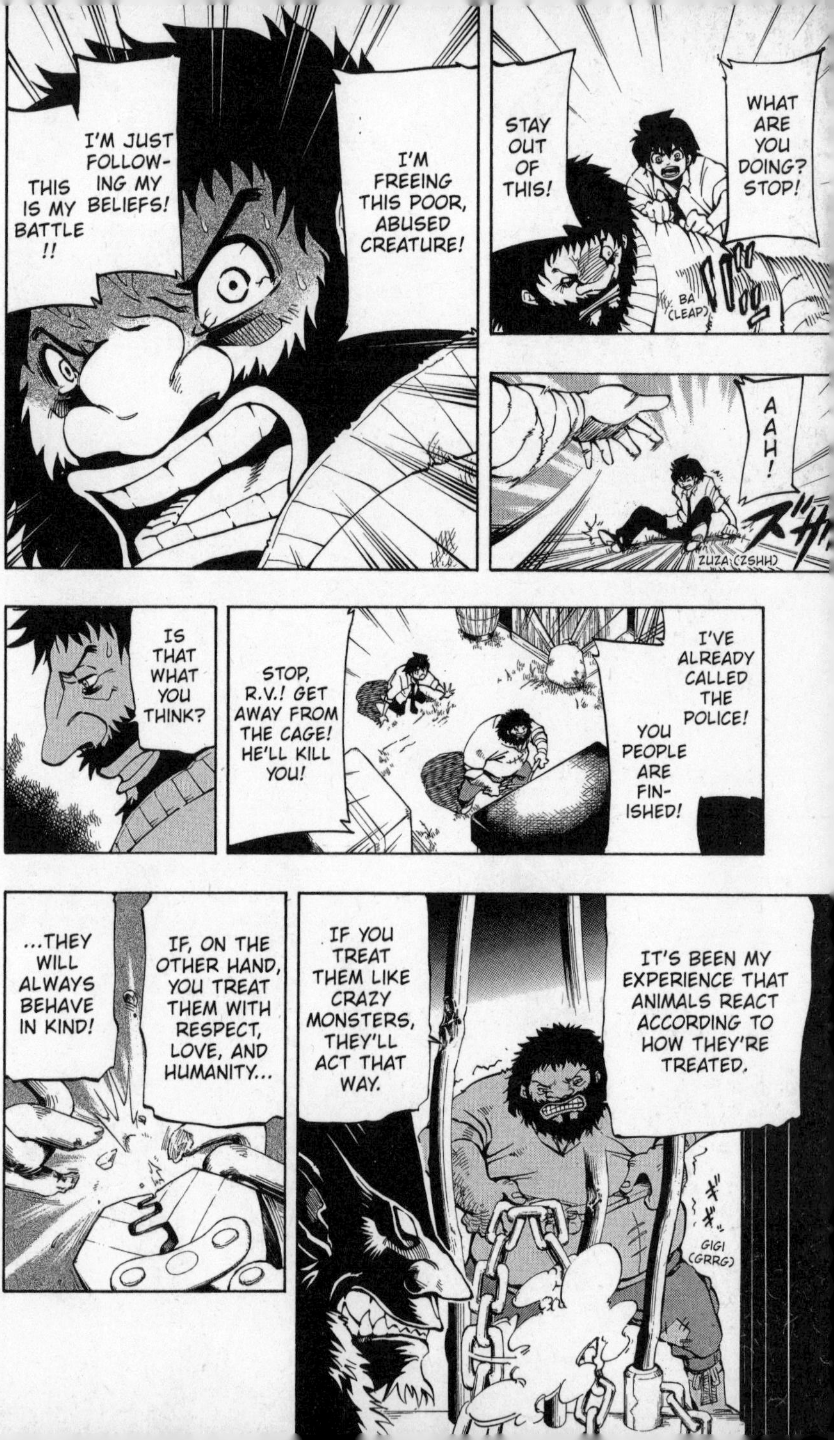
WHAT ARE YOU DOING? STOP!
STAY OUT OF THIS!
BA (LEAP)
AAH!
ZUZA (ZSHH)
I'M FREEING THIS POOR, ABUSED CREATURE!
I'M JUST FOLLOWING MY BELIEFS!
THIS IS MY BATTLE!!
I'VE ALREADY CALLED THE POLICE!
YOU PEOPLE ARE FINISHED!
STOP, R.V.! GET AWAY FROM THE CAGE! HE'LL KILL YOU!
IS THAT WHAT YOU THINK?
IT'S BEEN MY EXPERIENCE THAT ANIMALS REACT ACCORDING TO HOW THEY'RE TREATED.
GIGI (GRRG)
IF YOU TREAT THEM LIKE CRAZY MONSTERS, THEY'LL ACT THAT WAY.
IF, ON THE OTHER HAND, YOU TREAT THEM WITH RESPECT, LOVE, AND HUMANITY...
...THEY WILL ALWAYS BEHAVE IN KIND!

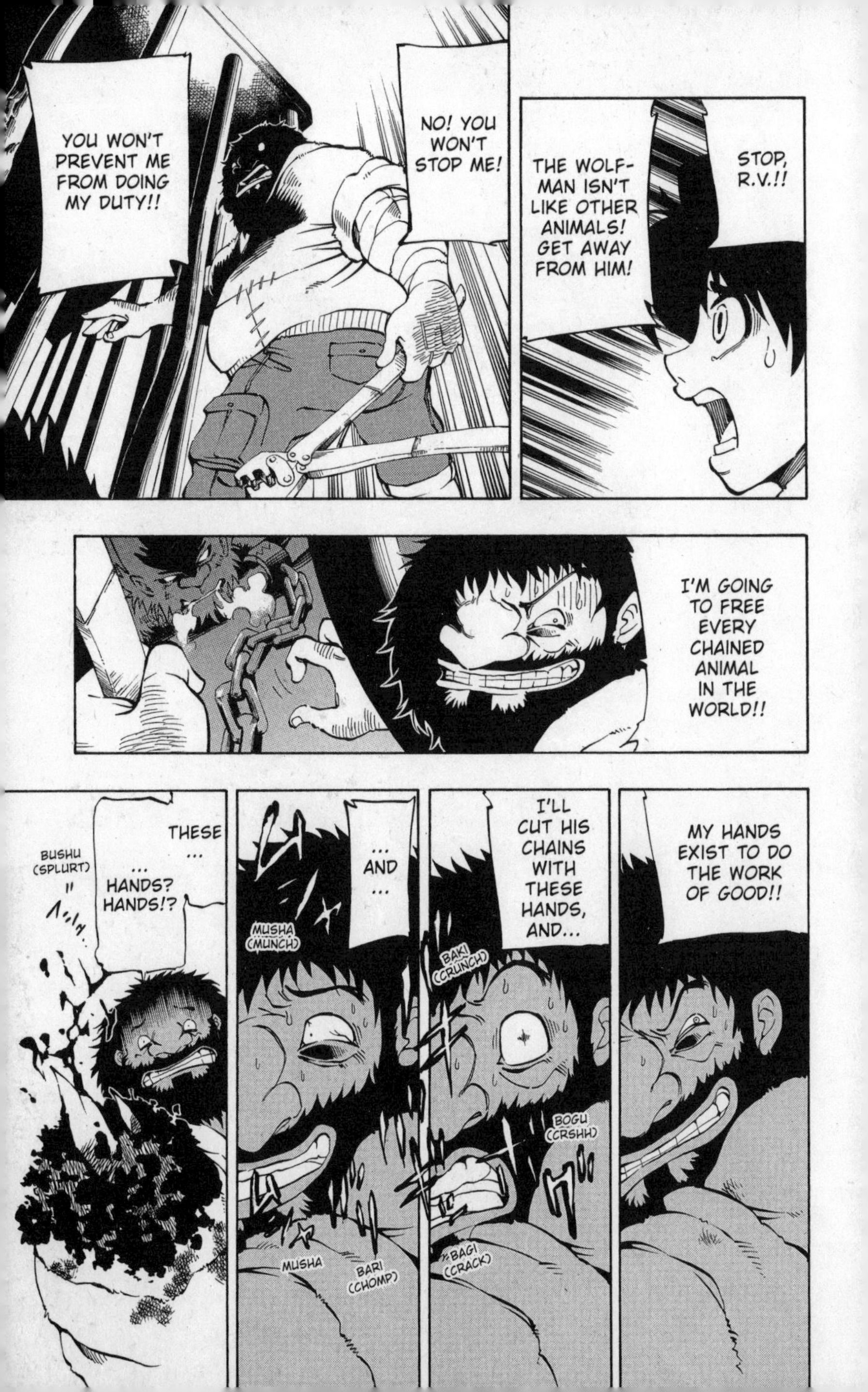
STOP, R.V.!!
THE WOLF-MAN ISN'T LIKE OTHER ANIMALS! GET AWAY FROM HIM!
NO! YOU WON'T STOP ME!
YOU WON'T PREVENT ME FROM DOING MY DUTY!!
I'M GOING TO FREE EVERY CHAINED ANIMAL IN THE WORLD!!
MY HANDS EXIST TO DO THE WORK OF GOOD!!
I'LL CUT HIS CHAINS WITH THESE HANDS, AND...
BAKI (CRUNCH)
BOGU (CRSHH)
BAGI (CRACK)
... AND ...
MUSHA (MUNCH)
MUSHA
BARI (CHOMP)
THESE ...
... HANDS? HANDS!?
BUSHU (SPLURT)

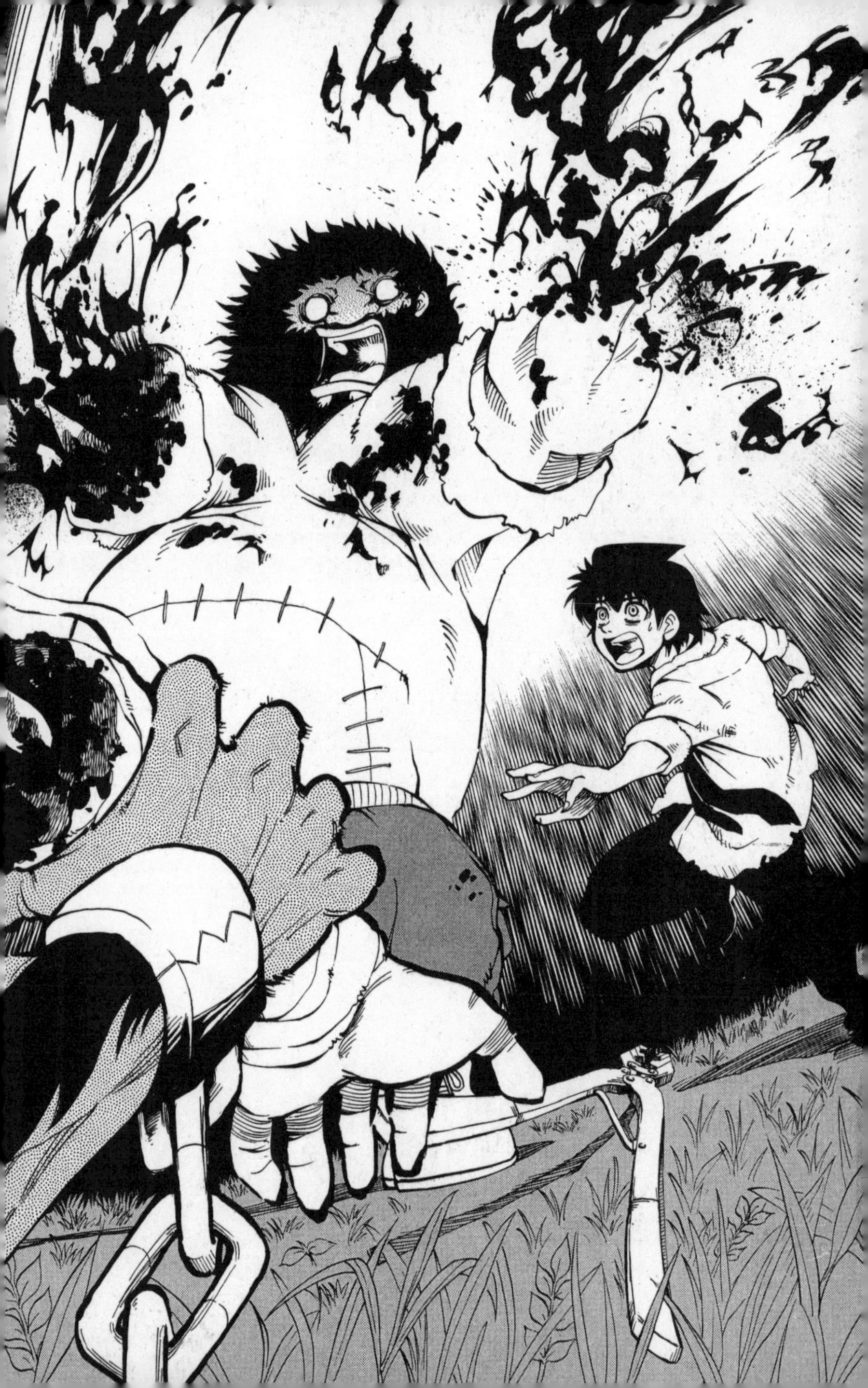

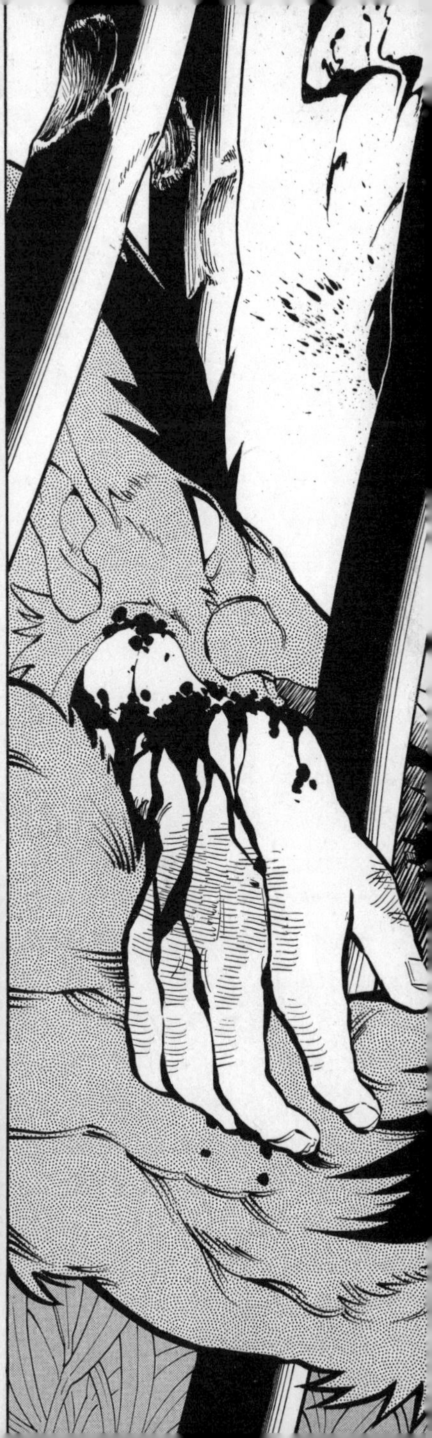

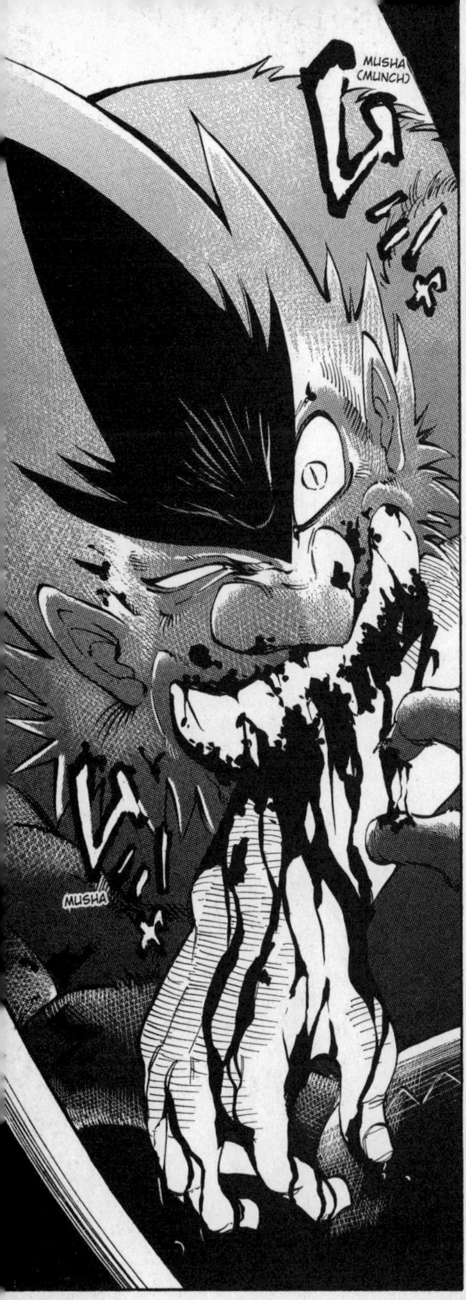
MUSHA
(MUNCH)
MUSHA

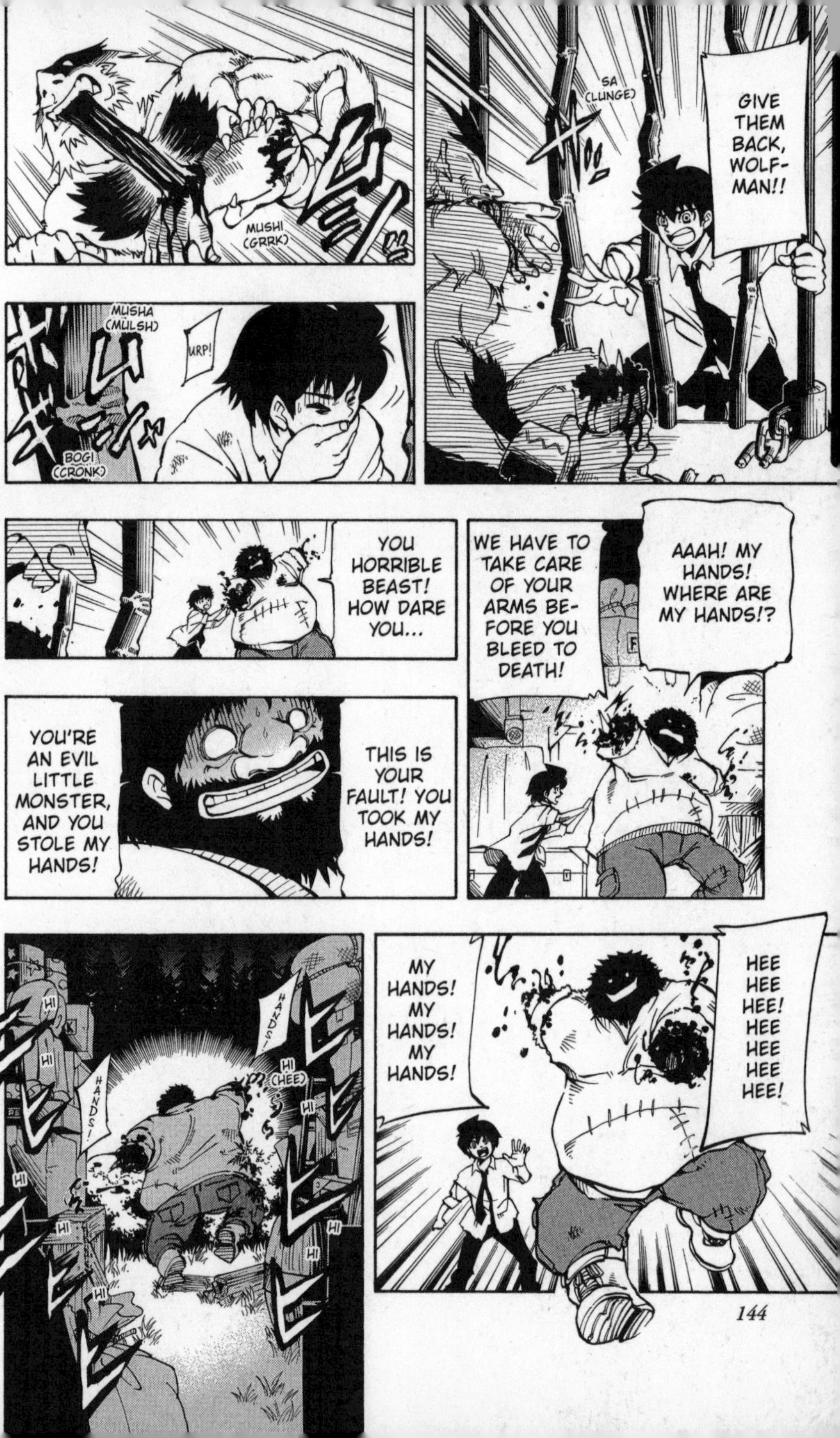
SA
(LUNGE)
GIVE THEM BACK, WOLF-MAN!!
MUSHI
(GRRK)
MUSHA
(MÜLSH)
URP!
BOGI
(CRONK)
AAAH! MY HANDS! WHERE ARE MY HANDS!?
WE HAVE TO TAKE CARE OF YOUR ARMS BE-FORE YOU BLEED TO DEATH!
YOU HORRIBLE BEAST! HOW DARE YOU...
THIS IS YOUR FAULT! YOU TOOK MY HANDS!
YOU'RE AN EVIL LITTLE MONSTER, AND YOU STOLE MY HANDS!
HEE HEE HEE! HEE HEE HEE HEE!
MY HANDS! MY HANDS! MY HANDS!
HANDS!
HI
(CHEE)
HANDS!
HI
HI
HI
HI
HI
HI
HI

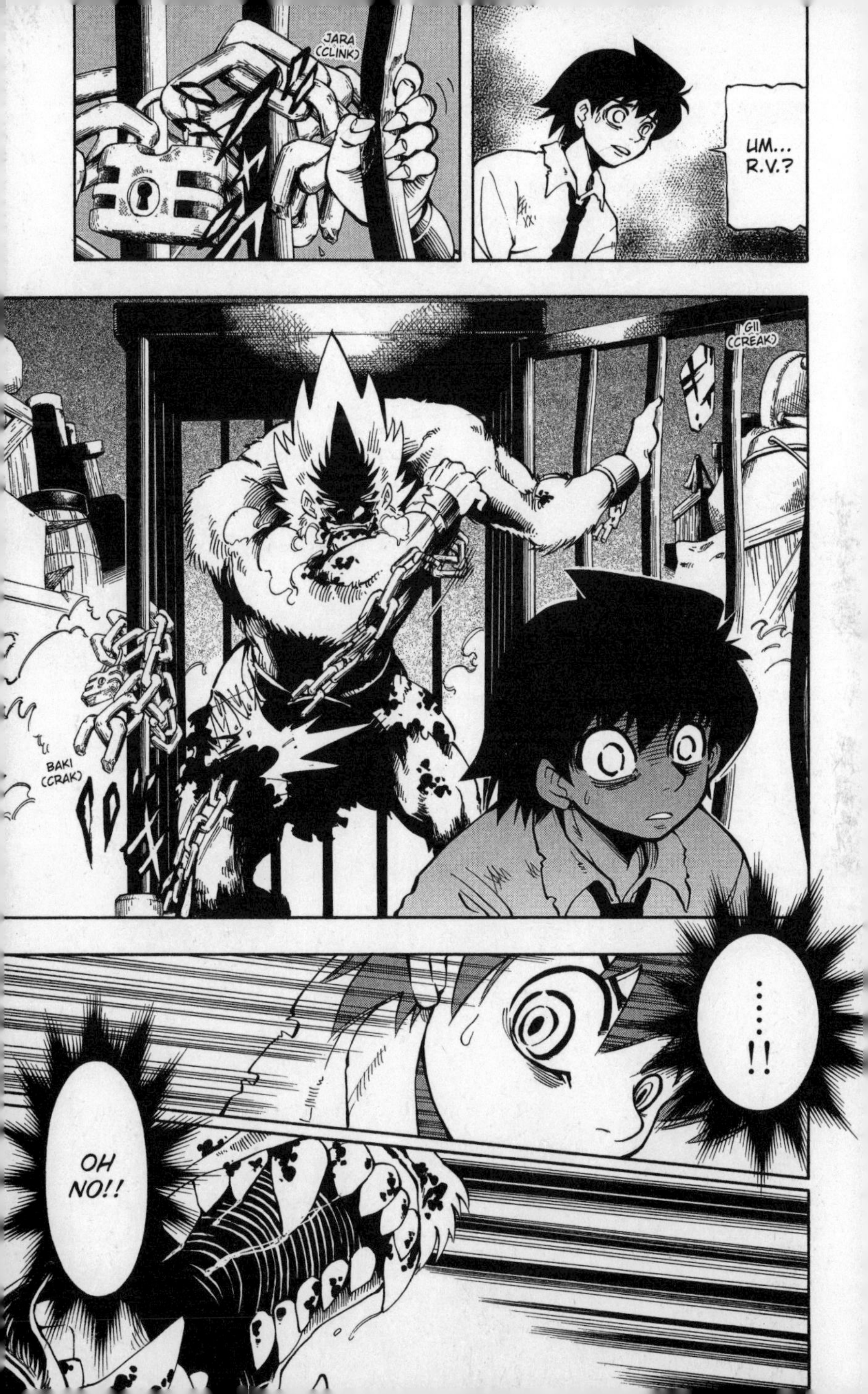
UM... R.V.?
JARA (CLINK)
GII (CREAK)
BAKI (CRAK)
.....!!
OH NO!!

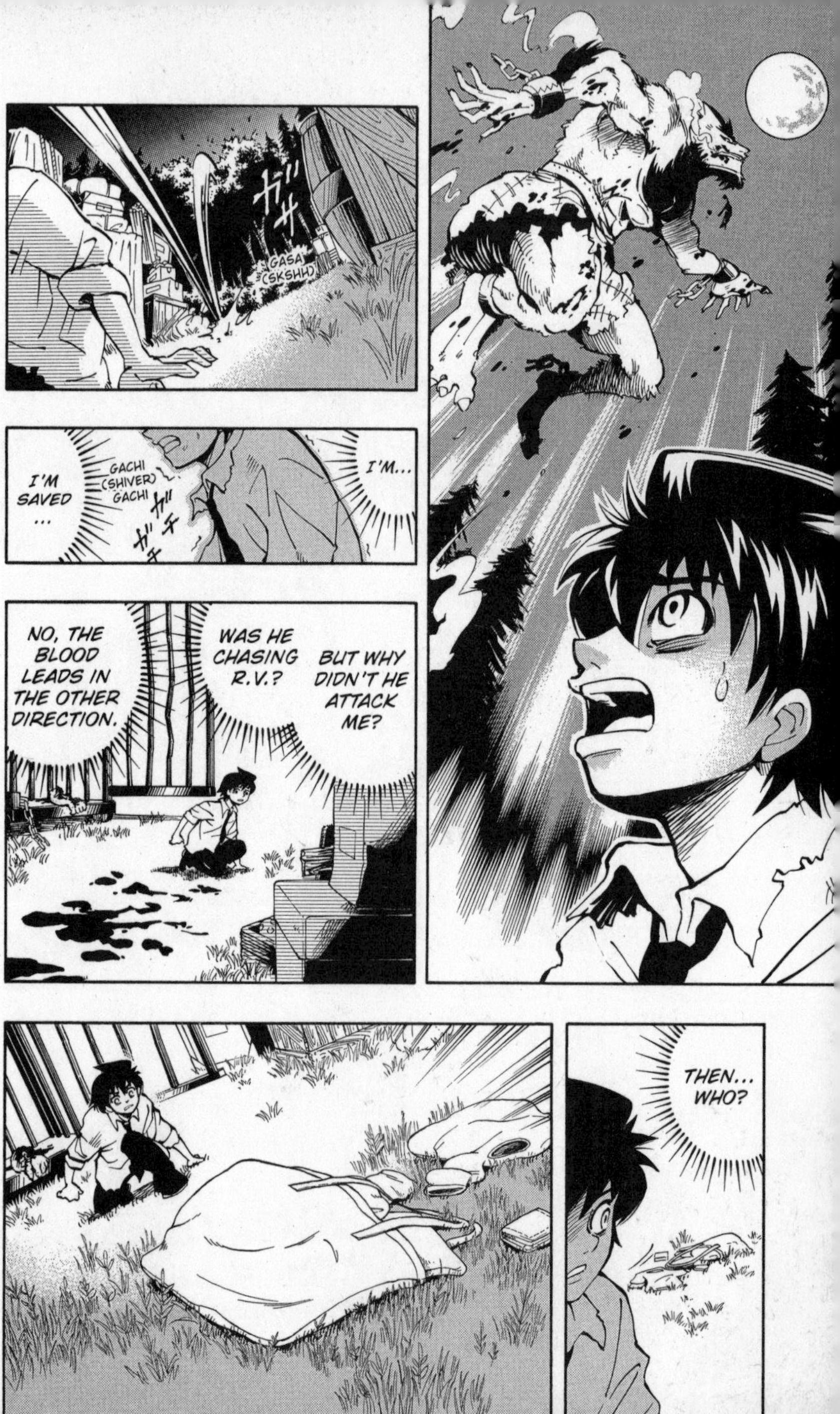
ガサ
GASA (SKSHH)
I'M...
ガチ ガチ
GACHI (SHIVER) GACHI
I'M SAVED...
BUT WHY DIDN'T HE ATTACK ME?
WAS HE CHASING R.V.?
NO, THE BLOOD LEADS IN THE OTHER DIRECTION.
THEN... WHO?

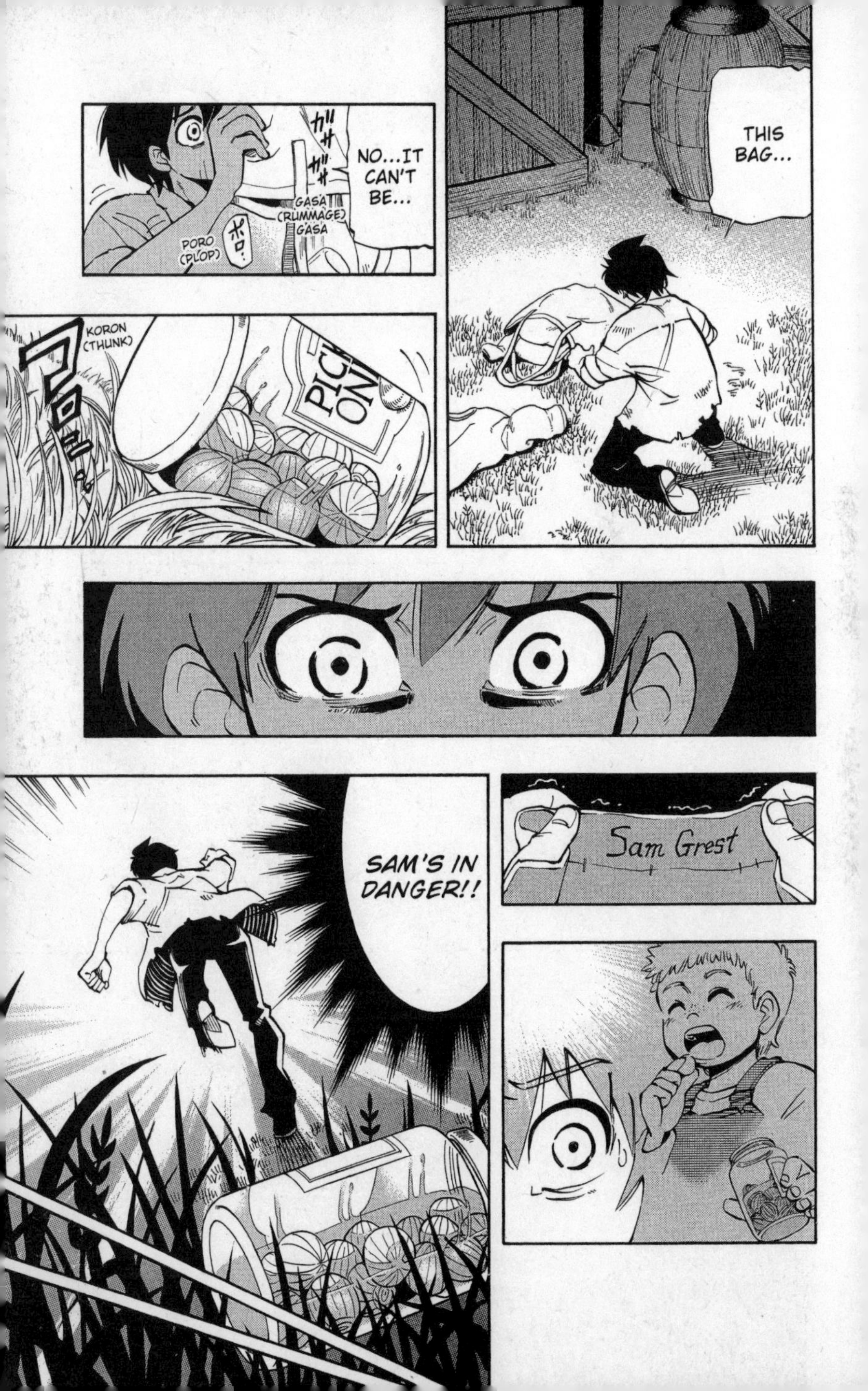
THIS BAG...
NO...IT CAN'T BE...
GASA (RUMMAGE) GASA
PORO (PLOP)
KORON (THUNK)
PIC ON
Sam Grest
SAM'S IN DANGER!!

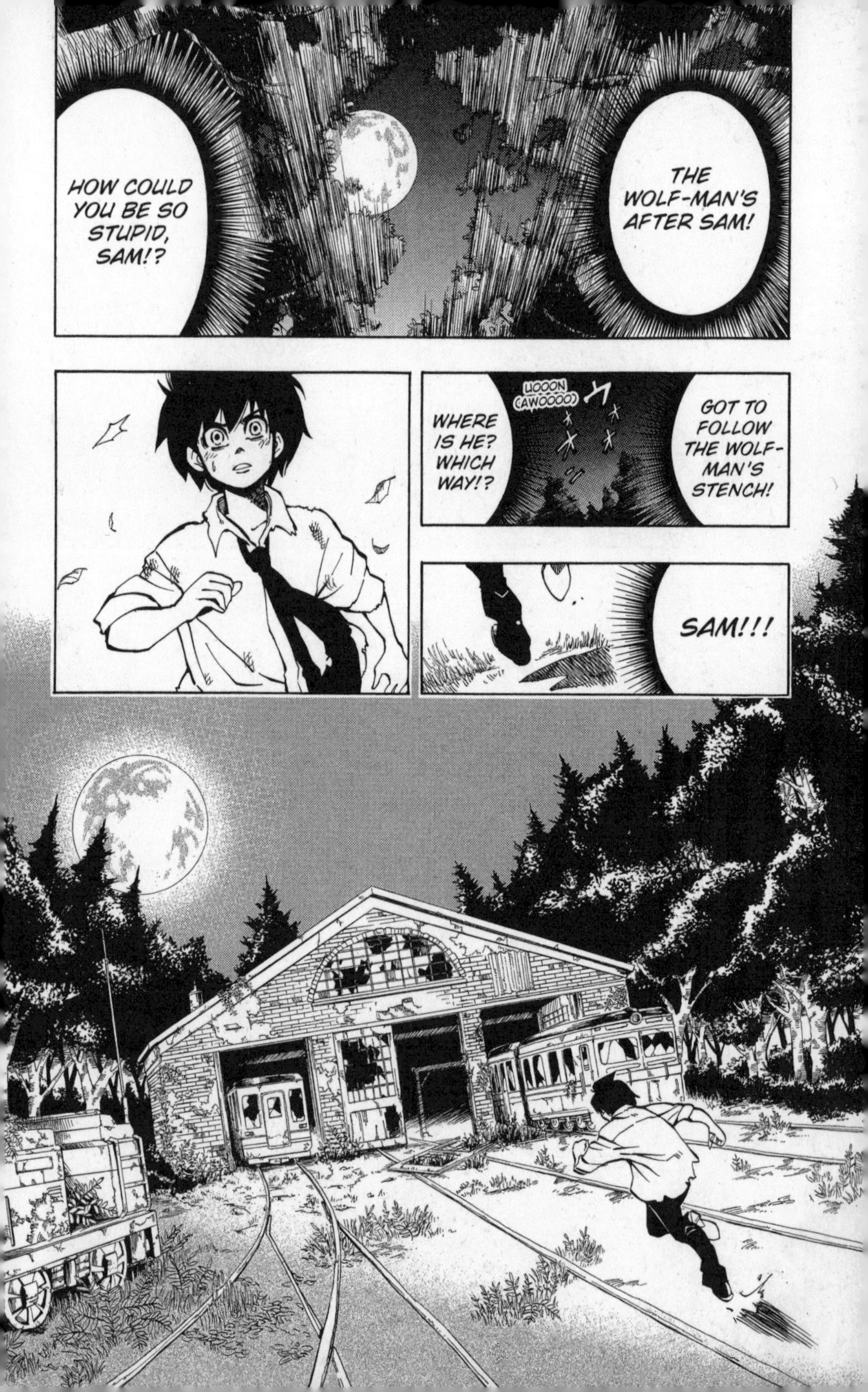
THE WOLF-MAN'S AFTER SAM!
HOW COULD YOU BE SO STUPID, SAM!?
GOT TO FOLLOW THE WOLF-MAN'S STENCH!
UOOON (AWOOOO)
WHERE IS HE? WHICH WAY!?
SAM!!!

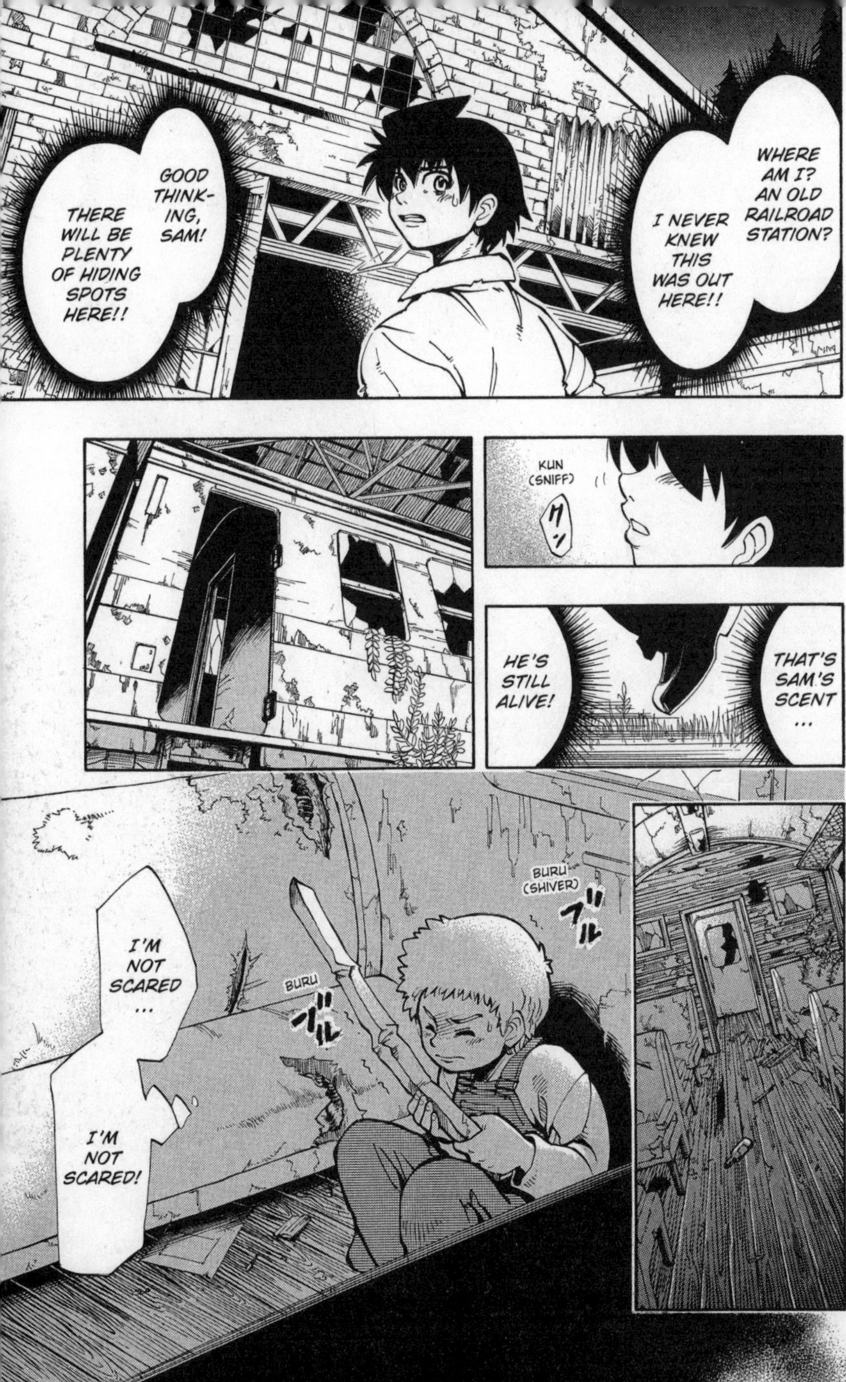
WHERE AM I? AN OLD RAILROAD STATION?
I NEVER KNEW THIS WAS OUT HERE!!
GOOD THINKING, SAM!
THERE WILL BE PLENTY OF HIDING SPOTS HERE!!
KUN (SNIFF)
クン
THAT'S SAM'S SCENT ...
HE'S STILL ALIVE!
BURU (SHIVER)
ブル
BURU
ブル
I'M NOT SCARED ...
I'M NOT SCARED!

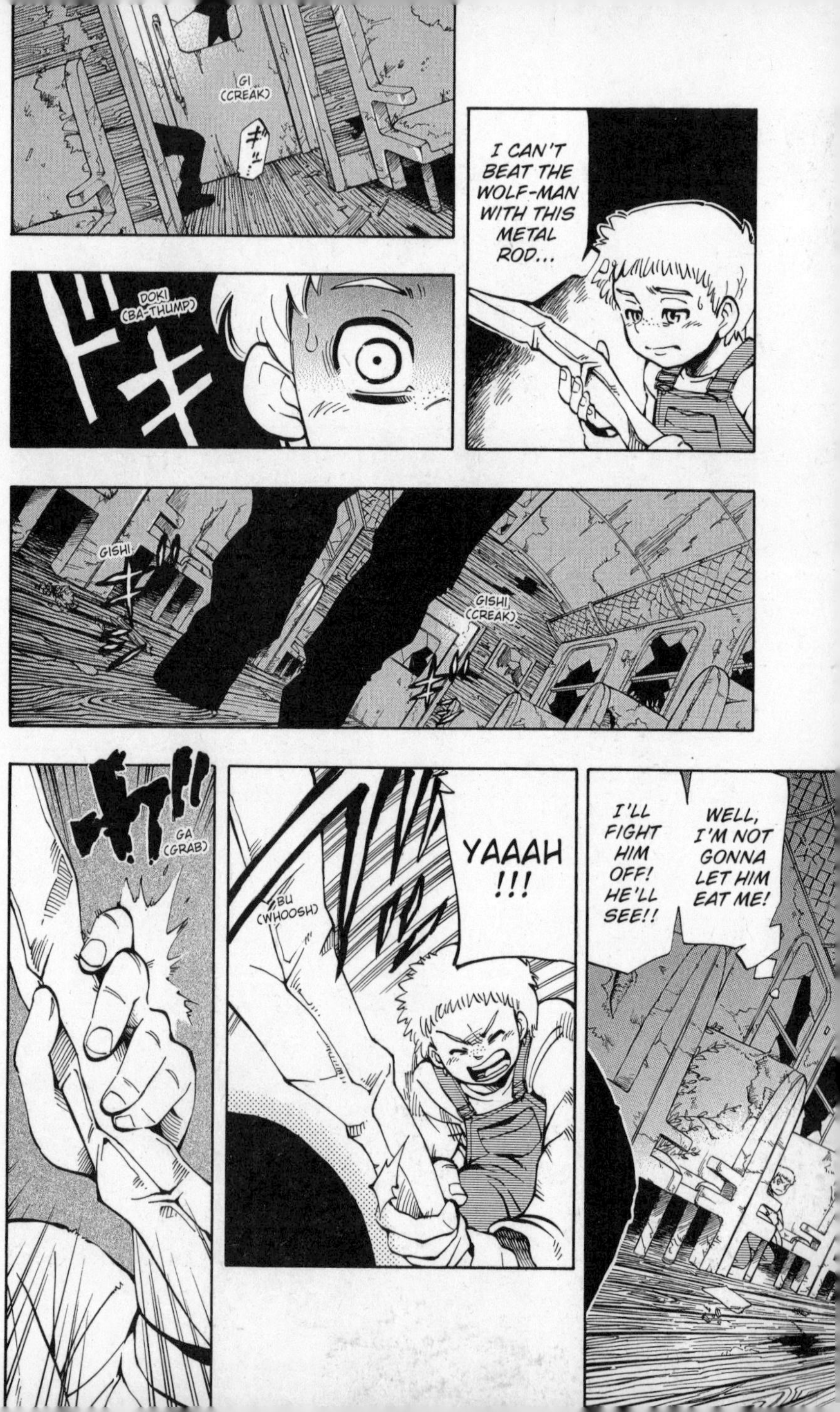
I CAN'T BEAT THE WOLF-MAN WITH THIS METAL ROD...
GI (CREAK)
DOKI (BA-THUMP)
GISHI
GISHI (CREAK)
WELL, I'M NOT GONNA LET HIM EAT ME!
I'LL FIGHT HIM OFF! HE'LL SEE!!
YAAAH!!!
BU (WHOOSH)
GA (GRAB)

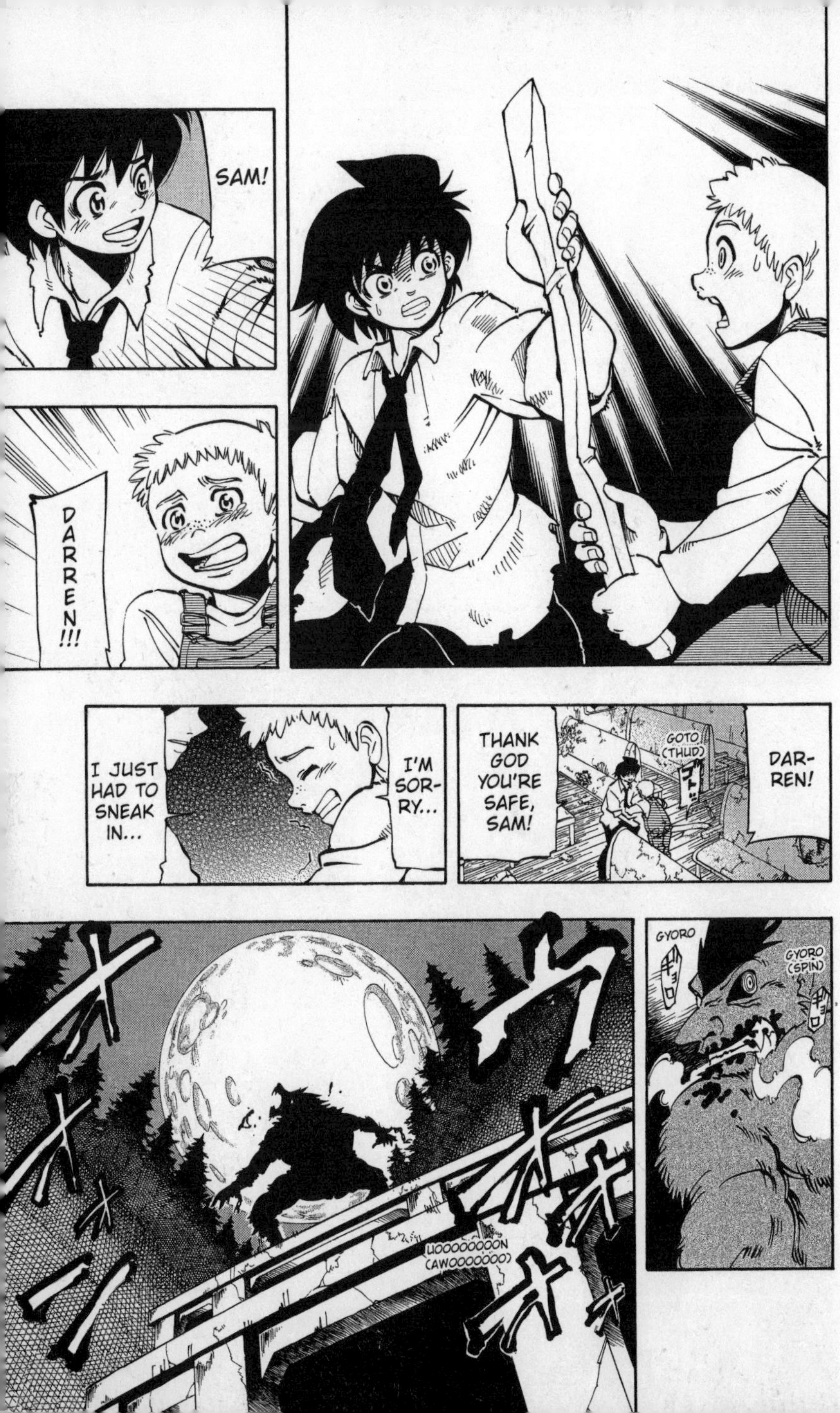
SAM!
DARREN!!!
DAR-REN!
THANK GOD YOU'RE SAFE, SAM!
GOTO (THUD)
I'M SOR-RY...
I JUST HAD TO SNEAK IN...
GYORO
GYORO (SPIN)
UOOOOOOOON (AWOOOOOOO)

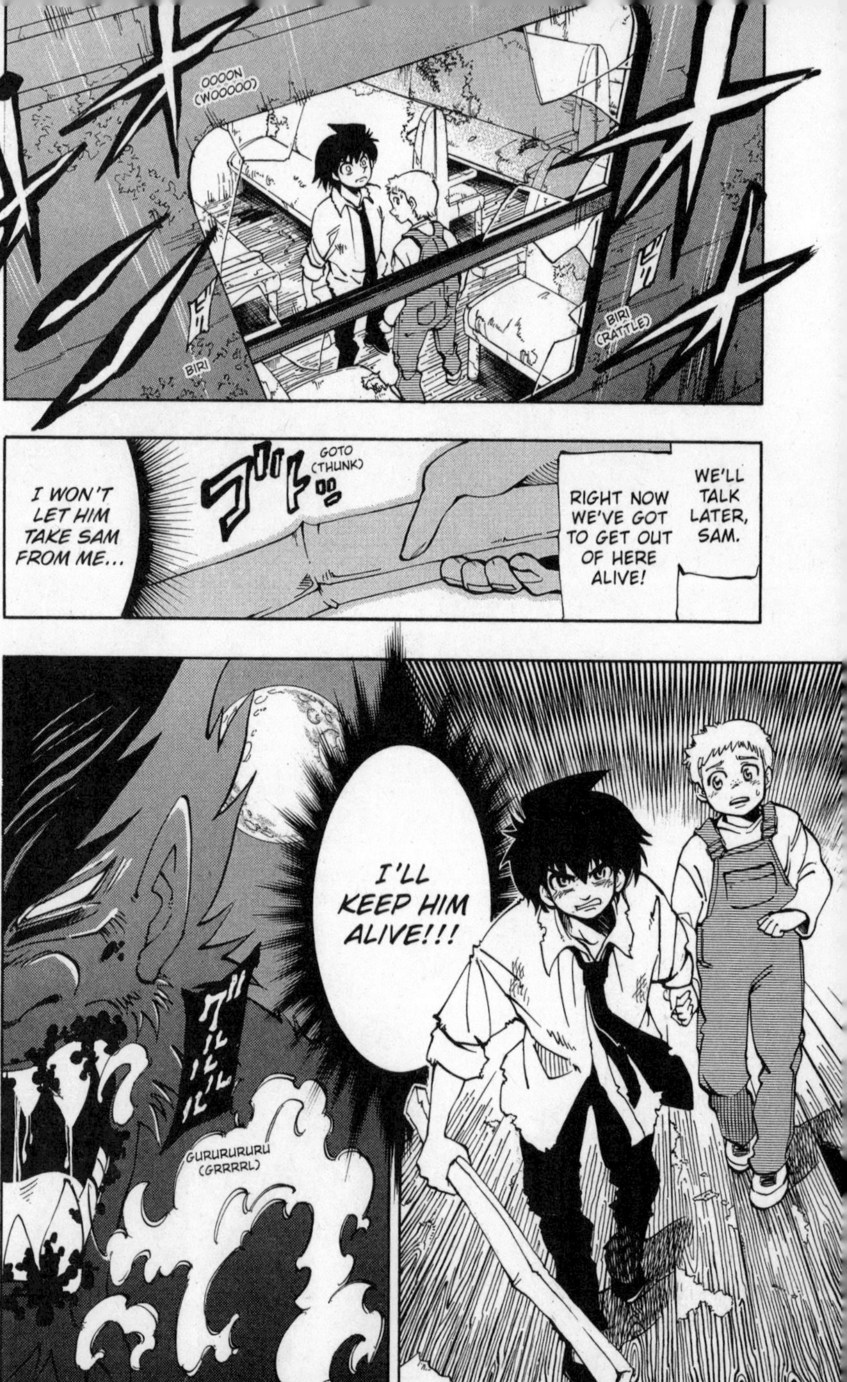
OOOON (WOOOOO)
BIRI (RATTLE)
BIRI
WE'LL TALK LATER, SAM.
RIGHT NOW WE'VE GOT TO GET OUT OF HERE ALIVE!
GOTO (THUNK)
I WON'T LET HIM TAKE SAM FROM ME...
I'LL KEEP HIM ALIVE!!!
GURURURURU (GRRRRL)

CHAPTER 13: BLOOD AND SPIRIT

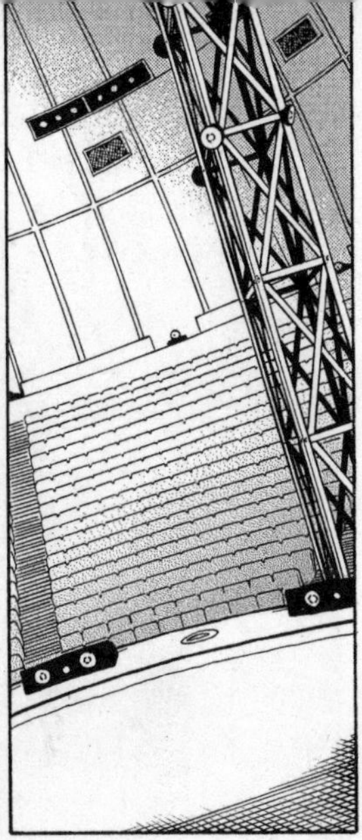

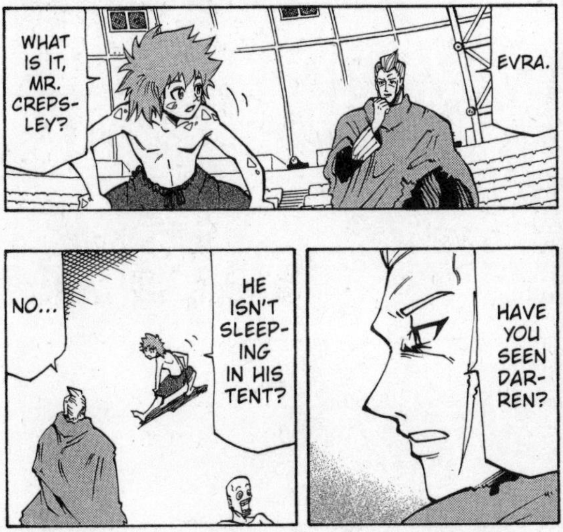
EVRA.
WHAT IS IT, MR. CREPSLEY?
HAVE YOU SEEN DARREN?
HE ISN'T SLEEPING IN HIS TENT?
NO...

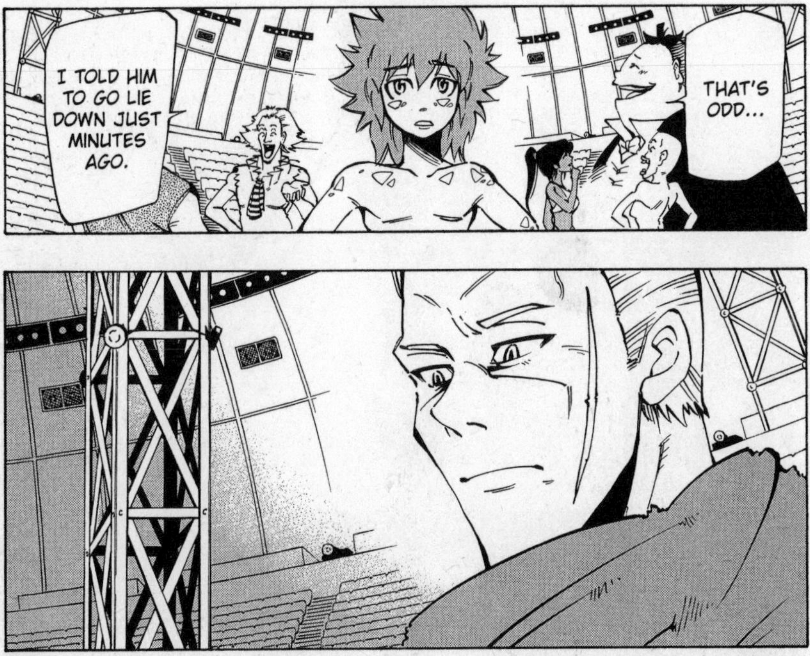
THAT'S ODD...
I TOLD HIM TO GO LIE DOWN JUST MINUTES AGO.

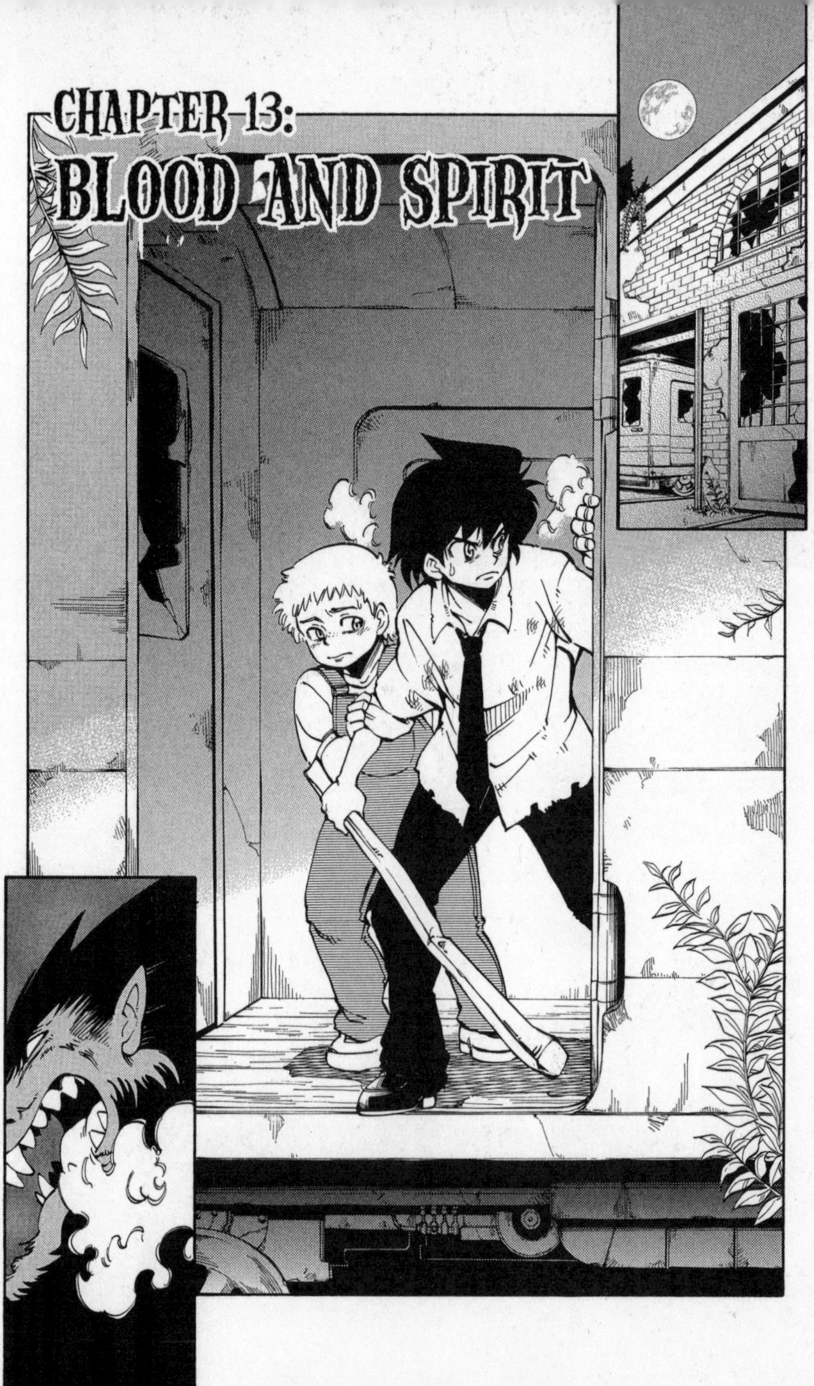
CHAPTER 13:
BLOOD AND SPIRIT

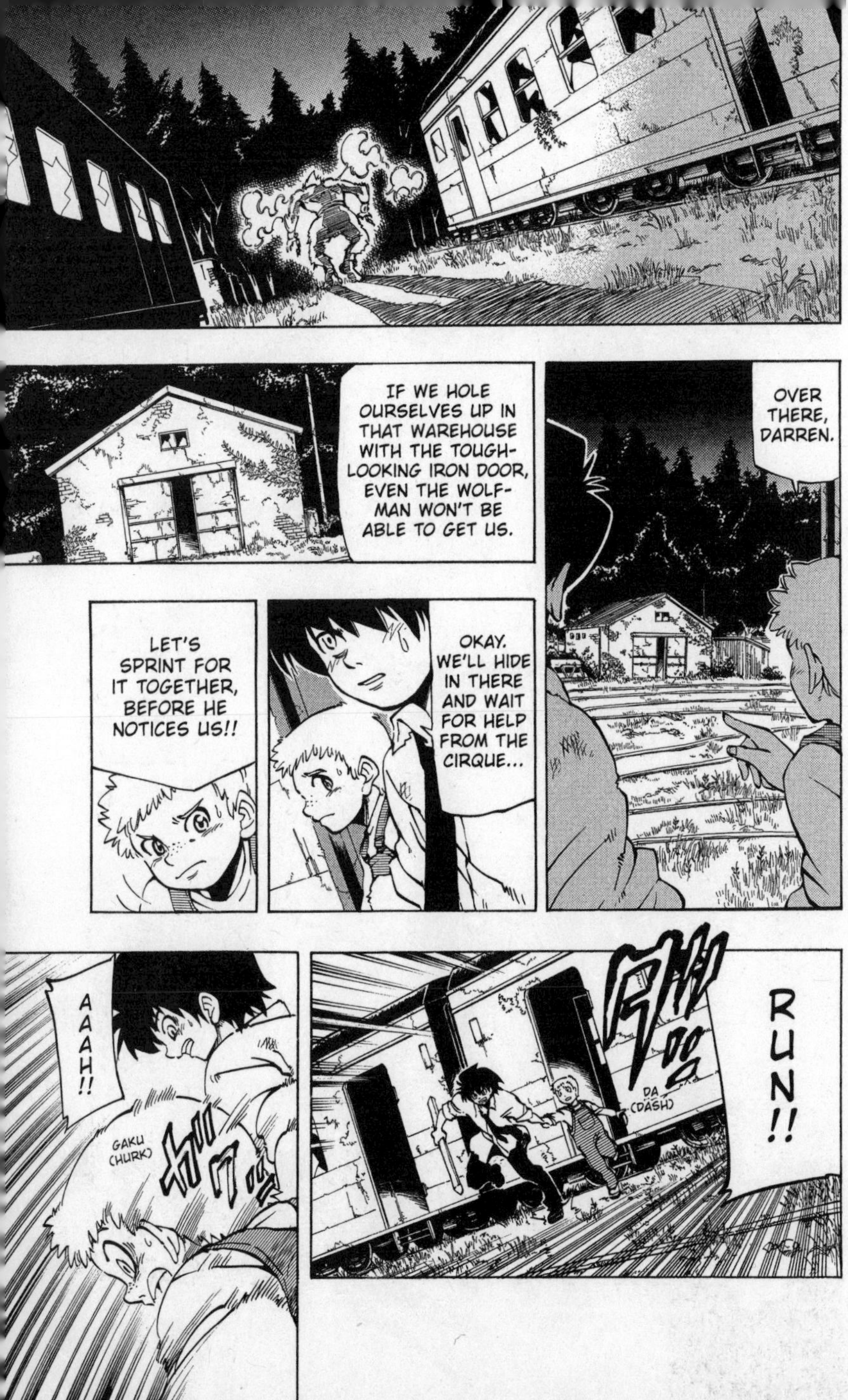
OVER THERE, DARREN.
IF WE HOLE OURSELVES UP IN THAT WAREHOUSE WITH THE TOUGH-LOOKING IRON DOOR, EVEN THE WOLF-MAN WON'T BE ABLE TO GET US.
OKAY. WE'LL HIDE IN THERE AND WAIT FOR HELP FROM THE CIRQUE...
LET'S SPRINT FOR IT TOGETHER, BEFORE HE NOTICES US!!
RUN!!
DA (DASH)
AAAH!!
GAKU (HURK)

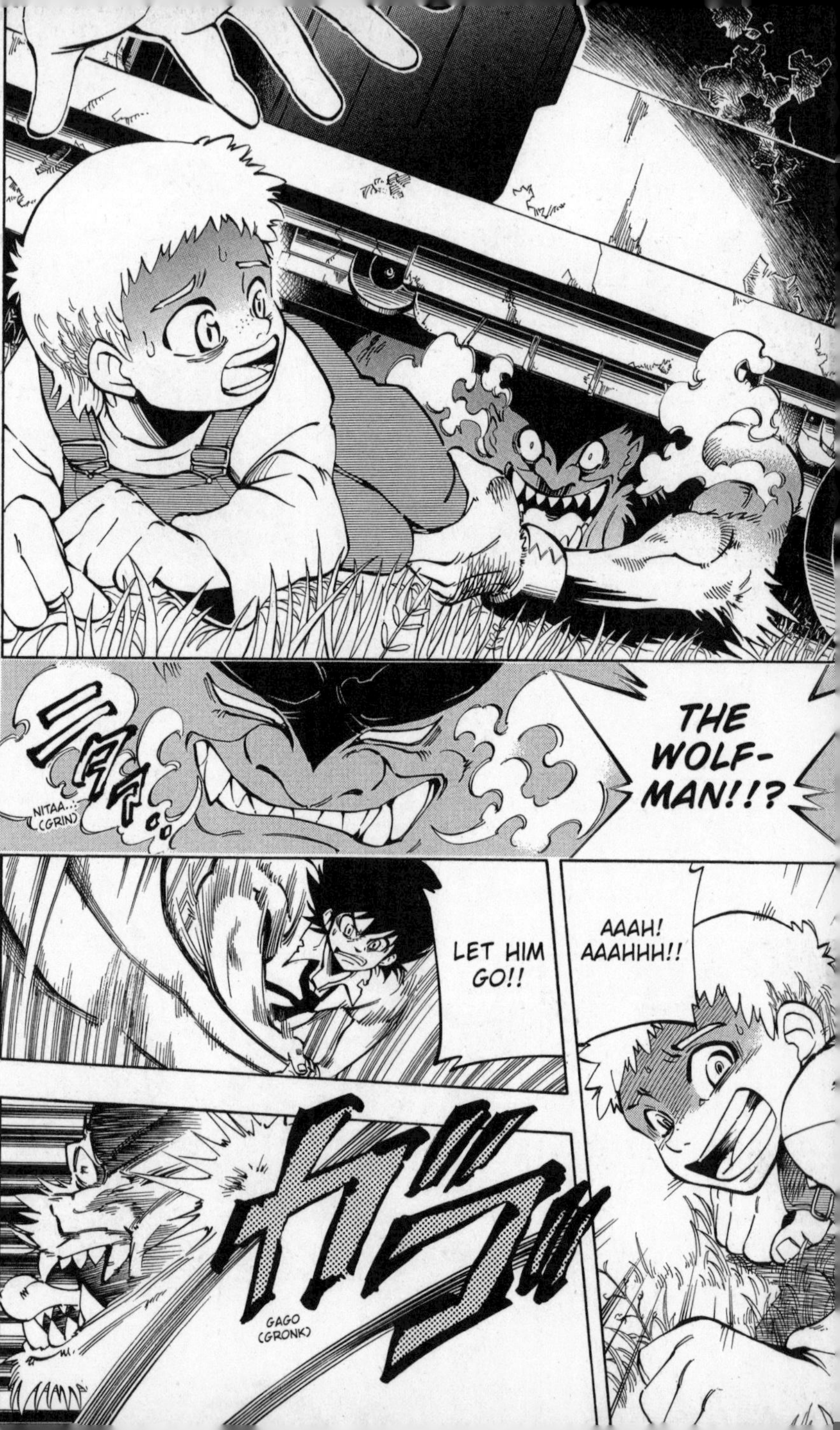
THE WOLF-MAN!!?
NITAA... (GRIN)
AAAH! AAAHHH!!
LET HIM GO!!
GAGO (GRONK)

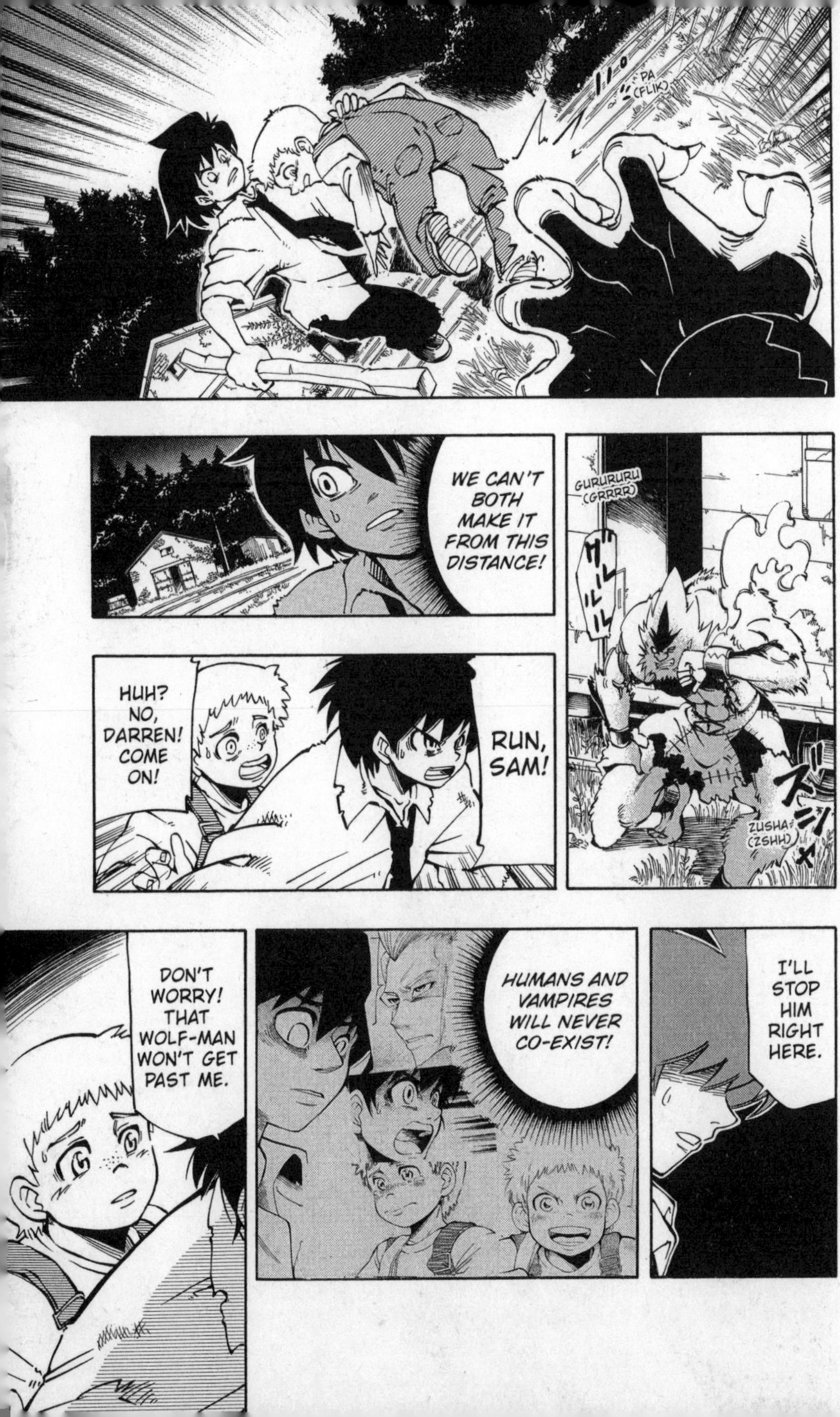
PA (FLIK)
GURURURU (GRRRR)
ZUSHA (ZSHH)
WE CAN'T BOTH MAKE IT FROM THIS DISTANCE!
RUN, SAM!
HUH? NO, DARREN! COME ON!
I'LL STOP HIM RIGHT HERE.
HUMANS AND VAMPIRES WILL NEVER CO-EXIST!
DON'T WORRY! THAT WOLF-MAN WON'T GET PAST ME.

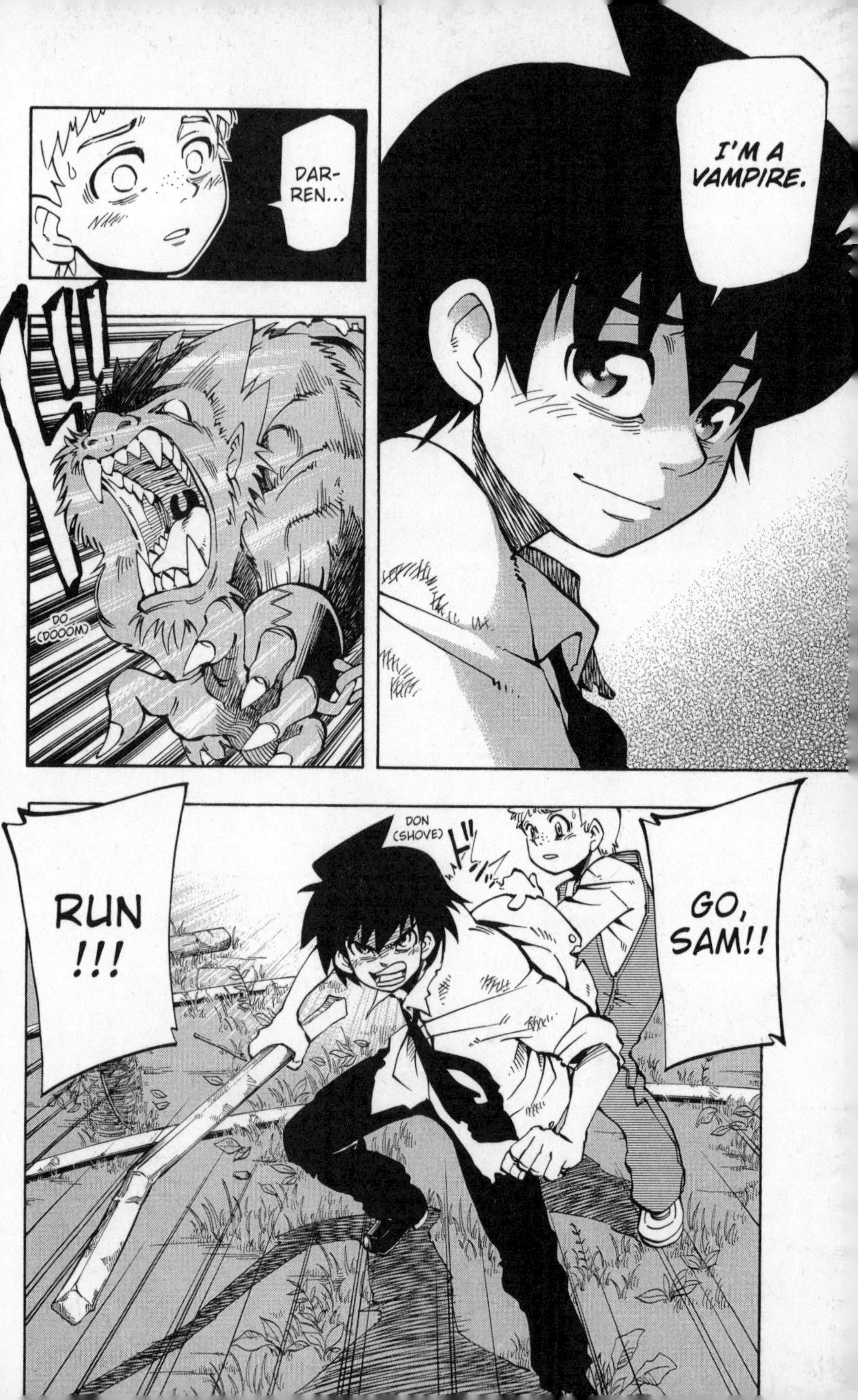
I'M A VAMPIRE.
DAR-REN...
DO (DOOOM)
GO, SAM!!
DON (SHOVE)
RUN !!!

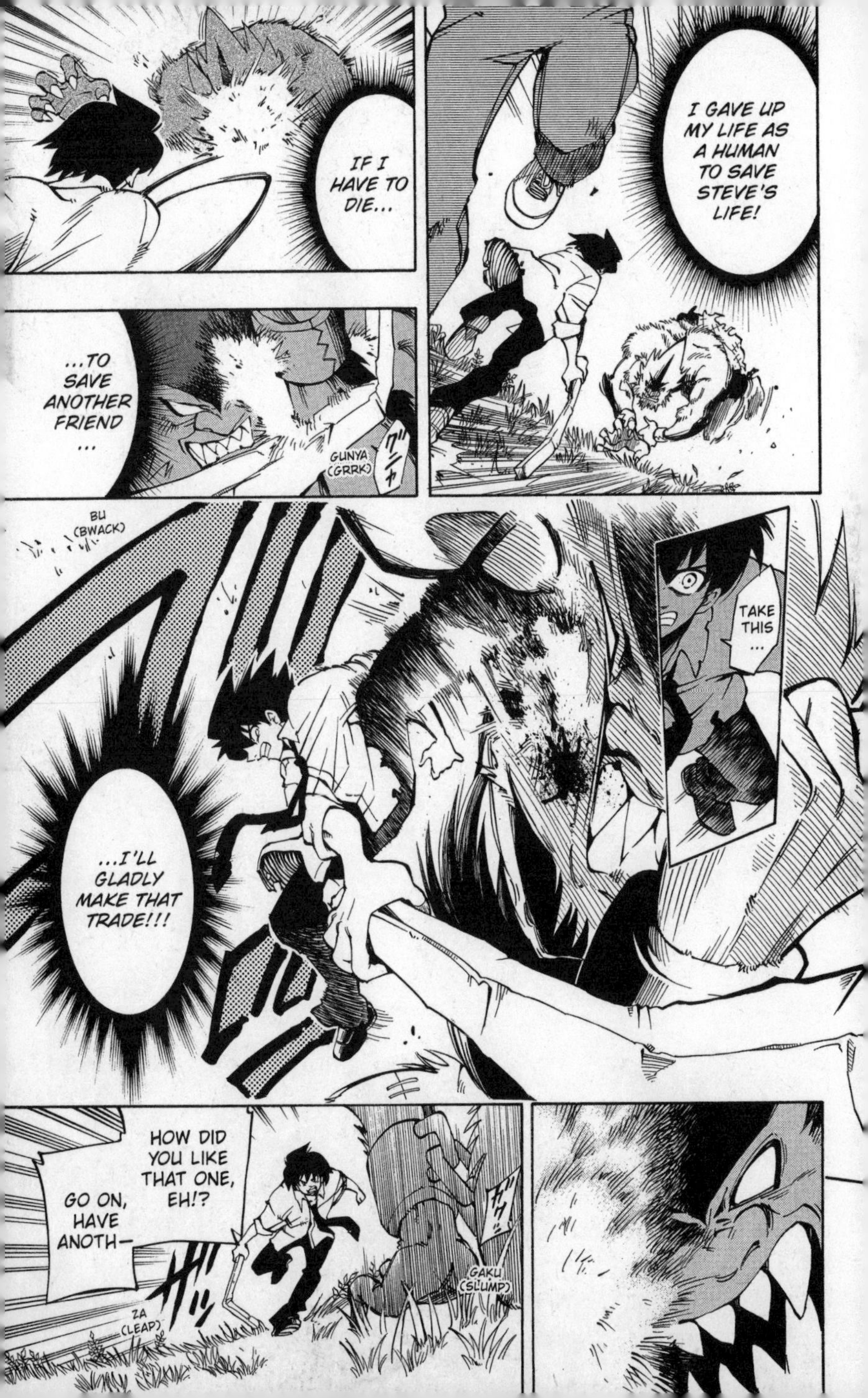
I GAVE UP MY LIFE AS A HUMAN TO SAVE STEVE'S LIFE!
IF I HAVE TO DIE...
...TO SAVE ANOTHER FRIEND ...
GUNYA (GRRK)
TAKE THIS ...
BU (BWACK)
...I'LL GLADLY MAKE THAT TRADE!!!
HOW DID YOU LIKE THAT ONE, EH!?
GO ON, HAVE ANOTH—
GAKU (SLUMP)
ZA (LEAP)

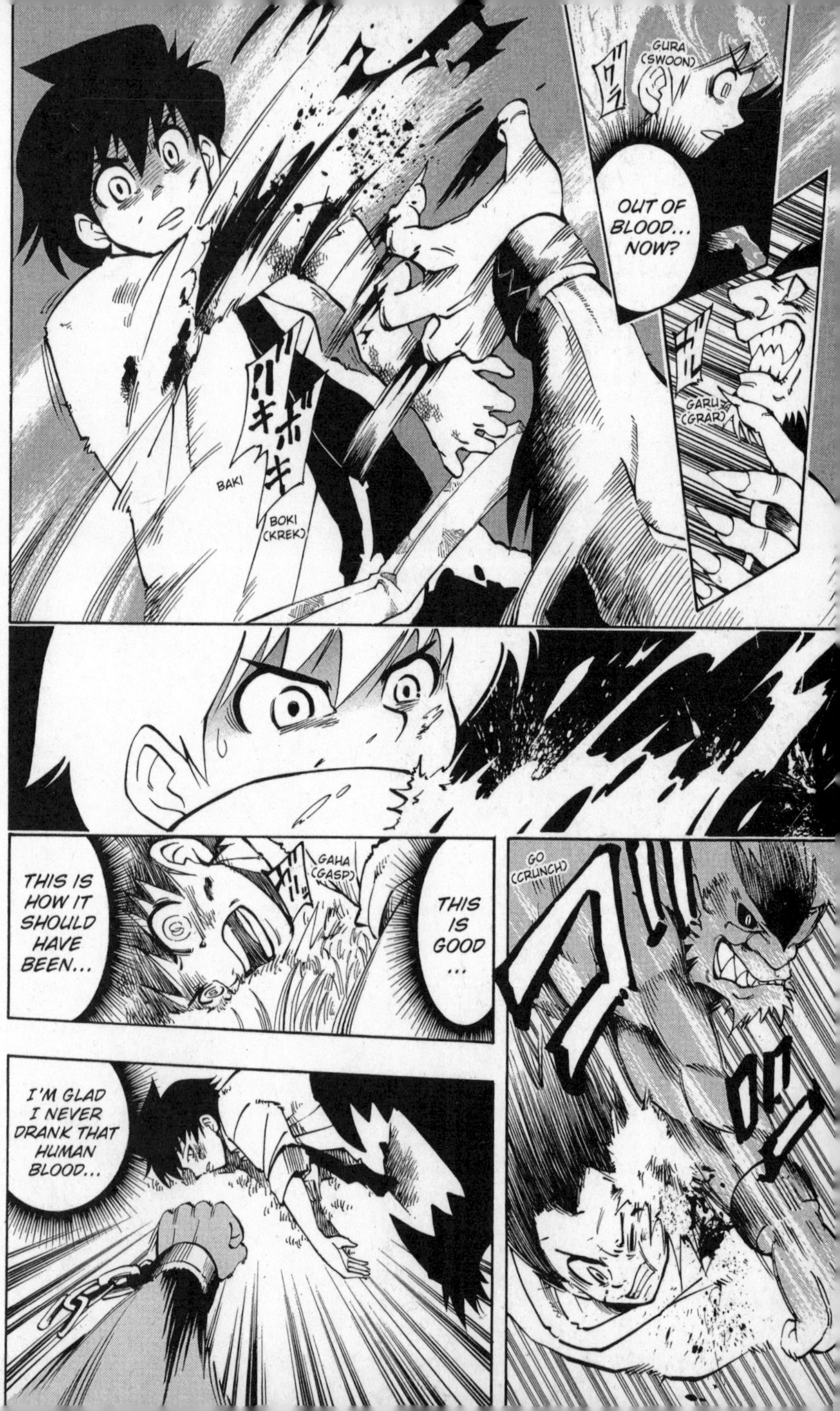
GURA (SWOON)
OUT OF BLOOD... NOW?
GARU (GRAR)
BAKI
BOKI (KREK)
GO (CRUNCH)
GAHA (GASP)
THIS IS GOOD...
THIS IS HOW IT SHOULD HAVE BEEN...
I'M GLAD I NEVER DRANK THAT HUMAN BLOOD...

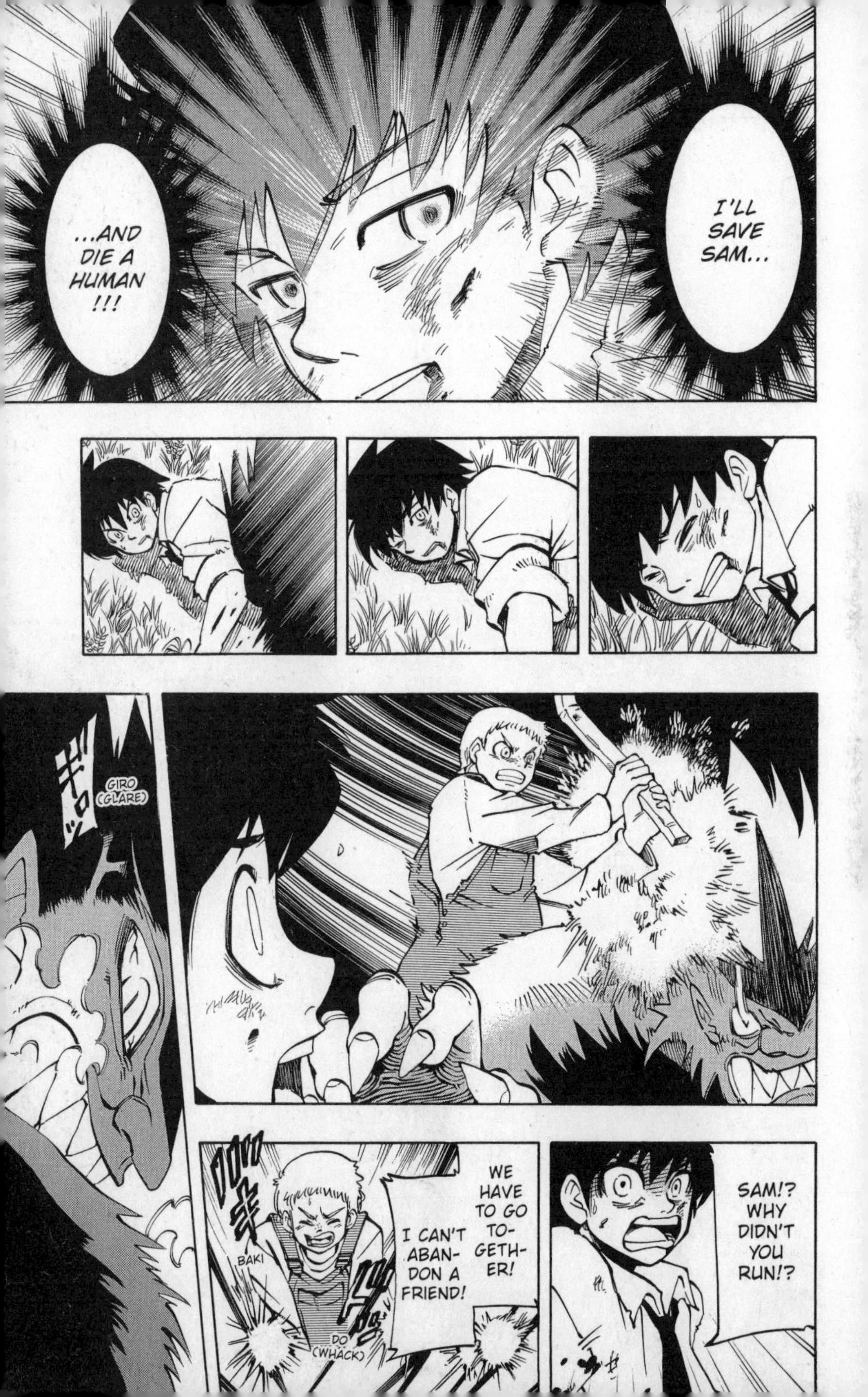
I'LL SAVE SAM...
...AND DIE A HUMAN!!!
SAM!? WHY DIDN'T YOU RUN!?
WE HAVE TO GO TO-GETH-ER!
I CAN'T ABAN-DON A FRIEND!
BAKI
DO (WHACK)
GIRO (GLARE)

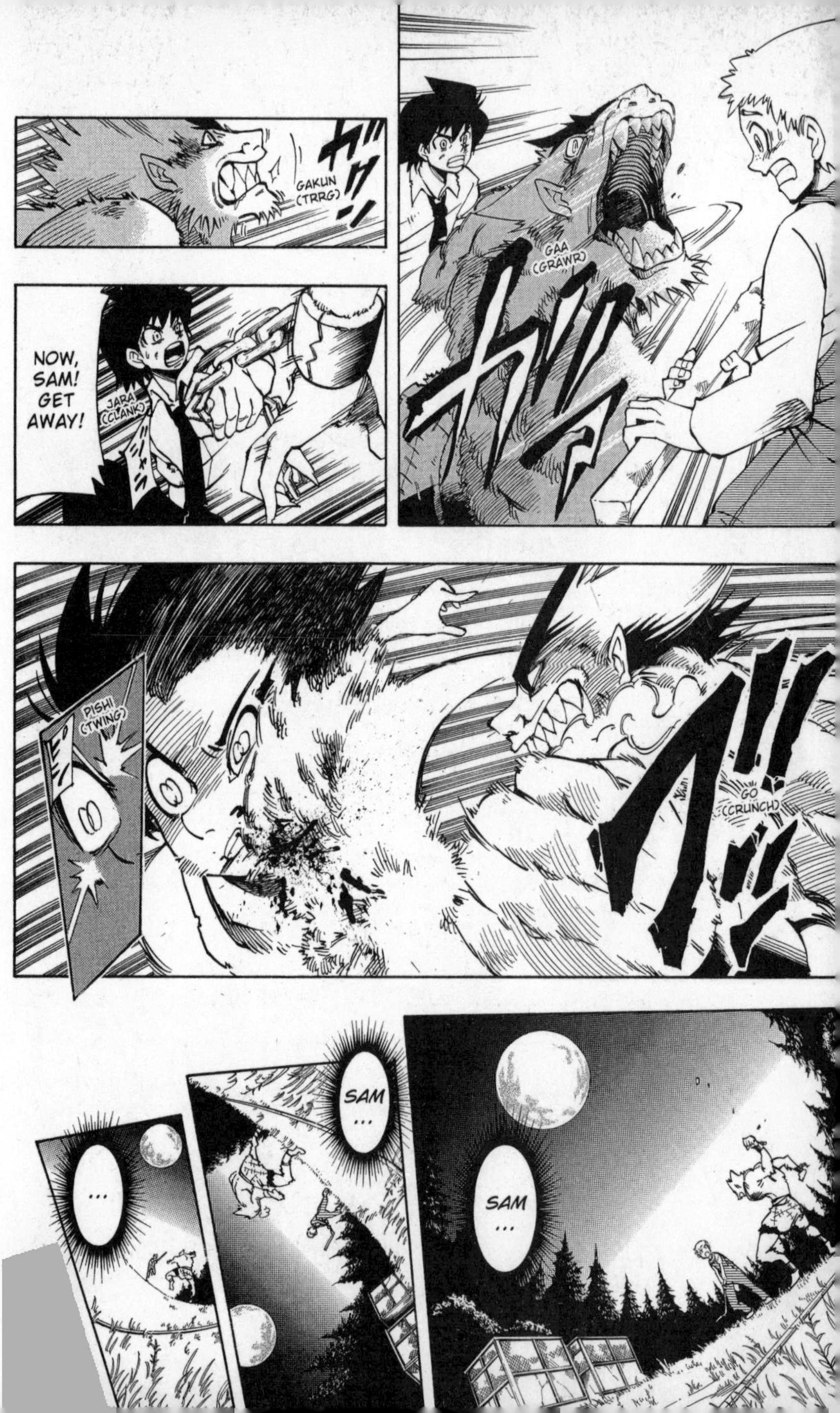
GAA (GRAWR)
GAKUN (TRRG)
NOW, SAM! GET AWAY!
JARA (CLANK)
GO (CRUNCH)
PISHI (TWING)
SAM ...
SAM ...
...

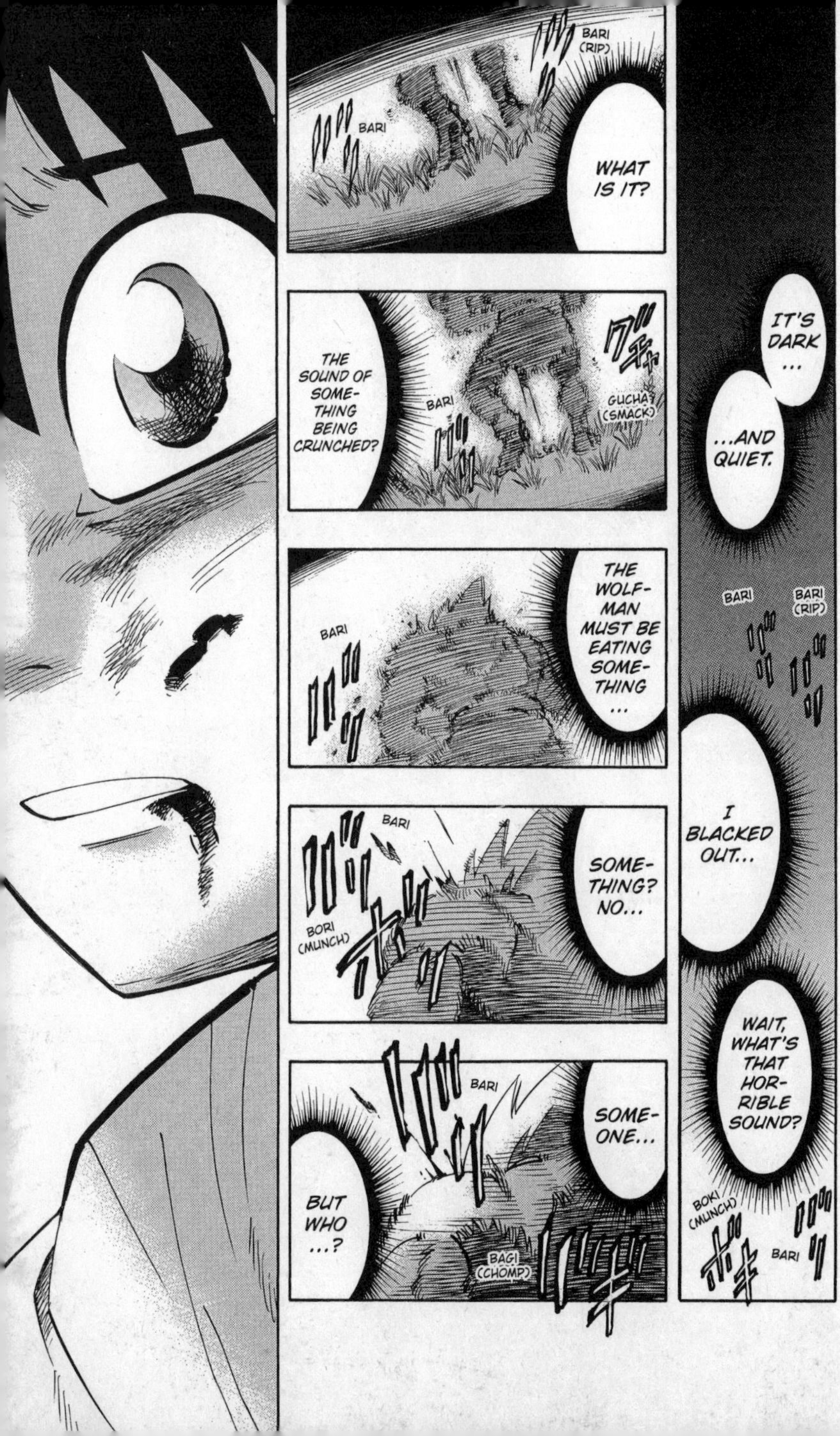
IT'S DARK...
...AND QUIET.
BARI (RIP)
BARI
I BLACKED OUT...
WAIT, WHAT'S THAT HORRIBLE SOUND?
BOKI (MUNCH)
BARI
WHAT IS IT?
BARI (RIP)
BARI
THE SOUND OF SOMETHING BEING CRUNCHED?
GUCHA (SMACK)
BARI
THE WOLFMAN MUST BE EATING SOMETHING...
BARI
SOMETHING? NO...
BARI
BORI (MUNCH)
SOMEONE...
BUT WHO...?
BARI
BAGI (CHOMP)

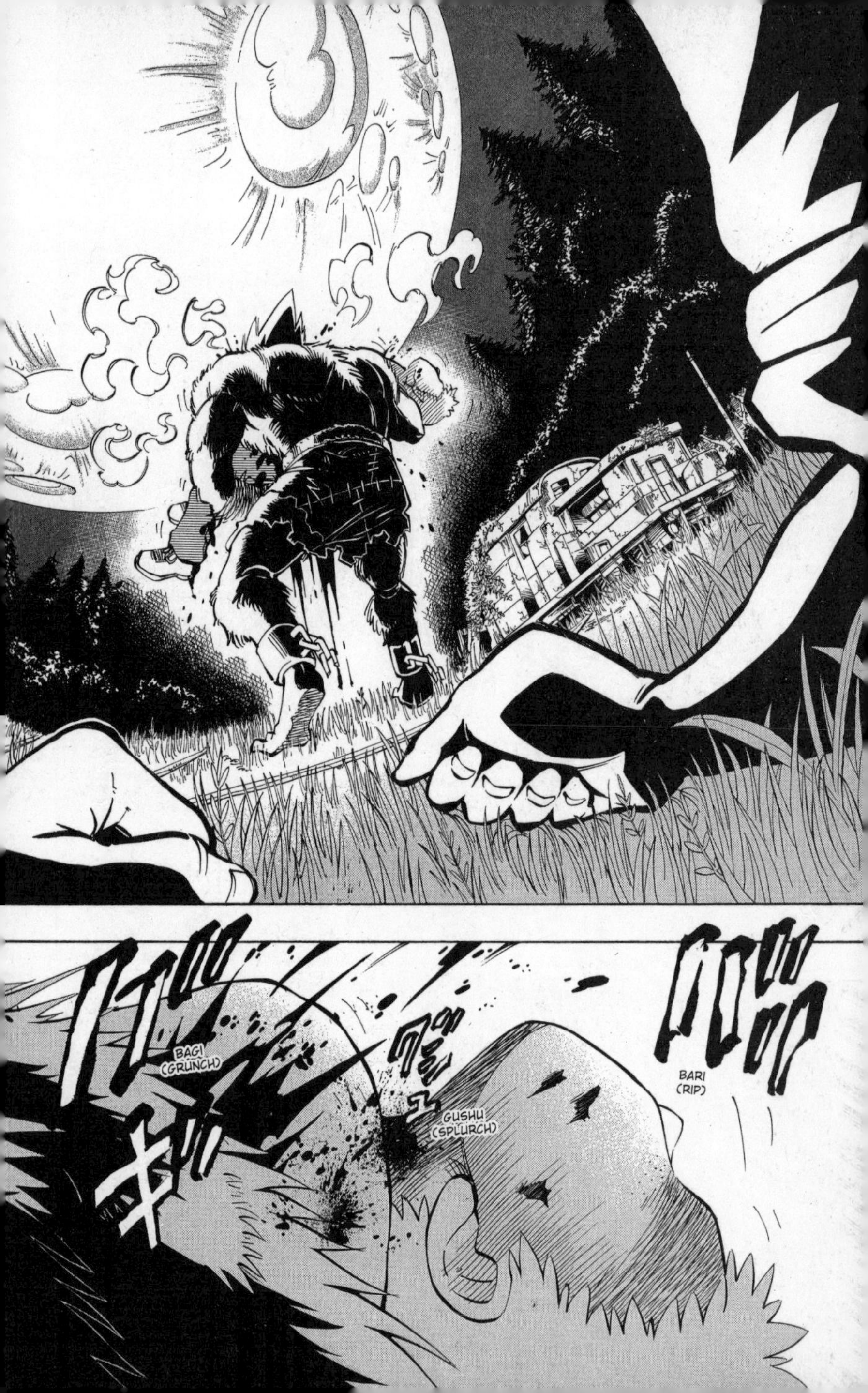
BARI
(RIP)
GUSHU
(SPLURCH)
BAGI
(GRUNCH)

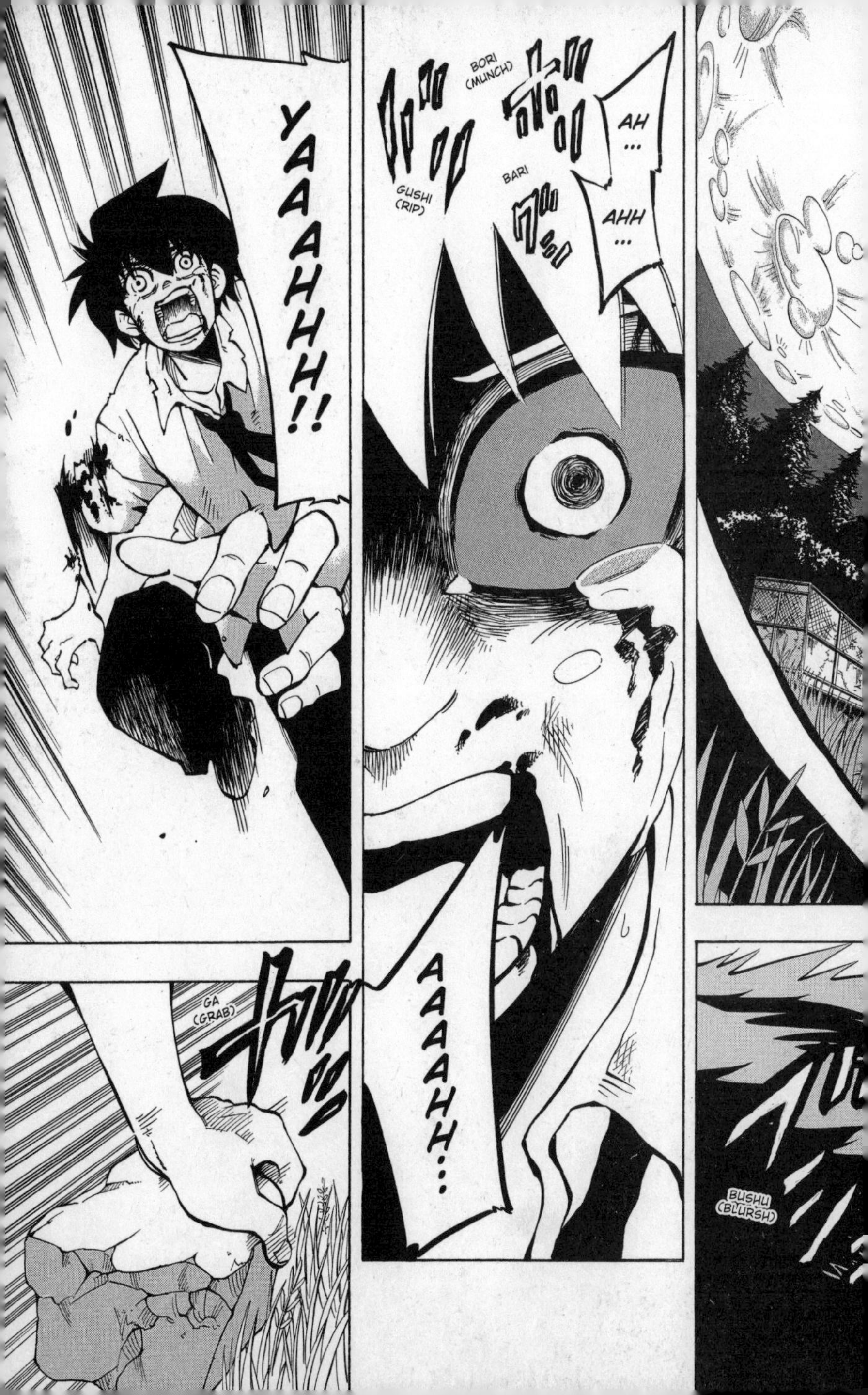
AH...
AHH...
BORI (MUNCH)
BARI
GUSHI (RIP)
AAAAAHH...
YAAAAHHHH!!
BUSHU (BLURSH)
GA (GRAB)

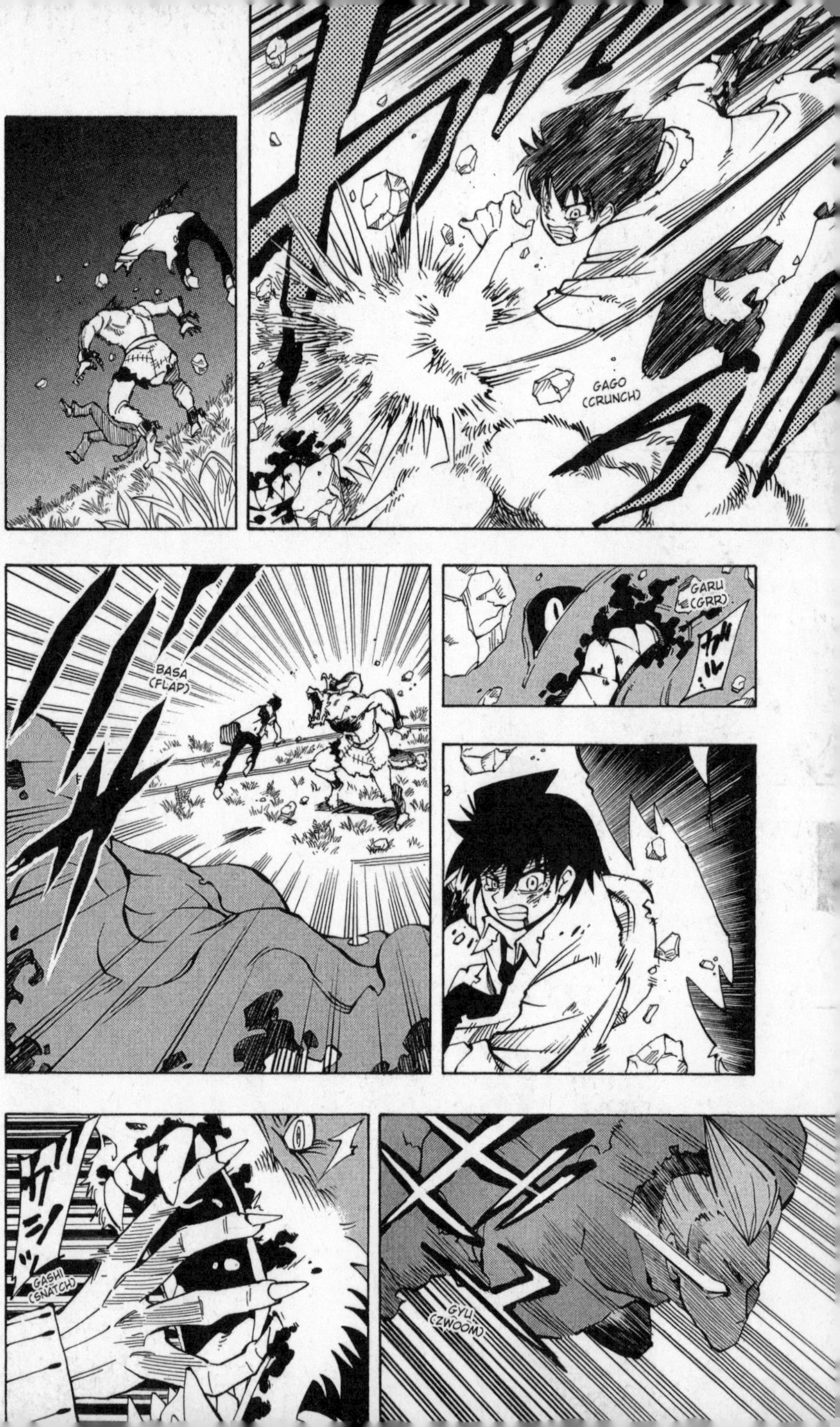
GAGO
(CRUNCH)
GARU
(GRR)
BASA
(FLAP)
GYU
(ZWOOM)
GASHI
(SNATCH)

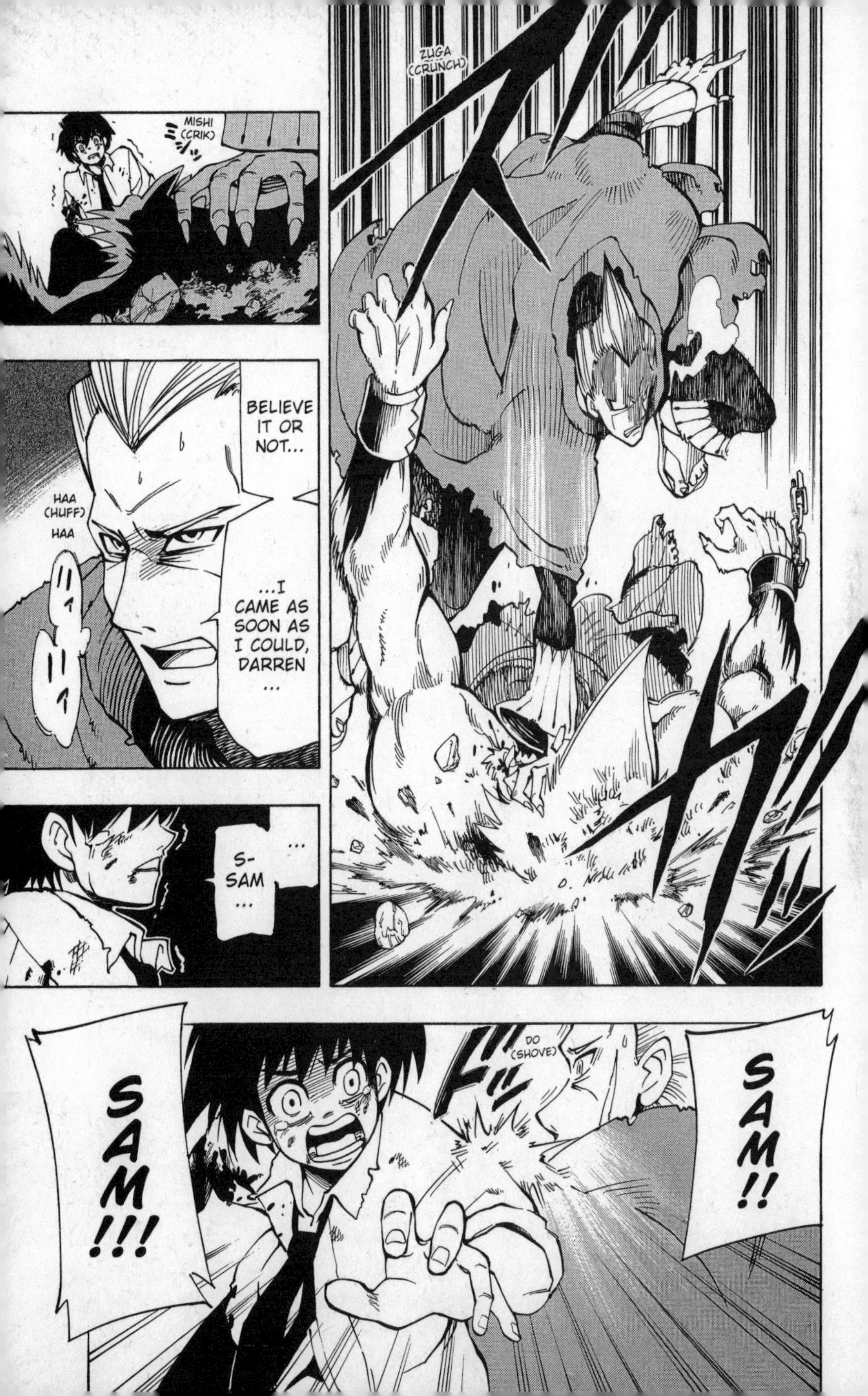
ZUGA (CRUNCH)
MISHI (CRIK)
BELIEVE IT OR NOT...
...I CAME AS SOON AS I COULD, DARREN ...
HAA (HUFF) HAA
...
S-SAM ...
SAM!!
DO (SHOVE)
SAM!!!

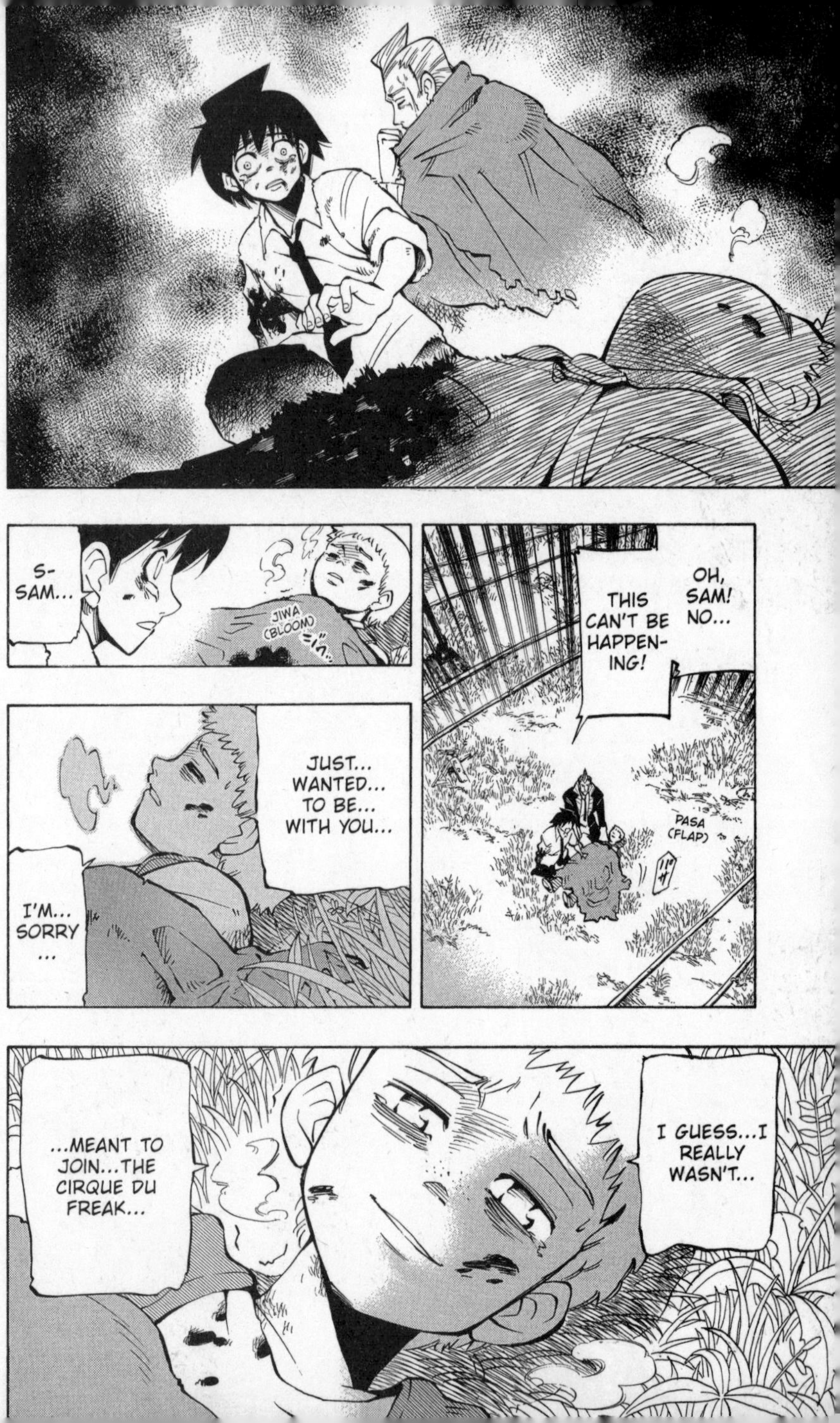
OH, SAM! NO...
THIS CAN'T BE HAPPENING!
PASA (FLAP)
S-SAM...
JIWA (BLOOM)
JUST... WANTED... TO BE... WITH YOU...
I'M... SORRY...
I GUESS...I REALLY WASN'T...
...MEANT TO JOIN...THE CIRQUE DU FREAK...

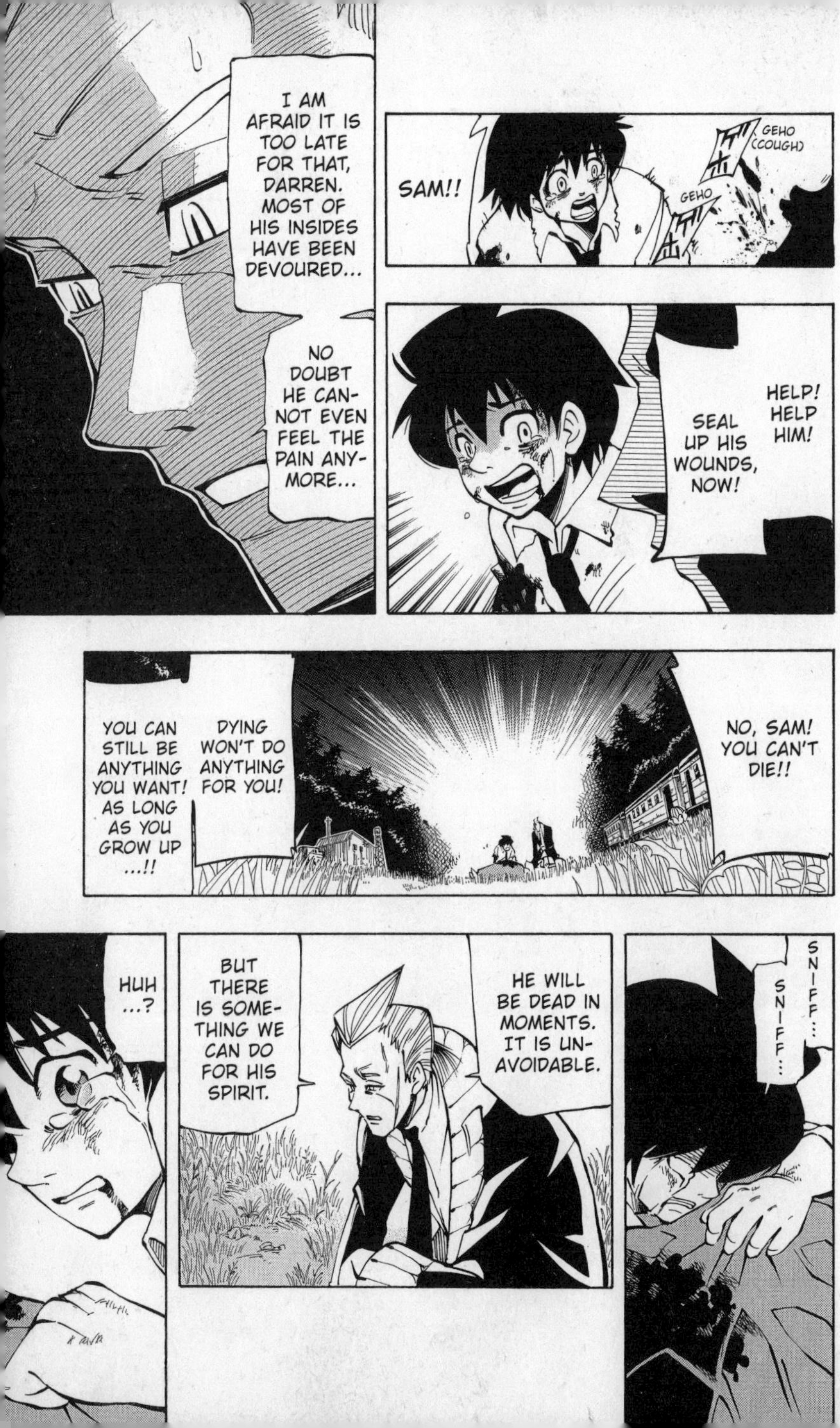
GEHO (COUGH)
SAM!!
GEHO
HELP! HELP HIM!
SEAL UP HIS WOUNDS, NOW!
I AM AFRAID IT IS TOO LATE FOR THAT, DARREN. MOST OF HIS INSIDES HAVE BEEN DEVOURED...
NO DOUBT HE CAN-NOT EVEN FEEL THE PAIN ANY-MORE...
NO, SAM! YOU CAN'T DIE!!
DYING WON'T DO ANYTHING FOR YOU!
YOU CAN STILL BE ANYTHING YOU WANT! AS LONG AS YOU GROW UP ...!!
SNIFF...
SNIFF...
HE WILL BE DEAD IN MOMENTS. IT IS UN-AVOIDABLE.
BUT THERE IS SOME-THING WE CAN DO FOR HIS SPIRIT.
HUH ...?

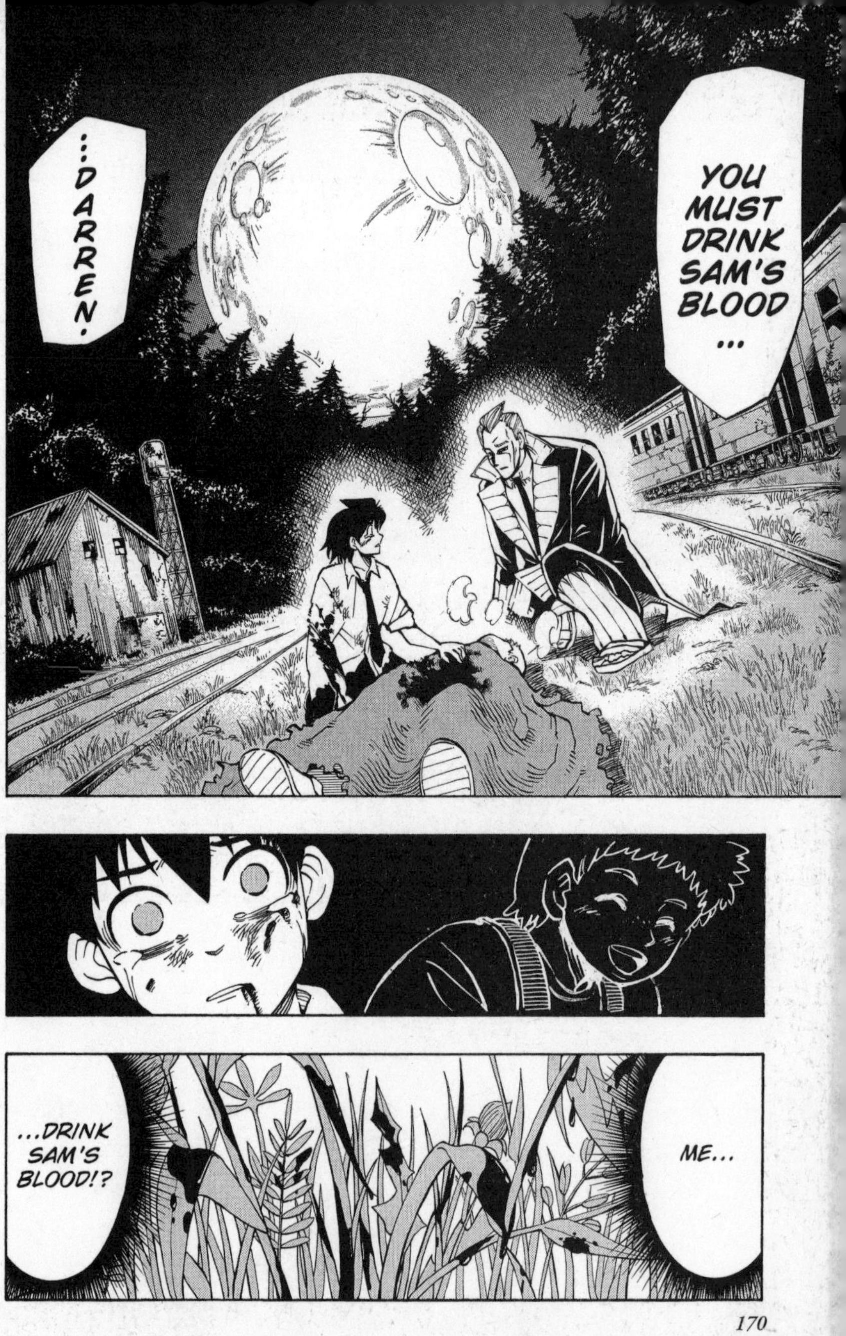
YOU MUST DRINK SAM'S BLOOD ...
...DARREN.
ME...
...DRINK SAM'S BLOOD!?

CHAPTER 13:
TOGETHER WITH SAM

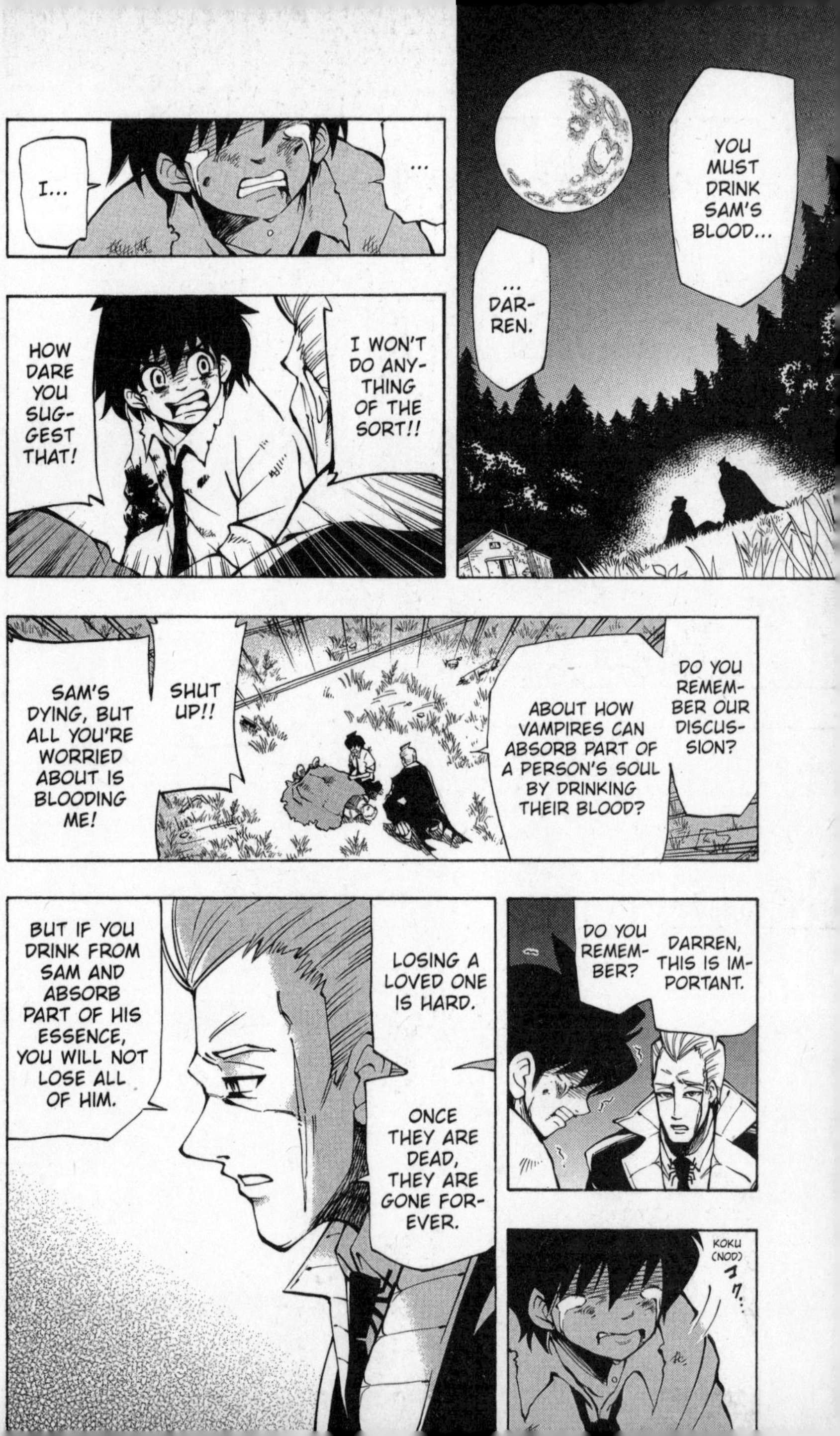
YOU MUST DRINK SAM'S BLOOD...
... DARREN.
...
I...
I WON'T DO ANYTHING OF THE SORT!!
HOW DARE YOU SUGGEST THAT!
DO YOU REMEMBER OUR DISCUSSION?
ABOUT HOW VAMPIRES CAN ABSORB PART OF A PERSON'S SOUL BY DRINKING THEIR BLOOD?
SHUT UP!!
SAM'S DYING, BUT ALL YOU'RE WORRIED ABOUT IS BLOODING ME!
DARREN, THIS IS IMPORTANT.
DO YOU REMEMBER?
KOKU (NOD)
LOSING A LOVED ONE IS HARD.
ONCE THEY ARE DEAD, THEY ARE GONE FOREVER.
BUT IF YOU DRINK FROM SAM AND ABSORB PART OF HIS ESSENCE, YOU WILL NOT LOSE ALL OF HIM.

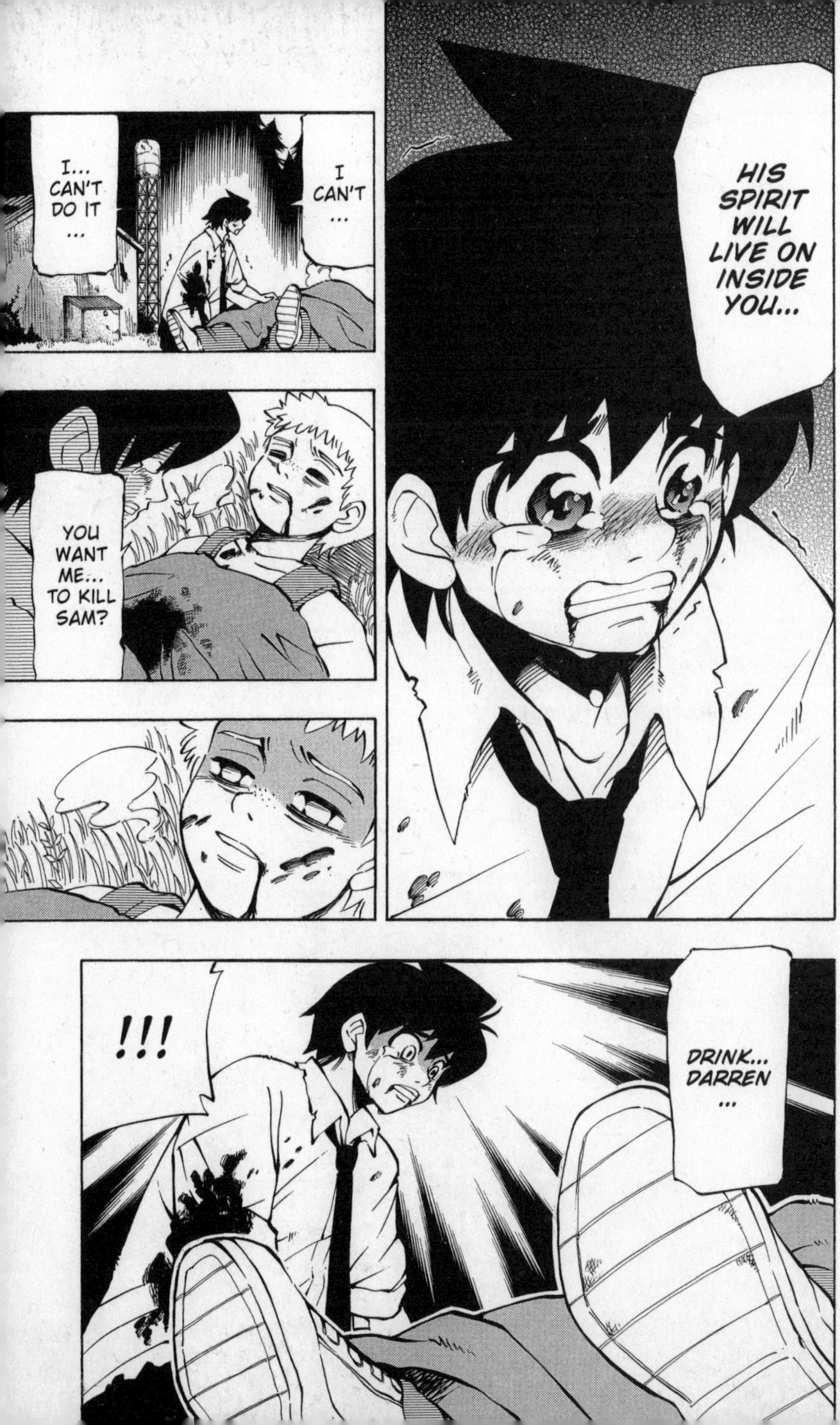
HIS SPIRIT WILL LIVE ON INSIDE YOU...
I CAN'T ...
I... CAN'T DO IT ...
YOU WANT ME... TO KILL SAM?
DRINK... DARREN ...
!!!

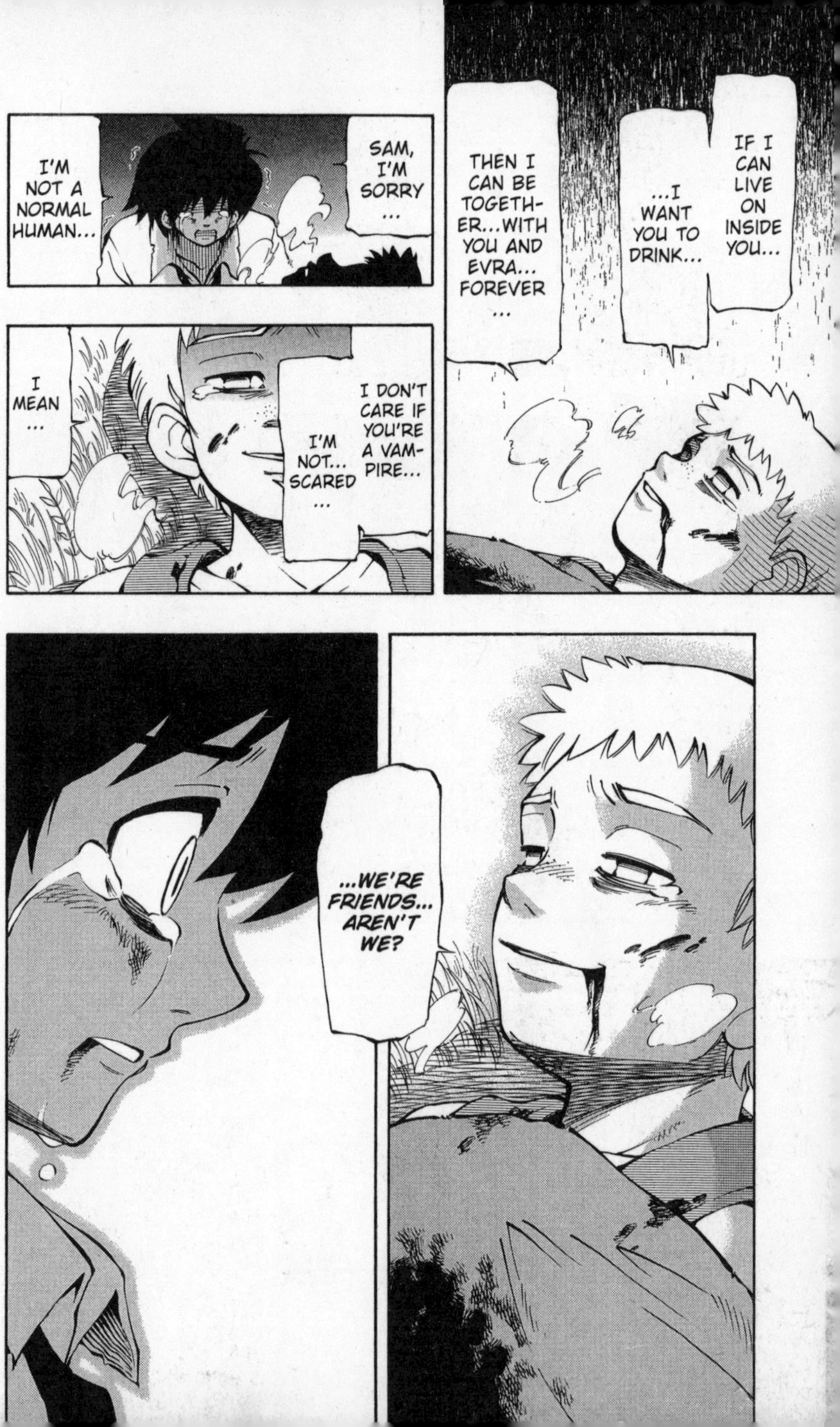
IF I CAN LIVE ON INSIDE YOU...
...I WANT YOU TO DRINK...
THEN I CAN BE TOGETH-ER...WITH YOU AND EVRA... FOREVER ...
SAM, I'M SORRY ...
I'M NOT A NORMAL HUMAN...
I DON'T CARE IF YOU'RE A VAM-PIRE...
I'M NOT... SCARED ...
I MEAN ...
...WE'RE FRIENDS... AREN'T WE?

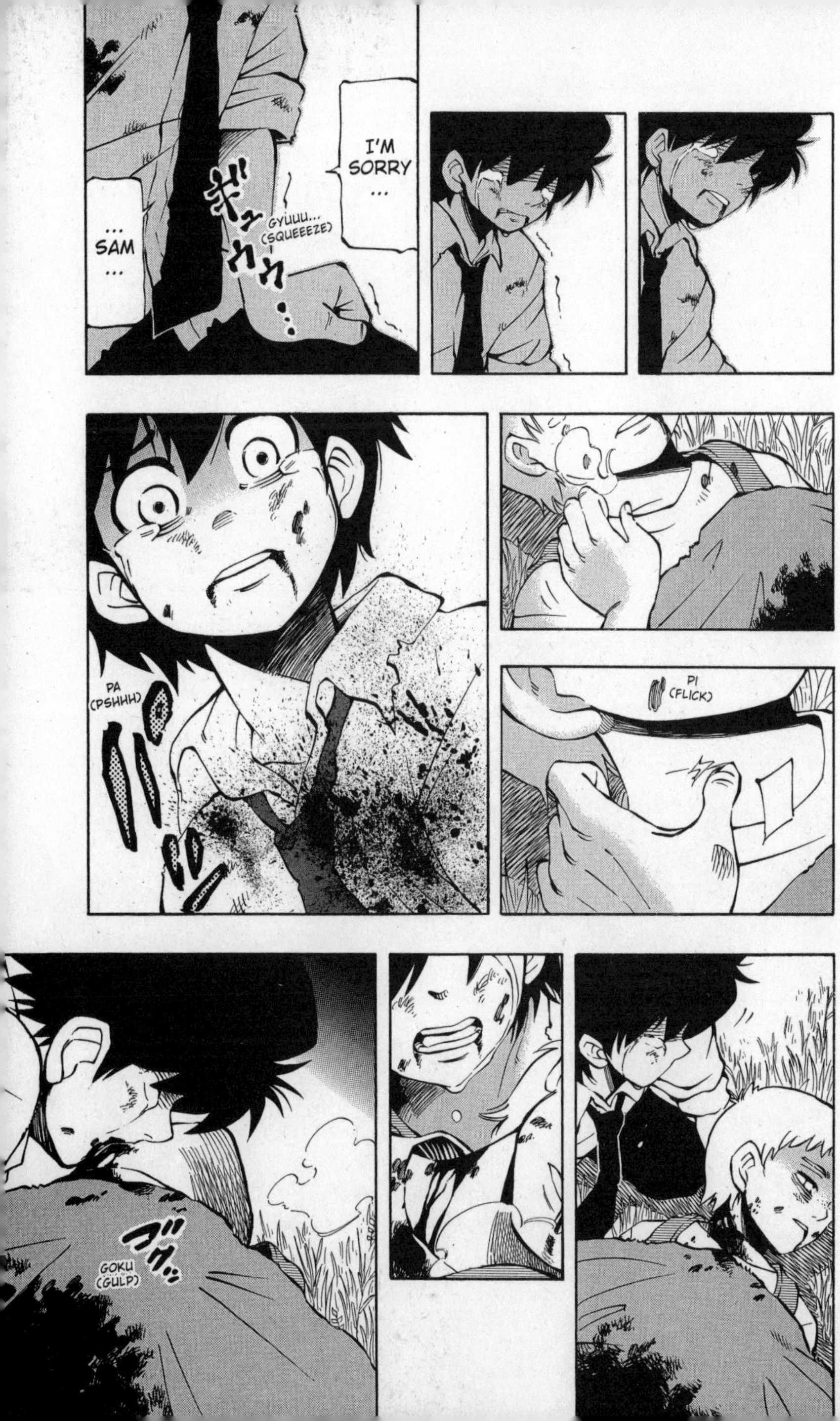
I'M SORRY ...
GYUUU... (SQUEEEZE)
... SAM ...
PI (FLICK)
PA (PSHHH)
GOKU (GULP)

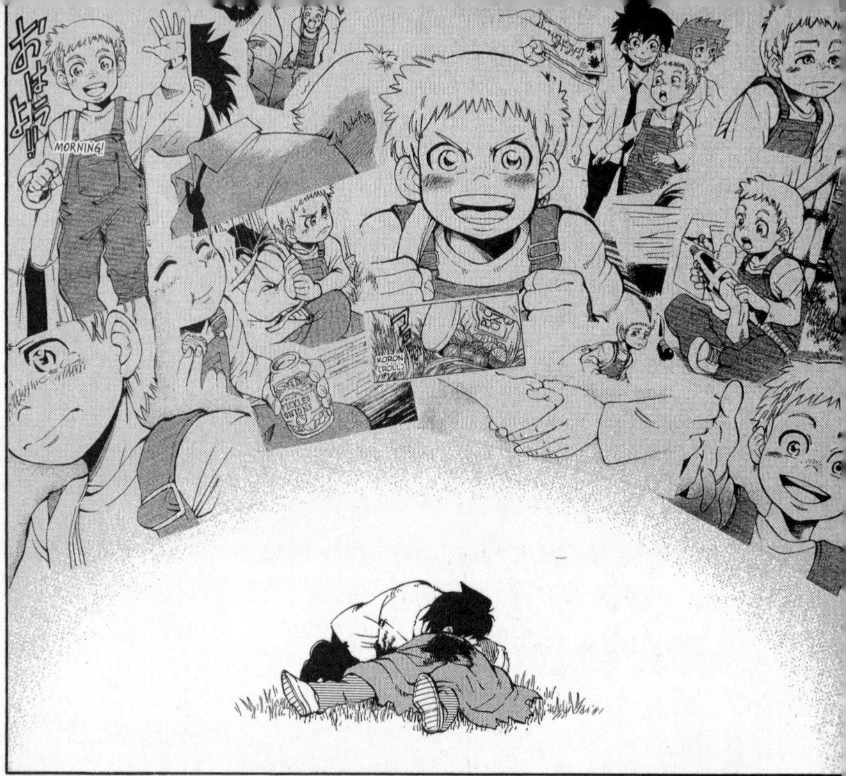
おはよう!!
MORNING!
KORON (ROLL)
PICKLED ONIONS

TICKET: CIRQUE DU FREAK

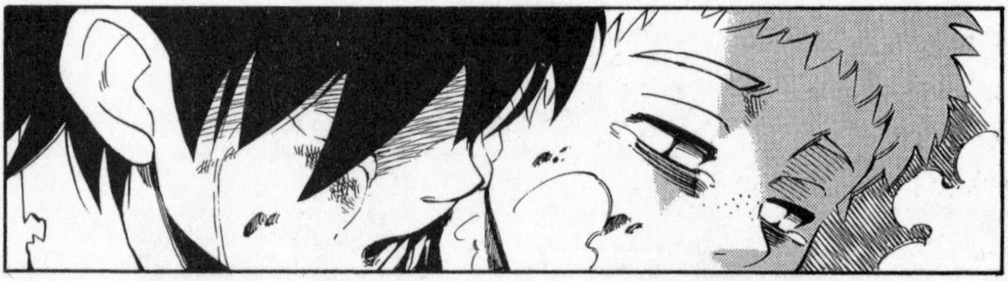

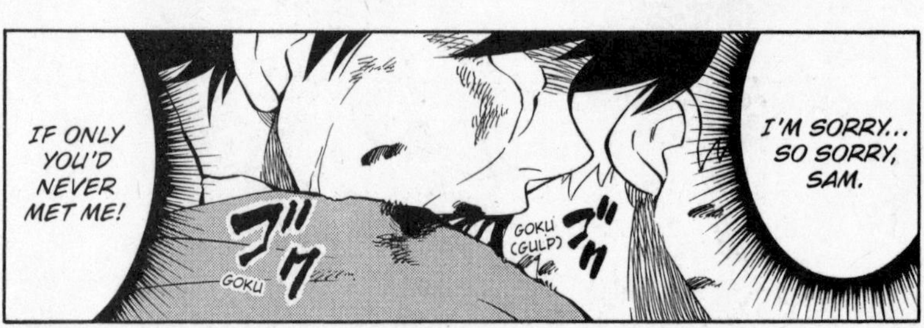
I'M SORRY... SO SORRY, SAM.
ゴク
GOKU (GULP)
IF ONLY YOU'D NEVER MET ME!
ゴク
GOKU

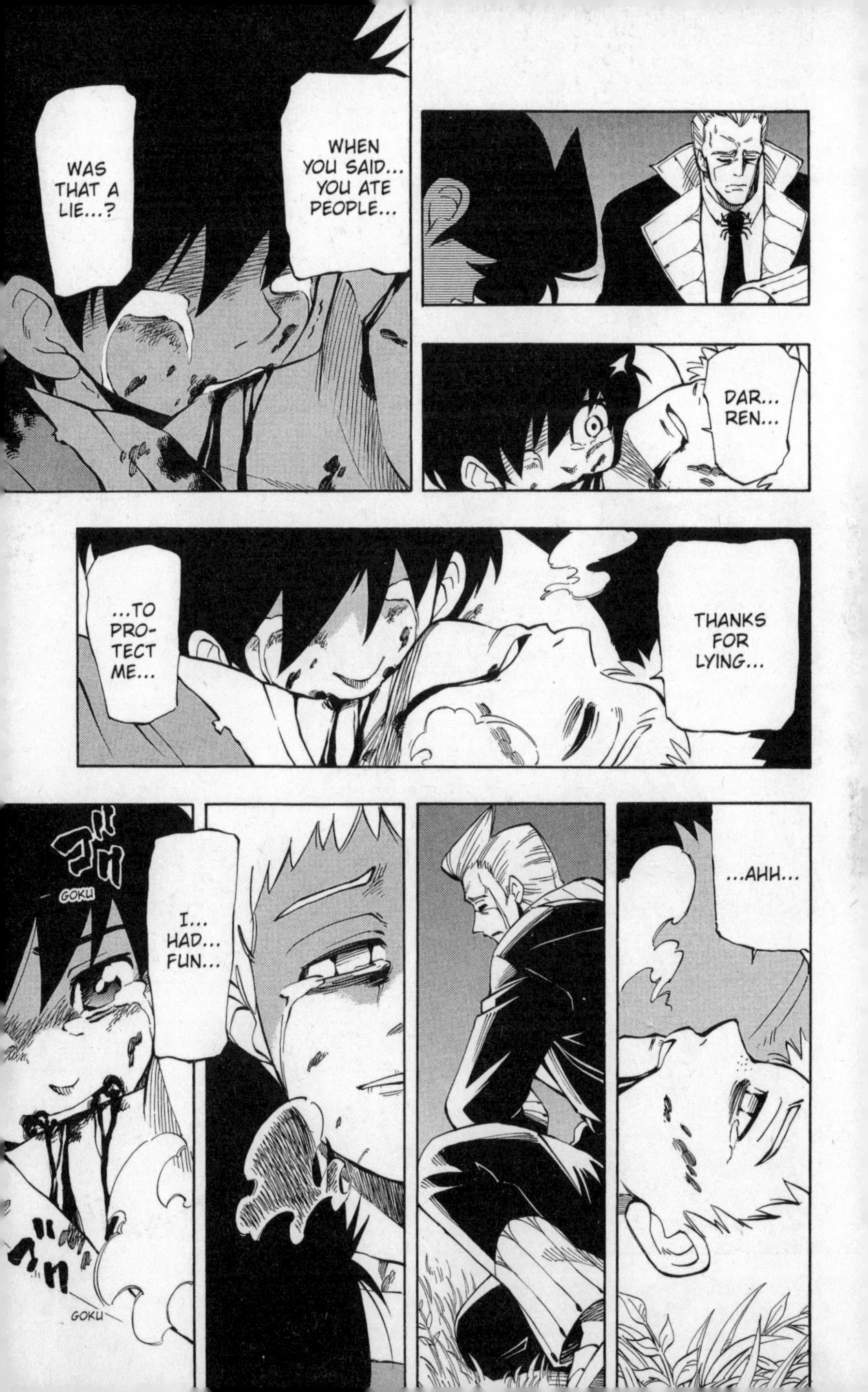
DAR... REN...
WHEN YOU SAID... YOU ATE PEOPLE...
WAS THAT A LIE...?
THANKS FOR LYING...
...TO PRO-TECT ME...
...AHH...
I... HAD... FUN...
GOKU
GOKU

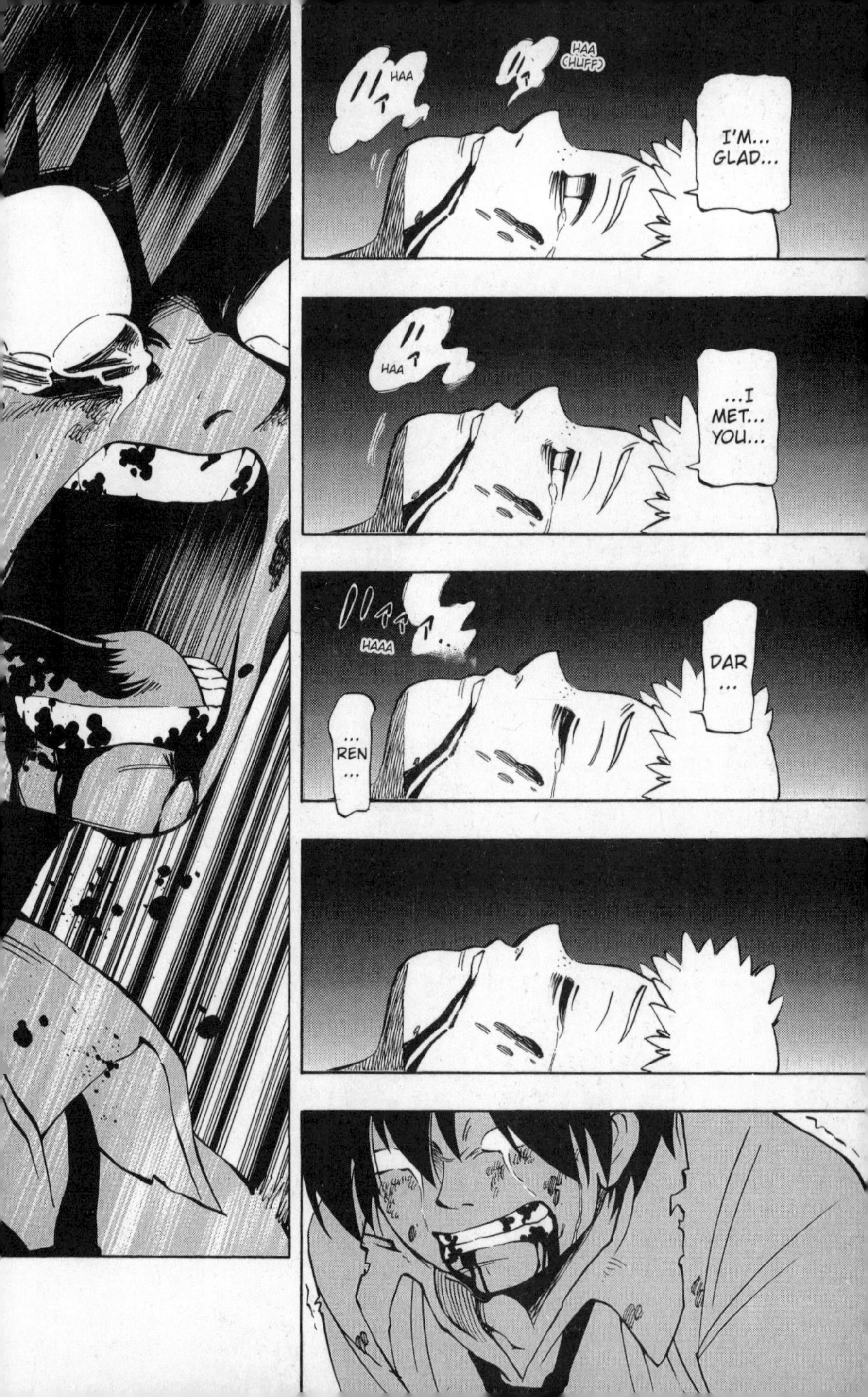
HAA (HUFF)
HAA
I'M... GLAD...
HAA
...I MET... YOU...
HAAA
DAR ...
... REN ...

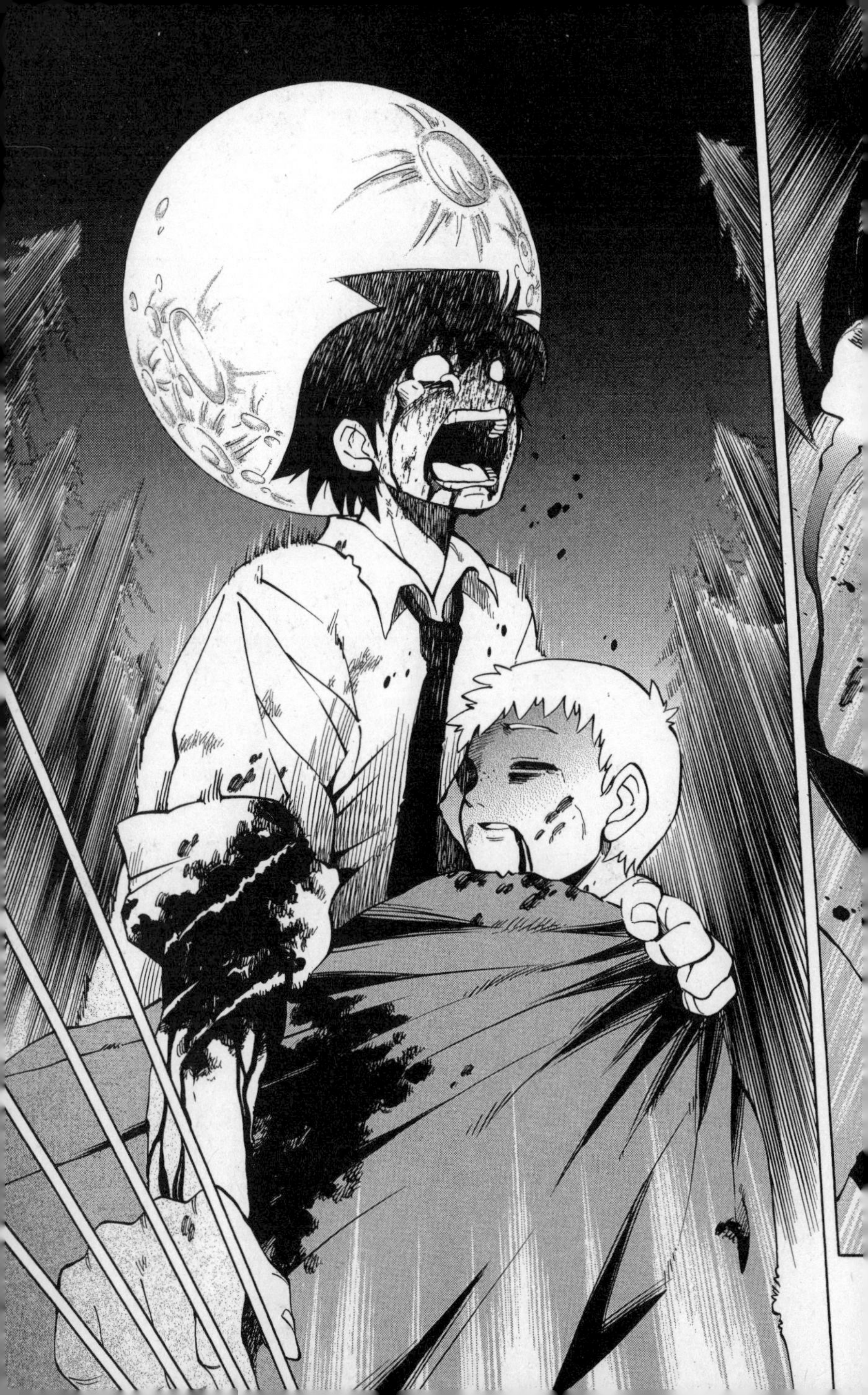

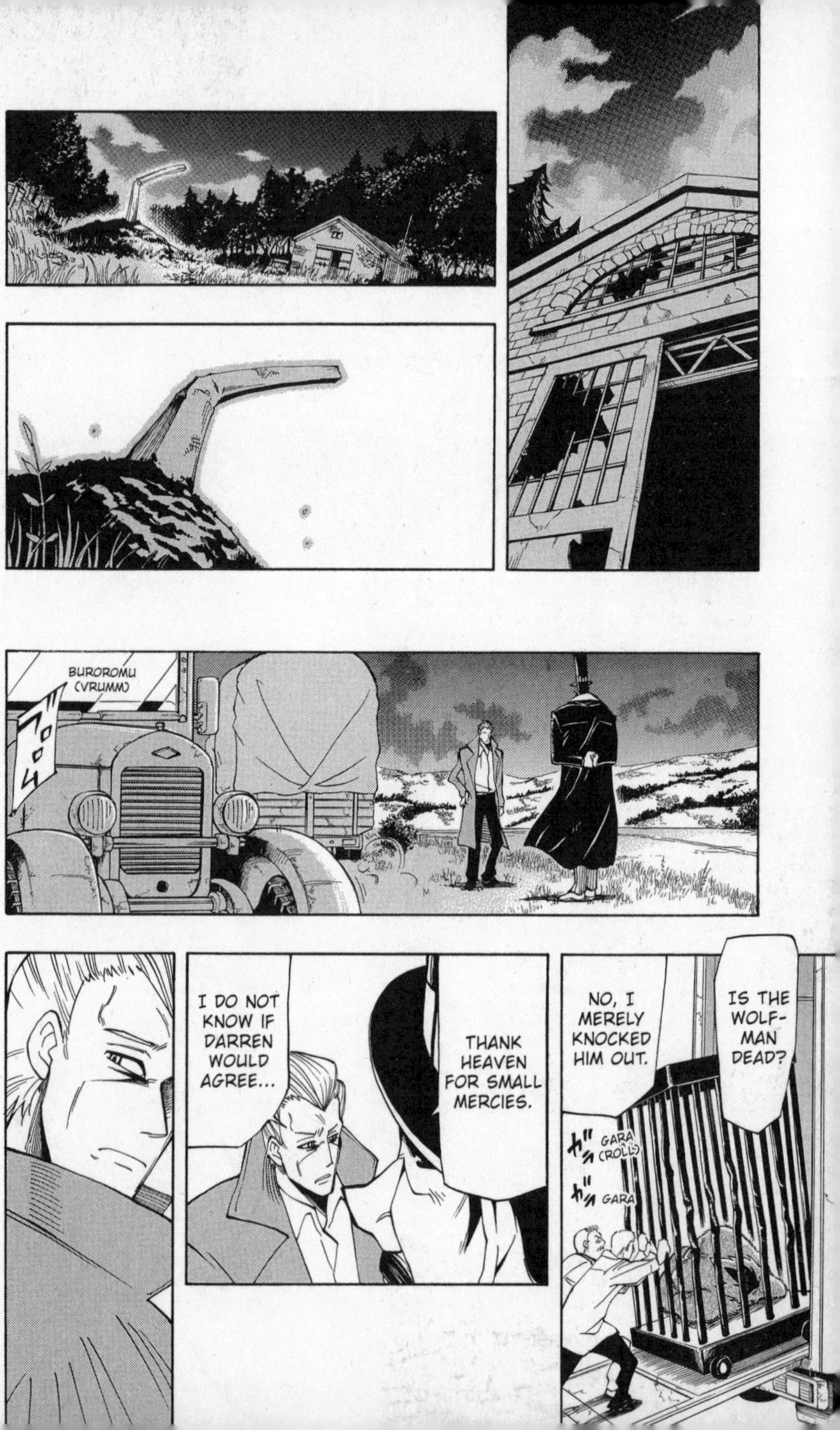
BUROROMU (VRUMM)
IS THE WOLF-MAN DEAD?
NO, I MERELY KNOCKED HIM OUT.
GARA (ROLL)
GARA
THANK HEAVEN FOR SMALL MERCIES.
I DO NOT KNOW IF DARREN WOULD AGREE...

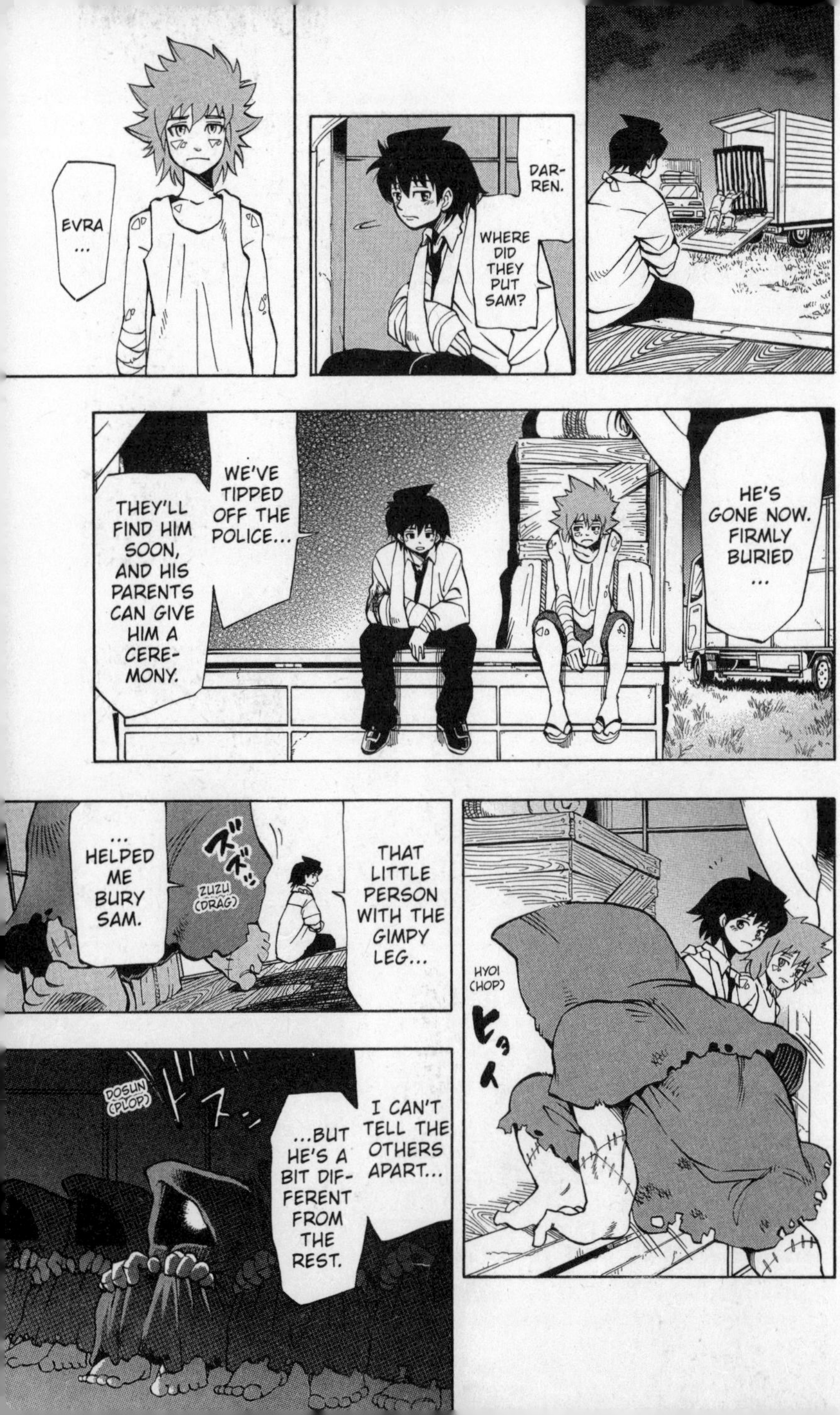
DAR-REN.
WHERE DID THEY PUT SAM?
EVRA ...
HE'S GONE NOW. FIRMLY BURIED ...
WE'VE TIPPED OFF THE POLICE...
THEY'LL FIND HIM SOON, AND HIS PARENTS CAN GIVE HIM A CERE-MONY.
HYOI (HOP)
THAT LITTLE PERSON WITH THE GIMPY LEG...
ZUZU (DRAG)
... HELPED ME BURY SAM.
I CAN'T TELL THE OTHERS APART...
...BUT HE'S A BIT DIF-FERENT FROM THE REST.
DOSUN (PLOP)

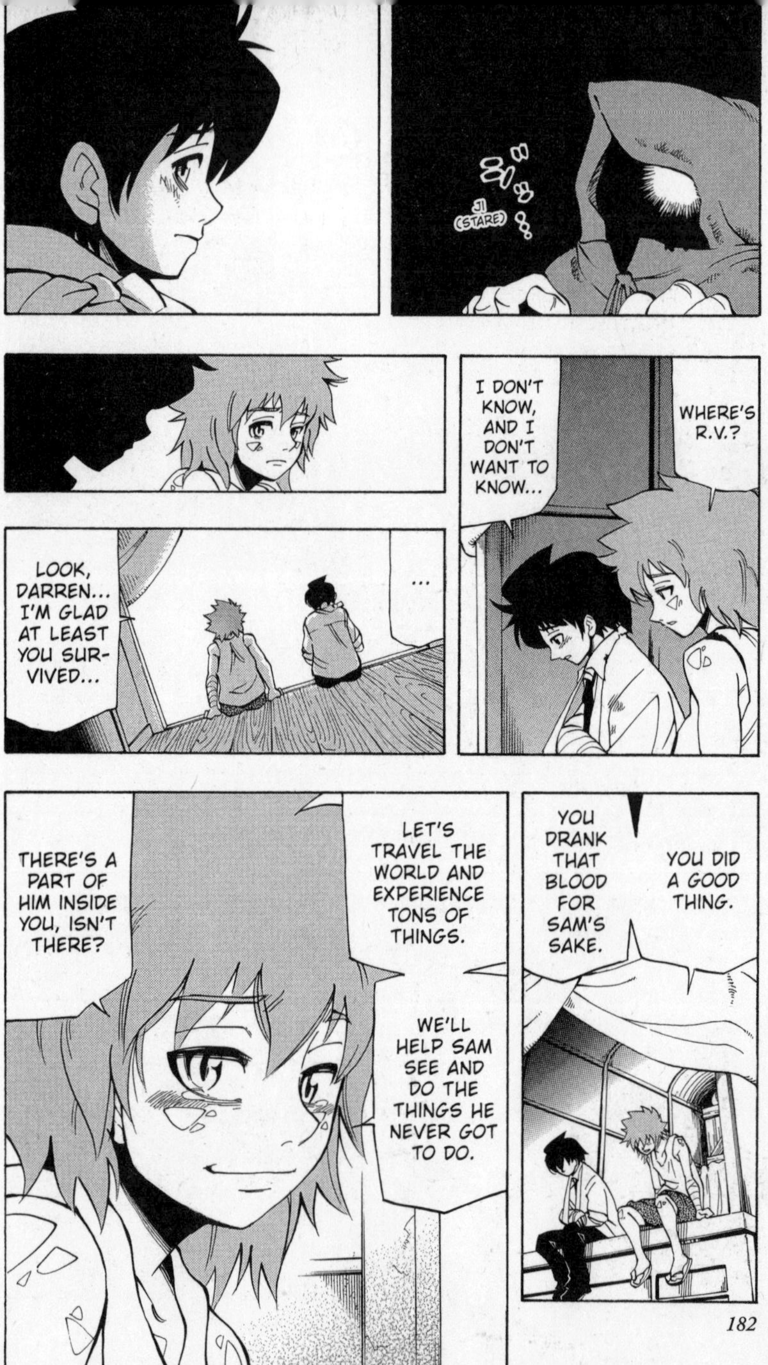

JI (STARE)
WHERE'S R.V.?
I DON'T KNOW, AND I DON'T WANT TO KNOW...
...
LOOK, DARREN... I'M GLAD AT LEAST YOU SURVIVED...
YOU DID A GOOD THING.
YOU DRANK THAT BLOOD FOR SAM'S SAKE.
LET'S TRAVEL THE WORLD AND EXPERIENCE TONS OF THINGS.
WE'LL HELP SAM SEE AND DO THE THINGS HE NEVER GOT TO DO.
THERE'S A PART OF HIM INSIDE YOU, ISN'T THERE?

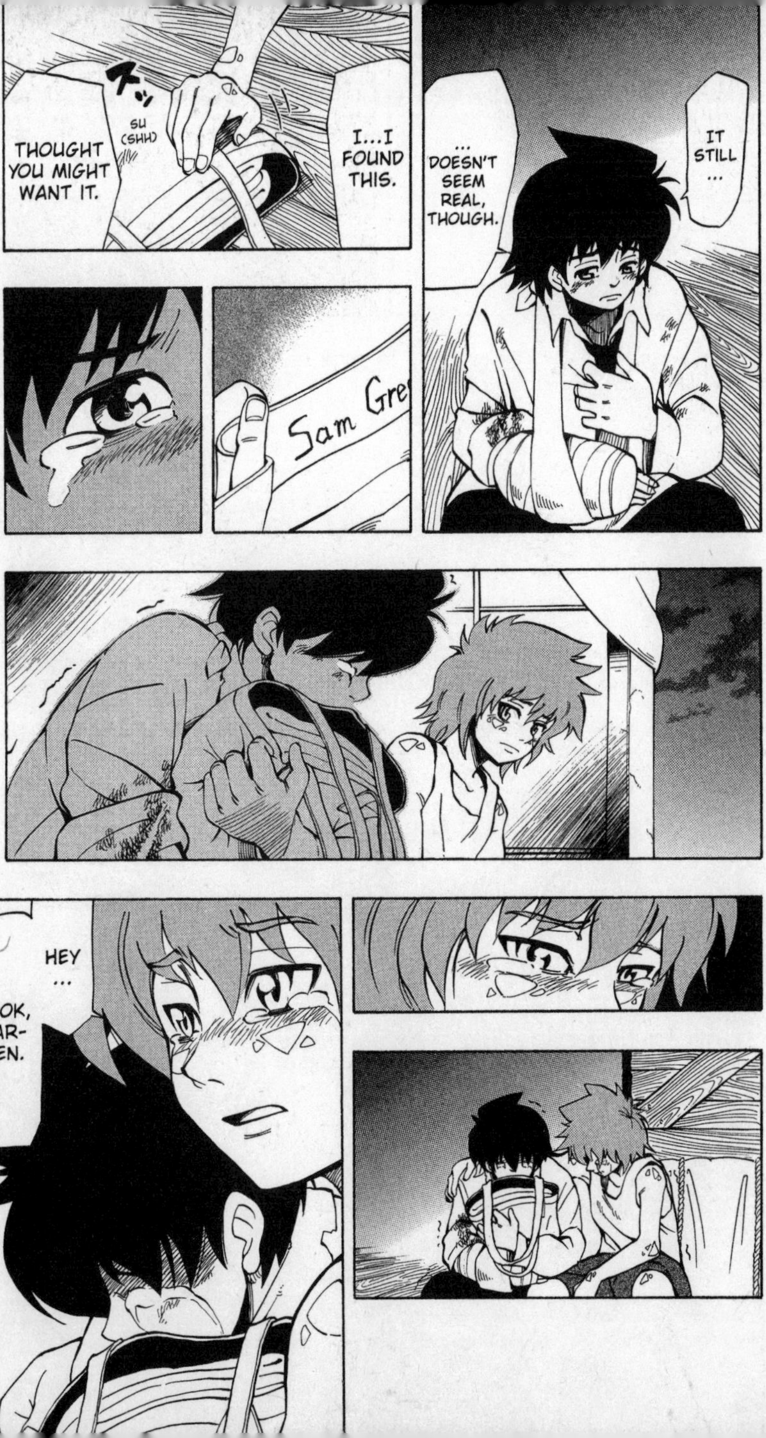
IT STILL ...
... DOESN'T SEEM REAL, THOUGH.
I...I FOUND THIS.
スッ
SU (SHH)
THOUGHT YOU MIGHT WANT IT.
Sam Gre
HEY ...
LOOK, DAR-REN.

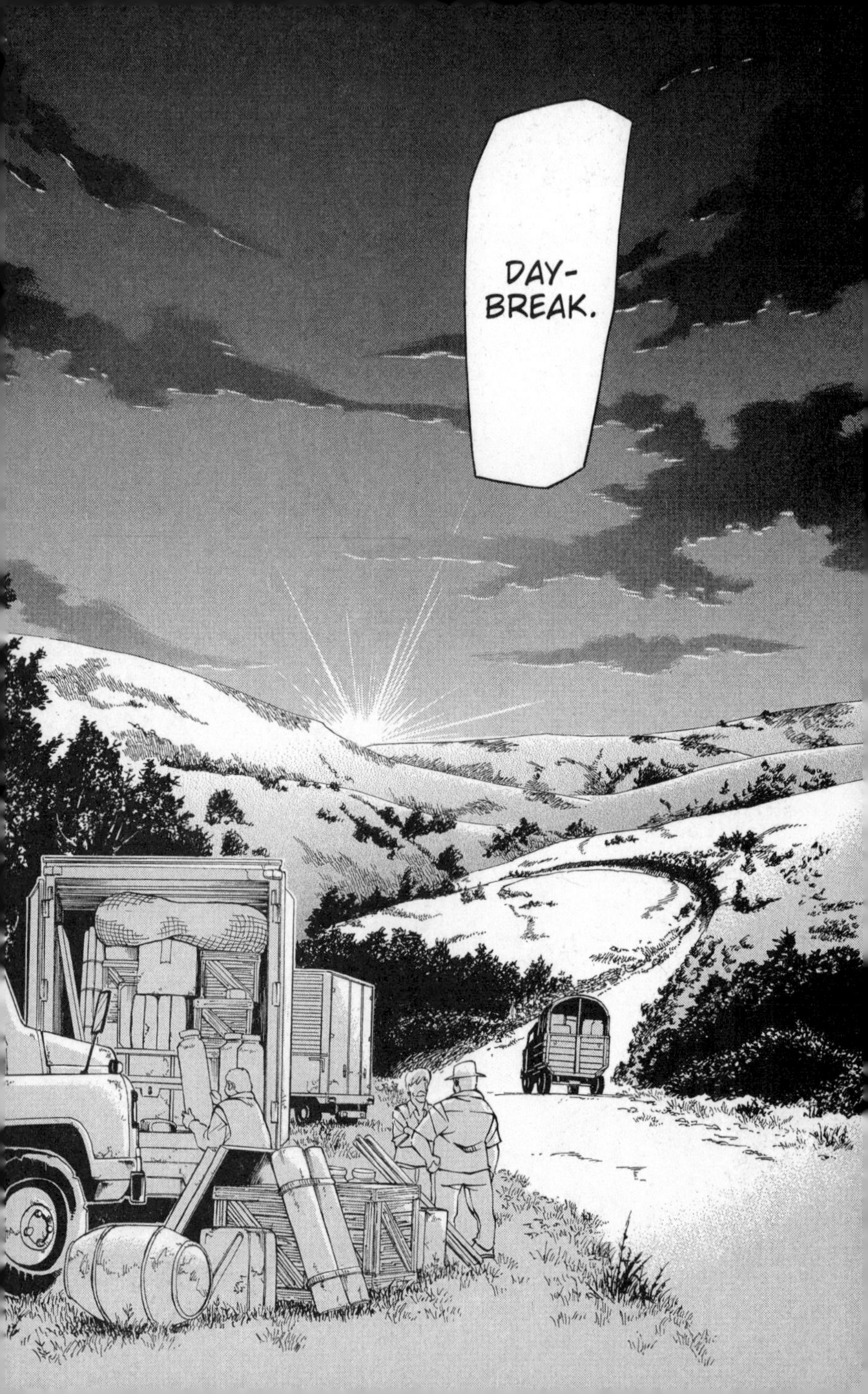
DAY-
BREAK.

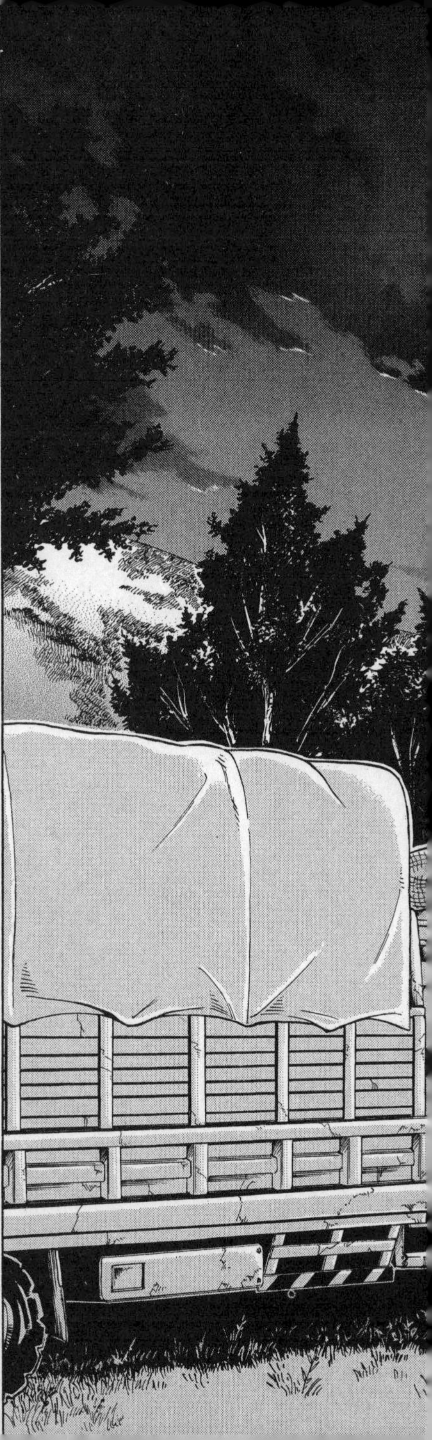
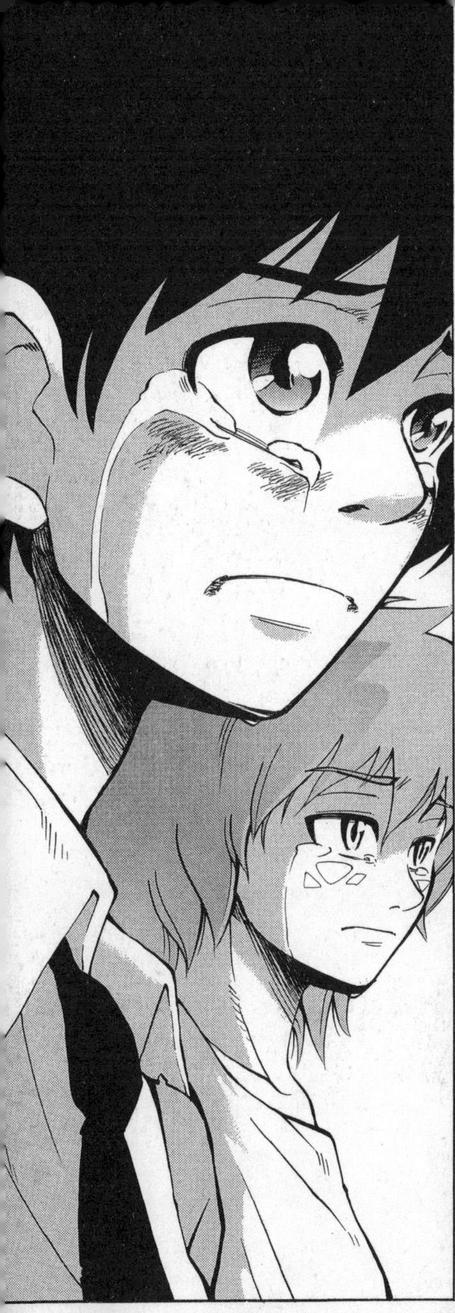

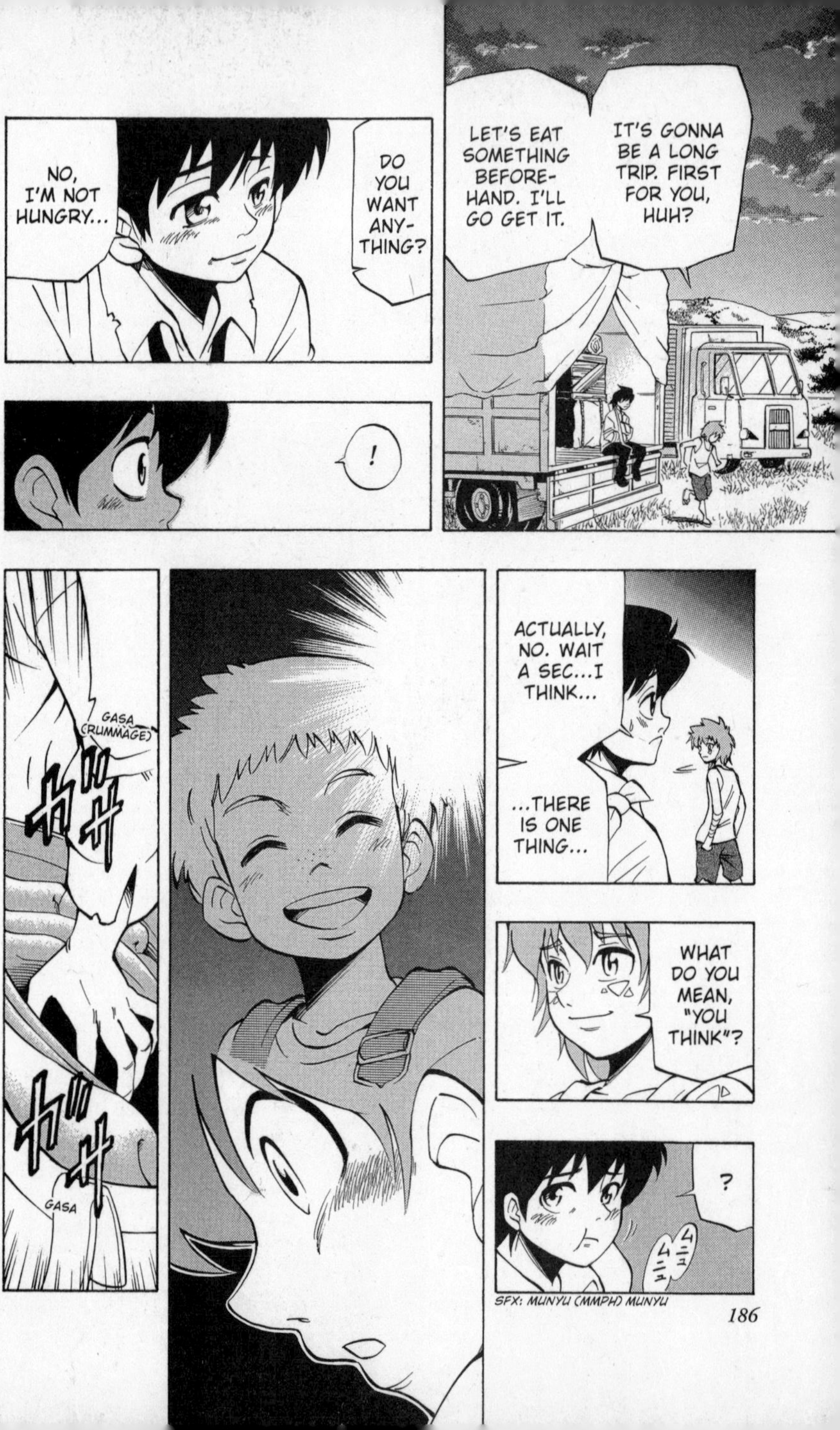
IT'S GONNA BE A LONG TRIP. FIRST FOR YOU, HUH?
LET'S EAT SOMETHING BEFORE-HAND. I'LL GO GET IT.
DO YOU WANT ANY-THING?
NO, I'M NOT HUNGRY...
!
ACTUALLY, NO. WAIT A SEC...I THINK...
...THERE IS ONE THING...
WHAT DO YOU MEAN, "YOU THINK"?
?
SFX: MUNYU (MMPH) MUNYU
GASA (RUMMAGE)
GASA

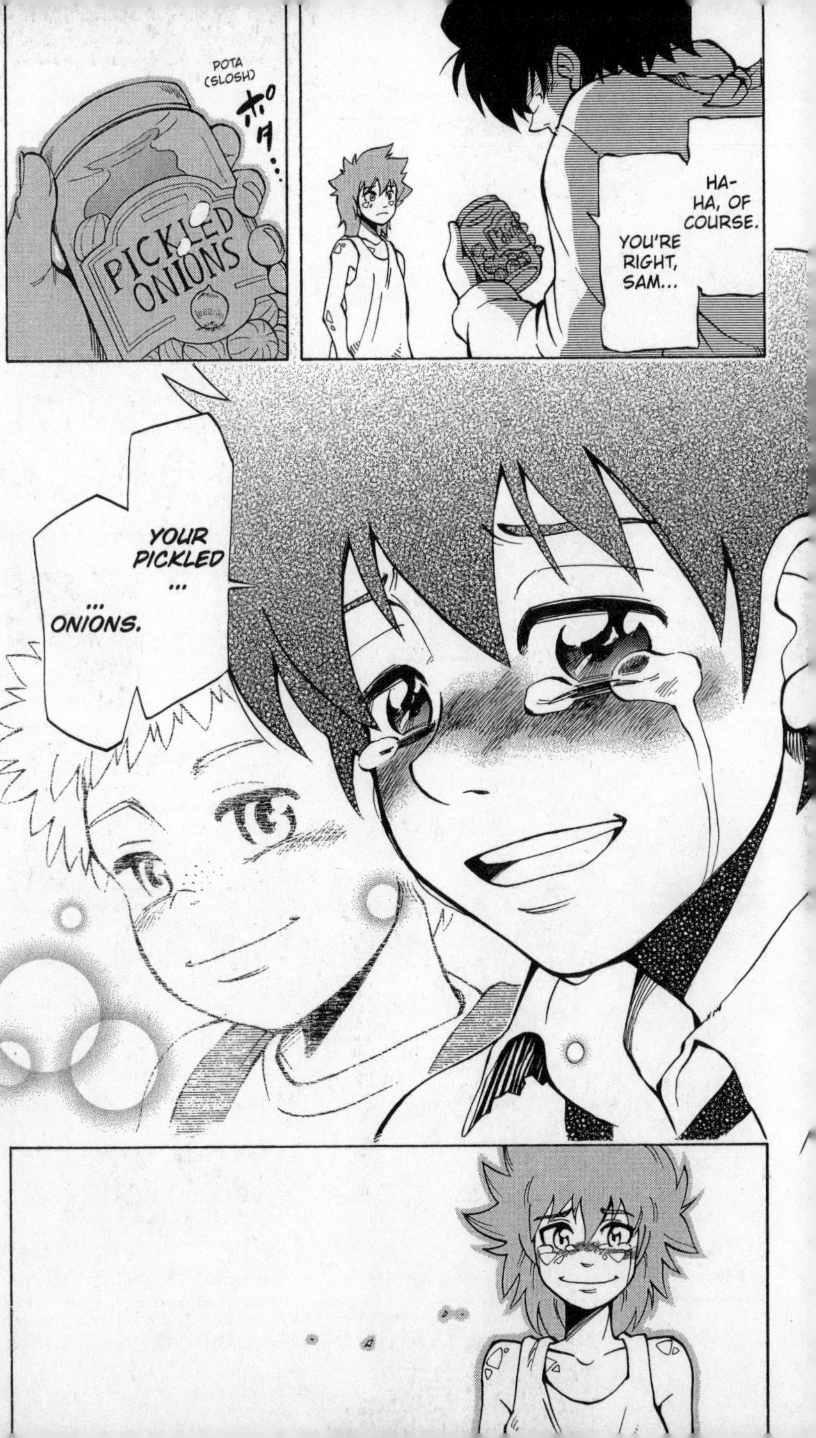
HA-HA, OF COURSE.
YOU'RE RIGHT, SAM...
POTA (SLOSH)
ポタ...
PICKLED ONIONS
YOUR PICKLED ... ... ONIONS.

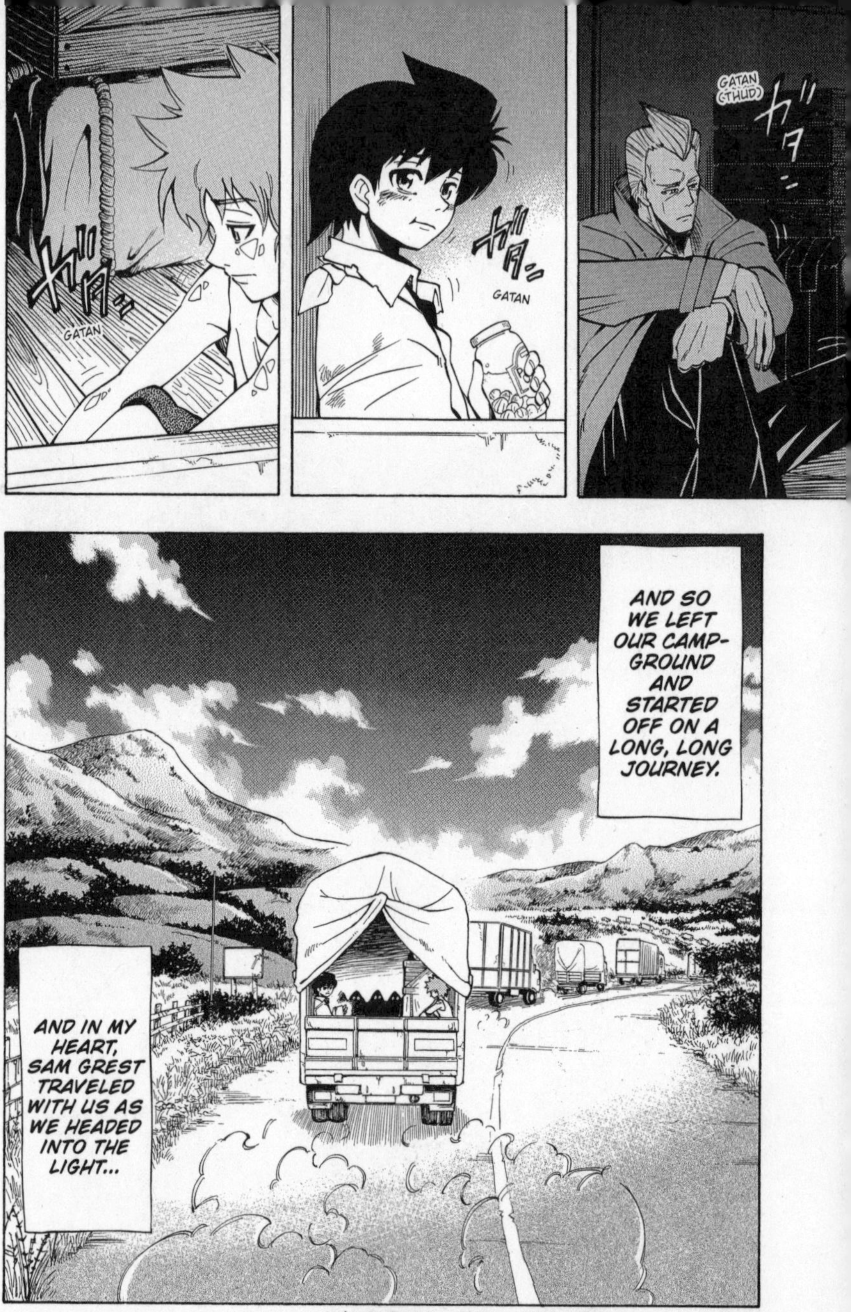
GATAN (THUD)
GATAN
GATAN
AND SO WE LEFT OUR CAMP-GROUND AND STARTED OFF ON A LONG, LONG JOURNEY.
AND IN MY HEART, SAM GREST TRAVELED WITH US AS WE HEADED INTO THE LIGHT...

CIRQUE DU FREAK 2 - END

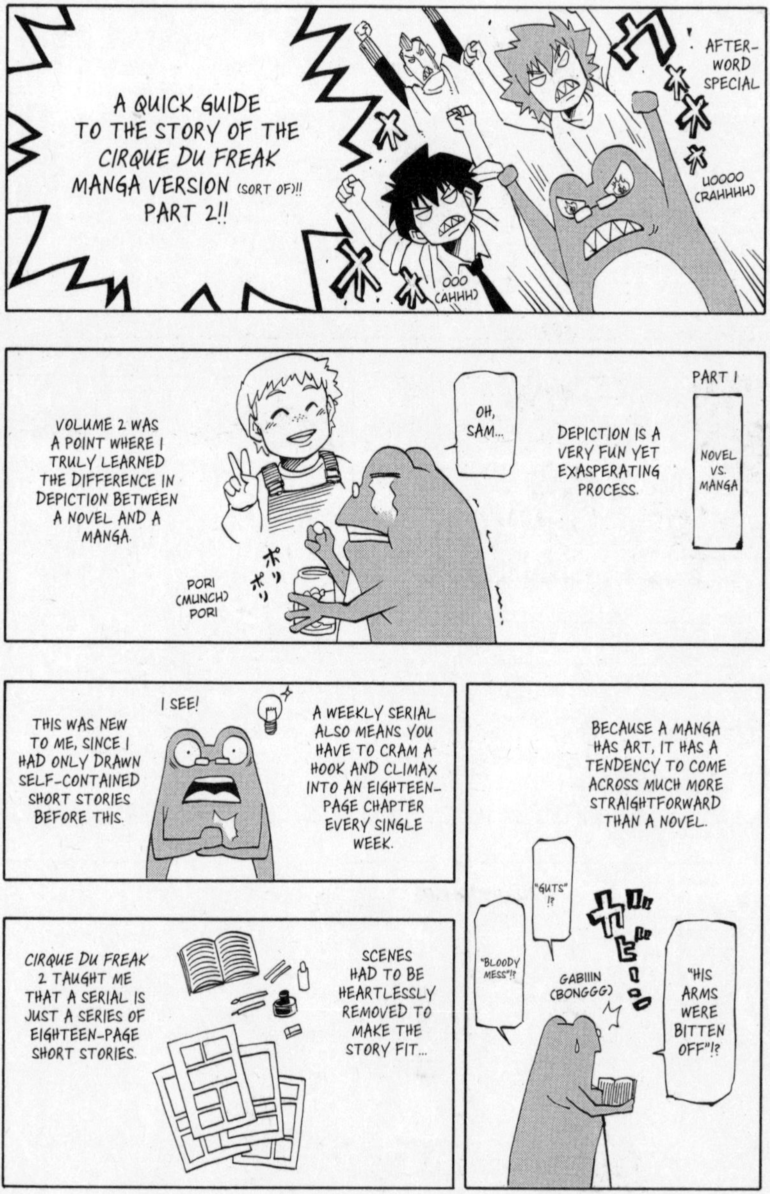
AFTER-WORD SPECIAL
UOOOO (RAHHHH)
OOO (AHHH)
A QUICK GUIDE TO THE STORY OF THE CIRQUE DU FREAK MANGA VERSION (SORT OF)!! PART 2!!
PART 1
NOVEL VS. MANGA
DEPICTION IS A VERY FUN YET EXASPERATING PROCESS.
OH, SAM...
VOLUME 2 WAS A POINT WHERE I TRULY LEARNED THE DIFFERENCE IN DEPICTION BETWEEN A NOVEL AND A MANGA.
ポリ
ポリ
PORI (MUNCH) PORI
BECAUSE A MANGA HAS ART, IT HAS A TENDENCY TO COME ACROSS MUCH MORE STRAIGHTFORWARD THAN A NOVEL.
"HIS ARMS WERE BITTEN OFF"!?
"GUTS"!?
"BLOODY MESS"!?
GABIIIN (BONGGG)
A WEEKLY SERIAL ALSO MEANS YOU HAVE TO CRAM A HOOK AND CLIMAX INTO AN EIGHTEEN-PAGE CHAPTER EVERY SINGLE WEEK.
I SEE!
THIS WAS NEW TO ME, SINCE I HAD ONLY DRAWN SELF-CONTAINED SHORT STORIES BEFORE THIS.
SCENES HAD TO BE HEARTLESSLY REMOVED TO MAKE THE STORY FIT...
CIRQUE DU FREAK 2 TAUGHT ME THAT A SERIAL IS JUST A SERIES OF EIGHTEEN-PAGE SHORT STORIES.

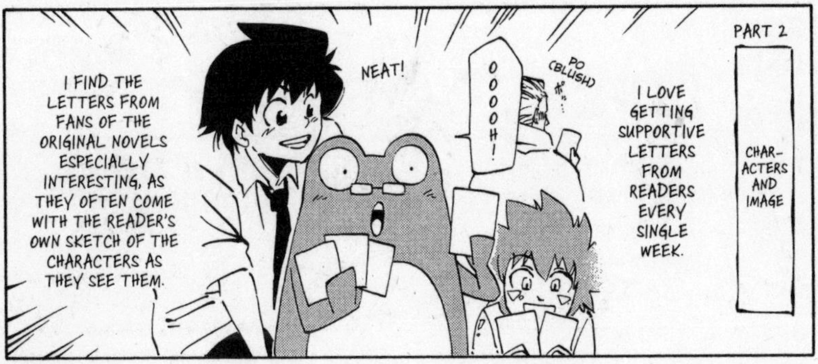
PART 2
CHAR-ACTERS AND IMAGE
I LOVE GETTING SUPPORTIVE LETTERS FROM READERS EVERY SINGLE WEEK.
PO (BLUSH)
OOOOOH!
NEAT!
I FIND THE LETTERS FROM FANS OF THE ORIGINAL NOVELS ESPECIALLY INTERESTING, AS THEY OFTEN COME WITH THE READER'S OWN SKETCH OF THE CHARACTERS AS THEY SEE THEM.

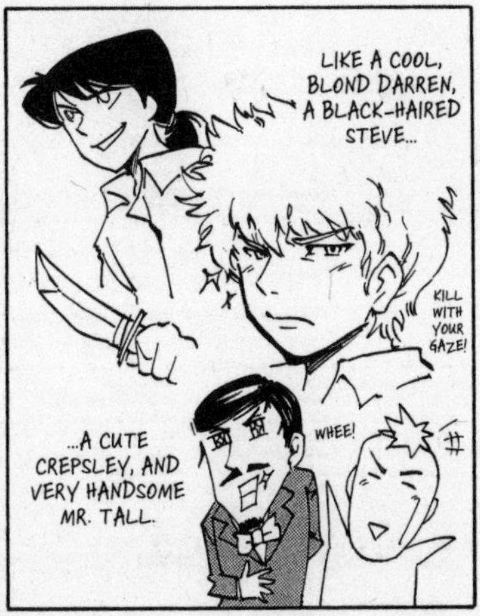
LIKE A COOL, BLOND DARREN, A BLACK-HAIRED STEVE...
KILL WITH YOUR GAZE!
WHEE!
...A CUTE CREPSLEY, AND VERY HANDSOME MR. TALL.

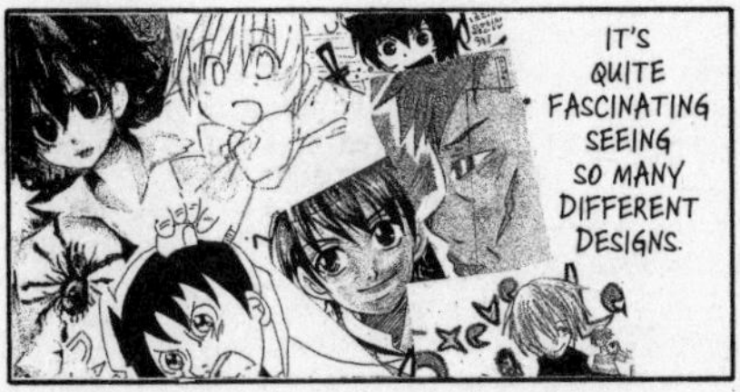
IT'S QUITE FASCINATING SEEING SO MANY DIFFERENT DESIGNS.

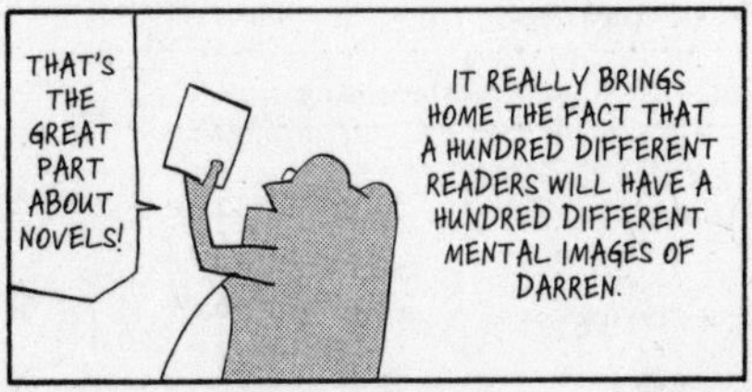
IT REALLY BRINGS HOME THE FACT THAT A HUNDRED DIFFERENT READERS WILL HAVE A HUNDRED DIFFERENT MENTAL IMAGES OF DARREN.
THAT'S THE GREAT PART ABOUT NOVELS!

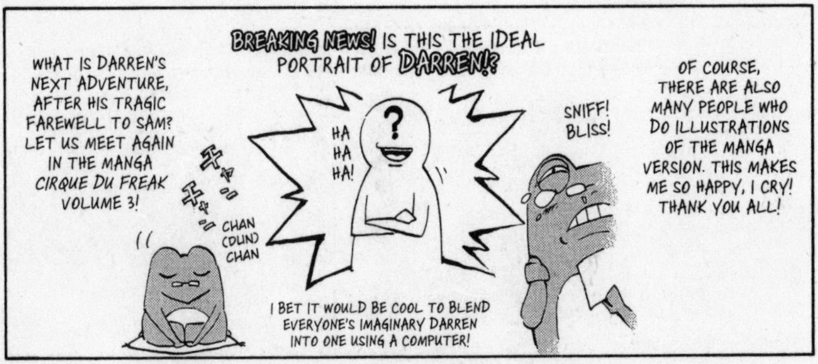
OF COURSE, THERE ARE ALSO MANY PEOPLE WHO DO ILLUSTRATIONS OF THE MANGA VERSION. THIS MAKES ME SO HAPPY, I CRY! THANK YOU ALL!
SNIFF! BLISS!
BREAKING NEWS! IS THIS THE IDEAL PORTRAIT OF DARREN!?
?
HA HA HA!
CHAN CDUND CHAN
WHAT IS DARREN'S NEXT ADVENTURE, AFTER HIS TRAGIC FAREWELL TO SAM? LET US MEET AGAIN IN THE MANGA CIRQUE DU FREAK VOLUME 3!
I BET IT WOULD BE COOL TO BLEND EVERYONE'S IMAGINARY DARREN INTO ONE USING A COMPUTER!

CIRQUE DU FREAK ②

DARREN SHAN
TAKAHIRO ARAI

Translation: Stephen Paul   •   Lettering: AndWorld Design
Original Cover Design: Hitoshi SHIRAYAMA + Bay Bridge Studio

DARREN SHAN Vol. 2 © 2007 by Darren Shan, Takahiro ARAI. All
rights reserved. Original Japanese edition published in Japan in 2007
by Shogakukan Inc., Tokyo. Artworks reproduction rights in U.S.A. and
Canada arranged with Shogakukan Inc. through Tuttle-Mori Agency,
Inc., Tokyo.

English translation © 2009 Darren Shan

Yen Press
Hachette Book Group
1290 Avenue of the Americas, New York, NY 10104

Visit our Web sites at www.HachetteBookGroup.com and
www.YenPress.com.

Yen Press is an imprint of Hachette Book Group, Inc. The Yen Press
name and logo are trademarks of Hachette Book Group, Inc.

First Yen Press Edition: July 2009

ISBN: 978-0-7595-3038-6

10 9 8

BVG

Printed in the United States of America